Reason and Conduct

NEW BEARINGS
IN MORAL PHILOSOPHY

REASON
AND
CONDUCT

New Bearings in Moral Philosophy

HENRY DAVID AIKEN

GREENWOOD PRESS, PUBLISHERS
WESTPORT, CONNECTICUT

208069

Library of Congress Cataloging in Publication Data

Aiken, Henry David, 1912–
  Reason and conduct.

    Reprint of the 1962 ed. published by Knopf,
New York.
    Includes index.
    1. Ethics—Addresses, essays, lectures. I. Title.
BJ1012.A37 1978   170   77-26079
ISBN 0-313-20083-1

F O R *Helen*

Reprinted with the permission of Alfred A. Knopf, Inc.

Reprinted in 1978 by Greenwood Press, Inc.
51 Riverside Avenue, Westport, CT 06880

Printed in the United States of America

ACKNOWLEDGMENTS

I WISH to acknowledge with gratitude the permission of the following publishers to reprint in this book extracts and articles from the following copyright works controlled by them. The copyright claimant in every case was the person or organization who has given permission to reprint the selection.

Constable & Co., Ltd.: from George Santayana, *The Sense of Beauty*, copyright 1936 for rights outside the U.S. and Canada; copyright 1936 by Charles Scribner's Sons for U.S. and Canadian rights.

J. M. Dent & Sons, Ltd.: from George Santayana, *Winds of Doctrine*, copyright 1940.

Harvard Educational Review: for permission to reprint the entire article by Henry D. Aiken: "Moral Philosophy and Education," Vol. XXV, No. 1, Winter, copyright 1955.

The Journal of Philosophy: for permission to reprint the following entire articles by Henry D. Aiken: "The Open Society and Its Enemies" (a review), Vol. XLIV, No. 17, August 14, 1947, copyright 1947, and "The Role of Conventions in Ethics," Vol. XLIX, No. 6, March 13, 1952, copyright 1952.

The Library of Living Philosophers, Inc.: from Paul A. Schilpp, ed., *The Philosophy of George Santayana*, Vol. II, copyright 1940.

Philosophical Review: for permission to reprint the following entire articles by Henry D. Aiken: "Definitions, Factual Premises and Ethical Conclusions," Vol. LXL, No. 3, July 1952, copyright 1952, and "What Is Value? An Essay in Philosophical Analysis," Vol. LXII, No. 2, April 1953, copyright 1953.

Philosophy and Phenomenological Research: for permission to reprint the following entire articles by Henry D. Aiken: "The Spectrum of Value Predictions," Vol. XIV, No. 1, September 1953, copyright 1953, and "The Authority of Moral Judgments," Vol. XII, No. 4, June 1952, copyright 1952.

Routledge & Kegan Paul, Ltd.: from Karl R. Popper, *The Open Society and Its Enemies*, 4th ed., copyright 1962.

Charles Scribner's Sons: from George Santayana, *The Sense of Beauty*, copyright 1936 for U.S. and Canadian rights; copyright 1936 by Constable & Co., Ltd. for rights outside the U.S. and Canada.

The University of Chicago Press: for permission to reprint the following entire articles from *Ethics* by Henry D. Aiken: "The Levels of Moral Discourse," Vol. LXII, No. 4, July 1952, copyright 1952; "Moral Reasoning," Vol. LXIV, No. 1, October 1953, copyright 1953, and "God and Evil: A Study of Some Relations between Faith and Morals," Vol. LXVIII, No. 2, January 1958, copyright 1958.

The Viking Press, Inc.: from Thorstein Veblen, *What Veblen Taught*, W. C. Mitchell, ed., copyright 1945.

PREFACE

Although the papers selected for inclusion in this volume have been written at various times and for a variety of occasions over a period of more than a decade, they are not in the usual sense occasional works. Much of the serious philosophical writing in our time has been in the form of the essay. In my own case, that form is suited precisely both to what I have hitherto had to say in philosophy and to the way in which I have wished to say it. I am content to let these papers speak for themselves, with a minimum of explanation and apology. Such unity as they possess is the natural unity imposed by a particular philosophical temperament and style, a characteristic way of going at problems, and a persistent concern with a group of problems that appear to me crucial for moral philosophy. Of course, some editorial revision has proved unavoidable. Now and then I have discerned an ambiguity or misleading statement which, upon reflection, has seemed to me unfaithful to what I remember of my original intention. In a few cases, I have rearranged, condensed, or expanded discussions in the interest of greater compression or clarity. But for the most part I have tried not to second-guess my earlier opinions or to remove all evidences of my philosophical development. In fact, it seems to me that the dialectic of that development may prove more instructive than any thesis or antithesis contained therein. By experimenting, I have also found that it is impossible, even were it desirable, to rewrite whole essays. For the result is always a new work which usually says less distinctly a very different thing. And it is these essays, not some others, that I have thought worthy, if any of my writings on moral philosophy are so, to be rescued from the oblivion of periodical publication. I am grateful to the editors of various philosophical and literary journals for their past indulgence toward my pieces; I also extend my thanks for their kind permission to reprint them here.

In arranging these essays, I have decided not to follow a strict chronological order. Instead, I have divided them into two main groups. The first represents my own successive efforts to find answers to the questions of analytical ethics. The second offers a selection of critical studies of particular works that reflect some of the prevailing winds of doctrine in contemporary moral philosophy and several essays dealing with a variety of topics, historical and substantive as well as methodological, which, at one time or another, have engaged my attention. Taken together, the papers do seem to me to provide a fairly comprehensive survey of a good many of the issues with which moral philosophers are now concerned. However, I most particularly desire not to give the impression that without really trying I have somehow managed to construct a new system of moral philosophy. These are "new bearings," nothing more.

On the whole the perceptive reader will find that the point of view of my more recent papers is rather more "protestant" and more "libertarian" than that of their predecessors. He will also find, especially in the second group of essays, an increasing preoccupation with certain limiting questions of moral philosophy and a corresponding broadening of my conception of its scope. Indeed, in the end it has become a question for me whether any sharp line at all can be drawn between moral philosophy and metaphysics or "first philosophy." But even in the earlier papers included in the present series I always insisted that, especially at its fringes, morality is necessarily something more, as well as something less, than a system of socially authoritative rules of action and that no such system could conceivably prescribe "the whole duty of man." A decade ago it seemed less important to "make a thing" of this fact than to insist upon the equally essential fact, which had temporarily been forgotten, that morality (like philosophy itself) is, through and through, a social phenomenon, and that the forms of deliberation and action which it countenances are not, in particular communities, as open-textured as proponents of the emotive theory of ethics previously had suggested. At the time, it needed to be said that what we ordinarily understand by the moral life is, in routine situations, subject to routine methods of correction to which ordinary persons normally submit without question. To a greater or lesser degree, most moral behavior is standardized behavior, and the built-in norms which most of us acknowledge as standards of what, in conventional situations, is right and proper tend at the same time to become *de facto* rules for the application of evaluative terms in those situations. Nor can there be any proper understanding of those levels of moral reflection which transcend such standardization that does not begin by noticing that transcendence always begins in resistance or rebellion, and that alienation from the "in-group" routines to which any individual is conditioned from birth presupposes that such routines are already in being as determinants of individual conscience and judgment.

This lesson, I take it, has now been sufficiently well learned. At present there is a danger that contemporary philosophers, who stress the ordinariness of the ordinary rule-governed language of morals, may have forgotten that, at least in our Western tradition, the "institution" of morality has always contained within itself the seeds of its own destruction as an institution. Other philosophers, from Bergson to Popper, have stressed that our Western moralities are essentially "open." What this means is that there has gradually been built into our very concept of morals the possibility of its continual reconstruction. Moreover, owing largely to the profound influence of great moral philosophers since the time of Socrates upon the language of morals itself, there has gradually been included within the compass of the idea of morality the notion of a philosophical or reflective morality, which, by the nature of the case, is the notion of a personal morality of spiritually free men who are not only determined to govern themselves, but also, in turn, determined by the idea or ideal of themselves as autonomous, self-governing moral agents. As I have increasingly come to see, that great philosophical idea is irremovable from our whole conception of the moral life. In brief, what philosophers have called the ordinary language of morals is there systematically ready for the use of reformers and revolutionaries as well as of conformists and conventionalists. This, in a culture which is incurably ideological, is a great boon, for it permits moralists of the right, center, and left to participate in an endless colloquy about man's spiritual destiny without finally having either to transcend or necessarily to abuse the language of good and evil.

It remains for me to acknowledge certain obligations and affinities and to define their limits. That I owe much to the English philosophers of ordinary language will be apparent to any informed reader. It is also a matter of record that on this side of the Atlantic I was one of the first writers on moral philosophy to make any use of their ideas. What may be less obvious perhaps is that I have read them for what I could learn from them, not for what they may have wished to teach me. From a logical point of view at least, they sometimes write as if they were revolutionaries who, breaking with everything that has gone before, are advocating a philosophy to end all philosophy. Such is not my conception of their work. In my view, they are in effect rebel loyalists who, after the prolonged "Russellian Protectorate" of "scientific philosophy," are now helping to restore, correct, and deepen the great humanistic, "common-law" tradition of British philosophy that has ever sought to preserve a continuity between philosophical sophistication and common sense and between new ways of "ideas" and tried ways of doing things. So far as it concerns me, their revolt is not meant to deny either the importance of science or the authority of its methods within their own proper sphere; nor is it meant to assert, as one follower of Wittgenstein has said, that ordinarily language is the one and only correct language. Rather is it meant to deny that what is significant in ordinary utterances can always be translated without loss of meaning into statements acceptable to scientists as such, and that only when such (unknown) translations have been made is it possible to determine the truth-value of ordinary statements. More important, it is meant to deny that preconceptions on the part of "scientific philosophers" concerning the methods of scientific inquiry are to be identified with cognition itself and that scientism is anything more than a rather stupid philosophical prejudice.

Bertrand Russell and his followers pretend that what they call "linguistic philosophy" is a know-nothing philosophy which uses ordinary language as a shield to defend its own ignorance of science and its methods. I believe this is a completely false issue. The preoccupation of the linguistic philosophers with the meanings of words or concepts represents no radical departure from their own investigations. Since the time of Occam, British philosophers of all schools have been incurably addicted to the study of language. Most of them, rightly or wrongly, have supposed that a sound philosophy of language would throw a flood of light upon many traditional metaphysical, epistemological, and ethical problems that have hitherto resisted solution. Russell's own best work as a philosopher has been concerned with the analysis of concepts, ordinary and otherwise. On this score, the only difference between him and the ordinary language philosophers is simply that the latter believe that many of the analyses offered by Russell and his followers are confused or mistaken, not only in detail, but in principle. So far as it is rational, this disagreement can be settled, not by pronunciamentos, but only by careful, piecemeal study of the uses of particular expressions in the contexts of *their* customary employment.

It has fallen to my lot for a good many years to teach British philosophy to Harvard students, both graduate and undergraduate. This duty has required me to do a certain amount of reading in original sources. What I have found there is not at all what the historians, including Russell, had led me to expect. To be sure I did find, for example, Berkeley's famous statement, *esse est percipi.* I also found many other things, including Berkeley's nearly forgotten *Alciphron,* in which there exist, as plain as day, many of the leading ideas lately celebrated by the followers of Wittgenstein. Something of the sort may also be said in the case of David Hume, whom Russell and the logical positivists have extolled as the true philosophical Copernicus. What both Berkeley and Hume came gradually to understand is that the meanings of the concepts which are the primary concern of the philosopher—such concepts, for example, as truth, beauty, validity, and goodness—can be better understood not simply by adhering more resolutely to the dictum, "Hunt the referent," but only by examining what men are *doing* with words when they assert the truth of particular propositions, when they affirm the validity of an inference, when they judge the beauty of a poem or the goodness of an object. This form of analysis, now so widespread among the linguistic philosophers, is brilliantly exemplified, for example, in Hume's analysis of promises. In fact it is exhibited throughout his *Treatise* with results that are inexhaustibly suggestive to the analytical moralist. In my own case, the reading of Hume, on whose moral philosophy I also wrote my doctoral dissertation, prepared me well for the ethical studies of the linguistic philosophers. And it is for this reason that neither their methods of analysis nor their results struck me as a bolt from the blue.

I fancy that not all of my English colleagues at Oxford and Cambridge will be thrilled by these protestations of affection. For some of them appear to agree with C. D. Broad that America is simply the place where English philosophies go after they are dead. From the beginning, of course, American philosophy has always been profoundly influenced by its British counterpart, and the situation is no different at the present time. The fact remains that British philosophy, like the language with which it has always been so preoccupied, always undergoes a sea-change in its passage to these States. This is true in the present instance. I am well aware that I have read Wittgenstein and Wisdom and Austin, as I also have read Berkeley and Hume, with glasses ground by the American pragmatists, Peirce, James, and Dewey. Like William James's great brother Henry, I too have regarded myself, since my nonage, as a pragmatist of sorts, and for this reason, it has never occurred to me that the study of language could be separated from the study of the various activities, scientific, moral, religious, or artistic, of which language forms but the leading part. But, for the same reason, I have also never supposed for a moment that for the philosopher the study of any form of words could ever be an end in itself. Philosophy is, or ought to be, the pursuit of wisdom, and the philosophical interest in language, as in any symbolic form, is therefore always impure. What the philosopher ultimately seeks, as Peirce said, is self-control and self-knowledge; he wants to know the ways of the concepts he employs only in order that he may use them more successfully in compassing his own ends, whether material or otherwise. It is precisely this pragmatic philosophical goal which the English linguistic philosophers have too often concealed from their readers, if not from themselves. As a pragmatist, I am bound to think that every philosopher, analytical or otherwise, is first and last a moralist, and that his study either of the "language" of morals or of any other language is merely preliminary to the conduct of life.

From the pragmatists I learned also that what men call "reason" is not a *Logos* written into the very constitution of being, but an all-too-human regimen or "sentiment," as James called it, whose claims are neither absolute nor unchangeable. The underlying insight, again, was Hume's, and it provided for him the basis of his thoroughgoing critique of rationalism. Its great philosophical point was also seen by Kant, who devoted his own greatest works to the critique of reason in all of its major deployments. However, both Hume and Kant lived before the age of the historical consciousness, and it remained for the great idealists to view reason historically and institutionally as a system of evolving norms or standards of validity, correctness, and truth. At the same time, the idealists intermittently understood that the "objective" standards of rationality embodied in such institutions as science, law, and education can exert no absolute claims upon the minds of men unless they themselves are prepared, as conscious subjects, to accept them. Moreover, history does not miraculously make itself; it is made by men. This means that what Spinoza called "the improvement of the understanding" (or reason) is not something which occurs by chance but in consequence of the deliberations and decisions of individual persons and groups. In short, the sentiment of rationality is at once an acquired and a variable sentiment, whose objective forms are in many cases the result of proposals which in the first instance can claim only a "subjective" validity for individuals who may be willing to adopt them. All this, in one way or another, I have learned primarily from the German philosophers of the nineteenth century, and their influence upon my thought has accordingly been profound.

One final turn of this screw remains to be made. Many of the German historicists tended, like Hegel, to become lost in a maze of cultural history in consequence of which they also tended to allow the history of reason to double in brass as its critique. This error lies at the root of the notorious "panlogism" of Hegel which Kierkegaard so violently attacked and which Nietzsche so brilliantly ridiculed. For Hegel, the history of philosophy tended to become its very principles. But the existentialists have plausibly argued, in effect, that any "discipline" whose only principles can be its own history is no discipline at all. They have concluded, and rightly in my opinion, that there can be no such thing as _the_ principles of philosophy, and that philosophy must therefore always be a first-personal activity whose only business, finally, is to discover what the "self" of the individual philosopher really is, or, better, is becoming. In short, as Socrates long ago perceived, philosophy at bottom is the search for self-knowledge and self-revelation. It may be obliged to do many things in conducting the search. Nor is it true, as some existentialists seem to think, that the best way of conducting it is simply to make a decision or else to stare at one's own navel. He who knows nothing of the world and of history will usually confuse genuine revelations of the self with idle dreams or else will discover a self that is impoverished, confused, and benighted. Here, it seems to me, Hegel's instincts were sounder than most of the existentialists who criticize him. I myself believe, at any rate, that, in Santayana's phrase, it is always "a

long way round to Nirvana," and that in the course of trying
to find out what I myself am and ought to be, I must make
many detours throughout the realms of being.

I am aware, finally, of a profound debt to Santayana himself, whose philosophy James once described as "the perfection of rottenness." Like that of the pragmatists, whom he
affected to despise, Santayana's is in essence a moral philosophy, and this is true, as it was also true in the case of James
and Peirce, even when he is doing metaphysics and epistemology. Perhaps the greatest value of Santayana's writings for
me is the almost fanatical detachment with which he examined the various symbolic forms that compose not only the
life of reason but also those supra-rational forms of life in
which the life of reason itself is always incysted. And in that
detachment I have found both a great wisdom and a method.
I suppose that I have returned oftener to Santayana's writings
than to those of any other single philosopher save Hume.
They have nourished me and given me assurance of my own
vocation. Were he the only American philosopher, that fact,
ironically, would suffice to prove that, like Greece and England, America has somehow managed to become a mother of
true philosophy.

To my own American contemporaries my debts are so
many and so extensive that it would be futile, as well as in-
vidious, to try to enumerate them all here. However, I cannot
forbear to express my continuing gratitude to a distinguished
teacher, Reginald Arragon of Reed College, from whom I first
learned both the excitement of philosophy and the importance
of understanding something of its history. My debt is only
less great to the writings and to the stimulating conversation
of my friends Raphael Demos, William Earle, William Frankena, John Ladd, Asher Moore, Everett Nelson, Ernest Nagel,
W. V. Quine, Israel Scheffler, Charles Stevenson, Donald
Williams, Morton White, and Paul Ziff. I have been blessed
also by a number of students, in particular Stanley Cavell,
Marshall Cohen, Thompson Clarke, Burton Dreben, Jan
Narveson, Moreland Perkins, and Irving Singer, to whom I
owe more for stimulus and criticism than any of them can

possibly realize. To have such students is itself sufficient compensation for the often dull and wearing grind of academic life. Finally, I must once again invoke the dear name of Ralph Barton Perry, whose memory provides for me an exemplary image of what it means to be a philosopher.

I dedicate this book to my wife, Helen Rowland Aiken, without whose encouragement the idea of gathering these essays together would never have seemed a serious matter.

HENRY DAVID AIKEN

Bedford, Massachusetts
November, 1961

CONTENTS

PART ONE

[I]

Moral Philosophy and Education

CURRENT PHILOSOPHY AND LIBERAL EDUCATION

The advancement of learning is rarely attended by a ready understanding of its relevance to liberal education. It is not hard to see why this should be so. On the one side is the scholar's desire to get on with his job without being continually side-tracked by importunate questions about the practical relevance of his researches; on the other is the understandable reluctance of educators to range too far from the highway of received ideas. From the nature of his calling the educator is bound to rely heavily upon theories and principles lying somewhat to the rear of current inquiry. The more radical its departure from tradition, therefore, the less likely is any new development in a branch of learning to find its way immediately into the core curriculum. When first introduced, it is almost necessarily restricted to courses intended for the specialist. The result is an inevitable, but not necessarily unhealthy, tension between the concerns of productive scholarship and the more conservative obligations of the common educational process. Occasionally, however, there sets in a more serious dissociation between research and education which can be exceedingly harmful to the permanent interests of both.

For some time such a situation has been developing in philosophy. This is doubly unfortunate, since a widespread revival of educational interest in philosophical problems is occurring precisely at a time in which there has been a very rapid development in the methods of philosophical analysis that promises results of great value to educated men. As rarely before, there is an intense conviction on the part both of educators and of the general public that a sound education must include forms of instruction that transcend the scope of the special sciences. The phenomenal growth of general education is itself evidence of a conviction, not always clearly articulated or understood, that only studies having a philosophical dimension can overcome the cultural parochialism and the trained incompetence that are thought to be the by-products of scientific specialization. In practice this has usually meant a headlong return to the study of the great philosophical classics, with a corresponding stress upon the history of philosophy and a tendency to ignore or even to disparage more recent achievements. The latter, so far as they are considered at all, tend to be regarded as horrible examples of scholastic logic-chopping that are wholly divorced from the profounder human needs of our time. Such phrases as "symbolic logic," "philosophical analysis," and "logical positivism" conjure up in many academic minds only images of an outlandish professional jargon and a *recherché* symbolism whose meaning is intelligible, if at all, only to a few godless initiates, and whose point is scarcely understood even by them. For all the external world knows or thinks it needs to know (and unfortunately this includes a good many teachers of philosophy), such symbol mongering is of interest only to a few monomaniacs who make a fetish of something they call the methodology of science and who thereby forfeit the philosopher's ancient prerogative to speak and be heard on the primordial problems of man's fate. The only contemporary philosophical ideas that have received any really widespread attention outside the seminar are those impressionistic, semi-literary doctrines, such as existentialism, which least adequately represent the hard and sober thinking which has quietly made of our age one of the few periods of genuine creative advance in philosophy. The result has been that philosophical theories of great relevance to general human enlightenment remain largely unknown or else are badly misrepresented, while at the same time, half-cooked ideas, whose very intelligibility is in doubt, are treated with polite respect and attention. Indeed the very classics themselves, which should be approached as precious harbingers of truth rather than as final or official statements of the views they represent, are set in prejudicial contrast to the present aims of philosophical research.

The truth is, of course, that any such opposition between the intellectual concerns of the great thinkers of the past, such as Aristotle, Locke, or Kant, and those of such original contemporaries as Russell, Wittgenstein, and Dewey is quite illusory. The present interest in problems of methodology and in the logical analysis of such concepts as meaning, truth, and value is merely a continuation of a perennial philosophical interest in the clarification of basic general ideas and techniques of inquiry that is older than Plato. If there is a difference, it lies rather in the fact that contemporary analytical philosophers have found ways of handling these ancient questions which are clearer and more precise, and which, therefore, hold the promise of answers upon which, for the first time, reasonable men might be expected to agree. Certainly the contemporary state of philosophy leaves much to be desired, but its insistence upon clarity, order, and exactitude is all that has ever distinguished philosophy as a discipline from common-sense speculation concerning the organizing concepts by which we live.

It is my purpose in what follows to correct in some measure the prevailing lack of understanding of the humane import of analytical philosophy by showing some of the broader implications of recent findings in ethical theory. Moral philosophy in the twentieth century has entered upon a period of important theoretical advances which, when properly understood, cannot fail to have a more general significance for reflective men. I shall first indicate what some of these developments are and then say something about their relevance to ordinary human affairs.

SUBSTANTIVE ETHICS AND ANALYTIC ETHICS

Most analytical philosophers are now agreed that a primary source of the faltering progress of earlier moral philosophy is the general failure to distinguish between two very different sorts of questions which we shall call questions of "substantive ethics" and "analytic ethics." As will presently be seen, these questions are not wholly unconnected. But even to understand how this may be so requires that at the outset the point of each should be clearly distinguished.

Substantive Ethics. The fundamental question of moral philosophy has always been "What is the good life?" From the attempt to answer it arise the endless comparisons and reappraisals of specific standards of value and systems of human conduct. Belonging to this side of the subject are such hoary but never irrelevant questions as "What, if any, is the highest good?", "What are the basic principles of right action?", and "What are the common rights and responsibilities of men?" These questions are commonly held to belong to "normative ethics." So to speak of them, however, is perhaps question begging, for it already suggests a certain generic theory as to the nature or function of moral judgments. In order not to prejudice the discussion in advance I shall refer to that side of moral philosophy which addresses itself to the question how we ought to live as "substantive ethics." In so doing I wish only to indicate that any other form of philosophical reflection about morals must take its rise from the fact that substantive problems of valuation and obligation already exist. Were it not for them, the analytical questions with which we shall here be mainly concerned, would have no subject matter.

Now the illusion prevails in certain quarters that the tasks of substantive ethics are, at bottom, not intellectual but merely decisional. On such a view analysis can have little or no bearing upon the problems of the moral life. In a later portion of this essay I shall try to show how mistaken such a view is. Meanwhile it must suffice to remark that the possibility of substantive moral *philosophy* as a discipline pre-supposes that, at least in some sense, moral ideals are not beyond the reach of rational reflection and comparison. It assumes, or seems to assume, that some ideals are not merely preferred to, but are also more reasonable and hence better than others. I do not doubt that the interests of substantive ethics are finally practical as well as speculative.[1] But they would appear to rest upon the conviction that in some relevant sense practice may be informed, and that moral criticism is not just expression of personal taste or feeling. At the moment, however, I do not wish to stress this point. For purposes of contrast I wish rather to emphasize the point that although, as I believe, substantive ethics cannot dispense with rational methods, its aims remain primarily delibera-tive, and hence are incomplete until they issue forth into choice, even though the choices with which it is concerned are at a certain remove from the immediate decisions of daily life.

Analytic Ethics. The questions of substantive ethics are no longer denied relevance to the concerns of liberal educa-tion. On the contrary, it is with them, I suppose, that general education as such is very largely preoccupied. It is the sec-ond sort of question, which marks the special province of analytical moral theory, that is more frequently thought to lie apart from the general educational interests of ordinary persons. Questions of this sort are the following: "What are the meanings or uses of 'ought,' 'right,' and 'value'?", "What are the roles of moral reasoning?", "What is the nature of moral disagreement and of moral justification?", "What is the relation of factual statements to moral judgments?". By call-ing such questions "analytic," I wish merely to indicate that they are concerned in the first instance with "second-level" problems of meaning and logic rather than with "first-level" problems of deliberation and choice. It is essential to bear in

[1] Speculation is not opposed to practice. Nor is it always directed to questions concerning what exists rather than what ought to exist. Prob-lems of conduct often require speculation, not only about matters of fact, but also about the validity of moral principles themselves.

mind at the outset, however, that interest in analytical questions is not new; in fact it is nearly as old as moral philosophy itself, and seems to have arisen spontaneously the moment that reflection upon moral problems went to fundamentals. In the dialogues of Plato, for example, Socrates constantly and insistently asks of his pupils, "What is justice?" or "What is the nature of goodness?" And from Aristotle onward questions concerning the "nature" or "essence" of virtue and obligation and concerning the logic of practical reason have preoccupied most first-ranking classical moral philosophers.

Confusion of Substantive with Analytic Questions. Until fairly recently, however, the import of such questions was not sharply distinguished from those of substantive ethics, with the result that even some of the greatest philosophers remained unclear as to the character of the problems to which they addressed themselves and were in consequence uncertain as to the sorts of arguments or evidence that might be relevant to their solution. Until very lately, in fact, the same tendency to confuse questions of meaning and logic with substantive ethical issues has plagued many contemporary analysts themselves. Even G. E. Moore,[2] who is perhaps as responsible as anyone for setting analytical ethics upon its present course of inquiry, tended to conceal from himself the nature of his task by asking his own analytical questions in a misleading form. He recognized intuitively that there is a fundamental difference between questions of the form "What things are good?" and those which ask "What does 'good' mean?" Yet particularly in his earlier writings he constantly phrased questions of the latter sort in various confusing ways. By assimilating the question "What is the meaning or (better) use of 'good'?" to such apparently similar questions as "What is the property of goodness?" or, more simply, "What is goodness?" he was led to suppose that by answering the *analytical* questions he had put himself, he would also be able, once and for all, to lay the cornerstone

[2] G. E. Moore, *Principia Ethica* (Cambridge: Cambridge University Press, 1929).

of a substantive "moral science." How dubious such a supposition is will be seen as we proceed.

The Linguistic Character of Analytic Problems. It is essential to understanding of the tasks of analytical ethics to see that all such questions are, at bottom, misleading ways of asking about the meanings or uses of words. They are objectionable because they tend to conceal from the questioner the point of his question and so obscure the sorts of answer that would be relevant to it. First of all, by asking about the *property* of goodness, it is assumed that there *is* such a property which can be discovered by inspection of and abstraction from the observable characteristics of good things. This implies that we may by-pass all linguistic considerations regarding the usage of words and proceed at once to the important matters of fact to which they supposedly refer. This is a basic error. For until we have examined the use of "good" in discourse, we cannot know whether it functions referentially at all.[3] Moreover, even when words do function referentially, we still cannot determine what they mean by ignoring them and inspecting their supposed referents. It is a wise referent indeed that knows what it is called, and a wise observer who can tell by "inspection" what color is named by the word "redness." However, once we see that problems of definition and meaning—in short, problems of analysis—can only be solved by close study of the uses of words, we gain at once a purchase upon the nature of our task. In this way we are able for the first time to delimit the range of relevant disagreement and hence seriously to hope for a settlement of the endless disputes that for centuries have divided the various schools of ethics.

The Human Relevance of Linguistic Analysis. At first

---

[3] I.e., whether there is in fact some objective quality or relation which it purports to designate; whether its purpose is, as a matter of fact, to designate, describe, or inform at all. The terms "referential," "descriptive," and "designative" are used interchangeably throughout.

sight problems of meaning may appear to have little relevance to the substantive problems of human conduct. The
question of how we are to use such words as "ought" and
"good" may be of theoretical interest to the logician or seman-
ticist, but the answer to it, as the saying goes, "butters no
bread." On this point not merely the opponents of analytical
philosophy but also a good many analysts have been agreed.
And it must be confessed that there is some initial plausibility
to the argument that analytic philosophy cannot have it both
ways: it cannot claim the complete irrelevance of substantive
or factual considerations to analytical questions without at
the same time admitting the irrelevance of its own verbal
and logical concerns to substantive or factual questions.

Such views I take to be ill-considered, and I shall try
subsequently to show that philosophical analysis is not
the academic concern of a few methodolatrists and word-
mongers who have thereby turned their backs upon the
pursuit of wisdom, but an indispensable means to clear
thinking and relevant argument in the conduct of practical affairs. Ways of life are articulated through words. If we
misunderstand the ways of the words through which they
are expressed, so also will our grasp of the ways of life themselves be faltering and confused. If we radically misconceive
the roles of moral judgment and the nature of moral reasoning, so also will we stumble in the use of moral discourse.
And if we are unclear as to the meanings of the great terms
that lay down the practical ends-in-view which are to guide
our lives, there can be no clarity in the ends themselves
and no settled direction to our conduct. In no domain of
human activity is there more linguistic confusion and fallacious thinking than in the domain of morality, and in none
therefore can a greater benefit be hoped for from the study
of the language in which the activity is clothed.

In order to give body to these remarks, however, it will first
be necessary to follow for a bit the progress of analytical
moral theory in recent decades. In this way we will be better
able to see just how recent findings in this domain may be of
use in the conduct of life.

THE DEVELOPMENT OF RECENT ANALYTIC ETHICS

Descriptivism and Its Defects.   Most earlier proponents
of analytical philosophy tended to take for granted that the
primary function of language is the communication of
knowledge or information about matters of fact. They assumed as a matter of course, that the task of the analyst is to
fix more clearly the supposed designata or referents of the
terms with which he is concerned. Such an assumption can
do relatively little harm so long as the words under analysis
happen to be used descriptively—so long, that is to say, as
the sentences in which they occur are employed to characterize and predict events. It is an egregious assumption, which
simply blocks the path of inquiry, when the role of expressions is not essentially informative. As we shall see, it is
fatal to the understanding of ethical terms whose primary
uses are commendatory and prescriptive, and which only
secondarily, and in certain special circumstances, serve
incidentally to characterize the things of which they are predicated. And in humanities generally, it at once results in
endless and futile disputation, and fortifies, where it does not
itself produce, profound confusions of value that have been
endemic throughout the history of our intellectualistic and
rationalistic culture. When what you want to know is the
"cash value" of such words as "yellow" or "buffalo," the rule
"Hunt the referent!" seems sound enough advice, although
even in such cases a flat-footed use of it can impede rather
than advance inquiry. But where words are not used referentially, and the utterances in which they occur are not intended to express anything which "corresponds to the facts,"
the rule actually produces unclarity. By implication, moreover, it has the disastrous effect of creating the impression
that when a referent cannot be found the word in question is
senseless and its use the business only of deceivers and
fools. Such an impression is inimical to the interests of literature and religion as well as morals; worse still, perhaps, it
endangers fruitful theory formation in science itself.

The Search for a Science of Morals: Intuitionists and Naturalists. The referential dogma, as it may be called, dominated nearly all of the work which was done in analytical moral theory during the first decades of the present century. Even a cursory examination shows that it controls the direction of the analyses both of such influential "intuitionists" as G. E. Moore,[4] W. D. Ross,[5] and C. D. Broad [6] in England and of the more influential American "naturalists" such as John Dewey [7] and R. B. Perry.[8] Under its influence, all of these important writers conceived the primary aim of moral philosophy to be that of reducing ethics to a science. They believed that only by means of a definition or clarification of the referent of the "primary" ethical terms, such as "good" or "value," would we be able to state precisely the conditions under which moral or value judgments, like other types of "scientific" statement, might be verified. Many of them also believed that, by defining such other ethical terms as "ought" and "right" in relation to the primary terms, it could be shown that the terms employed in various forms of valuation all have a common referent. In this way they sought to reduce or eliminate altogether the necessity for appeals to special acts of "insight" or "intuition" either in determining the meaning of ethical terms or in certifying the judgments in which they occur.

Certainly not all of these writers found precisely what they were looking for. Some of them, like Ross, came to despair of reducing "right" to "good" or of defining "obligation" in relation to "value." Some, like Moore, were also forced to conclude that "good" is not an empirical concept at all. Still,

[4] Moore, op. cit.

[5] W. D. Ross, *The Right and the Good* (Oxford: The Clarendon Press, 1930).

[6] C. D. Broad, *Five Types of Ethical Theory* (New York: Harcourt, Brace, 1930).

[7] John Dewey, *The Logical Conditions of a Scientific Treatment of Morality* (Chicago: University of Chicago Press, 1903); Dewey, *Theory of Valuation* (Chicago: University of Chicago Press, 1939); John Dewey and J. N. Tufts, *Ethics,* rev. ed. (New York: Henry Holt, 1932).

[8] R. B. Perry, *The General Theory of Value* (New York: Longmans, Green, 1926).

all of them hoped that the hitherto insolvable disagreements in ethics would be capable of a rational resolution if only the methods employed in the validation of moral judgments could be shown to have the same essential logical structure as that which has enabled the exact sciences to move into the thoroughfare of cumulative knowledge. For intuitionists and naturalists alike, this meant hunting and finding the common referents (objective qualities and relations) that are presumably designated by ethical terms. Thus, for example, Moore, in the opening pages of *Principia Ethica*, contrasts the hit or miss affair of ordinary "personal advice" and "exhortation" with the interest of "scientific ethics" which seeks to discover, amidst the apparently random assortment of things which men call "good" or "desirable," that common, objective quality through which alone we may truly know what things are really good. Subsequently he hoped to discover those objective principles of right action which would supply the objective grounds of valid moral judgment, thus removing from scientific moral deliberation that element of prejudice and vague surmise which characterizes the moral opinions of ordinary men.

Now superficially no ethical theory lies at a further remove from Moore's than that of John Dewey. Moore was an intuitionist whose loyalty to understanding and truth is deeper than any loyalty he might have to any particular method such as that of empirical science. For Dewey the two commitments are identical, and he remained throughout his later life an intransigent naturalist and experimentalist. What science could not enable him to say, he did not care to discuss. Yet despite basic epistemological differences in their respective analyses of ethical terms, Dewey's fundamental view of the task of moral theory differs little from that of Moore. The title of one of his most important and influential works in ethics, *The Logical Conditions of a Scientific Treatment of Morality*, itself shows that, like Moore, he took it for granted that the task of philosophical analysis was to show in detail how moral discourse is reducible to the status of a science. Numerous other examples might be given to

show the same underlying assumption that the language of
morals is or ought to be an objective, scientific language,
and that morality itself is or can be rendered intellectually
respectable only by specifying the intersubjective verifying
conditions of judgments of value and right action.

Beyond Descriptivism: Moore's Critique of Naturalists.
Gradually, however, a very different view concerning the use
of ethical terms and the role of moral judgments has
emerged. By a curious irony, the rise of this conception was
due in large part to conclusions implicit in Moore's own
acute analyses of ethical terms. Indeed one of the dramatic
turning points in the history of moral theory occurs when,
despite his own professed intention to reduce ethics to a
science, Moore's own arguments convinced him that any attempt to define moral notions empirically is bound to fail.[9]
As stated by Moore, these arguments were less conclusive
than he supposed. Yet they served to convince a whole
generation of moral philosophers of the essential wrong-
headedness of the whole naturalistic program in ethics. In
essence, the argument went something like this: Of any
empirical characteristic which may be designated by such
words as "desire," "pleasure," "satisfaction," or "adjustment"
(the words, that is to say, in terms of which naturalists have
perhaps most frequently defined the terms "good" or
"value"), one may always seriously ask, "But, after all, is it
really good?"[1] This eternally "open question," Moore believed, shows that the property of goodness or value cannot
be identified with any "natural" characteristic, and that the
word "good," which designates this property, can never have
the same meaning as any expression designating a "natural"
characteristic. In fact, Moore held that all attempts whatever to define ethical terms are at bottom guilty of the same
"naturalistic fallacy" of confusing questions concerning the
meaning of "good" with substantive problems as to the

[9] G. E. Moore, op. cit.
[1] Moore's question was intended to show the futility not only of
empirical, but also of "metaphysical" definitions of goodness.

things which in fact are good.[2] He concluded, in a way which is understandable given the premises of his analysis, that "good" must be assumed to designate a simple, unanalyzable, and (whatever that means) "non-natural" quality whose apprehension is entirely beyond the reach of our ordinary empirical faculties. It is for this reason that Moore is usually classified as an "intuitionist," even though that designation may appear to suggest a kind of philosopher very different from the common-sensical, "Let's-have-no-nonsense" sort of thinker Moore professed to be—and was. But Moore was no mystic or romantic advocate of private intuitions into what was never seen on land or sea. It was argument and logical analysis that convinced him that goodness is a non-natural quality, not insight which he might claim as a prophet or a seer.

Beyond Descriptivism: Ogden and Richards' Emotive Theory of Ethics. Moore's conclusion was plainly unacceptable to empirically-minded philosophers, even when they were impressed by the force of his arguments. To many of them, therefore, his analysis seemed to imply merely the failure of the program of "moral science." Negatively, his insistence upon the indefinability of "good" and upon the irreducible logical difference between "natural" and "moral" facts suggested that "moral facts" might not be facts at all. Evidently what was wanted was a more flexible conception of the roles of language that was not committed in advance to the dogma that in all significant uses words function essentially as signs. Such a conception was first introduced in recent times by C. K. Ogden and I. A. Richards,[3] the pioneers of the now flourishing discipline of semantics. In effect, Moore was compelled to invent a realm of "non-natural" entities in order to have something for his indefinable ethical terms to refer to. Ogden and Richards, on the other

[2] These arguments and their merits are discussed in more detail in later essays.

[3] C. K. Ogden and I. A. Richards, *The Meaning of Meaning* (New York: Harcourt, Brace, 1938).

hand, rejected altogether Moore's underlying assumptions about the meanings of words and so were free to draw an entirely different conclusion from Moore's own arguments. Such words as "good," they contended, are non-designative. They serve, not as names, but as emotive expressions of attitude and as imperative prods to action. Accordingly the utterances in which such words occur are not statements which might be verified as true or false. Even to raise the question as to the method of their verification involves at the outset a complete misconception of their linguistic function.

Beyond Descriptivism: The Logical Positivist' Approach to Ethics. In a very different quarter this view received support from a new generation of philosophers who were uncompromisingly empirical in their approach to the method of human knowledge, but were more impressed than the older empiricists had been with the potentialities of the new logic as a tool for the analysis of propositions and for the construction of a more exact or "ideal" language for the formation and transformation of scientific statements.[4] They accepted the directive that all "meaningful" statements must be capable in principle of reformulation in terms of an ideal language of science through which their verifying conditions would be more precisely expressed. At first, they contended that the method of their verification is literally constitutive of the meaning of all significant propositions, although in recent years they have been compelled to abandon so stringent a condition of "descriptive" meaning. It may appear from this that the "logical positivists" or 'logical empiricists" as they alternatively called themselves, were still subtly under the spell of descriptivism, and so, indeed, they were. Hence it might be supposed that they would follow the lead of the naturalists in trying to reconstruct the language of morals or valuation in such a way that it might be shown to conform to the requirements of "meaningful" discourse as they conceived it. Here, however, education took a hand. Nearly all of the original group of logical positivists were

[4] The work of I. A. Richards seems to have been largely independent of this movement, though it is clearly related to it.

educated in Austria and Germany where the idealist tradition was then still the dominant philosophy. Since Kant, the adherents of this tradition simply took it for granted that a radical bifurcation must be made between the logical and epistemological foundations of morality and those of empirical science. The positivists in effect took this bifurcation for granted, and so were not tempted to follow the lead of the American naturalists in trying to formulate a science of morality. But because of their commitment to the ideal of the "unity of science," they could not accept the idealists' view of morals as a form of *Geisteswissenschaft*. If there is no empirical property of goodness or value, so they maintained, there is no such property at all; if moral discourse does not conform to the canons of the scientific method, then morality is simply not a form of knowledge.[5] They concluded, therefore, that ethical concepts are "pseudo-propositions." [6]

Their analysis of moral discourse must be also viewed, however, in another way as an indirect corollary of an approach to the analysis of signs which regards ordinary language as an inadequate and logically imprecise vehicle of communication. Virtually no philosophers at this stage questioned that words are signs. The task of analysis, as the positivists conceived it, is not so much to determine the meanings of ordinary expressions, but to replace such expressions with a more exact or "ideal" language of science. Now as they are formulated in ordinary language, ethical sentences are grammatically indistinguishable from other sentences that express *bona fide* factual propositions. Because they are expressed in the indicative mood, as are ordinary factual statements, it appears at first that the predicate terms of such sentences are used to assign a corresponding property to the things designated by their subject terms. Logically, however, ethical sentences are indistinguishable from imperatives such as "Shut the door" or "Keep off of the

[5] See Rudolf Carnap, *Philosophy and Logical Syntax* (London: Kegan, Paul, Tench, Trubner, 1935).
[6] The same argument, of course, could be used to show that the concepts of pure mathematics and logic are also pseudo-concepts.

grass." It is indeed precisely this sort of misleading and confusing feature of ordinary language which, according to the positivists, renders it so poor a medium for clear thinking and exact statement; for this reason, so they contend, it must be replaced by a correct language which would contain no meaningless terms and would permit no pseudo-propositions.[7]

Since, then, there is no way of specifying verifying conditions for ethical judgments, there is no way of showing any party to an ethical disagreement to be in error. From a logical point of view, therefore, ethical disagreement is entirely pointless. But in that case what can be the sense of moral discourse? It may be nonsense. It is at any rate a very potent sort of nonsense in which empirically-minded philosophers and scientists also indulge themselves unofficially when they are not at work. If value judgments are without meaning, this would appear to be the proof perfect that man is the irrational animal, since he ostracizes those whom he pronounces "immoral" and is frequently quite prepared to sacrifice even his life for the sake of a pseudo-concept. The solution to this paradox was provided by the distinction, first formulated by Ogden and Richards,[8] between two radically different kinds of "meaning." One of them, which is characteristic of the language of science, is "cognitive meaning" or "descriptive meaning"; the other, which is exemplified in art, religion, and morality is "emotive meaning." The former is designative, and the statements involving it may be true or false; the latter is non-designative and the sentences involving it are essentially expressive and incitive.[9]

Problems of Emotive Theories of Ethics. Unfortunately, this distinction created almost as many problems as it at first appeared to solve. In the first place, what in the world *is* emotive meaning, and how is it possible? Many critics, such

[7] This view was perhaps most clearly stated by A. J. Ayer, *Language, Truth and Logic* (London: V. Gollancz, Ltd., 1936).

[8] Op. cit.

[9] This approach was carried to its greatest achievement in the work of Charles Stevenson, *Ethics and Language* (New Haven: Yale University Press, 1944).

as Max Black,[1] have questioned whether there can be such a "mode" of meaning at all; others have doubted whether the emotive effects of language can be accounted for in the absence of any element of cognitive meaning; some have also argued that it is merely a by-product of cognitive or descriptive meaning. But even if we waive these difficulties, there are other equally serious problems involved in the use of the notion of "emotive meaning" as a tool for analysis. If, for example, morality, poetry, and religion are all lumped together as "emotive," how is it possible to distinguish between them? Yet anyone who is actively concerned with these forms of discourse cannot believe that they have the same kind of effect or are employed in the service of the same kind of end. In a word, is not the term "emotive" simply another more pretentious, pseudo-technical way of saying "unscientific" which therefore tells us nothing positive whatever about the forms of words to which it is applied?

Were there space, even graver objections to the concept of emotive meaning might be raised. Nevertheless, it must be insisted that even this crude, vastly oversimplified classification of the meanings of words was a great step forward. Just because it was so crude and so vague, it has been a goad to further research and to subtler, more complex theories of language. And, once for all, it served to destroy the stultifying and pernicious illusion that language is merely an instrument of scientific thought. Under it, the question-begging rule "Hunt the referent!" gradually gave way to a more flexible and more realistic approach to the variable functions of symbols.

The Plural Uses of Ordinary Language. More recently, under the impact of the teaching and later writings of Ludwig Wittgenstein,[2] there has arisen within analytical philosophy a new movement [3] which, among other things, has helped

[1] Max Black, *Language and Philosophy* (Ithaca: Cornell University Press, 1949), Ch. 9.

[2] Ludwig Wittgenstein, *Philosophical Investigations* (Oxford: Baisell Blackwell, 1953).

[3] This school is most clearly and persuasively represented by the ethical writings of S. E. Toulmin, *An Examination of the Place of*

to make good the defects and limitations inherent in the positivistic approach to the analysis of language. Its proponents begin with the premise that ordinary language is multifunctional. They are concerned to determine, by careful study of particular forms of words, just what the various positive roles and uses of ordinary language may be. Their assumption is that, when properly used, ordinary expressions are never meaningless and that the normal use of words in ordinary language is never without point. The task of analysis is thus not to replace ordinary language, but to determine its uses, and through this to illuminate the wider practices of which such uses are a part. This school, therefore, radically rejects the contention of Bertrand Russell that ordinary language is a crude repository of outworn metaphysics which cannot be trusted for the clear articulation and communication of ideas. Like any language, ordinary language is a tool; and when correctly employed, it is a sufficiently precise and flexible tool for the ordinary conduct of human affairs. In practice it is not misleading. It is only when philosophers ignore the contexts of its normal uses and applications that it proves misleading. Thus, for example, it is only when we ask what goodness or obligation is, in and by itself, that we lose our logical bearings and are tempted to adopt wrong-headed models for the analysis of ethical terms. Viewed in context, moral discourse is not a crude, prescientific form of speech which must be reconstituted so as to render it more amenable to the requirements of a "moral science." Such a science is not even a possibility, and any such reconstruction, were it to prevail, would in effect mean the supercession of the institution of morality altogether. But neither is the language of morals a merely expressive language for the venting and inciting of private feeling or emotion. Were it to become such, in consequence of insensi-

---

Reason in Ethics (Cambridge: Cambridge University Press, 1950). As the reader will presently discover, the affinities of the present writer to this school are very close, although there are essential differences which should also be noted.

tive philosophical tampering, the general social consequences would be incalculable. All models for the analysis and interpretation of moral discourse provide, at best, only partially relevant analogies which are inevitably misleading and invariably subvert the aims of understanding when taken more seriously as bases for "logical reconstruction."

The Language of Conduct: Organization of Social Behavior. The philosophers who hold this view accept the thesis that the language of conduct is a practical and dynamic mode of speech whose primary role is the organization and control of behavior rather than the description or prediction of matters of fact. So far they agree with the emotivists. Otherwise, however, the two approaches have little in common; for the new approach takes seriously, as the emotive theory does not, the fundamental distinction between moral judgments, which profess a certain objectivity and impersonality, and mere expressions of taste or interest which neither have nor claim to have any inter-personal "authority" over the judgments or conduct of others. It takes seriously, also, the normal assumption that moral reasoning is not just a way of "irrigating" someone's attitudes (although it may be this also), but an impersonal rule-governed mode of justification to which the concept of validity may be relevantly applied. And in general the new approach regards moral discourse from an institutional viewpoint as a complex, if informal, machinery of regularized social adjustment and adaptation. Its adherents accept the imputation that there is a point in speaking of arguments as "irrational" and of decisions as "arbitrary"; and it takes seriously the prevailing assumption that in speaking of a supporting reason to a moral conclusion as a "good" or "bad" reason, we are expressing something more than our own first-personal approval or disapproval of it. The task of the moral philosopher is not to try to show what practical reasoning would be or ought to be if it were to conform to certain rules of inference which the formal logician or methodologist may prefer to regard as "valid." Rather it is to elucidate the patterns of deliberation and justification which, as they stand, determine what we mean in speaking of a process of moral argumentation as "invalid" or "irrational."

The Language of Conduct: Rule-Governed and Impersonal. In brief, the new approach takes seriously common-sense appearances in the light of which the characterizations of moral discourse offered by the descriptivists and the emotivists alike must inevitably seem paradoxical. Morality could not become a science without a radical reconstruction of the very uses of such terms as "good" and "ought"; but such a reconstitution would no longer enable us to say (or do) "the ethical thing." It would be better, because less misleading, if the descriptivists really wish to transform the language of morals into a descriptive, scientific form of speech, simply to say with Nietzsche that we should go beyond "good" and "evil" altogether. Such a view is worth considering; but it should not be allowed to masquerade paradoxically as a theory of morals. On the other hand, the terms of moral discourse are, in use, not such wildly "open-textured" expressions of emotion as the emotivists contend. Governing the use of ethical terms, in the various distinctive contexts in which they occur, are rules of application that prescribe the manner in which ordinary substantive prescriptions and commendations are to be made. Such rules, however vague or flexible, still set limits to the sort of judgment we are prepared to countenance as "ethical." Each time we apply moral rules we are not simply "venting" our own passing sentiments or wishes; rather, we are in such a case invoking an impersonal linguistic ritual which serves to keep practical deliberation and disagreement within certain socially acceptable bounds.

The point, then, is not that we do not express our own attitudes in using the language of morals—on the contrary. If, as we have suggested, the language of morals is an effective social device for the regulation of human relations, it would be exceedingly odd if moral judgments did not reflect certain basic social attitudes of the speaker. But moral judgments reflect our attitudes as social animals precisely because the latter have themselves been largely formed by habituation to the rules which govern the application of ethical terms. To parody Marx, it is not so much the individual conscience that determines the application of ethical terms, as it is the standard application of the terms which determines the conscience of the individual moral judge or agent. In short, it is through the constant employment of the language of morals that the individual is perforce obliged continually to re-enact certain impersonal social roles which willy-nilly render him, or at any rate his judgment, a "voice" or "conscience" of the social group. And when, for whatever reason, the individual misuses or misapplies the terms of moral discourse, he is automatically subject to the same forms of verbal rebuke which, in other domains, are directed against those who will not "talk sense" or "listen to reason."

These suggestions will be further explored in other essays in this volume. But enough has perhaps been said to indicate the increasing sensitivity and maturity of recent philosophical analyses of morals. What should be emphasized is that the errors to which philosophical analysis are subject, like those that occur within science itself, tend to be self-correcting, and that out of the successive misconceptions and exaggerations which we have had occasion to observe there is gradually emerging a more and more adequate grasp of an exceedingly complex symbolic process.[4] Certainly, the end is not yet. But enough is already understood concerning the language of conduct to be of use in the education of ordinary men. What remains to be shown is the relevance of these findings to general human enlightenment and to the conduct of life.

---

[4] For example, as I now believe, the remarks made on the preceding page concerning moral rules are in need of radical qualification and refinement.

THE PRACTICAL RELEVANCE OF ANALYTIC ETHICS

As I believe, there are two important respects in which this analytical study of morals may be relevant to the practical concerns of men. One of these pertains to the findings themselves, the other to the method of analysis employed in reaching these findings.

The Language of Conduct and the Life of the Community. Now if, as we have maintained, the language of morals is a dynamic language which at the same time is subject to relatively definite rules of application in various contexts, there follows at once a corollary which is pertinent to the present purpose. That is to say, the patterns of moral discourse, including the prevailing forms of commendation, prescription, and justification, provide a kind of mirror of the prevailing patterns of interpersonal relation and hence of the underlying way of life of the community. To the extent, also, that the individual himself is not deviant, the analysis of moral discourse will also provide a sort of map of his character as a social being. Any ambiguities, vaguenesses, or inconsistencies in the one will at the same time reflect confusions, indecisions, and tensions in the other. For example, where incompatible analyses arise from an inability to accept common instances and counter-instances in trying to determine the range of application of ethical terms, this will at once suggest, not a failure of analysis on the part of someone or other, but rather a lack of homogeneity in the moral attitudes of the social group. And conversely, where analysis is not stalled because of such disagreements, there is indicated the presence of a common system of moral habits. Again, a great deal of interest in defining and redefining ethical terms will tend to reflect a lack of clarity or consistency in interpersonal relations or else an inadequacy of communal moral standards and practices to the satisfaction of underlying human wants or drives.[5]

[5] These remarks are further developed in essay three, "Definitions, Factual Premises, and Ethical Conclusions."

All this being so, it would appear evident that anyone who seeks to know himself as a moral being will perforce be obliged to reflect with some care upon the nature of moral discourse. And if, as most of us profess to believe, a grasp of the communal way of life is essential to intelligent participation in the guidance and control of human affairs, then the study of the language of conduct must be a matter of general human concern.

Correcting Popular Misconceptions. In the second place, it is only through analysis of moral discourse that one gradually becomes aware of its limits. Such understanding is all the more important precisely because, unlike mathematical logic or the theory of induction, ethical theory, in one crude form or another, is already part of the public domain. As such it is constantly, if illicitly, used to bolster or lend prestige to various substantive prohibitions or demands. As any teacher of ethics soon discovers a great part of the difficulty of instruction arises from the fact that most of his pupils already hold theories—or prejudices—of their own which they have acquired in the home or school or church. I mean by this not merely the obvious fact that most persons, by the time they have entered college, have well-established moral habits and attitudes but rather that they have fairly well defined views concerning the meanings of ethical terms and the nature of moral principles. To one student, so-called Protagorean relativism seems virtually self-evident; to another, brought up perhaps in a parochial school, the view that moral "truths" are laws of nature or divine commandments needs little argument; to still another, morality itself is a form of prejudice to be replaced by hygiene and social engineering. In short, there abound in the popular consciousness a great many pre-analytic theories of morals, nearly all of which, unfortunately, involve profound misconceptions as to both the character of moral judgment and the possibilities of moral justification. And these, unhappily, deeply interpenetrate the whole moral consciousness of those afflicted with them. In what follows, I wish briefly to indicate how the findings of recent analysis may serve to correct some of these misconceptions and so to clarify the deliberative practices of the layman.

For example, if one clearly grasps the essentially practical or regulative role of value judgments generally and of the forms of reasoning intended to support them, one comes finally to understand, as one can in no other way, why it is that increased knowledge of matters of fact does not and cannot compel common agreement at the moral or ideological level.[6] In this way one may be fortified against a peculiarly prevalent and virulent sort of disillusionment either with morals or with science or with both which afflicts those who have been led to suppose that there is a necessary connection between knowledge and virtue. If one also understands the fact that our moral judgments and hence our moral practice are fashioned in the light of socially conditioned patterns of commendation and prescription, one is far less likely to misconstrue or to object in the wrong way to the moral faults or failures of "insight" of those who systematically disagree with us. And one will see thereby that the remedy for such faults and failures is not to be looked for in statements of principle or in appeals to "right reason" which beg the very point at issue. "Self-evidence" is nearly always a sign, not of god-given truth, but of thorough habituation. By properly learning this lesson through the study of the logic of moral justification and persuasion, one is thereby enabled to comprehend a matter of the greatest importance for intelligent cultural relations, namely, that the moral principles of one's own people, however beneficent, are not due to profounder insight into the metaphysical structure of the cosmos, but rather, for the most part, to a more fortunate cultural tradition. Conversely one may see that what we conceive to be moral obtuseness or bigotry is due, as a rule, not so much to stupidity or ignorance as to a less benignant human environment. In this way one may also gain a sense of the precariousness of any moral order and of

[6] For a fuller discussion of the concept of ideology and its relation to morals and to philosophy itself, see my *The Age of Ideology* (New York: Houghton Mifflin Co., 1957), esp. Chapter I.

the preciousness of those social and cultural circumstances in which alone a "reasonable" ethical system can grow and flourish.

With all this comes a gradual awareness of why it is that the basic problems of community and world order can never be resolved by direct religious or political propaganda, but only by a process of slow re-education. Such understanding is doubtless sobering; but it may protect the individual and the society against the self-destroying disillusionment which attends the inevitable failures of short-term moral crusades. At the same time it might help to save us from the now fashionable varieties of irrationalism which ascribe men's spiritual limitations to original sin and which make a fetish of human weakness or depravity without shedding any light whatever upon its causes or the means of its removal.

The Ultimacy of Conscience.   Possibly the greatest practical insight which the study of moral philosophy can impart is understanding of the fact, which Kant long ago expressed in another form, that there is no way of "deriving" moral principles from anything beyond the consciences of men, and hence that there is no way whatever of guaranteeing the validity of any moral code by trying to "ground" it in science, or the nature of the universe—or in the will of God. Or, better, because less misleading, one may see that any such "grounding" is, in practice, merely another symbolic device for articulating and regulating human attitudes which can be used effectively only among those who already have been practically conditioned to respond to it. The masks of conscience are many; the important thing is to understand them for what they are. Maturity comes when we finally realize that, however we may disguise the fact by the symbols by means of which we conduct our communal affairs, everything in this domain is finally "up to us." Then we see that ours is the only responsibility, and that it is our own constitutional loyalty to principles of liberty, justice, and welfare that can alone provide a relevant practical ground for the rights and duties which, as we believe, should be the prerogatives of every man.

This is altogether a matter of understanding what one can and cannot do with the language of conduct. The great trouble with dogmatic theories of moral obligation which insist upon referring it to "natural law" or "divine commandment" is precisely that they prevent those who accept them from seeing why they find such doctrines attractive or "true," and, conversely, why others do not. By helping to remove such forms of parochial self-deception and hence of eventual disillusionment, ethical theory may make a very considerable contribution to the advancement of common practical understanding.

In the preceding remarks I have tried to suggest a few of the ways in which philosophical study of moral discourse may have a beneficial effect upon our grasp of one important aspect of human relations. Before concluding I wish to show also that the very methods employed by the analyst in trying to penetrate the thicket of human conduct are also useful and even necessary within the more concrete domain of substantive ethics itself.

Clarifying Our Fundamental Goals in Life. Now it has been frequently maintained, and even today most philosophers would appear to hold, that the only practical relevance of reason in the conduct of life lies in its power to discover possible causes or means to ends upon which we have already decided. Since Aristotle many philosophers have argued that rational deliberation is and can be concerned only with the ways of achieving ends, but not with the formation of the ends themselves. This, I take it, is the primary point of Hume's paradoxical remark that reason is and ought to be the slave of the passions. Such a view clearly implies that at bottom the formation of a decision is a nonrational or supra-rational affair. (Those who have held it, incidentally, have not always seen that if this is so, it applies just as much at the level of means or proximate goals as at the level of so-called ends or ultimate goals.) Now undoubtedly there is an important grain of truth in such a view, although it is misleadingly expressed. This grain of truth is simply the logical point that a moral judgment, whether commendation, prescription, or imperative, cannot be logically derived from a theoretical or factual truth alone. Because it has been misleadingly formulated the theory has given rise to the notion that all we have to do or can do in reaching a decision is to let nature take its course, to wait, that is to say, until the strongest of our conflicting interests happens to manifest itself. Despite its patent irrationalistic implications, such a view curiously involves an extremely intellectualistic conception of purposive behavior which is contradicted both by common sense and by contemporary psychological theory. For it evidently assumes that although we may not know in advance how to get them, we all do know at the outset what our ultimate goals are, and hence that we must accept these as "given" in any process of deliberation.

How inconsistently such a position is usually held is evident from even a cursory examination of Aristotle's own *Nicomachean Ethics*. In that work, Aristotle, instead of directing his main effort to determining the means to happiness, which he considers the universal end of human action, expends his energy in trying to ascertain what the true nature of happiness is. From a practical point of view—and Aristotle's aim in the *Ethics* was thoroughly practical—such an analysis would be entirely pointless were it the case that the goal or end to which all men aspire is unambiguous, well-formed, and fixed. The fact of the matter is that the work of most great ethical thinkers has been directed not to questions of means but rather to the still more difficult task of clarifying the primary aims of the good life. And their own disagreements, uncertainties, and confusions are themselves sufficient evidence that whatever else may be true of them, our fundamental ways of life are neither clearly understood nor universally aspired to. Professor C. I. Lewis puts the point succinctly when he says, "At least half of the world's avoidable troubles are created by those who do not know what they want and pursue what would not satisfy them if they had it." A similar thesis is implicit in the findings of contemporary psychoanalytic and psychiatric theory. If Freud and his successors are even half right, most human action is governed by hidden motives that are imbedded in substitute symbols whose practical import we come to understand only with the greatest difficulty. Beyond all this, however, the lives of even "normal" human beings are largely controlled by words and symbols whose meanings are frequently ambiguous or misunderstood. It is because of this that the task of clarifying such golden words as "liberty," "justice," "democracy," "person," and love" is so essential to the well-being of any people whose way of life is expressed in terms of them. For if they are unclear or confused or inconsistent, then so also is the way of life.

It is no part of my intention, as my allusion to psychoanalysis might seem to indicate, to suggest that philosophical analysis can provide a complete therapy for mankind's ethical neuroses. What I do contend is that the clarification of ideals and the clarification of the terms by means of which they are articulated is a single process, and that in a humble way, every attempt to determine what sort of life one really wants to live involves essentially the same painful process of analyzing and clarifying the meanings and uses of words to which the analytical philosopher devotes himself professionally. The difference between them is not so much a difference in method as a difference in the thoroughness and sensitivity with which it is applied.

The point I am making might itself provide the topic for another book. It must suffice here to conclude this discussion with a few observations that may further illustrate my theme. Consider, for example, how frequently the hesitancy and confusion of our practice is correlated with lack of understanding of the import of ideals to which we think we have committed ourselves. Consider how often practical disagreements not only between individuals but also between whole societies are due to failures to recognize equivocations in the terms by means of which conflicting aims are expressed, and how baffled we frequently are as to the causes of such disagreements. Practical misunderstanding and conflict constantly arise from the fact that the same

terms are unwittingly used by both parties to express different or opposing aims, or, perhaps more tragically, from the
fact that different terms are unknowingly used to express
what are or would be common aspirations if only the terms
themselves were better understood. Communists and liberals
alike talk about something they call "democracy"; both appear to regard it as the consummation devoutly to be wished,
differing apparently only with respect to the means to be
employed; yet how profoundly unlikely such a characterization is. Or again, and on another plane, such different moralists as Epicurus, Marcus Aurelius, Jesus, Kant, Hobbes,
and John Stuart Mill expressed their respective conceptions
of the good life in terms which at least superficially express
different and in some cases opposing moral attitudes. How
can the man of pleasure, the stoic, the man of God and
Love, the incarnate rationalist, the incarnate egoist, and the
utilitarian all be supposed to aspire to the same ultimate
human condition? I do not say they can; I do maintain that
the only way such a question could be answered is through
the same sort of analysis which, on another level and in
another context, is employed in trying to determine the
meanings of "ought" or "good" and the logic of moral justification.

My contention is, then, that both the methods and the
results of contemporary analytical ethics are indispensable
adjuncts of enlightened moral practice, and that their study
is therefore a useful or even a necessary part of any truly
humane or liberal education. What this also means, if I am
right, is that the self-conscious analytical philosopher has not
at all abandoned philosophy's ancient search for wisdom, but
on the contrary is contributing his own important share to
the world's all too skimpy fund of practical understanding.
He makes his contribution partly by providing us with
sharper tools and a clearer notion of the search itself, and
partly in a more direct way by freeing us from ancient
myths and fetishes which have created endless confusion and
needless disagreement about matters that are not necessary

parts of the tragedy of human existence. If in no other way, he would have done his share toward the advancement of human enlightenment and freedom by showing us how and on what terms morality can be a part of action. And his only but mortal enemy is the obscurantist and the mystagogue.

The Multiple Roles of the
Language of Conduct

FALSE ISSUES IN MORAL PHILOSOPHY

In an essay summarizing the outstanding issues in contemporary moral philosophy,[1] Professor William Frankena divides the ethical theories now prevalent into three main types: (a) "naturalistic" theories which assert that ethical statements are cognitive and true or false and deny that such statements are non-descriptive or that ethical terms designate any unique, non-natural characteristics; (b) "intuitionistic" theories which agree with naturalism that ethical judgments are cognitive and true or false, but hold that ethical terms do designate at least one unique, non-natural characteristic and that they are (in the empirical sense) non-descriptive; and (c) "noncognitive" theories which agree with intuitionism that ethical statements are non-descriptive and with naturalism that ethical terms do not name any non-natural characteristics, but deny that ethical statements are cognitive and true or false. This is a very fair statement of the essential contents of these theories, and a very neat statement of the basic issues which divide—or appear to divide—moral philosophers at the present time.

Under each main rubric there are of course many sub-theories which shade by degrees into one another. Under

---

[1] William Frankena, "Moral Philosophy at Mid-Century," *The Philosophical Review*, Jan. 1951, pp. 44-55.

naturalism one finds the many pure and mixed types of voluntarism, hedonism, self-realizationism, and pragmatism. Under intuitionism one finds some philosophers holding that there is only one non-natural characteristic, others that there are more than one; some who define "right" and "ought" in terms of "good," some who define "good" in terms of "ought," and others who hold that they are mutually indefinable. Under "noncognitivism" one finds expressionists, individualistic imperativists, collectivistic imperativists, "rational" imperativists, ceremonialists, conventionalists, performists, and so on. Indeed, we are only beginning to see how wide is the variety of theories which fall under the general and misleading heading of "noncognitivism."

But as one reflects upon Professor Frankena's classification a number of disconcerting facts begin to emerge.[2] For one thing it provides no place for the eclectics whose analyses of moral discourse cut across party lines. Mixed theories, like their ideological counterparts, rarely make the philosophical headlines. It is worth noting, however, that some of the ablest thinkers in recent ethics have implied that no one of the above theories does justice, in their opinion, to the diversity of statements in moral discourse. For example, there are intimations that while Professor Frankena himself appears to be sympathetic with certain intuitionistic analyses of "ought," he is inclined toward a naturalistic, perhaps even a hedonistic analysis of "value." There is also the evidently mixed view of C. I. Lewis, who distinguishes sharply between "valuations," which are regarded as empirically verifiable statements of fact, and "ethical judgments," which, one gathers, are to be construed as imperatives of a certain sort. One recalls also that Professor Stevenson, whose earlier papers upheld a relatively pure version of the expressive-incitive theory, now holds that ethical terms have dual meanings which are partly descriptive. Even A. C. Ewing, the most intransigent advocate of intuitionism in the recent lit-

---

[2] I do not doubt that Professor Frankena himself is well aware of them. His classification was intended for convenient mapping purposes only.

erature, agrees that many senses of such terms as good" and "ought" are empirically descriptive. An excellent case could be made, moreover, for the thesis that such older intuitionists as Moore and Prichard held mixed theories. Their intuitionism seems to have been directed exclusively to some particular sense of "good" or "ought" which they considered "characteristically ethical."

Reflecting further, one finds that Frankena's classifications are misleading. For they may suggest that writers who are formally affiliated with a "naturalistic" account of ethical or value judgments really deny that such judgments have "noncognitive" effects or functions—or, if one prefers, "meanings." Such is far from true. Thus, long before the vogue of the emotive theory, R. B. Perry, the arch-defender of the empirical meaningfulness of "value" and the empirical verifiability of value judgments, attempted to account for the practical relevance and "moving appeal" of such judgments.[3] By this he meant explicitly their capacity to incite interest. And John Dewey, who also defends the "scientific" status of valuations, also distinguishes them as *de jure*, as distinct from merely *de facto* judgments. Whether any of the naturalists has successfully accounted for the non-descriptive or "normative" aspects of moral discourse is, to be sure, extremely debatable. But it is plain that most of them did not mean to deny that it has such aspects. On the contrary.

It should be borne in mind that until the last two decades, it was not the practice among philosophers of any school to regard the "noncognitive" intentions or effects of discourse as part of its "meaning." When such philosophers attempted to analyze the "meanings" of ethical terms they automatically concerned themselves with their purported significations alone. Even the earlier versions of the emotive theory itself tended to regard questions concerning the "meaning" of ethical judgments exclusively in descriptive terms. Hence

[3] R. B. Perry, "Value and its Moving Appeal," *The Philosophical Review*, XLI, 4 (July 1932), pp. 337-50. Perry's awareness of the emotive meanings of such words as "good" is quite evident, both in this article and in his "Value as Simply Value," *The Journal of Philosophy*, XXVIII, No. 10 (Sept. 1931), pp. 519-26.

the paradoxical thesis of Carnap and Ayer that ethical judgments are "meaningless." When we probe beneath the surface, however, we find that so staunch an emotivist as Ayer
admitted from the outset that such words as "good" sometimes are used "cognitively." [4] I do not suggest, of course,
that Ayer and Perry or Dewey are in complete agreement. I
do maintain that, when full account is taken of their views
concerning the functions and effects as well as the "meanings" of ethical terms and judgments, it is misleading to
classify the former exclusively as an emotivist or the latter
exclusively as naturalists.

Pondering the literature of moral philosophy during the
past half-century one is forced more and more to the conclusion that although there may be some real issues, many of
the issues that divide philosophers are really pseudo-issues.
By this I mean that they often arise from concealed and misleading terminological disagreements at the meta-ethical
level. Such meta-ethical expressions as "ethical term," "normative," "characteristically ethical," and so on, are not expressions having well-established or unambiguous meanings
in ordinary language. If they are to be significantly employed, therefore, they must be stipulatively defined, either
by enumerating the particular words or expressions in ordinary language to which they apply or else through some
descriptive phrase which clearly specifies some particular
class of expressions without regard to the individual words
which fall under it. But this is just what normally is not done.
One is left to infer as best one can from the context what
this philosopher means by "ethical term," or that philosopher
understands by "normative" or "characteristically ethical."
And when one attempts to determine from their examples or
from the sorts of "criteria" which their respective analyses
are designed to meet, it becomes evident that the terms, or
at least the meanings of the terms with which they are concerned are not always the same. One philosopher is preoccupied with the problem of accounting for the rhetorical

---

[4] A. J. Ayer, *Language, Truth and Logic* (London: Gollancz Ltd.,
1936), pp. 102-3.

or incitive aspects of statements in which such terms as "good" and "ought" occur, another with their informative aspects, still another with their critical or educational roles. Again, one philosopher is concerned with the "meaning" of "ought" in such a statement as "You ought not to have made a promise you didn't intend to keep"; another with the analysis of the whole class of statements, whatever the terms in which they may be formulated, that express attitudes; and yet another with the innocuous thesis that statements about desires and enjoyments and their necessary means are empirically verifiable.

The upshot of such reflections is that most of the supposedly opposing theories of ethics are but limited accounts of different "moments" of a complex and variable mode of discourse which serves, and indeed must serve, a wide variety of functions. As one reads a competent defense of any of the main theories one cannot help acknowledging that here is a kernel of truth, misleadingly stated. It is only when it is taken to imply a denial of what other theories assert that it appears indefensible. The various "criteria" which have been proposed for an adequate analysis of moral discourse turn out, on such an interpretation, to be nothing more than expressions of the different perspectives from which such discourse may be viewed. From a certain point of view each criterion is legitimate, and the attempt to provide analyses capable of meeting it often yields interesting and important accounts of certain otherwise neglected aspects of moral discourse. Yet none encompasses all of the roles which such discourse is called upon to fulfill in ordinary life. It would seem to follow, therefore, that the better part of philosophical good sense in moral philosophy would be to divide the spoils among the several theories, and to take seriously rather than merely to acknowledge formally the fact that in this sphere above all others our language is extremely flexible in function, purpose, and effect. In this light, I propose an end to, or at least a moratorium upon, futile disputation with imaginary opponents, and that we cease pitting part against part or the special perspective against the total context. Why should we spend our strength in senseless polemics against "types" of ethical theory, which at best are special theories of particular aspects of the language of conduct, when, without sacrificing any theoretical position worth defending, we may divide and conquer at our leisure?

THE COMPLEXITIES OF PRACTICAL DISCOURSE

Leaving this question to echo and, I hope, re-echo in the mind of the reader, let us turn from type theories of "good" and "ought" to the actual complexities of practical discourse itself. Here one discovers that whatever may be the truth about so-called "ethical terms" any adequate language of conduct must in principle provide a whole battery of concepts, rules, techniques, procedures, and other linguistic functions. To accomplish the purposes both of individual *and* of social life it is, at the very least, necessary that we be able to do the following things with words: (1) identify objects, (2) describe their characteristics, (3) predict their causes and effects, (4) infer from such descriptions and predictions what means are necessary to accomplish our ends and what ends are worth entertaining seriously, (5) express individual and collective attitudes and decisions, (6) adjudicate differences in attitude, (7) clarify aims, (8) commend, exhort, and persuade others to acts which we approve or deem desirable, (9) make promises, (10) assign responsibilities, (11) authorize, regularize, and correct behavior, and this on a variety of levels. If these requirements are to be met, we would then have to be able to formulate definitions, statements of fact (of various sorts), counter-factuals, arguments, rules, proposals, commands, and principles. In short, an adequate language of conduct would have to be able to marshal and deploy the entire gamut of human capacities. And if such a language did not exist, it would have to be invented.

The only question is whether ordinary language successfully mirrors the complexities of man's practical life. And as one turns back now and reflects upon the great variety of

ethical theories and the great number of "senses" of ethical
terms and roles or functions of practically oriented judgments
which such theories reflect, the only intelligible answer is
that ordinary language provides at any rate a vastly richer
and more supple instrument for expediting the conduct of
life than any ethical theory represents it to be. At certain
points, no doubt, this language is ambiguous; at others it
both permits and requires contextual qualification in order
to function properly as a vehicle of appraisal. There is no
more reason why ordinary language should be worshiped
as a sacred cow in the sphere of valuation than in that of
exact science. But, before attempting any philosophical reconstruction of it, we should see what this language is already capable of expressing. If we do we will find that in
broad outlines it fairly represents the multiplicity of functions which, in the sphere of human conduct, are required
of it.

I propose, then, that we adopt a more flexible, and pluralistic approach to the study of the language of conduct. As
here conceived, such a study would be prepared not merely
to acknowledge but also to explicate and relate the whole
gamut of "meaning" and the whole ensemble of roles to be
found in this form of discourse. One set of meanings would
then be considered as "essential" as any other; none would be
regarded as more "characteristically" ethical than the rest.
On such a view, "system" would be held suspect, if by this is
meant the attempt to formulate sets of definitions through
which all of the meanings of ethical terms are analytically
reduced to some supposedly "basic" concept of value. Nor
would the varieties of practical judgment and argument be
assumed to be merely species of a common genus. The
planting of axiological trees of Porphyry, to judge from the
literature, is not a fruitful occupation. At the very least
there would have to be an orchard, and a good many graft-
ings of branches before we could begin to cope with our
problems. What is wanted is the successive elucidation of
distinct but practically related levels or dimensions of moral
discourse, and an explication of the *movement* of evaluation

from reaction to gesture, from expression to demand, from puzzlement to deliberation and choice, from preference to criticism, from the envisagement of means and the prediction of consequences to the clarification or definition of ends.

It is not enough, however, to treat this movement as a series of separate "contexts" within which some particular meaning or role is elicited. Moral discourse, being practical, is free to draw upon whatever intellectual and motivational resources are necessary to clarify, appraise, alter, and organize its ends-in-view. Its ends-in-view exclude no interest or purpose to which human flesh is heir. It is the failure to acknowledge explicitly the dialectical fluidity and movement of practical discourse that is in part responsible for the sense of unreality we experience in contemplating the formalized philosophical reconstructions of what we are supposed to be doing when we engage in moral deliberation and criticism. The "examples" of moral discourse on this or that level which abound in works on ethics resemble nothing so much as the elegant but artificial period rooms which we see displayed in museums of art. In such a room each piece is a perfect example of its style; every appointment a marvel of congruity and fitness. Nothing is permitted to be "out of context." An actual living room, however, is a very different sort of thing. Its harmony is "functional," and its functions determined only in part by foresight and purpose. To the outsider, it often appears disorderly, confused, eclectic, perhaps even in bad taste. Nevertheless, to the person who uses and lives in it, its parts fit together in a way which is practically intelligible even if, taken as a whole, lacking in deliberate design. Similarly, actual moral arguments frequently involve a series of statements of different logical types which are nonetheless related to each other in ways that are practically relevant to the successive and shifting demands of the participants.

This is not intended to imply that there is no "form" to moral discourse, or that the philosopher, like the misguided critic who tries to recreate the aura of a work of art, should attempt to simulate the "infinite" flow and variety of moral discourse. On the contrary. As I have tried to show in other essays included in this volume, there are, on at least some levels of moral discourse, governing principles of relevance by means of which we can contain and legitimately correct an argument which tends to get unmanageable. In morals as well as in logic or science there are distinctions between appearance and reality, between inference and random association, and between justification and persuasion. But practical argumentation *as a whole* has to satisfy interest, not a book of rules. By necessity, therefore, it cannot be wholly confined by the rules and procedures which may be invoked at particular stages to channelize and order it. It cannot be too often insisted that the end product—the ulterior decision—is not clearly envisaged at the outset. A moral choice, like a finished work of artistic creation, emerges by degrees from a process of cumulative acts of expression, clarification, prediction, justification, and persuasion. And just because the real conclusion of a moral argument is a practical decision, there is no end to the questions and answers which at any point may become relevant to it. It would be foolish to deny, as some writers have done, that in deciding what we are to do, considerations of logical coherence or of empirical verifiability have their place. It would likewise be foolish to deny that on certain levels of deliberation, there are distinctive rules of relevance which determine the order of "moral" justification. We have standards which enable us to tell a "good" reason in ethics, just as we have standards which enable us to distinguish a valid inference in logic. But just because they involve the application of rules, these levels have limits which purposive activity as a whole does not. There just is no end to the possible emotional, cognitive, and volitional considerations which may have bearing upon our practical deliberations and choices.

Here it is not a matter of what the rules of a supposed

"moral game" permit but of what the active human being is prepared to accept, what his total fund of sensibilities and capacities permit or require. In action, every consideration is and must be subordinated to the exigencies of need. If one cannot find what one wants by way of an answer on one level of discourse, one must perforce search elsewhere. If one's practical hesitations cannot be removed by arguments which observe the amenities of one level, one is driven, willy-nilly, to seek answers on another. The steps, logical or otherwise, by means of which a critical conflict of interest is resolved are necessarily secondary to the controlling interests of both parties in reaching a basis of agreement. When our problem is to discover a goal which we may hold worthy of our effort, it is less important by what means—"ethical" or "unethical"—we arrive at our solution than that when we find it, it be genuinely satisfactory to us. Rationality, whether in the sphere of formal deduction, of factual prediction, or of ethical criticism, has proved its utility to countless generations of men. We violate its canons at our peril. But there are also occasions when free association may provide a better method of resolving a practical difficulty than close reasoning. When the problem is ennui or failure of nerve, the piling up of "reasons" and "justifications" may be irrelevant and even silly. What is wanted here is stimulation and example, and this of the most moving sort. And since rhetoric without imaginative objectification usually ends by being counterpersuasive, poetry in such a case may be the only effective means of moral persuasion. To acknowledge that the reading of a novel or the witnessing of a play may sometimes be a better way of reaching a decision than the endless and paralyzing reappraisal of consequences is neither to debase art nor to defend irrationalism in ethics; it is simply to recognize that the symbolic means by which we decide what is to be done are many, and that "nonrational" procedures also have their proper function in the moral life. Where reason may be invoked it may be "wrong" to ignore it, but where there is no motive to abide by the rules of "right reason," reasoning itself becomes pointless. In the last analysis, any method must justify itself as practical procedure to interest. Failing this it remains morally quite without relevance. For in the end, the "logic" of any practical discourse is grounded only in human need.

Definitions, Factual Premises, and Moral Conclusions

TWO FORMS OF THE NATURALISTIC FALLACY

"We have seen that the claim to infer significant ethical propositions from definitions of ethical terms, which appears to constitute the essence of what Professor Moore calls the naturalistic fallacy, is a special case of a more general fallacious claim, namely, the claim to deduce ethical propositions from ones which are admitted to be non-ethical." [1] In these words Mr. A. N. Prior sums up—I think very fairly— a view which many philosophers have come to regard as the fundamental point of departure for any adequate analysis of moral discourse. It, or something like it, is also popular among social scientists who like to insist upon the ethical "neutrality" of their disciplines.[2] Despite the fact, however, that some of the best minds in recent philosophy have, for a variety of reasons, maintained the view, it seems to me to be correct only in certain very limited respects. And even in these respects it is, as usually formulated, seriously misleading. There are other, more important senses in which, as

[1] A. N. Prior, *Logic and the Basis of Ethics* (London: Oxford University Press, 1949), p. 95.
[2] For example, see Max Weber, *The Methodology of the Social Sciences,* tr. by Edward Shils (Glenville, Ill.: The Free Press, 1949), pp. 1-113. For my part, Weber's prolonged discussion does little to clarify the problems at issue. Weber's powers as methodologist seem to me generally overrated.

I shall presently try to show, the contrary position must be upheld.[3]

Let us begin by reviewing those respects in which the view—I will henceforth refer to it as antidescriptivism— might plausibly be maintained.

Consider first the more general version, namely the thesis that the claim to deduce ethical propositions from ones admitted to be nonethical is fallacious. Now by "ethical proposition" let us here understand "any judgment containing such words as 'ought,' 'right,' and 'desirable' which is used normatively to prescribe that something is to be done or approved." And by "nonethical proposition" let us understand "any statement of fact or of logic to which the predicates 'true,' 'false,' or 'probable' may be ascribed, and in which no word functions essentially in the prescriptive or imperative mode." Let us agree also that the laws of logic, by which alone one statement can be validly deduced from another, apply only to propositions which are true or false.[4] Granted these assumptions, it is not hard to see in what sense it would be possible to say that ethical propositions are not deducible from nonethical premises. And anyone who maintained the contrary would seem to be involved in a fundamental confusion of logical categories.[5]

Consider next the narrower version of antidescriptivism, namely the thesis that significant ethical propositions cannot be validly inferred from definitions of ethical terms. For the moment let us understand roughly by "definition" "any statement in which the purely descriptive or logical mean-

[3] My reasons for this contention do not involve a defense of ethical naturalism.

[4] I am, of course, here using the terms "true" and "false" in their stricter or cognitive sense. Other looser and more figurative senses are irrelevant to the present point. In another place I will have something to say about these senses as employed in moral discourse.

[5] Careful reading of such versions of the emotive theory as that of Professor Ayer suggests that perhaps nothing more was implied by the proponents of the theory than I have stated in this and the following paragraphs. The not entirely unjustified opposition to the view was largely due to misleading formulations. See A. J. Ayer, *Language, Truth and Logic* (London: Gollancz, 1936), pp. 105-6.

ing of an expression is stipulated, analyzed or otherwise characterized." Here again, given the previous interpretation of "ethical propositions," it would be simply an egregious blunder to try to infer a significant ethical proposition from the definition of an ethical term—assuming, for the nonce, that it has one. Despite evident differences, the blunder would be comparable in some ways to the error of trying to infer a nonlinguistic statement of fact from the mere analysis of a concept.

So far, then, the contentions of antidescriptivism, in both its wider and its narrower versions, may be granted. To this extent, we may agree that at bottom there really *are* basic categorial mistakes inherent in the "naturalistic fallacy," even though the arguments intended to show this by Moore and his followers are quite inconclusive.[6] Unless these statements are immediately qualified, however, they tend to be misleading. For they appear to convey the impression, and indeed have conveyed the impression to a generation of moral philosophers, that statements of fact provide no logical support for ethical propositions, and that in no sense can significant ethical propositions be legitimately inferred from definitions of ethical terms.

SOME ROLES OF DEFINITION IN MORAL PHILOSOPHY

Let us see how such an impression has arisen. We may begin by considering a number of the most influential conceptions of "definition" in moral philosophy. First let us notice the view expressed by Moore in *Principia Ethica:* "What, then, is good? How is good to be defined? Now, it may be thought that this is a verbal question. A definition does mean the expressing of one word's meaning in other words. But this is not the sort of definition I am asking for. . . . My business is solely with that object or idea, which I hold, rightly or wrongly, that the word is generally used to stand for. What I

---

[6] See William Frankena, "The Naturalistic Fallacy," *Mind*, 1939, pp. 472 ff. See also A. N. Prior, op. cit., pp. 1-12, 95-107.

want to discover is the nature of that object or idea. . . ." [7]
And again, "definitions of the kind that I was asking for,
definitions which describe the real nature of the object or
notion denoted by a word, and which do not merely tell us
what the word is used to mean, are only possible when the
object or notion in question is something complex." [8] A
similar conception is to be found in R. B. Perry's *General
Theory of Value:* "No one would be disposed to deny that
there is a common something in truth, goodness, legality,
wealth, beauty and piety that distinguishes them from gravi-
tation and chemical affinity. It is the express business of
theory of value to discover what this something is; to define the genus, and discover the differentiae of the species.
By means of such definitions and systematic connections
theory of value may unify the special philosophical and social sciences enumerated above and arbitrate between
them." [9] Whether either of these conceptions of definition is
defensible as it stands we fortunately do not now have to
consider. What is of interest to us here is that both of them
regard definition as a purely explicative operation which is
to be performed only on the descriptive or referential meanings of words. Other functions of language and other forms
of clarification are simply ignored.

We are now faced with an interesting dilemma: if, on the
one hand, we insist on construing "definition" as Moore
and Perry do, many statements occurring in moral philosophy that are normally taken as definitions simply are not
really so at all; but if, on the other hand, we construe such
statements as bona fide definitions, then these theories of
definition must be regarded as faulty, since they completely
mischaracterize the statements in question. In either case,
however, we must conclude that the intentions of many
moral philosophers who have made such statements have
been radically misunderstood. And the source of the mis-

[7] G. E. Moore, *Principia Ethica* (London: Cambridge University
Press, 1929), p. 6.

[8] *Ibid.,* p. 7. Cf. also pp. 8-9.

[9] R. B. Perry, *General Theory of Value* (New York: Longmans,
Green, 1926), pp. 4-5.

understanding must be attributed to those who, like Moore, have carelessly applied the term "definition" to expressions whose roles are not to explicate the descriptive meanings of words. It is these analysts who are responsible for the misleading implications of the thesis that the claim to infer an ethical conclusion from the definition of an ethical term is fallacious. For although, as we have seen, they are correct in maintaining that in Moore's sense of the term "definition" ethical conclusions cannot be inferred from definitions of ethical terms, they mislead us into supposing that those charged with commission of the fallacy actually *did* claim to draw such inferences. The truth is that most of the moral philosophers charged with making this claim were really doing something utterly different. To be sure such philosophers often did purport to draw ethical conclusions from "definitions" of ethical terms (together with other premises which were usually factual). But their definitions were not, and were never intended to be construed as descriptive definitions in any of the senses considered above.

For purposes of illustration, let us briefly consider the ethical theory known traditionally as hedonism. I shall discuss it in the form popularized by Mill and subsequently reformulated and criticized by F. L. Bradley, Moore, and their followers. By hedonism let us understand here the doctrine which holds that "happiness (or pleasure) alone is good" or that "pleasure is desirable, and is the only thing that is desirable as an end." I may say, in passing, that I have no interest here in any of the reasons that might be given, or in fact were given by Mill and other writers, in defense of this doctrine. Nor do I wish to suggest that the doctrine is defensible. At this point, my concern is merely with the allegation that the hedonist is wrong when he infers from the thesis of hedonism that in particular situations we ought always to choose that alternative which will produce the most happiness or the least suffering. The thesis itself may be vulnerable; that is beside the point. What I maintain is that no fallacy whatever is involved in making the inference.

In order to show this, let us see how Mill himself regards

the thesis. First of all, it is fairly clear even in *Utilitarianism* that he does *not* regard it as a theoretical statement of any sort, whether analytic or synthetic. As he says repeatedly in this work,[1] it is a "principle" or "rule" of conduct. Morality, like legislation, is a "practical art"; its rules, as distinguished from the laws of science, are "practical principles" for the conduct of life.[2] This point is elaborated with the greatest clarity in the *Logic*, a work which, in this connection, none of his critics appears to have noticed. In that work, it may be remembered, Book VI is "The Logic of the Moral Sciences," at the end of which Mill devotes a chapter to what he calls "The Logic of Practice or Art, Including Morality or Policy."[3] In this chapter, he begins by sharply distinguishing "moral science"—we would now call it "social science" —which is concerned with inquiries into "the course of nature," from that "inquiry the results of which do not express themselves in the indicative, but in the imperative mode, or in paraphrases equivalent to it; what is *called* the knowledge of duties, practical ethics, or morality."[4] So understood, he tells us, the rules of morality do not consist in assertions respecting matters of fact. "The Method, therefore, of ethics, can be no other than that of the Art of Practice."[5] Now it is the function of Art to propose an end. This end having been proposed, it is handed to the sciences, which in turn treat it as an effect. They explore its causes, and then send it back to Art with a theorem which states the circumstances and conditions under which it could be produced. Art in turn considers these and asserts on its own authority that the attainment of the end is desirable. "But though the reasonings which connect the end or purpose of every art with its means, belong to the domain of Science, the *definition* of the

---

[1] J. S. Mill, *Utilitarianism*, Everymans Library ed. (London: J. M. Dent & Sons, 1944), pp. 2, 11, 32, etc.

[2] *Ibid.*, p. 2. Compare also the crucial first paragraph of the much criticized fourth chapter, p. 32.

[3] J. S. Mill, *A System of Logic*, 8th ed. (London: Parker, Son, & Bourn, 1862), Vol. II, pp. 652-9.

[4] Ibid., p. 653. (Italics mine.)

[5] Ibid.

end itself belongs exclusively to Art, and forms its peculiar province." [6] And then, as clearly as can be, "Propositions of science assert a matter of fact: an existence, a co-existence, a succession, or a resemblance. The propositions now spoken of [those of art] do not assert that anything is, but enjoin or recommend that something should be. They are a class by themselves. A proposition of which the predicate is expressed by the words *ought* or *should be*, is generically different from one which is expressed by *is* or *will be*." [7] Morality, Mill maintains, is the Art of Life, and its supreme principle, of course, is for him the thesis of hedonism. This thesis *defines* the end of conduct, and provides the basis for justifications of "secondary" moral rules that prescribe our particular duties, and through them for the justification of ethical propositions that prescribe what we should do in particular cases.

So far, then, is Mill from committing the *real* fallacies in question, that he himself formulates, with the greatest clarity and elegance of language, just what they might be presumed to consist in. To be sure, he claims to infer significant ethical conclusions from that definition which identifies the end of the Art of Life; but this is because the definition itself "enunciates the object aimed at, and affirms it to be a desirable object." [8] The definition does not provide a logical analysis of "desirable" or "good"—at least as "logical analysis" is now understood. *This* analysis is provided in his general account of "The Logic of Practice." The definition itself is nothing but the statement or, better, the *enunciation* of a norm or standard of conduct. And the "inferring" of significant conclusions from it is the business not of theoretical but of practical reason.[9] A fallacy would be involved here only if one attempted to infer an ethical conclusion from definitions concerned essentially with the explication of the descriptive meanings of symbols.

6 Ibid., p. 656. (Italics mine.)
7 Ibid., pp. 656-7. (Italics in text.)
8 Ibid., p. 656.
9 Cf. ibid., p. 657.

If we return now to *Utilitarianism* and interpret it, as Mill appears to have intended, not as a meta-ethical theory or analysis of moral discourse but as an enunciation of his doctrine of hedonism and as a defense of it against practical [1] objections, we will find that many (although not all) of the supposedly questionable or fallacious "claims" of that work involve no serious theoretical confusions whatever. On the point at issue, he is, I believe, quite consistent. To say, therefore, that for Mill the principle of hedonism constitutes a definition of the desirable, is to say in effect that it is *ipso facto* and by intention a practical or, if you like, a "persuasive" definition. But there is no confusion. Nor is there any deception. The imputation of confusion or deception arises solely from the mistaken and misleading application of descriptive definitional models in the interpretation of what plainly and explicitly is a normative ethical system. Given his own definition of desirable he is perfectly justified in inferring from it, in conjunction with the relevant "theorems" of science, those conclusions which prescribe in particular just what we ought to do. The categorial blunder, I submit, is not Mill's, but that of his critics.

Now I can imagine that certain readers may conclude from all this that we should have seized the first horn of our dilemma in the first place, namely, that many statements occurring in works of moral philosophy that are normally interpreted as definitions simply are not so at all. I do not agree. Acceptance of such an alternative rests upon an essentialist attitude toward definitions which I reject. But even if for the sake of argument we accept it, it still does not follow that any confusion is involved in Mill's doctrine on the point in question. For one cannot charge someone else with the commission of a fallacy on the ground that he claims to infer an ethical conclusion from a definition of ethical terms, when it is as plain as can be that *his* so-called definition was designed for a purpose very different from that which animates the conception of definition implicit in the first horn of our dilemma. Even more to the point,

[1] Cf. *Utilitarianism*, p. 5.

one had no right to suppose that, by means of such a conception of definition together with ordinary rules of logic, one can shed any light on the process involved in inferring ethical conclusions from what are *normally* interpreted as definitions by moral philosophers. Indeed, by so construing definition one thereby puts well-nigh insuperable difficulties in the way of properly interpreting what moral philosophers say and mean. By what is perhaps nothing more than a process of association of ideas one is led, when one sees the word "definition," or when one sees something that looks like a "definition," to an interpretation of it which at once utterly misses the point and results in a mistaken charge either of logical confusion or else of downright intention to deceive.

A more profitable procedure is to resist the temptation to cut the Gordian knots of meaning by essentialist definitions (they might as well be called stipulations) and to recognize instead the ambiguities and vagueness inherent in the normal use of "definition" and the variable functions of actual definitions. In this way one will approach a certain type of discourse without preconceptions concerning the model to which it ought to conform. And perhaps, if one is lucky, and manages to keep all the necessary distinctions in mind, one may be able to perform the difficult philosophical task of correctly interpreting a form of discourse. What is wanted is not an immediate cry of confusion, but the illumination of a normal function of language; not the implicit attribution of bad faith or of obscurantism, but the explanation of the nature of symbolic processes that answer to other needs than those of science or formal logic.

Any normal reader of Plato, Epicurus, or Mill recognizes at once that, for the most part, he is reading in moral philosophy, not *about* it. Such a reader, I submit, takes their "definitions" and "inferences" for what they are, namely, practical definitions of norms and practical reasonings to particular moral conclusions. I agree with Professor Stevenson and Professor Robinson that the *Republic* is a prolonged essay in the "persuasive" or practical definition of "justice." [2] For better or worse, Plato was desperately concerned to clarify and to defend a system of norms upon the acceptance of which, as he believed, the salvation of Athens depended. But there was nothing deceptive or illicit in what he was doing. The term "justice" no doubt has a strong aura of "emotive meaning." And like anyone else who attempts to define a norm in terms of "justice," he inevitably "traded" on its emotive meaning. But that he was proposing an "ideal," not explicating the use of a term in his famous definition of justice, seems to me as clear as day.

Therefore, I do not at all agree with Professor Robinson's remark, "A persuasive definition, it may be urged, is at best a mistake and at worst a lie, because it consists in getting someone to alter his valuations under the false impression that he is not altering his valuations but correcting his knowledge of facts. I am tentatively inclined to accept this view, with the practical conclusion that we should not use persuasive definitions." [3] I do not say that it never happens that emotive meanings are used illicitly to modify attitudes. Of course it does. I do say that in the context of normative ethics, where it is understood that a writer is making practical proposals for the guidance of conduct, no confusion and no deception is involved.

This is why I should prefer, in discussing Plato or Mill, to use the phrase "practical definition" rather than "persuasive definition" to characterize what they are doing. Perhaps unfortunately, the latter expression appears to suggest a process which involves confusions and lies. And it does so, it should

[2] C. L. Stevenson, *Ethics and Language* (New Haven: Yale University Press, 1944), pp. 224-6; Richard Robinson, *Definition* (London: Oxford University Press, 1950), p. 166.

[3] Robinson, op. cit., p. 170. It is instructive, I think, to see that in so many words Professor Robinson has drawn a "practical conclusion" from what he believes to be the statement of a fact. I applaud the inference, and, given his belief about the effects of persuasive definition, I consider it to have been his duty to have drawn it. If I do not make the inference, it is because I take a different view of the definitions in question.

be emphasized, precisely because of the tendency of analysts
to approach moral philosophers with descriptive models in
mind as *the* norms for correct definition and valid inference.
As I understand it, a practical definition is explicitly and
openly intended as the statement of a norm. Since it is
stated in ethical terms it also may be emotively loaded.
But this cannot be avoided in any case. No harm is done so
long as we know what is happening.

ON MISLEADING CLASSIFICATIONS
OF ETHICAL THEORIES

I wish, now, to say a word about current classifications of
"ethical theories." In my judgment most of them are misleading; and they are so precisely because they appear to be set
up for the purpose of classifying theories concerning the nature of ethical terms and moral judgments, whereas the doctrines so classified are abstracted from historical works in
moral philosophy, the purpose of which was to define the
right or the good only in the normative or practical sense.
Thus, for example, Professor Broad classifies "ethical theories" in accordance with certain principles that distinguish
among them according to their conceptions of "ethical characteristics." Clearly his classification concerns only metaethical
theories, not substantive normative systems. But then he applies his classification to such a writer as Mill who, in the
only work in moral philosophy to which his critics ever
refer, was *doing* ethics, not talking about it, and whose
definitions were definitions of ends, not theoretical analyses
of ethical "characteristics." Broad, in accordance with the
standard view, says that "Mill presumably meant to be a
naturalistic hedonist. But it is difficult to be sure in the case
of such an extremely confused writer that he really was
one." [4] And yet, if one looks at the *Logic* or at those passages
in *Utilitarianism* in which Mill does talk briefly *about* moral
judgments, it is, unless I am badly mistaken, quite evident

[4] C. D. Broad, *Five Types of Ethical Theory* (New York, Harcourt,
Brace, 1930), pp. 258-9.

that, in Broad's sense of the terms, Mill is neither a naturalist nor a hedonist in his theoretical ethics. Rather, he was primarily a noncognitivist with a strong prejudice *against* descriptivism or "naturalism." His affiliation is with the emotivists and imperativists, rather than the naturalists. Only in his normative ethics is Mill a hedonist of sorts.

Indeed I am not at all sure that one can find a clear case of a naturalistic hedonist in Broad's sense, i.e., one who believes that "good" is analyzable without remainder in terms of "pleasure." A number of eighteenth-century writers do seem to have held that "good" in its "natural" use does mean the same thing as "agreeable" or "pleasant." But they were usually at pains to distinguish this use from "moral goodness" which, for them, carries with it normative or practical implications. Even Bentham, who said in his downright way that the words "ought" and "right" have a meaning only when applied to actions conformable to the principle of utility, is only an apparent exception.[5] As Mr. Stuart Hampshire has suggested, it was really Bentham's concern to replace all this fiddle-faddle of "morality" with scientific social engineering guided exclusively by the social norm of greatest happiness.[6]

But perhaps even these remarks may be indirectly misleading. For in saying that the great classical moral philosophers were not primarily interested in "the analysis of ethical terms" I may have created the impression, which I most certainly wish to avoid, that the term "analysis" should be pre-empted in ethics for the kind of thing that analytical ethicists generally do nowadays.[7] I believe that the effect would be altogether desirable if philosophers somewhat enlarged their conceptions of the roles of analysis itself so as to acknowledge explicitly its normative and practical functions. In my judgment, the clarification of aims is at least as important a task for analytical philosophers as is the descrip-

[5] See *British Moralists*, ed. by L. A. Selby-Bigge (Oxford: The Clarendon Press, 1897), Vol. I, p. 342.

[6] Stuart Hampshire, "Fallacies in Moral Philosophy," *Mind*, 1949, p. 473.

[7] Professor Karl Popper is a notable exception.

tion and elucidation of moral discourse itself. However much one may disagree with it in detail, Professor Popper's *The Open Society and Its Enemies*[8] is a brilliant example of what the philosopher may do in the way of clarification of purposes and in sweeping away the manifold confusions which produce practical misunderstanding.

Disagreement at the practical or moral level frequently arises, not so much from differences of opinion about matters of fact or from well-defined and outright conflicts in interest, as from confusions of language and thought and from ambiguity and vagueness in the formulation of aims, and hence in the aims themselves. Hedonists, for example, have been called "pig philosophers" by those who, had they only understood them, might have found more with which to agree than to disagree. And on the other hand, as we shall see, hedonists have frequently provoked disagreement by faulty statements of their fundamental principle. The interminable disagreements in contemporary moral philosophy among those who have called themselves "hedonists," "voluntarists," "eudaemonists," and "instrumentalists" are often due not to well-defined differences of aim as to opposing expressions of what, if we could get clear about them, might turn out to be common aims.

The reason for this is due largely to the vagueness and the ambiguities latent in such notions as desire, will, satisfaction, pleasure, pain, end, feeling, attitude, and belief—precisely the terms, in short, in which basic norms have so often been expressed. It is, or should be, the business of the moral philosopher not merely to codify and adumbrate the principles by which we are to live, but also to remove misconceptions standing in the way of their acceptance, and to provide them with such determinateness of meaning as may enable them to function adequately as practical guides to conduct.

Only by such processes of reflection or analysis are we at last able to grasp *what* we are enjoined to accept as right or

[8] Two volumes (London: Routledge and Kegan Paul, Ltd.), 4th edition.

good; only so can we intelligently deliberate on the appropriate means to its realization. It is simply not true that the only function of deliberations or practical reason is to devise means to the fulfillment of already given ends-in-view. As often as not it is the means that are clear, not the end. Not knowing what is wanted, or confusion as to its nature, is at least as common as, and perhaps an even more tragic privation than not knowing how to acquire a known goal. Utilitarianism, as it stands, is unquestionably inadequate as a moral philosophy. But, comparatively speaking, its failure is due mainly to a very fundamental lack of clarity with respect to its own governing purposes. Thus when Mill tells us that "human nature is so constituted as to desire nothing which is not either a part of happiness or a means of happiness," [9] it would seem that he did not mean to assert that we desire what we desire. One is forced to conclude that in such a passage, "happiness" or "pleasure" (for Mill, of course, they are equivalent) are not to be understood simply as synonyms for "object of desire" or "realization of desire." Surely, one supposes, Mill, with his awareness of human ignorance and his fear of the uncorrected impulses of the mob, did not wish to assert that in our dealings with others what we should regard as intrinsically desirable is the realization of their desires *as they stand*. Surely, as a consequentialist who put his emphasis not on motives but on their fruits, he did not mean to enjoin us to regard objects of desire alone as intrinsically worthy of our respect and solicitude. And yet, to our confusion and despair, we find him saying almost in the same breath that "desiring a thing and finding it pleasant" are not merely "two parts of the same phenomenon," but "in strictness of language, two modes of naming the same psychological fact." [1] So construed, it would seem there is no difference whatever between ethical hedonism and ethical voluntarism, and that psychological hedonism is a vacuous tautology, not a theory at all. The truth of the matter is that, by an inattention to a funda-

[9] *Utilitarianism*, p. 36.
[1] Ibid.

mental ambiguity in the term "pleasure" and its derivatives, Mill allowed himself to fall into a confusion which is fatal not for his meta-ethics but for his normative moral philosophy.

Now in one sense, of course, Mill was quite within his right in equating "desiring" and "finding pleasant"; both expressions, as Professor Ryle tells us,[2] do refer to inclination, which is a sort of proneness or readiness to do certain sorts of things on purpose. And in another sense, he is also justified in talking, as he so often does, about a "desire for pleasure." But this latter expression requires that "pleasure" and "desire" be distinguished and, indeed, contrasted. So understood, "pleasure," as opposed to "desire," does *not* refer to inclinations, but rather to certain distinctive feelings or moods which we designate by such expressions as delight, joy, contentment, the sense of well-being, and (in one sense) satisfaction. But it obviously makes a tremendous difference, for moral philosophy and for those who are enjoined to base their deliberations on the assumption that pleasure alone is desirable, which of these senses of "pleasure" is intended. On one interpretation we are, in effect, enjoined to contribute as much as we can to the delight, joy, contentment, well-being, and satisfaction of ourselves and others. On the other interpretation we are enjoined, I suppose, to respect (or coddle) other people's inclinations and wishes, to help them to get what they happen to be aiming at. No greater ethical difference, I submit, can be imagined. For my part, it is plain that after all it is the former sort of thing toward which Mill's hedonism was fundamentally oriented.[3]

[2] Gilbert Ryle, *The Concept of Mind* (London: Hutchinson, 1955), pp. 83 ff.

[3] Much the same sort of difficulty appears when we turn to Mill's discussion of "qualities of pleasure." The phrase means one thing if "pleasure" is construed as a feeling word, but means quite another thing if "pleasure" is taken as equivalent to "desire." And if "quality of pleasure" is construed as "kind of feeling," a different thing is meant by regarding some kinds of pleasure as "higher" than others than is meant if, as Mill suggests, "quality of pleasure" means nothing more than "decided preference." Again Mill is simply confused. And in any

I have dwelt again on Mill merely to illustrate once again my contention that philosophical analysis is an indispensable tool for normative ethics itself, and that the clarification and subsequent definition of aims is an indispensable part of successful practical deliberation. Other illustrious examples of moral confusion and of the use of analysis toward its removal come readily to mind. The history of egoism, as everyone knows, is one long history of equivocation, ambiguity, and vagueness. Its plausibility or attractiveness for many thoughtless people has depended largely, I think, upon these factors. When they are eliminated by such superb essays in clarification as the second appendix to Hume's second *Enquiry,* the business of normative moral philosophy is thereby immeasurably advanced.

ON INFERRING ETHICAL CONCLUSIONS FROM FACTUAL STATEMENTS

We have now to consider the second part of Mr. Prior's statement, namely, the wider thesis that a fallacy is involved whenever we attempt to deduce or claim to deduce moral conclusions from statements of fact. I have already indicated in what sense this seems to me to be plausible. I shall now try to show in what sense it is mistaken and misleading. Let me again emphasize that my reason for believing that moral conclusions may be inferred from statements of fact does not in the least depend upon the tacit assumption that moral conclusions are, after all, a species of factual statement, or that the ethical terms occurring in the conclusions are analytically synonymous with descriptive

case, to promote or support other people's preferences, when well-considered, is one thing; to promote certain "higher" qualities of feeling or certain *experiences* of pleasure such as those involving the exercise of our so-called higher faculties, is something else. All through Mill's moral and social philosophy one can find a tension which arises primarily on the fact that he had not sufficiently clarified *what* he regarded as intrinsically valuable. I do not say that the tension would automatically disappear once the ambiguities in the term "pleasure" were brought into the open. But I do say that only then could one intelligently decide, as a putative hedonist, what one was really for.

or empirical predicates occurring in the premises. This is as
it may be. I have already indicated elsewhere that I do
think that in certain contexts "good" and "right" tend to
acquire fairly well-defined descriptive meanings. But my
present argument does not depend upon this fact. Nor do I
wish, at this point, to cavil at the difficulties involved in
such ill-defined expressions as "ethical terms," "ethical conclusion," "nonethical term," "empirical or natural predicate,"
"nonethical premise," and the like. The difficulties implicit
in the ordinary use of these expressions in contemporary
ethical theory I have also pointed out elsewhere.[4] In his
essay, "A Finitistic Approach to Philosophical Theses,"
Morton White has shown how tenuous is the thesis of an-
tinaturalism in its ordinary "infinitistic" formulations.[5] There
will be some naturalists who may choose to avail themselves
of Frankena's and White's criticisms of the question-begging assumptions and imponderable infinitistic theses involved in the usual arguments provided by antinatural-
ists in their attack upon the naturalistic fallacy.[6] I do not wish
to avail myself of these criticisms, just though they are, for I
do believe that, when all the question-begging assumptions
and the infinitism have been removed, there remains a sense
in which the naturalistic fallacy really *is* a fallacy.

In spite of this, I believe that under certain conditions it is
entirely proper to infer (not deduce), ethical conclusions
from factual premises. (The quotation, on page 53, from
Professor Robinson provides an interesting example of this.)
And the reasons why some philosophers have supposed that
a fallacy is involved in such inferences are (*a*) the tenacious
hold which descriptive models have upon all of us in all
our interpretation of language, and, more important, (*b*) the
ingrained tendency to regard the processes of validation ob-
taining the formal logic and in inductive reasoning as the

[4] See my "Evaluation and Obligation: Two Functions of Judgments
in the Language of Conduct," *Journal of Philosophy*, XLVII, No. 1
(Jan. 1950), pp. 5-7.
[5] See M. G. White, "A Finitistic Approach to Philosophical Theses,"
Philosophical Review, July 1951, pp. 307-11.
[6] See ibid.; also Frankena, op. cit., pp. 472 ff.

only processes in which questions of validity can ever arise. So tenacious are these assumptions that, when certain philosophers get even the vaguest inkling that there may be informal contextual standards of relevance in art and morals, they leap immediately to the absurd conclusion that a work of art is a deductive system or that a moral code is one of the social sciences. Perhaps the most fantastic example of this sort of thing in recent literature may be found in Professor James Feibleman's *Aesthetics*. According to him, the act of artistic creation is simply a deduction of the logical consequences implicit in the artist's initial idea.[7] He says, in so many words, that the relations holding between a theme and its variations are not merely analogous (in some sense) to, but identical with those which hold between the axioms and theorems of a deductive system. Such a view, you may say, is absurd and I agree. It is logicism gone mad. But I am convinced that nestled at the heart of the absurdity is a genuine insight, if he only knew how to make use of it. This insight, however, is concealed from its author by virtue of his unconscious addiction to the idea that validity and relevance are notions which are exemplified only in logical systems. The insight is this: there are relations of relevance —some people call them relations of "propriety" or "fittingness"—which hold between the parts of a successful work of art.[8] And in the same way, although it is absurd to say that ethical conclusions can be *deduced* from factual premises (since here we are dealing with propositions, the absurdity is less palpable), there is still an insight of sorts concealed within the absurdity. For there are conditions of relevance which permit, in certain circumstances, the inference of significant ethical judgments from statements of fact. Some of these I will mention shortly.

Meanwhile it must be remarked that in recent years moral philosophers have been more prone to see the ab-

[7] See James K. Feibleman, *Aesthetics* (New York: Duell, Sloan & Pearce, 1949), pp. 12 ff.

[8] See my "The Concept of Relevance in Aesthetics," *Journal of Aesthetics and Art Criticism*, Dec. 1949, pp. 152-61.

surdity than the insight within it. And this is due, again, to a
subtle addiction to descriptivistic attitudes implicit in the
above-mentioned notion concerning validity. Thus, for example, although Professor Charles Stevenson is perhaps more
sensitive than any other philosopher to the reality of persuasive definition, he himself falls into it when he refuses,
for no reason sanctioned by ordinary language, to accept the
possibility that there are any "rational methods" other than
those of formal logic and science. Although he freely allows
the right of moralists to use, *inter alia,* what he regards as
rational methods when they happen to be appropriate for
the purpose of "irrigating" ethical judgments, he nevertheless
insists there are no criteria of validity with respect to ethical
disputation as such. But why should he fear lest the notion of "validity" be extended so as to include forms of inference which are neither demonstrative nor inductive? As
he himself wisely says, "When an inference does not purport
to comply with the usual rules, any insistence on its failure to do so is gratuitous." [9] And yet he maintains, to my
mind quite unconvincingly, that it is "wholly impracticable
and injudicious" (sic) to sanction a definition of validity
which extends its usage beyond its applications to logic and
to science.[1] Apart from a tenacious desire to reserve the
emotive meaning of such expressions as "rational" and "valid"
for processes of reasoning involved in formal logic and inductive science, what is there to commend Stevenson's position? Again, why must it be misleading to say that "validity,"
not in special "philosophical" senses but in normal common-
sensical applications, is a normative as well as perhaps (in
some uses) a descriptive term? Surely it is so. To say that
"*x* is invalid" is, in effect, to say "*x* fails to conform to certain
accepted conditions; do not accept *x*." In the realm of logic,
its function is to control and direct belief. In the realm of
ethics, it is not only to control belief, but also to control and
direct practical second-level attitudes.

I submit that Professor Stevenson is still, in an extremely

[9] Stevenson, op. cit., p. 153.
[1] Ibid., p. 154.

subtle and involved way, under the spell of descriptive and logical models in his approach to nonscientific forms of *reasoning*, even though he is quite free from such models in his analysis of nonscientific *terms*. To be sure, he does not, like Perry, make the mistake of interpreting moral disputation simply as a variety of scientific and logical inference, albeit with a subject matter that cuts across the special sciences. On the contrary. Yet he does appear to regard science and logic as *the* proper models in regard to all questions of relevance and validity. And it is because of this, I believe, that he is forced to conclude that there is no such thing as validity in morals except by accident, when purely factual or logical issues are momentarily in view.

In principle, of course, he is free, on his view, to *disapprove* those who employ "invalid" arguments in the process of supporting ethical judgments. That is his privilege as a moral being. But as an analyst he is bound to regard such arguments, from the standpoint of moral discourse itself, as entirely within the proprieties. Thus although he may, as an individual, be against certain forms of "irrationality" in ethics, he is obliged, as an ethical theorist, to accept them as integral parts of moral persuasion and argument.

The issue here, I realize, is exceedingly delicate—so much so, indeed, that I am not altogether sure that I too have not been unintentionally misleading. Perhaps, in the end, all one can do is to go on indefinitely correcting the misleading impressions of one's own preceding remarks. This may, in fact, be all that writing a book in philosophy amounts to. I must state, in any case, that I get the strongest sort of impression from Professor Stevenson's writings that he is almost as much concerned to protect science and logic as the only *valid* methods of argumentation as he is to free ethics itself from bondage to a false god of rationality.

Now I agree once and for all that there are no formal logical rules by means of which one can deduce the ethical proposition "*x* ought to be done" from any combination of purely factual statements. What I do maintain is that, according to ordinary usage, it is entirely permissible to *infer*

ethical conclusions from factual premises. I should now like
to support this contention with some examples. Suppose that
it could be shown that a certain act would cause another person unnecessary hardship or suffering; I think that any normal person in our society would regard this as a good, if
not sufficient, reason for inferring that, other things remaining equal, the act in question ought not to be performed.
Again, suppose it could be shown that the fulfillment of a
certain promise would probably cause the person to whom
one made it to destroy himself; here also, I think that normal
persons would, perhaps reluctantly, conclude from this that
the promise ought to be broken. Other examples come to
mind.

I conclude from this that, however difficult they may be
to specify, there are nevertheless broad principles of relevance or valid inference in moral discourse which enable us,
in certain circumstances, to infer ethical conclusions from
nonethical premises. But I do not in the least wish to imply
by this that the ordinary laws of logic should be amended
or broadened. Such laws have no immediate application
to the kinds of inference in question. My contention is
merely that within the universe of discourse called "moral"
or "ethical," certain types of inference are viewed as reasonable, others not. Nor do I wish to say that moral judgments
may be "logically derived" from nonethical statements of
fact.[2] I think, nothing is gained from such an unnecessary
and really misleading extension of the expression "logical
derivation." All that needs defending is the thesis that
moral reasoning has its own proprieties which, while certainly not written into the starry heavens above, are at least
constant and extensive enough to enable the members of a
given civilization to distinguish a good reason from a bad one.

[2] Cf. Hampshire, op. cit., pp. 470 ff. Let me state here that, although
apparently different sorts of stimuli have given rise to our respective
reflections on moral philosophy, I find myself in agreement with much,
although not all, of Mr. Hampshire's admirable essay. In my judgment
the most stimulating thinking about ethics to be found in contemporary
philosophy is being done at Oxford by Mr. Hampshire and his colleagues.

Levels of Moral Discourse

THE POINT OF VIEW OF THE PRESENT ESSAY

As a matter of principle most contemporary moral philosophers pay lip service to the diversity and complexity of human problems. One might reasonably assume, therefore, that they should regard it as axiomatic that the forms of discourse most intimately related to these problems would reflect their diversity and complexity. Yet when we survey the prevailing contemporary moral philosophies, we find that all or nearly all of them are monistic in their approach to the meanings of so-called "ethical" terms and reductivistic in their treatment of the roles of so-called "ethical" judgments. If they succeed momentarily in avoiding the "one and only one meaning fallacy," they do so only to fall directly into the "one and only one function fallacy." Even when there is a passing acknowledgment of the "ambiguities" of such terms as "good" and "ought," there is usually an immediate narrowing of the subject for analysis to some "essentially" or "characteristically" ethical sense of these words. Essences, however, always follow our interests, and where interests differ, what seems essential to one will appear merely accidental to another. Because of this it is not surprising that there should be disagreement among moral philosophers as to what is characteristically, or essentially, ethical in the meanings of ethical terms and in the roles of ethical judgments. The unfortunate consequence of this, as one might anticipate, is an interminable debate among the various ethical theories which is profitless because it is insoluble.

The only way to resolve such controversies, which merely block the progress of moral philosophy toward a more comprehensive grasp of its problems, is simply and resolutely to ignore all the essentialistic and reductivistic questions upon which they depend and to proceed at once to a detailed and unpolemical examination of the several levels upon which practical discourse proceeds. The resulting analysis will not be classifiable under any of the main "types" of ethical theory that now prevail. It will be neither a cognitive nor an emotive theory, though it will be prepared to acknowledge both the many cognitive and the many emotive aspects of the language of conduct. It will be neither subjectivistic nor objectivistic, though it will attempt to show that moral discourse has, and must have, both subjective and objective phases. It will acknowledge the importance of reasoning in conduct, but it will also recognize its limits. It will see that, while there is such a thing as "justification" in ethics, there is no one form to which all the justifications occurring within moral discourse can be reduced. In short, such a theory will be pluralistic in orientation, and hence fundamentally opposed to all of the "type" theories whose exposition and defense occupy so large a place in the current literature. It will not, of course, oppose reduction indiscriminately; but it will be prepared from the outset to acknowledge irreducible differences in meaning and irreducible differentiations of function. Nor will it be misled by the countercharges of "eclecticism" or "lack of system." "Logical" or "analytic" connections of meaning are not the only relations among concepts or judgments that require explanation, nor is there only one way in which "system" can be achieved.

Such, at any rate, is the point of view of the present essay. Its purpose is to show that there are at least four distinctive levels upon which such terms as "good," "right," and "ought" are employed, and to explain the roles of judgment on each of these levels.

For purposes of identification I shall speak of these levels respectively as (1) the "expressive-evocative" level, (2) the "moral" level, (3) the "ethical" level, and (4) the "post-ethical" or "human" level. Such labels are perhaps arbitrary. They are here defined exclusively with reference to specific contexts of moral discourse. To dispute about them in any intelligible way is to argue the adequacy of the analysis of a particular context or level. By which name we *call* the level is a question of secondary importance.

Before proceeding to a detailed examination of these levels, however, several preliminary remarks need to be made. Without them any schematic survey of the sort provided here must inevitably prove misleading. In the first place, then, any moral argument which goes on at any length is likely to proceed on more than one level. As questions become more probing or more urgent, more and profounder resources of the language of conduct will be brought into play. This means that the context of moral discussion is, or tends to be, a *shifting* context. Second, the nature of moral discussion being, as it is, practical both in intention and in effect, the connections between the successive levels must be understood primarily in pragmatic rather than in "logical" terms. Such systematic relations as may be discerned in the shifts from level to level will be functional rather than deductive or evidential in character. But, third, this should not be taken to imply that on a given level there are no criteria of relevance or validity. On at least two levels—2 and 3— such criteria do obtain, as I shall presently show. Only at the extremes do we pass beyond the bounds of "propriety" or "rationality" to the open sea of individual feeling or human aspiration. Here also there may be relevancies and irrelevancies, but they are of a different sort altogether, and can be determined, if at all, only by appealing directly to the irremovable needs of the individual agent. This is why, as we shall see in more detail later, there is in moral discourse a variety of modes of justification. Some are in an intelligible sense "objective"; others, whether we like it or not, are necessarily "subjective." The differences between them can be explained only with reference to presence or absence of intersubjective "rules" or "principles" to which one may confidently make appeal in carrying out a justification. An objective justification, since it involves an appeal to intersubjective rules, is indifferent to the immediate claims of personal inclination or preference. Indeed, it is on this basis alone that we can make out a clear distinction between the "desirable" and the "desired," or between "apparent goods" and "real goods." But in the end any justification which is practical in intent must provide a justification *to* interest. So far it must be subjective or it has no relevance to action. Such a justification cannot in the end be indifferent to the demands of inclination, since here there is nothing in the last analysis to appeal to save human passion itself. Passion is prior to rules, if, within limits, it is also governed by rules. Both forms of justification have their place in ethics. The danger lies in failing to distinguish them.

THE EXPRESSIVE LEVEL

Our initial responses to any situation are likely to be of the unreflective, stock variety. We see something and like it; we hear something and dislike it; we think of someone and are at once attracted or repelled, we know not why. Unless there is something unstable or ambiguous in the situation which requires reflection or deliberation, we are usually content, if we make any comment at all, simply to express our passing feelings of favor or disfavor. "Bravo!" we cry as the curtain goes down. "What a fine day for a picnic!" we exclaim as we step out on the porch on a sunny day in June; "What rotten luck that the attic has to be cleaned out." "Good play!" we shout as the first baseman on the home team fields a line drive headed for the bleachers. Such expressions of spontaneous pleasure or displeasure serve merely to vent our emotions; they pose no problems nor call for any reply. They are immediately construed by others for what in fact they are, namely, as conventional expressions of personal feeling. To challenge them or to raise questions of "truth" or "validity" with respect to them would be pointless. They do not solicit agreement or invite a reply.

Such uses of "good," "bad," and their equivalents have received much, perhaps too much, attention of late, due to the advent of the emotive theory. It would be a mistake to disregard them, however, or to fail to recognize that, even at this most elementary of the levels upon which the language of conduct is employed, there are more complexities than are usually noticed. Failure to discriminate them can cause trouble later on at the levels which perhaps interest us more. A full account of the expressive level would have to distinguish at least the following: (*a*) the conventional use of words as vehicles for the expression of emotion; (*b*) the varying degrees of intensity and rhetorical force of such expressions; (*c*) the expressive or "venting" relation holding between the speaker and the expression itself; (*d*) the symptomatic relation in virtue of which the expression functions as a natural sign to an interpreter; (*e*) the incitive or rhetorical effect of the expression upon an interpreter, in virtue of which we speak of a relation of communication between him and the speaker; and (*f*) the intentions of the speaker in thus giving vent to his emotion. Here already it is clear that several modes of "meaning" may be distinguished. And in the case of *d* at least, it is plain that, as early as the expressive level, "cognitive" meanings begin to emerge, even though nothing is "designated" or "named" as such. Even here, therefore, a pure emotive theory would not account for all the facts.

THE LEVEL OF MORAL RULES

At the purely expressive level, as such, no question of justification can possibly arise. Nor can there be any problem whether what is directly responded to or reported as "good" or "bad" really is so. Here everything is as it appears to be. Such diversity of expression as may arise signifies nothing more than the venting of contrary—or perhaps merely different—emotions. To ask who is right in such a context or whether the expressions "good" or "bad" are really appropriate to the objects toward which they are directed would be senseless—or rather, which is closer to the facts of the matter, it would be to shift the discourse at once to another level.

The first level upon which serious questions are asked and serious answers given in ethical terms I have called the "moral" level. Here questions for the first time begin to emerge: "What ought I to do in this situation?" "Is this object that I admire so much, really good?" "Is it really worth having?" Here, in short, there now appears a problem of conduct and a problem for appraisal and ultimate decision. On this level two sorts of utterance are involved in attempting to justify one's answer to such a problem: (*a*) factual appraisals of relevant means and consequences and (*b*) rules or procedures in relation to which alone the moral relevance of such appraisals can be established. Frequently one of these goes unmentioned. When the facts are sufficiently plain, attention may be directed exclusively to the interpretation and ordering of the relevant rules. At other times there may be no question concerning the meanings, order, or application of the rules, but only a problem as to the facts themselves. Moral discourse, being practical and frequently urgent in intent, is full of such ellipses and elisions. The justifying reasons for many of the things that we ought to do go without saying. Because of this, so discerning an analyst as Prichard could argue very plausibly that our particular obligations are really self-evident.[1] That they are really not so, however, is sufficiently indicated by the facts of moral perplexity and disagreement. It is always legitimate, if often fatiguing, to ask "Why?" when a particular moral judgment is proposed. And in such a case, if we are reasonable, there is no escape from an appraisal of the relevant facts and, if necessary, an explicit appeal to the appropriate rules.

The tacitness of so many of the understandings governing our moral deliberations has caused many philosophers to ig-

[1] Cf. H. A. Prichard, *Moral Obligation* (London: Oxford University Press, 1950), pp. 1-18.

nore one or the other of the roles of factual reasoning and rules in moral discourse. The neglect of either, however, invariably results in a form of irrationalism. When, on the one hand, the role and relevance of factual premises in our inferences to moral conclusions is overlooked, the distinction between what is and what ought to be becomes a total diremption, with the consequence that "insight," as in the case of Prichard, or "sentiment" as in the case of Hume (in some passages), is substituted, at the wrong place, for rational reflection. When, on the other hand, the role of moral rules is ignored, as in the case of Stevenson, the whole conception of validity or relevance in ethics tends to lose its meaning altogether, with the result that "justifying" reasons of all sorts collapse at once into "exciting reasons."

Moral rules still govern the course of our factual reasonings in ethics, for all the fact that, unless an issue of interpretation or precedence arises, there is usually no need to refer explicitly to them. But in the last analysis, they alone determine what factual reasons are to be accepted as relevant. Not just any facts or consequences have bearing upon a moral problem. The besetting weakness of the instrumentalist account of moral deliberation is that it provides no criteria as to the relevance of the consequences upon which it enjoins us to reflect. Hence, in spite of their desire to render moral deliberation "scientific," the instrumentalists neglect the very considerations which might conceivably turn science to a moral use. The emotivists are more candid. They hold that there are no criteria of relevance or validity in moral deliberation at all. Any statement of fact, in their view, is *ipso facto* appropriate to the extent that it proves efficacious in reinforcing or modifying the attitudes which we wish to fortify or change. But in practice, moral reasoning is not so deucedly liberal. For better or worse, it presents to us certain standards of propriety to which we regard ourselves as bound. Some reasons it acknowledges to be "good," if perhaps, in some cases, insufficient; others it holds to be "bad," despite their rhetorical effectiveness. On this level, a

good reason is one whose relevance to the problem at issue
is determined by the rules of the communal code itself. A
bad reason on this level is one which is *merely* "exciting."

Now the rules of moral codes vary considerably in number, clarity, flexibility, and well-orderedness. In "closed" societies they are likely to be many, specific, rigid, and well
ordered. The studies of such anthropologists as Malinowski or
Ruth Benedict amply confirm this fact. In more open societies
rules are usually fewer in number, highly general, capable
of indefinite reinterpretation, subject to exceptions, and
rather vague in order of precedence. When a problem of
interpretation arises, as it frequently does in such a "system,"
the individual is frequently forced to fall back upon another
concept, which is nonetheless important because it is even
vaguer than the procedures between which it is required to
adjudicate. This is the notion of "good sense," "normality,"
"reasonableness," or "competence." To suppose, however, as
some writers have done, that this principle does all the procedural work in moral deliberation is as serious as the analogous supposition would be in regard to the law. We must, to
be sure, be "sensible" if we are properly to resolve our moral
perplexities. But this is not to say that good sense works in
a vacuum without the guidance of more explicit rules of
conduct.

In this connection it may be useful to compare my views
with those of Stephen Toulmin and John Rawls. In his discerning review of Toulmin's *An Examination of the Place of
Reason in Ethics,* John Rawls makes the following remark in
criticism of his author: "The point is that a reason is any
consideration which competent persons in their reflective
moments feel bound to give some weight to whether or not
they think the consideration sufficient in itself to settle the
case." [2] I should myself amend this to read: A reason (in
ethics) is any consideration, including those covered by
acknowledged rules of the moral code, which "competent"
persons in their reflective moments feel bound to give some
weight to whether or not they think the consideration suffi-

[2] *Philosophical Review,* LX, No. 4, 572-80.

cient in itself to settle the case. I agree with Rawls that Toulmin's account of moral reasoning is far too rigid. But I agree with Toulmin that there are moral rules, although it seems to me that he supposes them to be more objective, definite, and inflexible than they are. My own view, in short, is somewhere midway between that of Toulmin and that of Rawls.

In the spheres of logic and factual explanation there is, or so we like to suppose, only one set of correct or valid principles of reasoning.[3] But in morals, unfortunately, there just is no one set of universally valid principles of deliberation to which all peoples, regardless of cultural heritage, are in conscience bound. In saying this, I am not preaching moral relativism; I am simply stating a fact. It is a fundamental *theoretical* blunder to treat the particular procedures of moral deliberation current in our own culture as paradigmatic for morality in general.

Here is another point on which Stephen Toulmin seems to me to be somewhat unguarded. His emphasis upon utili-

---

[3] I take no great pleasure in the thought, but this statement may be more debatable than some of my more sanguine empiricist allies would admit. The issues which it raises, however, cannot be argued here. Fortunately, they do not immediately affect the problems with which we are here concerned, although I must warn my colleagues against the tendency to identify "good sense" in the sphere of factual assertion with the criteria which they themselves accept as correct or proper. Cf. Professor Herbert Feigl's essay, "De Principiis non disputandum . . . ?" in the volume *Philosophical Analysis,* edited by Max Black (Ithaca, N.Y.: Cornell University Press, 1950). Says Feigl: "The vindication of the principles of meaning and knowledge is so trivial precisely because, given the purposes of language and knowledge, there are no genuine alternatives for fulfilling them. But we do know of alternative systems of moral norms." (p. 143). I wish Feigl were right. He certainly convinces me that given the uses I have, if not for language, then for "knowledge," there are no alternatives for fulfilling them but the principles he has in mind. Unfortunately, mine are not the only uses that have prevailed in the history of thought. Nor are his criteria, which are —broadly speaking—my own, the only ones to which reflective persons have appealed, even in our own tradition. I am curious to know how Feigl deals with the "thoughtful" persons for whom Thomas Aquinas is the spokesman. I condone their standards no more than Feigl does, but I think that they have different purposes for and different principles of "knowledge" than he and I do.

tarian arguments which show that actions not otherwise
prescribed as duties will cause other members of the community some inconvenience, annoyance, or suffering is, I
think, largely correct for "our" system. That it is a correct
characterization of other codes seems to me very doubtful.
This mistake, if such it be, is, I think, a consequence of the
tendency to argue from the general social effect of morality,
which is usually to prevent or reduce conflict, to the nature
of the types of reasoning that govern it. Even the edicts of a
totalitarian system prevent conflict in many cases, but I
doubt whether anyone would care to argue that this is more
than a by-product.

We must not assume, therefore, simply on the basis of our
own conviction, that the proper end of moral reasoning
should be the harmonization of actions, that the principle of
harmony is everywhere the standard of validity in moral
reasoning. The initial plausibility of the assumption is, I
admit, somewhat increased by the fact that a common social
effect of morality is, as a rule, to prevent conflict and insure
order. But this is, within limits, the usual effect of any rule-
governed activity or institution. It does not follow that it is
to be acknowledged as a principle of "right reason" in moral
deliberation. Again, such humanistic principles as "harmony,"
"adjustment," and "least suffering" are implicit to a greater
or less degree in the codes of many "civilized" peoples.
But however desirable they may be from our point of view,
they are still not universally definitive of what it is to be a
moral rule or principle. The conclusion cannot be avoided,
therefore, that at present there just is not one set of procedures or rules for the validation of moral reasoning to which,
regardless of cultural differences, every person is "objectively"
bound. On the other hand, it is not necessary to infer from
this, as some writers have done, that the very concept of
validity has no meaning when applied to moral arguments
and deliberations.

What I here call "moral rules" at once specify certain types
of behavior which ordinary non-deviant persons within a
given community would approve and which demand that

the addressee, in so far as he is "normal," likewise approve and, if appropriate, act accordingly.[4] The moral judge, so understood, functions primarily as a middleman or agent. He voices the claims of society but is not the primary source of their moral authority. This does not imply, of course, that the moral judgment does not express the sentiments of the judges. It may; but though, as normal persons, we tend to adopt the attitudes which we express in our moral judgments, this fact is not essential to their characteristic meaning or role. It is the social press of "morality" itself which disposes us to present its claims, not the personal interests we may muster in its defense. This is reflected in the fact that at the phenomenological level morality normally appears to us as a constraint, not as an expression of our inclinations.

THE LEVEL OF ETHICAL PRINCIPLES

Ordinarily, we do not need to proceed beyond the "moral" level in our deliberations. But answers of the sort hitherto considered do not necessarily put an end to the ethical questions that may relevantly be raised. Occasionally one is obliged to ask whether an action which is prescribed by existing moral rules *really* is right and whether, therefore, one ought to continue to obey them. When pressed in a certain way, the effect of such a question is to throw doubt upon the validity of the rules themselves. And in that case, there is usually no alternative to a fundamental reconsideration of the whole moral code.

Such questions have many causes. It may be that the moral rules conflict, or that a consistent adherence to them would result in general inconvenience or suffering. It may be that they run too persistently against the grain of human need or inclination. It may be that changing social conditions render them inapplicable or inadequate for the adjudication of communal disagreements. We must distinguish, however, between the various causes which may animate what I here

[4] For a more detailed defense of this characterization see "A Pluralistic Analysis of the Ethical 'Ought.'"

distinguish as "ethical" criticism and the procedures which give it its status as a valid mode of practical reasoning.

Several aspects of ethical criticism require comment. In the first place, it must be constantly borne in mind that when we question the propriety or fitness of a moral code our question remains practical, both in intention and in effect. Ethical questions are never purely theoretical or speculative. But there are many ways of raising practical questions. When they are raised in ethical terms, the effect, first of all, is to place the questions on a level of impersonality which requires the subordination of personal bias or preference. It is their function to establish a mood in which the particular moral rule or the moral code as a whole is considered impartially or, as we say, "objectively," without regard to our own inclinations or benefits. In this guise, the incitive or normative effect of ethical terms appears to consciousness as something which is independent of and even in opposition to "interest." A second characteristic effect of this use of ethical terms is their tendency to "frame" or set apart the questions and answers in which they occur from ordinary practical deliberations. The language of ethics is, among other things, a ceremonial or ritual language. Our "lay" deliberations and appraisals may be fully as important for our ultimate well-being as those couched in ethical terms. In certain situations they may be even more intensely incitive. What they lack is the distinctive "aura" of impersonal authority which sets ethical judgments apart from the ruck of practical demands. "Would it be beneficial to everyone considered if the moral code were revised?" has nothing like the distinctive authority of "Would it be right to revise it?" or "Ought we to alter the moral code?" Here the only illuminating comparison is with other ceremonial languages such as those of religion or the law. Each of these institutions has its own characteristic rituals, each of which is incitive in a somewhat different way. Each has its own characteristic "style" which signifies a different sort of press and different trains of reflection. The ceremonies of the law are impersonal and authoritative, but they carry with them the suggestion of ulterior punishment or confinement. They are inevitably threatening in their effect in a way that the language of ethics is not. On the other hand, the distinctive ceremonies of religion, although impersonal, are primarily devotional in character; the press which they evoke is one of worship, prayer, and meditation. Their function is discharged when they have evoked the proper moods and feelings. The attitudes aroused by ethical terms on the level of discourse which we are considering, however, are not worshipful but critical, not meditative but, by intention at least, practical.

Perhaps the most distinctive feature of ethical discourse is its so-called "autonomy." It makes no promises of future benefit to the individual; nor are its principles justified by an ulterior consideration of expediency. If such a justification is made, it has nothing directly to do with ethical criticism as such. Indeed, it is precisely the effect of ethical terms to short-circuit questions of this sort, to shame them, in effect, out of countenance. To ask whether a proposed reform of the moral code will make one happier or more prosperous is to declare one's self so far immoral, and hence subject to moral censure. But the only "threat" implicit in moral judgment is the impersonal disapproval which is embodied and projected in the judgment itself. Psychogenetically, the "source" of the authority of the language of morals is closely connected with the sanctions of parental approval and disapproval. Gradually, however, "ought" and "right" become incitive substitutes, not merely for the parent, but for the social group. And at the level of ethical criticism they appear to voice a claim which is wholly ideal and universal. The point is, however, that in fact there is nothing apart from the attitudes which these terms evoke in one's self to substantiate or enforce the claim. One may give "reasons" in support of this or that demand for a change in the moral code. But at last one can only justify such reasons, from an ethical point of view, by appealing to ideals or standards which themselves establish what we mean by an ethical reason. To require their justification is simply to go beyond "ethics" altogether.

Now, as Hume understood, more clearly, perhaps, than anyone else, the interests which support "morality" are many. Custom, habit, sympathy, fear, the love of reputation, and a thousand other motives, together with the myriadic nonmoral "reasons" that reinforce them, combine to secure moral action upon a far more solid base than would be possible were we to rely exclusively on moral justifications. In the same way, a thousand and one nonethical motives and reasons may support the ethical reasonings in the light of which a reform of the moral code may be demanded. There is no need to impugn such nonmoral considerations or to deny them their place in the sphere of practical reasoning and deliberation in general. Indeed, when such ulterior supporting considerations are long absent, morality tends to die of sheer attrition. To acknowledge this, however, is not even by implication to blur the distinction between ethical and nonethical reasons or between ethical principles and individual preferences.

The same sort of point is frequently made in regard to questions of logic or questions of fact. In trying to convince someone of the truth of a certain statement, we often find it necessary to introduce supporting reasons that are not strictly relevant from a logical point of view. It is sometimes actually, if unfortunately, the case that people will not listen to "reason." When this happens, we have to employ other methods of persuasion. But this does not in the least mean that we confuse a "good" reason in logic or in factual reasoning with one which simply happens to work. Nor does it mean that we are impelled to question, in their own spheres, the autonomy of the validating methods of logic and inductive science. If someone challenges these methods or asks us to supply a better reason than they afford in answer to the questions they enable us to answer, we would simply not know how, within logic or science, to make a reply. Pragmatic "justifications" of the rules of inquiry doubtless have their function, but they do not determine in general what a "valid" inquiry is.

The same thing is true in the case of ethical appeals. One

may question, if one must, the "justice" of the rules governing the duties of wives or mothers in our society. But if one should question the legitimacy of the standard of justice itself, in virtue of which alone a question becomes ethical, there is simply no way of answering without moving outside of ethics altogether. Someone may ask, "Shall I accept ethical standards of criticism?" if by this he wishes to challenge the procedures of ethics as a whole. But he cannot expect an answer to which it would be possible to ascribe the characteristic of "validity." At the ethical level, "ought" and "good" are simply not appropriately used save in connection with such principles as "justice" or "least suffering." Their whole function here is to "put us in mind" of such principles. Both are parts of an indivisible level of discourse, whose boundaries are set by the interlocking relations of such terms themselves.

How many justifying principles or rules of relevance there are in our system is very hard to say. One such principle is that of "benevolence" or "least suffering." It is always legitimate to question the legitimacy of a moral rule when it can be shown that continued adherence to it would cause unnecessary or undue hardship or misery. It is likewise proper to ask for a reform of the moral code when it can be shown that continued adherence to it would result in some fundamental indignity to the "persons" of certain individuals. On the other hand, it is not legitimate to demand a modification of the code on the ground that adherence to it would cause personal inconvenience to ourselves. Nor is it valid to demand a change on the ground that the drift of history is against it. In my judgment, there is, in our system, no one principle of ethical criticism to which alone we may properly make appeal in justifying a demand for moral reform. Various attempts have been made to reduce the principles of welfare or least suffering to those of justice, equality, and respect for persons, or vice versa—always, I believe, without success. Other efforts have been made to justify the one group in terms of the other. Hume and Mill, for example, were able to show, within limits, the benefits which accrue to society as a whole from a strict adherence to rules of justice. But they usually avoided "hard cases" when so doing. The benefit to society as a whole never provides a conclusive ethical reason for acting unjustly. Nor does the justice of an act which would cause irreparable harm to society as a whole certainly establish the act's validity. It might be supposed that here we must appeal to some vaguer but more general standard of "reasonableness" or "competence." But in this case such an appeal would be of no avail if, as I suspect, most reasonable men, faced with the necessity of choosing between the two sorts of principles, would find no final or certain answer as to which is preferable.

It is precisely at such a point as this that ethical tragedy occurs. When we reflect upon the essential tragedies of *Antigone* or *Job*, it is no "fatal flaw" in the individuals involved that lies at the heart of the tragedy but, as Hegel saw, a fundamental and inescapable conflict of ethical principles, both of which are "right." In both cases adherence to one principle of right action involves the protagonist in head-on collision with another. The conflict cannot be avoided, but it is ethically insoluble. Hence the tragedy. Wherever such tragedies as *Antigone* may occur, there is a plurality of basic ethical principles. Indeed, the very possibility of tragedies of this sort is itself an index of such a plurality.

In a strictly ethical appeal, then, such principles as those of justice and least suffering define the relevant applications of the ethical "ought," and it in turn sets them apart as the distinctive rules of the ethical "game." Together they constitute a universe of discourse which is so far autonomous and self-justifying. In this sense, even in "open" societies, morality is a closed system in a way that the laws of politically organized society are not. Laws are not, at least in open societies, self-justifying. The authority of any moral system, however, is grounded in the very terms of morality itself. When we "criticize" a particular moral code it is usually on grounds that are themselves ethical.

One can, of course, go "outside" morality altogether and question its "value" from some ulterior point of view. Or one may propose, in the manner of Bentham, to dispense with "morals" altogether and deliberate exclusively in terms of felicific consequences without regard to their moral worth. But such a question or such a proposal has no more place within ethical criticism as here conceived than analogous questions or proposals would have within the "games" of logic and science. To propose that science adopt "agreeable consequences" as a criterion of truth would, in effect, be a proposal to abandon science altogether for something else. And in the same way the proposal that morality should submit to some "higher" or "more fundamental" authority in justification of its rules is tantamount to the suggestion that ethical discourse be replaced by some other form of deliberation.

One criticism that has frequently been leveled against ethical principles of the sort in question is that they are "empty." To a person faced with the problem of making up his mind what he ought to do in a particular situation, such principles will inevitably appear trite, empty, and vague. This, as Mill recognized, is just as true of the principle of utility as it is of Kant's categorical imperative. Such principles are principles of criticism by means of which lower-order moral rules are justified. "Secondary" rules, as Mill called them, are not to be replaced by the greatest happiness principle. In attempting to justify particular actions it is to "secondary" rules rather than to the latter principle that we must appeal. What must be recognized here is simply the difference of level to which moral rules and ethical principles apply.

To criticize the principle regarding respect for persons on the ground that it is "empty" would be analogous to a criticism of the rules of inductive inference which argued against them on the ground that no substantive law of nature could be deduced from them. Such criticisms are based upon a complete misunderstanding of what such principles are designed to accomplish. As we move up the ladder of moral criticism from justification to justification and from subordinate rule to superordinate "procedure," we

also move from attitudes that are relatively determinate
to others which are relatively indeterminate. The former
are directed to the solution of particular problems of conduct
or concerned with the realization of particular goals. The
latter, on the contrary, are directed rather to the organization,
regulation, and correction of lower-order attitudes. Second-
level ethical principles, therefore, are procedural rather than
substantive in aim. Their role is not to tell us what to do in
particular cases but to provide us with standards of relevance or "reasonableness" when appraisal of lower-order
rules is required. Vague and formal though they may be,
the lack of them would force the would-be critic to resort altogether to supra-ethical special pleading controlled by nothing save his own interests.

Kant's formulation of the categorical imperative has often
been criticized as an empty form from which no "duties"
could be inferred. But such a criticism, as C. D. Broad has
pointed out, is based upon a complete misapprehension of
Kant's intention. What Kant was trying to do—with what
success we do not have to consider here—was to characterize
the general validating procedure by which, as he believed,
all moral imperatives are ethically justified. It is not a rule
of conduct but a formula for testing rules of conduct. It had
to be "empty," it had to be formal, if it was to do the job
assigned to it. To enrich its content would be *ipso facto* to
transform its role and hence to deprive it of its power as
a general principle of ethical criticism. The trouble with
Kant is not that he provides us with an empty formula but that
the one he provides will not bear the burden of justification
required of it. What he saw, with an unrivaled clarity, is
that moral criticism which is something more than an *ad hoc*
expression of individual attitudes is impossible save on the
assumption that there are ethical principles which are general in normative appeal.

THE POST-ETHICAL LEVEL

We come now to the final or, so I have called it, the "post-ethical" or "human" level of moral discourse. The problem at this level can perhaps best be understood in terms of the paradoxical question "Why should I be moral?" This question has been roughly handled by many philosophers ever since Bradley. But in Kant it was already given, if not its quietus, then its comeuppance. For the whole point of Kant's sharp distinction between moral rules and counsels of prudence and between the heteronomy of hypothetical imperatives and the autonomy of the moral law was to render the question "Why should I be moral?" meaningless. If one is a rational being, one recognizes that one is bound by moral laws; if one questions such laws, nothing that a rational being might say in reply would make sense, for by one's question one has declared oneself unamenable to the rules of ethical reasoning. To be sure, consequentialists have sometimes claimed to justify particular moral rules in terms of their effects. But this merely transfers the burden of obligation to something else which is taken to be intrinsically desirable on its own account. When this point is reached, the consequentialist, whether he knows it or not, is at the end of *his* rope. His principle provides a justification of secondary moral rules or prima facie duties, and through them particular moral imperatives; but the rule itself has and can have no such justification. If the consequentialist supposes the contrary, he is simply confused and fails to understand the logic of his own consequential arguments. All that he or anyone can do in the end is to reiterate the intrinsic desirability of the end which he believes to be the proper goal of moral action. And if someone should stubbornly ask, "Why should I accept that as intrinsically desirable?" he has and can have no answer. For him the question must be simply tantamount to the question "Why should I accept as intrinsically desirable what really is so?" which is tantamount to the tautology "Why should I do what I really ought to do?"

The point, as we have seen, is that on its second and third levels morality is a limited sphere of discourse with its own distinctive criteria of relevance and validity. One can question the morality of an act and answer the question by appeal to a moral rule; that rule in turn may be questioned in relation to some more ultimate principle. But at last one reaches a point at which no further ethical question can be raised. The only possible way of *validly* answering the question "Why should I approve *x?*" is to invoke some rule which itself enunciates and delimits the sphere of moral action.

All this must be assented to if one is to avoid confusion. Yet I am convinced that many people have asked such questions as "Why should I be moral?" without posing senseless philosophical puzzles and without wishing to "reduce" the moral or the ethical to something else which it is not. And I think that such persons are not invariably silly in asking them, even though they perhaps have no clear notion of precisely the kind of question they are asking or the kind of answer they would in principle be prepared to accept. But they would not be satisfied, nor would they be adequately answered, if we should try to remove their moral "cramps" by pointing out that the question is linguistically out of bounds. For, although it is out of bounds on certain levels, there is another, as I shall try to show, on which the rules governing the usage of "ethical terms" cannot prevent it from being raised.

In thinking about ethics, philosophers usually fail to bear in mind the whole gamut of its dimensions, roles, and relations. In discussing the "ground" of moral obligation, they fail to see that the metaphorical ambiguity of "ground" conceals a plurality of legitimate or, at any rate, of inescapable questions. In emphasizing the limits of moral reasoning which govern the strictly "ethical" applications of "ought" or "right," they forget that such limits are themselves man-made and that the autonomy which, as social beings, we normally grant to moral rules can itself be transcended by the raising of questions which require the whole enterprise of morality to justify itself before some other court of appeal. Finally, they forget that "justification" is a many-sided process and that what is an adequate justification from one point of view, is, from another standpoint, no more than the posing of a problem. Especially is this so when we proceed from limited questions that presuppose an institutionalized framework of ideas and rules to unlimited ones which embrace the institution as a whole. If morality, like science, is a systematic process which, at least up to a point, raises no questions about itself, this does not mean that as human beings we are bound to raise no questions concerning it, even though, upon reflection, we may find that we no longer wish to raise them. There is a sense in which man transcends all his works and is "free," albeit at his peril, to junk any of them at any time. I am bound by the rules of morality so long as I am responsive to the demands of a "rational" moral being. But nothing can give them authority over my conduct unless I, in virtue of my attitudes and wants, am moved by them. Moreover, no man is responsive to the rules of morality and nothing else. It is, we are frequently told, the office of morality to oppose and correct our inclinations. This is true. But, if so, then it follows from the very nature and function of morality itself that man is more if also less than a moral being. And, as such, he may have questions to ask of morality which it itself is unable to answer.

Nor is there anything to prevent him raising them in what are *called* "ethical terms." To be sure, I cannot, or, if I would avoid confusion, should not raise every question at once that can be expressed in terms of "good," "right," or "ought." But such terms have so broad a *spread* or spectrum of meanings that there is simply no way of confining their use to those levels we may agree to call "characteristically moral or ethical." But there are occasions upon which I may ask, à la Bentham, "Well, now, what's the good of all this business of morality anyway?" And I should surely regard my answerer as an ass if he merely replied, "I'm sorry, dear fellow, your question doesn't make sense. Your question simply commits a fault against usage. One *cannot* ask what the good of

morality is, because it is only in relation to the rules of
morality itself that you can even ask such a question."

Rather than appeal to purely supposititious linguistic rules
which prohibit the raising of the question "Why should I
be moral?" let us try to see what kind of question it is, and
in what sort of context it might conceivably be raised.

We may get a purchase on our problem by comparing
the question with others which have a similar ring: "What's
the point in living morally anyway?" "Morality is well
enough for those who choose to go in for that sort of thing,
but why, with one life to live, should I be bound by such conventions?" Such questions have no single answer, nor is there
any criterion save interest itself which can determine when
an answer to the question is satisfactory. I am "satisfied" and
the question is "answered" not when some objective conditions have been met but when my practical indecision or
doubt has been removed—when, that is to say, I have been
provided with an adequate motive for playing the moral
game. Here the only sort of justification possible is of the subjective sort which provides an "exciting occasion" capable of
motivating the will.

It is at this point, it seems to me, that the existentialists,
for all their strange way of saying things, have really understood a fundamental fact of the moral life. When they speak
of man's "freedom" in the moral situation, what they mean, I
think, is that no purely logical or metaphysical "reason" can
bind a man to any obligation whatsoever, that only by a gratuitous decision can one in the end ever answer the question
"Why should I be moral?" I am more than my commitments. I
am bound by my commitment only so long as I continue to
be moved by it. No existential situation can compel my loyalty
unless, for *whatever* reason or for no reason at all, I choose
to be bound by it. Every situation, from the standpoint of
my loyalty, is a new situation, every reaffirmation of past
loyalties a new affirmation. If I choose, I may at any point
refuse to abide by past loyalties. This is not an expression
of disloyalty or of readiness to act thenceforth in an irresponsible way but rather a statement of the fundamental

character of the moral situation itself. The continual possibility of rejection or indifference thus renders the authority of moral rules constantly dependent upon what I, as an agent, elect to be or to do.

In the end, then, the fundamental *human* problem is not to provide an answer to the question "Why should I do x?" but "Why should I do anything?" This is a question which is beyond reason. If it is senseless, then, as human beings, we are at bottom committed to the posing of senseless questions. Decision is king.

[V]

Moral Reasoning

ON THE NEW APPROACH IN MORAL PHILOSOPHY

Recently Stephen Toulmin, Stuart Hampshire, and others have called for a radical shift of perspective in moral philosophy. They tell us that "traditional" approaches, which begin with questions concerning the meanings of ethical terms, must be abandoned. We are now enjoined to by-pass the problem of meaning in order to reach more directly the only really interesting philosophical issue, which concerns the nature of moral reasoning and the use of moral judgment. We are to ask not "What does 'good' mean?" but rather "What sorts of reasons count as good in defending moral decisions?" and not "How is 'ought' to be defined?" but "What is the logic of reasoning to a conclusion that prescribes what we ought to do?" The problem of definition, so it is said, belongs, if anywhere, to lexicography; philosophers are now to be saved from the necessity of going out of business by the fact that lexicographers are not logicians. Thus, apparently does Samuel Johnson leave a place in the sun for David Hume.

Opinions well may differ in regard to the virtues of the philosophical commitments underlying the "new" approach. Remembering Aristotle, Hume, and Kant (to mention only the greatest names), one may argue that it is, at best, a second and weaker bolt from the same old blue. At any rate, the classical moral philosophers were mainly concerned with the problem of practical reason; nor did they waste much time debating the question, "What is the correct analysis of 'right'?" Plato himself is only an apparent exception. Still, the new-old approach has already helped us to break fresh ground, or, if not this, then at any rate to sharpen the shovels with which we dig up the old. The now ancient and interminable debates between the naturalists, emotivists, and intuitionists plainly reached an impenetrable impasse by the turn of the mid-century. The only way out has seemed to require that we go around the problem of meaning which has stopped the "istists" dead in their tracks.

Yet it would be premature to claim that the problem of meaning has been successfully by-passed or that the logic of moral reasoning can be adequately explicated without regard to the meanings of "good" and "ought." One might, of course, question whether any very sharp boundary can be made between meaning and implication or between the sense of a term and the conditions governing its range of application. At bottom, meaning is a matter of our responses to words, and our responses to words are affected by their interconnections with other words. If the meaning of a word is to be *fully* grasped only when viewed in relation to their own wider logical contexts of argument and inference, it is perhaps reasonable to hold that, in order to know the *full* meaning of a word, one must grasp the whole syntax or logic of the sentences in which it normally functions. Simple-minded questions get simple-minded answers. To the question "What does 'good' *as such* mean?" no simple answer is possible.

The trick word, here, is "fully." It does not follow that, since full understanding of "good" requires knowledge of the logic of its normal use, no understanding of it can come from knowing its definitions. Nor does it follow that, since no sharp distinction between meaning and implication can be drawn, there is no distinction whatever. If the full significance of a term is revealed only when its logic has been explored, it is at least a question whether it could have a logic at all unless it has a core meaning which remains the same, to all practical purposes, in the different sentential contexts in which it is used. Just as coherence theories of truth, of whatever origin, are bound in the end to come a cropper, so also coherence theories of meaning or use are likely to lead us only to an undifferentiated ooze of larger and larger significances.[1]

It is worth bearing in mind, moreover, that preoccupation with the problem of the definability of "good" was not due to myopic perversity on the part of Moore and his followers. Both Moore and his teacher Sidgwick were no less interested in the central problem of ethical methodology than their predecessors. They found, however, that theories of practical reason that are detached from close study of such words as "good" and "ought" are built upon shifting sands. Indeed, it was precisely their desire to come to closer grips with the methods employed in moral justification and reasoning which forced them to consider whether, and in what terms, "good" may be defined. The besetting sin of the then traditional approaches to the logic of morals consisted entirely in the fact that they tended to prejudge the methodological issue from the outset by tacitly begging crucial questions as to the meanings of ethical terms. By challenging such question-begging presuppositions, Sidgwick and Moore were able, almost at a single stroke, to place in extreme jeopardy all so-called "naturalistic theories" of the validation of moral judgments. For unless "good" *is* a descriptive predicate, and unless the property which it supposedly designates *can* be identified, how can the proposal be maintained that moral judgments are verifiable, and hence justifiable, by the

---

[1] To say, for example, "The sky is blue" can be understood only in so far as it is viewed as part of or in relation to something called "the whole of science" is, in effect, to deny the possibility of knowing what "The sky is blue" conveys to all. It is also to preclude the possibility of knowing what logically follows from "The sky is blue." Rational puddle-jumping presupposes islands of distinguishable meaning. If "blue" has no distinguishable sense or meaning apart from the sentential contexts in which it may be placed, then it becomes problematic how significant assertion and denial could even occur. Possibly the radical piecemeal "meaning analyses" of the first half of the century went too far. But one must not forget that, in part, such analyses were a much-needed reaction against the coherence theories of the preceding generation which, when pushed to their logical conclusions, made of predication an incomprehensible muddle.

methods of empirical science? If, in short, one is to maintain that "*x* is good" is capable of a certain type of validation, one must also be prepared to argue that "good" is the sort of term whose use permits that type of validation. This requires attention to the question of meaning itself. More generally, it may be argued that the sorts of "reasons" that are permissible in ethics depend upon the kinds of terms involved in asserting that something is right or good or that a certain act ought to be performed.

In order to determine why this may be so, let us for a moment consider the background of the new approach itself. Now there can be little doubt that the present preoccupation with the problem of moral reasoning is itself largely due to the challenge which the emotive theory has offered to the whole notion of rational justification in moral discourse. I dare say no one would have been upset by the emotive theory had it not appeared to imply the impossibility of committing an error in reasoning to a moral conclusion —if, in short, it had not seemed to entail that the entire substance of an ethical disagreement consists in nothing more than an opposition of first-personal attitudes, the removal of which can be effected only by so-called "persuasive methods." Not all the attacks on the emotive theory were well founded; many seem almost perversely bent upon misinterpreting its intention, which was meta-ethical rather than moral. Nevertheless, beneath the confusion lay a well-founded apprehension. For if the emotive theory be true, not only most philosophers but most ordinary men have been laboring for centuries under a profound misapprehension in seeking by supposedly rational means to establish the validity of their moral judgments and decisions.

What is the nature of the challenge presented by the emotive theory? In essence it consists almost entirely in a radical hypothesis as to the meanings of ethical terms. In this view, it is because ethical terms have no "cognitive meaning" or else, in their crucial ethical role, are independently emotive that ethical arguments to a moral conclusion are alleged to have no logical cogency whatever. The point

may be more forcibly put in another way. It has been widely
assumed that the rationality of moral discourse depends
upon the cognitive meaningfulness of its terms. Validity,
Stevenson has maintained (and many cognitivists would
agree), applies only within the spheres of logical and factual
reasoning. It does not apply to mixed trains of thought,
association, and feeling, or to utterances which are merely
expressions of feelings or prods to action. Therefore, if the
fundamental meaning of ethical terms is merely expressive
and incitive, no argument to a moral conclusion can be
either valid or invalid, and one argument is as valid or invalid as any other.

Thus did the emotive theory of ethical terms entail, or
appear to entail, a corresponding view regardng the uses
and limits of reason in ethics. Without this the emotive
theory of ethical methods would have little to recommend
it. But the moral is clear: if the emotive theory is to be
effectively overthrown, then its claims concerning the meanings of ethical terms will sooner or later have to be refuted
or else qualified. One will have to show either that such
terms have a different sort of meaning, which permits the
application of rational methods to statements containing
them, or that even if their meaning is noncognitive, it is
still such that rational processes of validation may still apply
to moral judgments. In either case one will have finally to
come to grips with the problem concerning the nature of
ethical terms.

It is no good arguing, as Toulmin does, for example, that
the emotive theory must be false since there are such things
as good and bad reasons in ethics. This will not for a moment faze proponents of the emotive theory, for they may
immediately reply that when we say that x is a good
reason, we are merely expressing our own personal approval of it and recommending that others do so as well.
Persuasive methods are plainly not limited to so-called "ob-
ject-level" statements. They may be employed on any level
of discourse whatever. The fact of emotive meaning, if such
it be, must be reckoned with not only in sentences pre-

scribing what we ought to do but also in sentences prescribing how we ought to argue or how we ought to weigh
statements introduced in the support of a moral conclusion.
The emotive meaning of "good" does not disappear when
we predicate it of statements or arguments rather than of
acts or objects. And when applied in the former case, or
so it may be argued, its use is no more rational than when
applied in the latter.

Nor does it much help to argue, as Toulmin also does,
that "good reason" may be translated as "valid reason."
For a skillful emotivist may easily reply that, when applied
beyond the spheres of formal logic and induction, the term
"valid" is itself merely emotive and rhetorical. Stevenson
himself simply fell into his own trap when he sought persuasively to restrict "validity" to the methods of formal logic
and empirical science. The issue here concerns the meaning
of the terms predicated of an argument or process of justification, not the mere vocabulary employed in the predication. It is not, in short, a question of whether we can say
that an ethical justification is good or valid or reasonable,
but what we mean and what we do when we say this. If, at
bottom, all we are doing when we say that such and such
an argument is valid is to put upon it our own personal
stamp of approval, then it would appear that there is
logically no way of telling another who disagrees with our
reasons that he has made a mistake. For how can one make
a mistake unless there is some rule or procedure or usage
which tells us when a mistake has occurred? The emotivist
claims that ethical arguments may be defeated; he denies
that they are in any ordinary sense corrigible. To outflank
the emotivist, therefore, one must at last come to grips
with the question of how terms such as "good" or "ought,"
the force of which is prescriptive or incitive, may be subject
to rules of application and transformation.

In the end, I submit, questions of meaning and questions
of logic or reason must be made to ride tandem. Neither can
be successfully treated without regard to the other. In the
next sections I shall consider certain aspects of the logic of

moral discourse; then I shall return once more to the question of meaning.

THE MORAL USES OF DEDUCTIVE REASONING

Another feature of the new approach is its contention that in ethics we are faced with a special sort of reasoning which is different in kind from those employed in formal logic or in empirical science. But here again we do well not to dismiss too soon more traditional views.

Because ethical arguments are, at certain junctures, subject to special "moral" rules of inference, it does not follow that, at other junctures, ordinary deductive and inductive methods do not also apply.

Now one of the reasons why it has been argued that the logic of moral discourse is peculiar is that it has been taken for granted that ordinary deductive and inductive methods are applicable only to statements which are cognitively meaningful. Ethical judgments are, at least in part, noncognitive. Hence, if they are to be regarded as rationally justifiable, there must be special rules of normative inference applicable to them. This conclusion, I am now convinced, is also premature. Philosophers have no very precise notion of what they mean by "cognitive meaning," and hence no clear idea of the range of deductive and inductive procedures, even when it is granted that they are to be restricted to cognitively meaningful statements. But, apart from this, there is no compelling reason to suppose that the application of such procedures to normative statements or to mixed reasonings which are partly cognitive and partly normative is illicit. For example, we all constantly seek to justify particular moral conclusions by subsuming them under general moral principles. Granted that the terms of the conclusion are, as we say, contained in those of the premises, we are all prepared to acknowledge, in certain cases at least, that the conclusion follows logically from the premises. All that is required for deductive methods to apply is that the sentences in question be capable of quantification and of some lawful form of negation or opposition. Sometimes the logic required is two-valued; sometimes it may have to be three-valued. That is as it may be. But the cogency of a logical inference does not presuppose the "cognitive" status of its premises or of its conclusion; it depends only upon the question whether certain rules of transformation have been observed. All that we have to do in performing deductions in ethics is simply to carry through the appropriate substitutions of ethical terms for the variables of the appropriate syntactical or logical forms.

Indeed, it may well be argued that, just because formal logic is indifferent to questions of modes of meaning, the only serious logical question, in the wider sense of the term, concerns the use or meaning of such words as "good," "right," and "ought." Once this problem has been resolved, no special logical issue remains. If so, the only remaining task for theoretical ethics concerns what has been called the "epistemology of morals," that is, the process whereby the general principles of moral discourse are themselves validated or verified.

It is possible to reply, however, that such a view is ill advised and question-begging, since it neglects the possibility, brought forcibly to our attention by the emotive theory, that the distinctively nonreferential meanings characteristic of ethical terms preclude altogether the application of logical procedures of any sort in the validation of moral conclusions. The logic of the books, whether two-valued or three-valued, applies only to statements which are true, false, or probable. Ethical judgments, however, are or contain recommendations, proposals, prescriptions, and incitements to act. These can be neither true nor false nor probable in any intelligible sense. How, then, it may be asked, can one speak of relations of entailment or logical implication holding between them and other expressions? The appeal to general normative principles is not like the appeal to universal premises from which particular conclusions are inferred. If I accept a universal moral rule, I am bound by no law of logic whatever to accept any particular moral conclusion. It is true that we continually do assert moral principles in support of particular moral conclusions. But here the relation is again purely psychological. When we find ourselves adhering to moral principles which conflict with our particular moral decisions, no question of logical inconsistency is involved. There is merely a material opposition of attitudes which happen to conflict with one another in action.

To this it must be rejoined that, while there can be no logical opposition between individual attitudes, it does not follow from this that there is no logical opposition between sentences which express such attitudes. Again we must focus upon the question whether, as normally used, ethical judgments are related to one another in ways that accord with the syntactical rules of logic. That we do normally so relate them is plain. Nor does formal logic itself preclude the possibility. If all s's are p, and a is an s, then a is a p regardless of whether p is a descriptive predicate such as "yellow" or a normative predicate such as "good." There is no rule that I have been able to discover in the logic books which restricts the values of the variables of any ordinary sentential function to so-called "cognitive" or descriptive terms. There is no formulated condition that they must mean in some particular mode of meaning. If it be replied that there is at any rate a presumption that the sentences derived by substitution from such functions must be either true or false, then it must be rejoined that there is no good reason to deny that ethical judgments are not properly spoken of as true or false. Toulmin tells us that ethical judgments may be valid or invalid but not true or false. But if his appeal is to our ordinary moral practices, as it is, then the reply is clear; it is far more appropriate to say that it is false that I ought to beat my grandmother than to say that it is invalid. Toulmin's contention is incompatible with the most obvious facts of ordinary moral discourse. He may then wish to say that, if we so speak, we *ought* not to do so. But to this the reply must be that in saying this he changes the question and that, when he has given us valid reasons for such a recommendation, we will be delighted to consider them.

For my part, I have discovered no sound reason whatever for denying to our ethical judgments, even if they be admitted not to be factual descriptions or predictions, the right to be regarded as true or false. Notice that no one objects when it is said that a certain statement in formal logic is true or false. Nor does anyone object to the use of the phrase "logical truth." The interesting question is thus not whether moral judgments may be true or false but rather in what sense they are so; nor is the issue whether this sense is identical with that intended when we hold a statement of fact to be true or false but rather whether there is a sufficient analogy to permit the application of logical procedures in both cases. The application of "truth" and "falsity" in either case signifies primarily that the statements in question are validatable or certifiable in accordance with certain governing rules or procedures.

Let me make the point of these remarks more explicit. It is not denied that, in certain respects, the process of justification in morals differs from that involved in formal logic. It is maintained only that there is no sound reason for denying that ordinary deductive methods do apply, not merely to the factual parts of an argument to a moral conclusion, but also to the distinctively normative aspects. Logical subsumption occurs as well in ethics or in the law as in science or pure logic. If this requires us to believe that other than factual statements may have logical implications or relevancies, then we must make the best of it. And if it requires us to adopt the view that words having noncognitive meanings are themselves sometimes subject to proprieties, that in the ascription of a noncognitive term we may make significant mistakes, and that we sometimes may be required to withdraw normative judgments on pain of inconsistency and error, then we have our work cut out for us. For my part I welcome the result. What is wanted is a better theory of "noncognitive" terms.

COMPETING CLAIMS AND
THE WEIGHING OF ALTERNATIVES

But granted that formal logic has its uses in the normative as well as in the factual aspects of moral discourse, I fear that this does not take us very far. Our moral perplexities are rarely removed simply by introducing general rules under which our particular moral conclusions may be subsumed. Normally the appropriate moral rule occurs to us, as we say, intuitively, without effort or thought. In a way, all that has been done through the process of logical subsumption is to guarantee that we really are involved in a moral situation. What usually needs further to be considered is whether the duty laid upon us by the principle is itself to go unchallenged. If it is merely a question of our inclination not to keep a promise, then, granted that I have made a promise, the moral question is easily resolved. If I am tempted to tell a whopper merely for the fun of it, then, if there is a chance of my being believed, it is perhaps plain that I ought not to tell it, since it is generally agreed that we ought to tell the truth when any question of belief is at issue. There is little room for perplexity here. If we have trouble finding the appropriate rule, something has usually gone wrong with our moral training. More frequently, moral perplexities arise, not from problems of subsumption, but rather from problems of adjudicating between competing moral claims, each of which has its accepted justifying moral principle or rule. The usual trouble is that our actions have complex characteristics or effects, some of which jeopardize or infringe upon other acknowledged claims and responsibilities.

In such cases how can we rationally decide what we ought to do? Is it here simply a question of discovering a more general principle under which lower-order principles may be subsumed? Does the justification of promise-keeping or of respect for the liberty of persons depend ultimately merely on the fact that the principles of promise-keeping and respect for the liberty of persons are specific cases or applications of some more universal principle such, for example, as the principle of least suffering? This would seem to imply that there is no obligation to keep promises or to respect the liberty of others unless it can be shown that promise-keeping and respect for the liberty of others is required in order to reduce suffering. In that case, however, we could hardly speak accurately of a conflict of duties at all, for then we would really have only one duty which is prescribed by the principle of least suffering. The obligation to keep promises or to tell the truth would then be no more than an application of this more general duty to certain specific sorts of action in which there is a presumption that the sort of action in question usually results in less suffering than its opposite. This seems to me to be highly dubious. Let us see why.

Suppose that there is a question whether we should keep a promise which we have made in good faith. Two considerations need to be observed. In the first place, the very making of a promise may reasonably be said to carry with it an obligation to keep it. Other things remaining equal, any promise creates an obligation which cannot be denied without committing a moral fault. But other things are not always equal, and in certain situations it may be that I ought not to fulfill my obligation to keep my promises. No one would deny that, although we ought normally to keep our promises, other claims may be introduced which may challenge the obligation to keep a promise. Suppose, for example, that the net effects of keeping my promise will most probably result in a greater suffering than the effects of breaking it. Then it may be argued that a genuine perplexity has arisen, which in effect requires us to choose between competing principles of conduct. Now it may be held that unless the suffering entailed by keeping a promise were substantially greater than that entailed by breaking it, the promise should be kept. The principle of least suffering does not automatically take precedence over the principle of promises. It does so only at a certain point, when a great deal of suffering would result from the keeping of a promise. It is only in this sense that the principle of least suffering takes precedence over the other. But how much suffering is required to make the principle of least suffering take precedence? Here, I think, there is no exact prescription and no clear way of guaranteeing that, granted equal knowledge of the facts of the case, reasonable men may not disagree about the point at which the deleterious effects of keeping a promise absolve one from keeping it.

Nevertheless, I believe that most interested persons in our society would agree that in extreme cases the principle of least suffering does take precedence over that involved in making promises. But let us consider a more serious perplexity. Suppose there arises a question whether we should perform an act which, as we believe, will result in less net suffering for the people concerned than any feasible alternative but which cannot be performed without serious injustice, that is to say, without piling up unequal misery upon a single person. Now the ordinary utilitarian would have to hold here that, our only obligation being to maximize the happiness or minimize the misery of those who are in any way affected by our conduct, the obligation not to act unjustly is derivable solely from that to maximize happiness or reduce misery. There are also some philosophers who would admit that the demands of justice impose independent obligations but who would also argue that these obligations must give way when they seriously conflict with the demands of the principle of least suffering.

To the ordinary utilitarian we must reply that most of us raise no question about our obligations to be just in our dealings with others unless, in a particular case, it is alleged that by fulfilling the obligation a greater moral evil would result than by violating it. We ask for a reason when someone tells us that we should act unjustly; we do not ask, other things apart, why we should be just. The principles of justice are binding upon us in their own right. They belong to the fundamental commitments of our moral universe, as the events of recent years have forcibly brought home to us. To ask us to regard them otherwise would be tantamount to asking us to give up some of the very justifying principles in terms of which we conduct our deliberations. There is no "because clause" attached to the principles of justice, for they are among the principles in terms of which reasons are given in trying to justify our actions. To ask why one should be just is tantamount to asking why one should be moral. To this no answer can be given within the framework of moral discourse as we know it. The utilitarian, in effect, simply asks us to renounce what, for us, is the moral life itself.

But what shall we say to the moralist who maintains that, though the principles of justice may be independently binding, they must give way when they require the performance of actions which conflict with the principle of happiness or least suffering? Here, I think, we may ask for a reason. One cannot just appeal to the principle of least suffering itself, since it has been shown that the principles of justice do not derive their moral force entirely from the former. Is it, then, a matter of self-evidence? This is easily shown not to be the case. Suppose that an act of great injustice would result in a very slight reduction in suffering to the greatest number of persons involved. In that case surely we would hold that the principle of justice takes precedence and that it would be wrong to perform the unjust act. And in cases where the injustice is as great as the utilitarian advantage from acting unjustly, most of us would say that there is no clear answer to the question of which is morally preferable.

It is my contention that, although in many cases it is normally possible to decide which, among competing claims, is to be accepted, in at least three sorts of cases there is no conclusive reason for always giving one claim the right of way over the rest. I shall call these the claims of least suffering or humanity, the claims of justice or fair treatment, and the claims of liberty of persons.[2]

[2] Consider, for example, the case of Skinner's *Walden Two*. Suppose you are a very kind and extremely knowledgeable person who is in a

Now it may be argued that no reason worthy of the name can accept such a situation and that beyond any commitments of the sorts I have mentioned there is still another and more fundamental one which enjoins us, whenever we find ourselves involved in a conflict of duties, to search for a further principle or procedure that will enable us to adjudicate decisively between them. It has been said that the supreme principle of rationality is the commitment to be consistent in thought and action, so that, if we find that our moral code involves us in inconsistency, the code is so far irrational and must be modified. However we act, whether in the name of least suffering, or justice, or liberty, or whatever, we are bound as rational agents to choose as our principle one which would be equally binding upon all rational agents in a similar situation. Either one is committed, then, to choose once and for all one of the preceding claims as prior, and to hold it as unconditionally and equally binding upon all rational beings, or else one is committed to search for some still higher principle which takes precedence over

position to institute, at your pleasure, a society of happy, carefree men, on the sole condition that you deprive them of all liberties of person. This means, in part, that they will have no choice with respect to their vocations or their mates; that they will not have the right to criticize the policies or theories of their rulers; and that there will be, in short, no important area of human activity in which they will be free from the benevolent supervision and control of the ruler. Privacy and freedom from benevolent interference in such a society will have no place. We must, of course, play the game fairly. We will suppose, therefore, that our happy people have been given an elixir so that they will not know or, if they know, then not resent what they have lost; that, in short, they will no longer care for privacy or for the freedom of their persons at all. On the other hand, although they will be manipulated by the ruler, it will always be for their own good, so that they themselves will never dream of making a complaint that the liberties which they do not enjoy have been violated. It is my contention that, although such a choice, if presented to us as possible rulers, would have something to commend it, we would still not be able to say that a sufficient reason has been given for adopting it. For I think we would maintain that the freedom of persons ought categorically to be respected and that, when they seriously conflict, the principles of least suffering and happiness do not always override the demands of freedom. What are at stake here are the basic commitments of a whole way of life, neither of which is finally and unconditionally prior to the other.

any of these and, through it, to reach a decision which would also be so binding.

In this form, the argument is pretty clearly mistaken. For in the first place, although it is true that, as rational agents, we are bound to try, as far as possible, to be consistent in our actions, and that we should never rest in a conflict of principles without first carefully searching for a more ultimate principle, it can scarcely be held that we are bound to discover such a principle or that we may not in conscience find that among our ultimate commitments there will be some that, in practice, do seriously conflict. After centuries of search, moral philosophers have found no one supreme principle which in hard cases all reasonable men must in conscience acknowledge as prior in its claims to every other. On the contrary, I believe that, if we are candid, we will have to admit that we are morally certain that there are equally binding principles which, at least in hard cases, do involve us in fundamental conflicts of duties. It cannot reasonably be asked that I renounce the very principles in terms of which the whole process of moral justification is carried on or that I must choose between them once and for all when they appear co-equal. How shall I do so, and on what grounds? It is nothing to the point to argue that another sort of being might find himself involved in no such conflict of principles or that in Paradise the demands of freedom or justice might be held to be secondary or even practically meaningless. We do not inhabit Paradise. The only sort of practical reason which is relevant for us to consider is that which involves the procedures of justification to which we ourselves are committed and in terms of which alone *we* give reasons for what we ought to do. In one sense, ultimate moral principles are, as some philosophers say, given; it may be that to certain other creatures they would not be given and that for them other procedures of justification might appear quite as proper or sensible as ours to ourselves. But it is our business, as moral philosophers, to uncover if we can the principles which are given to ourselves and which define what we ourselves understand by sound or unsound reasons in moral deliberation. It is our own moral consciousness that concerns us here. If someone wishes to move that this be changed, he may; that is another matter. But his recommendation will not of itself carry any rational obligation on our part to accept it. It does not matter to us that in 1984 no one will be bothered by the demands of justice or that in *Walden Two* no one will miss his lost liberty; that is not our affair. It is our own procedures of justification or of practical reason that we have to analyze. With respect to them, I maintain, fundamental conflicts of principle are clearly possible.

In the second place, I submit that in our system it is assumed that in certain situations, and with all evidence before them, men may still reasonably disagree and that, upon reflection, they may properly decide differently as to the weights to be attached to the respective claims of liberty, justice, or least suffering without fear of justifiable recrimination or blame on the part of their peers. But, if this is so, then it cannot be maintained that, as a rational moral agent, I must always decide precisely in such a way as all other men would decide in a similar situation or even as I myself would subsequently decide in the same sort of circumstances. Upon reflection I may decide to weigh the conflicting claims differently without involving myself in the charge that either in one case or in the other I have acted unreasonably. Formulas here are of no help.

Nevertheless, it does seem that something further may be said about the demands of reason in such a situation. For it may be said that, when I am involved in a conflict of basic commitments, I must decide between them and that I cannot justifiably renounce them both. Moreover, it is always in order to demand that a man reconsider and that he review both the facts and the principles in question in order to make certain that no vital point has been missed. In short, I am always bound to listen to reason, and this means, in part, that the process of moral reconsideration and justification is never finally closed, even when, for the time being, I find that I must provisionally make up my mind. But, having reconsidered, then as a rational agent I am free to choose for myself between the conflicting principles, and, in so doing, I may claim to have done everything a reasonable man may be required to do in order to reach an impartial and objective decision. And my decision in such a case will be impartial and objective, since no one may fairly claim that I have failed to do what any man ought to have done in the same circumstances, even though some men might reasonably have decided differently.

What emerges, here, is that there is finally a direct appeal to "reason" itself rather than to the specific principles that bear its name.[3] I am bound to be just; but I am also bound to listen to reason when justice conflicts or appears to conflict with welfare. This does not commit me to decide against justice, but it does commit me to consider the possibility that I may have been mistaken and that the weight should perhaps go the other way. This means not that we are here appealing to some special faculty of moral intuition but that we are invoking still another regulative procedure which claims governance over the process of deliberation itself. It does not tell us in particular what our first-level duties may be; it provides no formula for weighing the respective claims of conflicting obligations. It tells us only that we must take an impartial or general view, that we must consider how others in our predicament have acted, and that we be prepared to review the facts of the case upon demand. It tells us, in short, what steps we must have taken in our process of justification if our choice is to be held free from blame. This is a procedure to be used in trying to make up our minds about claims, but it is not itself an injunction to make up our minds in a specific way. Like Kant's supreme principle of categorical imperatives, it prescribes the form which the deliberation prior to a justifiable decision must take, not what the decision itself must be.

[3] Cf. essay VII, "Global Conventions in Ethics," pp. 128-33.

THE MEANINGS OF ETHICAL TERMS AGAIN

It was my contention earlier in this essay that questions of meaning and questions of reason in ethics cannot be completely separated and that an adequate theory of reason-giving involves a theory regarding the nature of ethical terms. I wish now to go a step further in trying to make good this claim. In so doing, I hope to shed a further light upon the character of the deliberative processes involved in moral justification.

On all levels ethical terms have a normative aspect which cannot be adequately explicated in terms of their contextual descriptive meanings.[4] This is true also of the processes of justification in ethics; they too are normative in intention and in use. Such terms as "valid" and "invalid," "relevant" and "irrelevant," "ethical" or "unethical," and, finally, "rational" and "irrational" are themselves normative. They are used to commend or condemn supporting arguments and, indirectly through them, the choices or decisions which may depend upon them. To some this may suggest that after all the present view differs in no important respect from the emotive theory and that all the preceding talk about principles and reasons was simply an elaborate way of commending certain ways of resolving moral perplexities, without any theoretical significance.

I think that this is not true, and I shall now explain briefly wherein the present view differs from ordinary emotive theories like that of Stevenson. Let me say at the outset, however, that I do not wish to deny that we often do use words like "good" or even "ought" in order to express our first-personal sentiments or to issue first-personal directives regarding which there is no thought of rational justification. If I should say "Good play!" at a football game, I would

[4] That ethical terms *are* used descriptively, as well as normatively, is a thesis which underlies all of my work in ethics and value theory. This thesis, if correct, precludes the need for serious controversy between so-called "cognitivists" and "noncognitivists."

perhaps merely be expressing my own emotions and inciting others to similarly vent theirs. And when I reply, "Right," when asked if I plan to be at a certain place at a certain time, I may be simply expressing my own intention to be there. But there are other occasions when the ordinary emotivist characterization of these predicates seems to be plainly inadequate. For, in the first place, there are, as I have indicated, systematic connections between sentences containing these terms which are by no means arbitrary. Some reasons, regardless of how we may personally feel about them, are generally accorded a relevance which is quite independent of their capacity to win an argument for us in the purely rhetorical sense. In speaking of a reason as irrelevant, we do not mean simply that we ourselves wish it to be discounted; we are condemning it from the standpoint of a system of justifying procedures that are felt to be equally binding upon all members of our moral community. We speak of certain reasons as valid or invalid and of certain moral decisions as reasonable or unreasonable. When we do, we are asserting claims—not in our own persons, but rather in the name of a set of principles to which all normal persons in our moral community are committed. In short, the moral judge or critic acts as the voice of an impersonal system of prescriptions and procedures which are impersonally regulative of our deliberations.

To speak of a reason as "valid" is, then, to commend it. But it is not just to commend it; it is, rather, to commend it in a certain way and in accord with a general method of commendation. What needs to be remembered is that there may be impersonal conventions of praising and blaming just as there are impersonal methods of validating logical or factual truths. There is a vast difference, not merely in tone, but in meaning or use, between "Please pass the butter" and "You ought to keep your promise," or between "Fine weather we're having" and "Every human being ought to be at liberty." The difference lies precisely in the fact that moral recommendations are subject to a social ritual of impersonal justification or authorization which limits the way in which supporting reasons are introduced and corrects us when we make a mistake. In short, there are normally tacit "because clauses" and "unless clauses" written into particular moral prescriptions which cannot be correctly or properly filled out in any way we please. And what is meant here by speaking of "properly" filling out such a clause differs in no important way from what is meant when we speak of errors or improprieties in any other sphere. Terms such as "proper" are, if you like, evocative and persuasive. But they are no more mere first-personal evocations of feeling when used by the moralist than when used by the logician or by the grammarian.

When the question "Why?" is raised, it functions, so to say, as a signal which shifts the context of the use of ethical terms to a systematic plane where the concepts of validity and relevance may begin to gain a purchase. At this level it becomes legitimate to ask for bona fide reasons and to speak of reasons which meet or fail to meet certain conditions as "sound" or "unsound." In so doing, we have not passed beyond the normative sphere. We have merely introduced a framework of systematically related procedures of justification by which, as we say, rational persons within our community are governed. Such procedures are themselves expressive; but what they express are not just the first-personal sentiments of the person who invokes them but rather, the impersonal social presses of the whole community of law-abiding men. This is why their "weight" upon us is so ponderous and why we are so loath to violate them.

In partial justification of this view, we may consider how we normally interpret the norms of morality when viewed as natural signs. What, in fact, do we normally take them to signify? I submit that no one regards them merely as signs of the sentiments of the speaker. Rather do we construe them as indicative of certain general social attitudes or sentiments which we refer to by such expressions as the "conscience of the community" or even perhaps as the "conscience of mankind." The moral critic, in using the language of reason, speaks for and in his person represents the presumed collective sentiments of a group. On its prescriptive side, moreover, the moral judgment is not an isolated or blind evocation of passion or feeling toward an object. The presence of the because clause, and the admission of the relevance of "Why?" indicates that the incitive role of "ought" is qualified—that it carries with it a train of normative conditions and implications which cannot be turned on or off at will. Moreover, the ethical "ought" appeals to us as men and not as individuals. It addresses us, not as particular John Smiths or Bill Joneses, but anonymously, as rational men who are governed by the procedures of an impersonal moral order. This framework of rules and principles, enables us to speak of the misuse of "ought" or of the falsity or invalidity of a particular "moral judgment." In virtue of it we carry on a regularized process of correction when errors in judgment or in reasoning are made. In a word, it is possible to make a mistake in morals.

Second-level words of moral discourse, such as "valid," place a stamp of collective approval upon certain modes of deliberation and justification. They prescribe, as the case may be, what is socially permissible, what is mandatory, and what is prohibited in the matter of forming our decisions. He who uses such terms is at once caught up in a process of regularized reason-giving which has nothing to do whatever with his personal preferences or wishes in the matter.

I do not wish to claim too much. I have not said that the moral rules of rational men cannot be altered; nor have I held that the procedures for justifying first-order moral decisions yield sufficient reasons in every case. Quite the contrary. There can be no question here of a calculus. Even to speak of decision procedures would be misleading if it suggested that we possess well-formed rules for the weighing of obligations in cases of conflict. There is perhaps a greater openness of texture in moral reasoning than in ordinary factual reasoning. This does not imply, however, that in morals anything goes so long as it is effective or that the concept of validity has no legitimate application in moral deliberation. Reasonable men may reasonably disagree, but there

are still many alternatives which all of them acknowledge
to be arbitrary and irrational. If that is so, then any simple
emotive theory is surely mistaken, and this on its own
grounds.

The Authority
of Moral Judgments

PREVAILING ANALYTICAL MODELS
IN ETHICAL THEORY

Until recently, most philosophers have taken the statement of fact as their model in analyzing the meaning of ethical judgments. This is true not only of the naturalists, who have sought to reduce ethical judgments to empirically verifiable statements, but also of the non-naturalists, who deny that such a reduction is possible. For both groups questions of fact are posed as the primary concern of ethical controversy, and the authority of any ethical judgment is accordingly assumed to be directly proportional to the validity of its factual truth-claim. When any question is raised concerning one's commitment to do what the moral judgment asserts or demands that one ought to do, the descriptivists—for so I shall call them here—usually brush it aside as a "psychological question" which is therefore irrelevant to the problems of ethics. To be sure, some descriptivists such as Dewey have emphasized the decisional or practical context of moral discourse; but its *de jure* or normative status is generally treated as a simple function of its claim to truly describe the objective characteristics of actions conceived as processes or as events.

However, if by the "normative" status of a judgment is meant its role as a guide to conduct, then it is clear that the normative status of ethical judgments cannot be adequately understood in terms of a descriptive model whose primary function is to convey factual information. For the relevance of any description of fact to the principles which control our actions is not logical, but motivational; or, put in another way, it is not what a statement descriptively asserts which establishes its authority as a guide to action, but its power, by whatever means, to influence the will. It is for this reason, I believe, that the emotive theory of ethics has had such a vogue in recent years. For the emotive theory, whatever its merits in other respects, is designed explicitly to account for the practical or normative aspects of moral discourse.

Now the proponents of the emotive theory, like the non-naturalists, usually begin by insisting that ethical judgments in their characteristic use are not empirically verifiable, or, what comes to the same thing, that ethical terms cannot be defined through other terms which stand for natural or empirical properties. But here the resemblance ceases. For the non-naturalists, still clinging to the model of the factual statement, are compelled to invent a realm of non-natural facts or quasi-facts in order to give countenance to the ostensible truth-claim of the moral judgment, while the emotivist, proceeding on the basis of a completely different model, is free to draw an entirely different concluson from the same assumption.

The earlier versions of the emotive theory, however, were formulated not by specialists directly concerned to characterize the peculiar functions of moral discourse, but by methodologists of science, such as Rudolf Carnap, who were primarily interested in the problems of descriptive meaning and truth, and by semanticists, such as I. A. Richards, whose approach to the non-descriptive aspects of language was through the study of literature. For the former group the category of "expression" provided a convenient semantical wastebasket into which could be dumped all forms of discourse—metaphysical, poetic, or moral—that failed to meet the descriptive canons of empirical verifiability. For the latter group, the primary interest in non-descriptive discourse was in its immediate emotional effect. And for both, therefore, the personal utterance or evocation of feeling became the principal model for the interpretation of ethical judgments.

Gradually, however, it became apparent that such a model, although stimulating and suggestive, failed to do justice to the specific differentiae of moral judgments even when conceived as a sub-class of "expressive judgments." In the first place, as John Dewey and others insisted, the relation of "venting" or "expression" which holds between a statement and a speaker sheds no light whatever on the distinctively practical intention and effect of moral persuasion. What is wanted, in short, is not a theory of the *causes* of the moral judgment but rather an analysis of its conventional use as a guide to conduct. And from this standpoint, a linguistic venting of emotion is not more but less relevant than a trusted statement of fact which at least directs our attention to something to which we actually do aspire.

This point is, I believe, a pertinent criticism of those versions of the emotive theory which characterize the non-descriptive aspects of the moral judgment simply in terms of personal emotional expression. More particularly, it is a fair criticism of Carnap, Ayer, and even of Stevenson's "working models." It does not, however, impugn the importance of the theory in bringing forcibly to the attention of ethical theorists the urgent necessity of going beyond purely descriptivist analyses of ethical terms and judgments, if they hope to account for the normative functions of the latter. Moreover, it is only fair to say that some of the emotivists —and this is particularly true of Stevenson—never sought to construe ethical judgments exclusively in terms of the expressive model. From the first Stevenson has insisted upon the "magnetism" of ethical terms,[1] and his whole analysis of persuasive definitions assumes that such terms have mean-

---

[1] See Stevenson, "The Emotive Meanings of Ethical Terms," *Mind*, 1947, pp. 14-37.

ings which are independently incitive as well as expressive in character.

Also Karl Popper, despite his radical separation of factual from ethical assertions, regards the latter not as mere expressions of feeling but as "statements of norms," which have, according to him, an objective thrust which is analogous, although never reducible, to the statement of a fact.

It is significant, however, that even for Stevenson and Popper, the closest analogue of the moral judgment, in its active function, is the decision or command whose force or authority derives primarily from the interests of the participants in a moral colloquy. This is evident, in the case of Popper, from his reiterated emphasis upon the fact that we are always "free" to choose our norms as we please, and that the authority of the norm derives from our avowal of it, rather than vice versa. It is apparent also, in the case of Stevenson, in his tendency to characterize an exchange of moral judgments as the expression of two opposing commands whose incitive appeal seems, at least, to be identified with the fact that the respective speakers have expressed them.

NEW WORKING MODELS IN
RECENT ETHICAL THEORY

Thus, the characteristic model in terms of which more recent proponents of the emotive theory have conceived the moral judgment is essentially that of the individual proposal, decision, or command. But it is precisely the adequacy of even this model to do justice to the full significance of moral judgments on their normative side which has recently been challenged by two philosophers—Margaret MacDonald and C. E. M. Joad—who otherwise have next to nothing in common. Indeed, their agreement on this point is all the more striking precisely because they have such diametrically opposed axes to grind, and because their own respective ways of accounting for the normative significance of moral judgments are so utterly different.

Mr. Joad's opposition to the emotive theory seems to be

based as much upon moral as upon theoretical grounds. And I am not concerned with the former.[2] What interests me is his contention that "ethical judgments are recognized as claiming an authority and a publicity that feeling judgments do not. We expect other people to share our ethical judgments and feel that they are morally obtuse if they do not, and we expect ourselves and others to act in accordance with their dictates and feel that we and they are wrong if we do not."[3] If this statement is even roughly true, and I think that most persons would tend to agree intuitively that it is, then no ethical theory that regards ethical judgments as merely expressions of personal decisions or as individual incitements of attitudes can possibly be regarded as providing an adequate general analysis of the normative functions of ethical judgments. Whether we like it or not, an impersonal, public authoritativeness is frequently claimed for and perhaps voiced in moral judgments on certain levels that is independent of and, indeed, precisely opposed to the private inclinations or preferences of either the person judging or the person judged. And this poses a problem of interpretation, therefore, for which the ethical theorist must provide some answer.

[2] There are the all too familiar charges that to deny the objective truth-claim of moral judgments is, in effect, to open the floodgates of unreason and moral irresponsibility, to encourage cynicism in others, and to irrevocably weaken the hold of one's own moral commitments. Most of this, of course, in the sense in which Joad means it, is itself a form of irresponsible nonsense. It cannot too often or too forcibly be expressed that such writers as Carnap, Stevenson, and Popper have no intention of belittling the importance of rationality in the conduct of life. On the contrary, and this is particularly true of Popper, the whole polemic is directed to the defense of reason in conduct against those misguided crypto-rationalists who identify "goodness" and "obligation" with some trans-empirical or non-natural quality which can be discerned only by some supra-rational intuition. Indeed, their writings should provide a source of comfort to those who still retain some faith in the principles of Enlightenment, and would have the deliberations of men directed toward the probable means to their own well-being rather than clouded or swayed by the power of words disguised as the will of God or as the voice of some transcendental "moral order of the universe."

[3] C. E. M. Joad, *A Critique of Logical Positivism* (Chicago: The University of Chicago Press, 1950), p. 139.

The person voicing a moral judgment is, or is usually regarded as, merely the spokesman of morality; and the person judged is singled out for reprobation primarily as the violator of a rule that applies not merely to him but to all members of a certain class or group. But if this is so, then the full prescriptive meaning of "This act ought not to be done" cannot be adequately represented in terms of the usual emotional schema which characterizes it as "I approve of this; please do so also."

Now it may well be true that we rarely do utter moral judgments unless our own feelings partially coincide with the attitudes which they prescribe. And as a rule the incitive appeal of such judgments has and is expected to have a bearing upon the conduct of the particular persons to whom we address them. This is not here in question. What is questioned is that the kind of authority expressed in and exerted by the moral judgment is adequately characterized in terms of the emotional dispositions of the particular individuals engaged in a moral discussion. On the contrary, just as what we call "the" meaning of a word in ordinary language is an interpersonal rule which *thereby* functions prescriptively for those who use the word, so also the moral authority of an ethical judgment is primarily due to the fact that it is validatable by a general rule of conduct which is binding upon the individual person only because it is regarded as binding upon all moral persons.

THE CEREMONIAL USE OF LANGUAGE IN ETHICS

It is at this point that it becomes relevant to consider Margaret MacDonald's important recent essay, "Ethics and the Ceremonial Use of Language." Miss MacDonald offers an explanation of precisely those normative aspects of moral judgments which are not accounted for by the usual versions of the emotive theory, without, however, resorting to the questionable metaphysics of Mr. Joad. In what follows I shall make use of parts of Miss MacDonald's analysis in my own way, qualifying it or amplifying it as I see fit.

Now according to Miss MacDonald there are five general characteristics which hold of all moral judgments. Such judgments she maintains, are all "certainly (1) normative, (2) authoritative, (3) public, (4) indicative in grammatical form, (5) practical." [4]

It is Miss MacDonald's primary contention that moral judgments derive these peculiar characteristics partly from the fact that they are used in a way which is akin to, although not identical with, the use of language in the performance and facilitation of common tasks or actions. In this use, language may also have a "cognitive" or descriptive meaning, but its function is not primarily to say something about a proposed act nor to express or incite feelings, but rather to expedite action. Similarly moral judgments are neither mere speculations as to what might be a good thing to do under such and such conditions nor mere initiatory incitements to feeling; they are, rather, integral parts of larger processes of action which we designate by the term "conduct." [5]

But not just any common task or regularized action is a form of "conduct" in the moral sense. And not just any active or performatory use of language is thereby ethical. We have still the problem, therefore, of finding the specific characteristics which differentiate moral discourse from other forms of performatory utterance. To solve this problem, Miss MacDonald, following certain clues of the anthropologist Malinowski, proposes the analogy (which she is careful to insist is merely an analogy) of the ceremonial and ritualistic uses of language. And the suggestion is a happy one, for as Malinowski describes it, ceremonial language does have precisely those traits of publicity, normativeness, and authority which are characteristic of so much moral discourse.

Miss MacDonald has neglected, however, one vital part of Malinowski's brilliant analysis of primitive rite and ritual. [6]

---

[4] Cf. *Philosophical Analysis*, p. 212. A collection of Essays, edited by Max Black (Ithaca, N.Y.: Cornell University Press, 1950), pp. 211-29.
[5] This last point is my own.
[6] See Bronislaw Malinowski, for example, *Magic, Science and Re-*

As he conclusively shows, no ritual can give significance to an act which is without an independent interest or vital function of its own. In primitive societies, the death ritual, the marriage ceremony, the rites of hunting and of war, are all rooted in activities or events which have, quite apart from their ceremonial emphasis, a profound social and psychological importance to the persons involved. The ritual, in short, does not so much create the value as to "frame" and solemnize it. In part, it serves notice, as it were, that the acts are to be approached in a special mood and performed with special seriousness. Yet it is never more than an aspect of some wider activity which has a significance of its own, without which the ceremonial language would be an empty shell, without interest or power to move.

But what, more precisely, does the ritual do to the acts which it solemnizes? To say that it sets apart and deepens their significance is only partially true. For as in the case of the death ritual, the effect is not to augment the sorrow and fear of those who perform it, but to transmute and alleviate it. But whatever the effect in the particular case, the ritual invariably provides a social vehicle by means of which the interests of the individual are emotionally tied to or identified with those of the group to which he belongs. Invariably the effective ritual is traditional, formal, and impersonal. Through it the individual joy or sorrow, love or hate, is regularized and ordered in such a way as to transform it into a social gesture which reaffirms the individual's solidarity with the tribe or clan and vice versa.

For our present purpose, then, the important thing is that the ceremonial provides an authoritative social sanction to acts which are already in their own right important both to the individual person and to the group. By implicitly underlining the communal importance of the ritual act, the symbols help to effect a unification of personal interests within a framework of common customs and rules. Thus they achieve

---

ligion (Garden City, N.Y.: Doubleday, 1954), pp. 47 ff.; see also his *Crime and Custom in a Savage Society* (New York: Harcourt, Brace, 1926).

their effective authority both from the private sentiments which the separate individuals bring to the ceremony and from the traditional social and interpersonal context into which the ceremony automatically places the individual. The meaning of the ritual is reinforced and, hence, subsequently revitalized by the special concern or emotion which the individual brings to its performance; but it is never simply an expression of personal feeling nor a vehicle of personal exhortation or supplication. It always has the effect of a social "rule" the authority of which is "in" the rule itself, but only as a symbolic surrogate of the collective interests which it represents.

Coming to still closer grips with the problem, Miss Mac-Donald next introduces the model of law which itself is an instance of the ceremonial use of language. The legal verdict, as she says, is not merely a statement of fact, although it may "contain" such a statement, and although it emerges from and "rests" upon evidence and reasoning.[7] It acquires its special status and authority, not primarily from the cogency of the arguments which have occasioned it, but rather from its ritualistic setting. The law thus does not describe, it imposes; it not merely announces the opinions of the jury or the attitude of the judge, it pronounces through them upon the individual in the name of society, or more figuratively, it *is* society in any visible and articulate sense.

One may of course always "question" the authority of a law. But what does this mean? It means primarily that the spell of the ceremony of the law has, for the nonce, been broken, that it has run counter to interests which are so exigent that the prestige of the law for the moment is impugned. In short, to question the authority of a law is, in part, to oppose to the sanctions of public reprobation the more urgent motives of personal need. Merely to express

---

[7] It is worth pointing out in passing that legal "evidence" and legal "reasoning" are themselves shot through with ritual. Hence even the "supports" upon which a verdict is based are more than *mere* facts and deductions. Their proper weight is a function of the way in which they are introduced. Thus, for example, facts which are not "sworn to" on oath have no status as evidence which can be used against a defendant.

one's need, however, is socially ineffectual. As a rule, therefore, such a question is stated, not as a bald expression of individual preference but, rather, as an impersonal appeal to some higher legal authority. And this authority in turn is effectively derived from a further ceremony. Miss MacDonald concludes from this that "Even in an authoritarian state, the Leader must distinguish, by some formalities, laws from other personal decisions. So the authority of law itself is inexplicable without the ceremonies conducted by their characteristic modes of utterance, which attend its introduction." [8]

Following these ceremonial analogies, we may perhaps begin to understand the peculiar impersonal social authority and publicity of moral judgments without inventing a supersensory realm of "values" to account for the fact. We may also see why they are usually stated in the indicative rather than in some other form which would distinguish the norm as emanating from a personal source alone. "Do this" in many contexts frequently provokes a counter response which defeats its own purpose. But "It is wrong to do this" removes the arbitrary decisional aspect of the explicit personal command or imperative. So understood, the moral judgment derives its authority neither from the emotional tone of the speaker nor from his physical presence alone. As such it appeals not to the private inclinations of the listener but to the socialized dispositions which he possesses as a member of society. The speaker pronounces the judgment, as it were, not as an agent, but as a *carrier* of meanings whose effective appeal is determined elsewhere. And the listener is moved by it, not simply because it happens to coincide with some half-aroused private emotion which he happens already to feel, but because he is a socially conditioned organism, and the rules of society are already written into his nervous system as conditioned patterns of response.

There is, however, one important hitch. And to this Miss MacDonald herself provides the principal hint. In com-

[8] Op. cit., p. 226.

menting upon the limitations of the emotive theory she says:

> The emotive theory dissolves the hardness of moral judgments into the softness of a romantic preoccupation with a personal gospel and a private missionary society. It is a lucky accident that our gospels sometimes agree and that intercommunication occurs between the one-man sects. This seems an exaggerated moral protestantism.[9]

Precisely. But I wonder if the implications of this passage are not somewhat different from those Miss MacDonald has drawn from it.

THE LIMITATIONS OF THE CEREMONIAL THEORY

Let me begin by pointing out that the ceremonial theory may itself be regarded as a species of emotive theory. It does not, to be sure, interpret the moral term along the lines of Stevenson's first pattern analysis. But as Stevenson himself emphasizes again and again, his first pattern schema does not fit all of the inflections of the moral judgment. In certain contexts "x is good" may be perhaps most appropriately characterized as "I approve of this; do so as well." But it may also mean "we approve of this; do so as well," or "it is approved, do so as well." The important thing, in any case, is not the expressive side of the emotivist translation, but rather, its "incitive" aspect. This incitive meaning may be dependent or independent of descriptive meaning, and it may have the force of an invitation, a supplication, a command, or an impersonal rule.

But this is perhaps not so important as the next point to be made. The fact of the matter is that the ceremonial theory provides a special pattern of analysis which works very well in certain situations but not in others. And, in the long run, even in those situations to which it does apply it cannot be fully understood if we fail to bear constantly in mind the nonceremonial context as well as the nonceremonial content of

[9] Op. cit., p. 220.

the moral-judgment itself. Let us consider the analogy between morals and religion to which Miss MacDonald herself calls attention. Perhaps we will find that it is closer than she realizes. Now as she describes moral discourse, it must always be, in effect, "catholic." That is to say, it represents a universal, public, impersonal authority which is wholly independent of individual choice or preference. And the acts which it enjoins or prescribes are distinguished as "moral," not by the characteristic sentiments or feelings which they may incidently express, but by the sacred forms or patterns of the utterances themselves. In a word, it is not my emotion which sanctifies the rite; it is the rite which sanctifies my emotion. From the standpoint of Catholicism, I am known as a Christian, not by the purity of my motives or the intensity of my private conviction but rather by my acquiescence in the public ceremonials of the Church. Just so, my judgment is not rendered "moral" by the special "moral sentiment" which may animate it; rather, my moral motive is known to be such because I express it in ethical terms. The feeling does not, in short, invest the judgment with moral authority or persuasiveness, but the judgment itself gives the stamp of moral authority to the act of personal approval or disapproval.

But, just as the independent authority of a religious ritual is gradually weakened when it ceases to be the effective symbolic surrogate of collective social interests which "back it up," so, in the ethical sphere, the moral judgment will tend to lose its independent authority when it ceases to be regarded as the symbolic equivalent of the common demands of a unified social order. The moving appeal of religious myth begins to dry up when it ceases to express an independent collective attitude or belief of the group as a whole. And similarly, when the actual prescriptions that are expressed through the forms of the moral judgment no longer express genuine social demands, the forms of the judgments themselves will be incapable of long retaining their moving appeal.

What is religious protestantism? It is, above all, the practical denial of the efficacy of general social and institutional procedures in the matter of individual salvation. It is in principle an assertion of the right of the individual to employ the forms of religious utterance as an expression of personal faith and private feeling. The religious authority, so the protestant claims, does not lie in the ritual, but derives exclusively from the personal conviction and piety which alone give religious significance to the forms. What protestantism means, therefore, from the standpoint of the vehicular symbols by means of which the Christian, whether catholic or protestant, affirms his loyalty to his religion, is precisely a denial of the objective, public authoritativeness of the symbols as such. The protestant continues to use the symbols, but only because he can pour into them an expression of his own passion and devotion. *This alone* is what gives them their authority for him.

Now just as the independent social authority of religious ceremonials is inevitably weakened by the rise of protestant religious attitudes, so, in the sphere of morals, it may be argued that the authority of the forms of the moral judgment lose their independent normative appeal when they are regarded as deriving their proper authority from the individual conscience itself. And just as in the sphere of religion, the emergence of protestantism marks a gradual breakdown in the efficacy of the established ceremonials and their accredited ministers, so the emergence of a spirit of protestantism in morality results gradually in the breakdown of the efficacy of the moral judgment itself as authoritative public rite.

To generalize, I suggest that in the sphere of morality, the rise of individualism has carried with it a gradual decline in the special ceremonial status of the moral judgment, and a gradual weakening of the sheer persuasiveness of moral expressions as such. Personally, I am inclined to think that this may be a good thing, but I am here concerned to describe a fact, not to evaluate a tendency. If I am correct, then just to the extent that an individualistic normative ethic becomes dominant, the interpersonal ceremonial theory of Miss

MacDonald ceases to apply, and patterns of analysis similar to Stevenson's working models come into their own. The applicability of the ceremonial theory presupposes, in short, a people bound together by profound "organic" ritual and ceremonial ties which are reinforced continually by independent common concerns. But just to the extent that these ties are loosened, the moral judgment is transformed from an impersonally authoritative ritual into an expression of personal attitudes or decisions.

Another parallel between religion and morality may also be instructive. It should be pointed out in the first place that protestantism is not a wholesale repudiation of traditional religious formulae. On the contrary, although their meanings are profoundly altered, the ritualistic patterns at first remain precisely what they were. Thus, for example, the protestant, like the catholic, continues to recite the Lord's Prayer and to observe the ritual of baptism. The old forms remain; they are simply invested with a new and more intimate personal significance which emphasizes the feelings of the individual rather than the common authority of the group. "Our Father" becomes, in effect, "My Father," and the confessional is replaced by private meditation and prayer. The verbal expression remains the same, but the way in which it is said, and its effect upon the sayer is utterly different.

Similarly in ethics, the repudiation of the ostensible authority of the old social mores does not necessarily or even usually involve a wholesale refusal to invoke the verbal forms by means of which they were expressed. On the contrary, precisely because of their inherent normative appeal, they are usually retained—with a shift in their areas of application.

But if the objects to which different individuals apply the ritualistic terms of moral discourse are widely different or opposed, so that in the end each moral judgment becomes merely the private celebration of a personal moral rite that is dishonored by one's fellows, then in the end the suasion of the terms themselves will tend to disappear. The authority of the moral judgment helps to solidify, but it also in turn depends upon a sense of community with others. When it ceases to be thought of as a symbol of a larger common interest with which, in part, oneself is in sympathy, it loses its distinctive moral status as something which can oppose the inclinations of the individual as an impersonal or public "ought." Hence, when the objects to which we attach or seek to attach moral significance are widely different from those to which the moral judgment is traditionally applied, it becomes necessary, if the forms of moral discourse are to retain their public authoritativeness, that we successfully redefine their scope or areas of application so that henceforth they will be applied both by ourselves and others to classes of objects of which we already jointly approve on other grounds. And it is at this point that the functional significance of Stevenson's theory of persuasive definition in ethics becomes ethically relevant.

However, it is of the first importance to observe that the process of "irrigation" works both ways, and that the persuasive redefinition is quite as important as a means of "irrigating" the ceremonial forms of moral judgment themselves as it is as a means of redirecting attitudes, through the use of emotive language, toward new classes of objects. As a rule no one attempts to redefine the scope of an ethical term unless he also believes that the objects which fall within that scope are more useful or agreeable than those to which the term was previously applied. But unless the objects to which the definition directs attention are themselves already in the process of becoming socially desirable, the definition will simply fail to be accepted. What happens in the case of persuasive definition is, then, a two-way modification of meaning, and a two-way modification or reinforcement of attitudes. The ceremonial meaning of the ethical term invests the objects to which it is reapplied with the aura of special importance which the notion of moral obligation tends to convey. But they, in turn, because of our independent interest in them, reactivate the ceremony of the moral judgment.

In general, I believe, too much attention has been paid by analysts to the predicates of the moral judgment, and too little to the subjects to which, in different ages, they have applied. Not only do ethical terms have a meaning of their own, but also they have conditions of sentential intersignificance which limit the range of their application. These conditions, I submit, are a function above all of common interests which, quite apart from their moral significance, are of basic social importance.

To be sure, the range of application of ethical terms is always vague and variable. But indefinite as their range may be, it is still true that there is at any given time a fairly clear area in which we have no doubt as to the applicability of moral terms, and another in which we have little doubts as to their inapplicability. These areas conform, roughly, to those areas which are and are not, respectively, matters in which the group as a whole is seriously interested. When, as in our own time, these areas become confused, either through indiscriminate redefinition or through their persistent application to objects in which there is no independent common interest, ethical terms will tend to lose their authority.

Broadly speaking, then, the ceremonial use of ethical terms cannot long remain effective where there are no underlying common focal aims to which most members of society are committed. Where the objects to which they are applied are objects of indifference or revulsion, then not merely will the moral ceremony lose its appeal but it may, in the end, even become counter-incitive. Such a process is sufficiently familiar in the sphere of religion, but it sometimes occurs also in the sphere of morality.

There are other considerations which also tend to support the present thesis. One of these is the well-known fact that unless a conditioned response is at least occasionally reinforced by a correlated reduction of the underlying drive, the stimulus gradually looses its efficacy to incite the response. If this is so, then it would appear to follow that the emotive appeal of any symbol will tend to fade unless the objects toward which it directs attention are themselves genuine satisfiers. Secondly, it appears that negative reinforcement is generally far less effective as a means of determining attitudes than is positive reinforcement. But if this is so, then moral judgments which are reinforced merely by a vague threat of social disapproval will tend to be less effective as determinants of conduct than those which direct the energies of the individual toward goals which are objects of some positive satisfaction.

This suggests that when the force of "morality" declines, it may be due not so much to a general lack of seriousness in the conduct of life, or to the perversity of certain moral philosophers, but, rather, to the emptiness of a system of ceremonial rules which have lost their positive social utility. Whether men may live without "morals" I do not know. I believe, however, that moral judgments cannot long retain their public authority as incitors when the ends which they enjoin do not serve the permanent communal interests of men.

Global Conventions in Ethics[1]

No one seriously doubts any longer that the full normative sense of a moral judgment cannot be wholly explicated in terms of its descriptive meaning, and that although such a judgment may "contain" a proposition which is true or false, its distinctive normative claim does not rest exclusively in this fact alone. What was less evident before the clamor over the emotive theory subsided is that there are conditions of relevance in moral deliberation and argumentation. No reason is a "good" reason just because it proves effective in sustaining attitudes prescribed by the moral judgment it-self. There are, in short, governing normative conventions in ethics which control our vagrant attitudes and correct the associations that psychologically determine them. These conventions are embodied in the notions of "normality," "reason-ableness," "disinterestedness," "sensible person," and the like. It is with the special characteristics and functions of these conventions that this brief essay is concerned.

It is not profitable, I think, to debate the question whether these expressions have any "cognitive" meaning. It would be absurd to say that I do not "understand" anything by them. But *what* it is that I understand is somewhat vague. As we shall see, this does not in the least impair the useful-ness of such expressions.

[1] I owe the term "global" here to Philip Blair Rice. See his *On the Knowledge of Good and Evil* (New York: Random House, 1955), which is discussed at some length in essay XII of this volume, pp. 240-62.

As in so many other places in moral philosophy, the initial insights are Hume's. Now most of Hume's critics have classified him as a characteristic representative of the sentimental school, according to which natural benevolence is the source of all moral approval and sympathy is the psychological mechanism whereby benevolence is "irrigated." What they have usually failed to observe is that an analysis of moral judgments which reduces them to expressions of sympathetic benevolence cannot account for the characteristic "corrective" role which Hume assigned to "morals." According to him, we have no instinctual love of mankind as such. Our natural sympathies are strongest in relation to those who most closely resemble ourselves, weakest toward those who appear most dissimilar. It is evident also, Hume contends, that our sentiments vary in accordance with the distance of their objects in relation to ourselves. Hence our ordinary benevolent impulses and our individual acts of praise and blame tend to be fluctuating and parochial. This, however, does not greatly affect our moral judgments of human motives and actions.

In judging the *moral* character of any person or act, we ignore our variable personal feelings and take a "more general view." Yet we do this, *not because of any particular decision on our part,* but rather because of our habitual use of certain impersonal social conventions which dispose us to discount our variable temporary attitudes and "still apply the terms expressive of our liking or dislike in the same manner as if we remained in one point of view. Experience soon teaches us this method of correcting our sentiments, or at least of correcting our language, where the sentiments are more stubborn and unalterable." [2] "Such corrections," he adds by way of comparison and elucidation, "are common with regard to all the senses; and, indeed, it were impossible we could ever make use of language or communicate our sentiments to one another, did we not correct the momentary appearances of things and overlook our

---

[2] *Hume's Moral and Political Philosophy,* edited by H. D. Aiken (New York, Hafner, 1948), pp. 137-8.

present situation." [3] It is also worth remarking in this connection that Hume also speaks analogously of the corrective role of aesthetic judgments which serve to offset our variable individual responses to works of art. In the essay "On the Standard of Taste" he points out how, despite the inescapable truth of the dictum that there is no disputing about tastes, it is also from a common-sense viewpoint absurd to deny that there is an order of merit among works of art which is somehow public and independent of the variations of our tastes. By this latter "species of common sense," he says suggestively, the former is "modified" and "restrained."

These suggestions are immensely fruitful. At this point, however, Hume leaves us to our own devices. Let us compare, then, for what it may be worth, the concept of "objective red" and analogous conceptions in ethics. In both cases, first of all, a distinction is made between appearance and reality. In both cases a means is provided for offsetting fluctuations due to the "accidental" factors affecting our changing views of things. In both cases we are enabled by the distinctions to make communications in which the subject under discussion is responded to in similar ways by both parties. But there are also important differences. The function of the judgment "x is really or objectively red" is to describe the appearance of x under certain standard conditions and to correct hasty beliefs based upon appearances which may be abnormal. The result of such a judgment, for the addressee, is information. He is thereby enabled to predict how the object will appear to him if he looks at it in a certain way. However, the function of the moral judgment is not primarily informative and predictive. What it aims to correct is not our beliefs about matters of fact but our attitudes towards actions, motives, and persons. It "restrains" our feelings, not our perceptions—or, better, it determines us, in those deliberations upon which our "general decisions" are based, to consider the object imaginatively without regard to our more personal interest. When we ask whether something is really or ob-

[3] Ibid.

jectively right, we are, in effect, enjoined to perform one of the "imaginative experiments" so frequently employed in books on moral philosophy. More than this, a type of attitude is appealed to which regards the objects reflected upon from a certain point of view, which we call "disinterested" or "social." We are induced, so to speak, to impersonate the role of a person imbued with only the fundamental social presses of the community. The effect of ethical discourse is thus to standardize and coordinate our deliberations and general decisions, just as the effect of statements about objective predicates is to standardize and coordinate our beliefs about matters of fact.

In ethics, several normative conventions prevail which, although they do not precisely correspond to any actual individual sentiment, nevertheless serve to induce certain relatively uniform attitudes in most persons to whom they are addressed. They serve to "correct" our sentiments, and yet "they" are also dimensions of our natures; otherwise their normative appeal would be nil. It is, after all, only because we are social animals that they retain any normative hold upon us.

There is another difference between "really red" and "really right." Both, as we have seen, involve notions of "objectivity," "competence," or "reasonableness." But in the latter case, the conditions of normality cannot be precisely stated. Perhaps the difference is one of degree; if so, the degree of vagueness in the latter concept is far greater. But if we bear in mind the different roles of the respective concepts, we shall see that the vagueness of "competence" in ethical criticism is proper to it. The point is that the functions of ethical criticism are (*a*) to dispose us to reflect deliberately and dispassionately, not to predict precisely what will occur, and (*b*) to produce agreement in our general decisions and in our procedures for resolving lower-order disagreements that inevitably arise in applications and criticisms of the prevailing moral code. For such purposes the operative concepts need to be flexible and vague. Too much rigidity in meaning would render them practically useless. The "realities" with which

ethical criticism is mainly concerned are "sober second
thoughts" and "calm passions," the settled convictions which
determine our long-range behavior as moral agents. It has
no particular objective or goal in view, merely a way of
settling differences that arise from our particular passions
and preoccupations.

In speaking of "global conventions" in ethics I do not mean
"decisions" as this term is ordinarily used by philosophers. I
may decide to go to the grocery store; I may decide to let
the word "value," in a particular essay, mean "object of desire." But just as the ordinary meanings of words are not established by decisions or stipulations, but rather by unconscious processes of association and imitation, so the conventional principles that govern and correct our moral reflections
and deliberations are learned ideo-motor dispositions, not
particular "acts of will." This is part of what is meant in saying that ethical norms are "social": they are acquired by
processes of social conditioning and imitation of which we
are largely unaware.

It may be worth while, at this point, to compare the role
of global ethical conventions with what recent writers have
misleadingly called "myths" in the sphere of political ideology. Both expressions may confuse the unwary. Just as the
former term may mislead the unwary into supposing that
ethical norms are personal decisions, so the latter term may
suggest to some that a political myth is a deliberately per-
petrated lie by means of which the rulers control the ruled.
But as Professors Harold D. Lasswell and Abraham Kaplan
observe in connection with their own discerning analysis of
political myths, the expression need not be interpreted as
necessarily imputing a fictional, false, or irrational character
to ideological symbols.[4] As they put it, "myth" refers to an
aspect of "their functioning" not "their properties." [5] A political myth does not describe any existing or historical state
of affairs. Nor does it prescribe any particular political act or

----

[4] H. D. Lasswell and Abraham Kaplan, *Power and Society* (New
Haven: Yale University Press, 1950), pp. 116 ff.
[5] Ibid., p. 117.

obligation. Rather, its role is to set in motion and to direct certain general attitudes toward existing political institutions.

But whereas myths function, as Lasswell and Kaplan point out, in preserving or supplanting the existing political order, ethical conventions, as here conceived, have a dual role. Since they permit the "objective" criticism of existing moral rules, they do not serve to preserve the existing moral order altogether. But since they themselves involve impersonal standards of propriety or reasonableness, they are not calculated to produce a complete or revolutionary transformation of lower-order moral attitudes already in operation. In short, they neither wholly supplant the existing moral code nor wholly sustain it. Rather do they enable its equitable correction or modification within a broader framework of general norms which itself changes slowly by processes of accretion and reinterpretation.

I suggest, then, by way of conclusion, that the role of such notions as "reasonable" in ethics is to dispose us (*a*) to take a "second look," to consider a wider variety of alternatives and a longer range of consequences than we have hitherto considered, and (*b*) to judge without regard to our present or merely personal feelings. The injunction "Be reasonable" or "Be objective," in ethics, does not tell us what to look for or what to approve. It does not prescribe any particular attitude of favor or disfavor. Instead, it induces a disinterested point of view or press which invites imaginative experiments and the impersonation of the role of the "social man." For no two persons will the point of view have precisely the "same" meaning. For no person will its meaning be exact. But again, this is not a serious handicap, given the function which such concepts perform.

[VIII]

The Concept
of Moral Objectivity

INTRODUCTION

What are ordinary persons, including philosophers in their ordinary moments, doing when they raise doubts about the objectivity of particular moral judgments? And how, as moral agents and critics, do they go about resolving such doubts? These questions, one would think, must have occurred to anyone who in an idle moment bethought himself about the nature of moral objectivity. Yet they seem rarely, if ever, to be considered by the ethical objectivists and their critics, in spite of the interminable debate between them—or more likely, because of it. In the case of the subjectivists this is hardly surprising, since it would be fatal to their cause to admit that such questions may be seriously raised at all. But the objectivists make no use of this advantage; in fact, they manage merely to create the impression that the notion of moral objectivity is question-begging. The reason for this is evident: no objectivist has examined the use of the concept of objectivity in moral contexts without preconceptions about its generic meaning derived from a continuing philosophical tradition for which formal logic and natural science have provided not only exemplary, but paradigm cases of objective discourse. Suppose that we challenge these presuppositions. Why, for example, should it be assumed in advance of analysis that moral judgments cannot be objective unless such words as "right" and "good" are terms of "objective reference," or unless such judgments are true or false statements about something called "objective reality"? For that matter, why should we not take that reality to be whatever, in context, answers to our objective questions? Why should we assume that proper application of the concept of objectivity in all contexts involves the notion of a consensus of "competent," "rational," or "ideal" observers? And, if we do not, why must we assume that meaningful application of the concept involves definitive disciplinary procedures or rules to which anyone who sets up for a moralist is logically bound to submit?

When I first came within range of the ideas underlying the preceding remarks, they at once appeared to me to open a path through a swamp of controversy to a firm and neutral ground where I could proceed without ado to a constructive analysis of the concept of moral objectivity. The questions raised at the beginning of this essay seemed completely irenic; they were calculated, so I thought, not to increase pre-existing philosophical doubts about the possibility of objective moral judgments, but rather to allay them. For if these questions can be asked at all, then such doubts, as well as the controversies to which they give rise, must surely be both gratuitous and perverse. The implication, plainly, is that instead of endlessly arguing whether, in principle, objective moral judgments are possible, philosophers would do better to ask themselves how a serious problem about the objectivity of morals could even arise. But there, precisely, is the rub. Whether or not my questions are neutral, they at any rate are not pointless. Why not? Let us consider an analogy. Why is it that since Plato there has been no philosophical interest or stake in the concept of mud? To be sure, lexicographers have asked (and to their satisfaction, have quickly found answers to) the question "What is the meaning of 'mud'?" But among philosophers, only Plato has ever thought of asking that question, and he himself did so merely in order to illustrate a point, without staying for an answer. The philosophical interest in the concept of moral

objectivity is of another sort. In this essay I am not trying
to illustrate a point at all, but rather to resolve genuine
philosophical doubts, not only about the meaning, but also
about the meaningfulness of the concept of moral objectivity. The fact is that philosophers, unlike lexicographers, never
inquire into the meaning of any concept in a purely speculative frame of mind. For them there are always two questions to be asked: (*a*) "What is the meaning of '*x*'?" and
(*b*) "Why ask such a question?" This means that within a
philosophical context, no question about the meaning of a
word, or the use of an expression, is ever purely irenic,
and no answer to it is significant until it is shown how it
bears upon the perplexities, at once intellectual and practical,
that dispose us to ask it. Indeed, it is only its power to resolve such perplexities that convinces us that the answer
itself is substantially correct. The trouble is that the perplexities themselves prevent us from seeing where the answer lies.

These remarks apply directly to the case at hand. There
would be no philosophical reason to undertake an analysis
of the concept of moral objectivity were it not for the widespread, morally destructive doubts about the meaningfulness
of such a concept. Such doubts may once have been gratuitous; they are no longer. On the contrary, philosophical
preconceptions about the nature and conditions of any objective discourse have, in one form or another, so conditioned our thinking that laymen, as well as philosophers,
take it for granted that rejection of ethical objectivism automatically commits us to the thesis that, despite appearances,
moral objectivity is an illusion and hence that the ordinary
language of morals is systematically misleading. Thus, those
who accept the responsibilities of objective judgment in
morals have been impelled to reinstate their own principles
as laws of nature or as definitive principles of morals which
cannot be challenged without declaring either one's immorality or one's incompetence as a moral being. On the other
hand, those who regard all such positions as morally untenable, on the ground that they profoundly jeopardize the

principle of moral autonomy or freedom, seem thereby committed to some form of moral subjectivism which precludes one, on principle, from asking whether one's judgments and principles are objective. Meanwhile, our ordinary moral practices are hobbled for want of a clear and morally suitable conception of their critique, and the whole institution of morality gradually acquires the appearance of a system of arbitrary dicta which have not yet attained the status of positive laws. The moralist is demoted to the rank of a busybody who has fortunately not yet discovered his vocation for politics, and the immoralist assumes the status of a cultural hero whose bad conscience is treated as a badge of courage. The rest of us—which, I suspect, includes practically everyone for whom neither immorality nor morality is a vocation—find ourselves, when we reflect, involved in a practical dilemma which forces us to vacillate perpetually between the bad conscience of objectivism and the equally bad conscience of subjectivism. Our unhappy situation is this: we wish to honor, indeed, we cannot escape, the obligation to be objective in our moral decisions, yet we seem unable to do so without at the same time committing ourselves to a conception of morality which, if taken seriously, destroys our autonomy as moral agents and critics. On the other hand, we find ourselves committed to a principle of moral freedom which apparently dooms us to acquiesce in a radical ethical subjectivism that renders meaningless the very effort to search for objective moral judgments. This predicament, let me emphasize, is not merely theoretical— it is practical; or better, the problems with which it confronts us are not speculative problems about moral discourse, but theoretical problems that arise within it whenever we are obliged by moral necessity to go to the fundamental principles underlying our moral practices. Until they are solved—or resolved—judicious men who wish to view moral reflection as a part of the life of reason must continue to have grave, even paralyzing, doubts about the mutual consistency of the basic critical practices from which our familiar notions of the moral life are ultimately derived. Thus, although I still take seriously the questions posed at the beginning of this essay and hope presently to find answers to them, it would be philosophically pointless to proceed to a constructive analysis of the concept of moral objectivity without regard to the philosophical perplexities which provide the only reason for understanding it. This delay, however, is not without its reward. As I have found, it is precisely by facing these perplexities that we come gradually in sight of a conception of moral objectivity to which, without illusion, practicing moralists as well as moral philosophers can give credence.

My first task, then, will be to spell out the ethical antinomy which gives rise to the question of how objective moral judgments are possible. My second task will be to find a way out of this antinomy which, without compromising what seems essential to the principle of moral autonomy, nevertheless preserves intact the basic minimal claims embodied in the principle of moral objectivity. Such a solution, of course, is possible only at a price. In this case, fortunately, the price is not exorbitant; indeed, it can be readily paid without in the least compromising what remains of our common moral sense. The conclusion I am forced to is that, at least so far as ethics is concerned, traditional philosophical notions concerning the meanings of the terms "objective" and "subjective" must be abandoned once for all, and that neither empirical science nor formal logic can any longer serve philosophers as the models of objective discourse. I shall argue that it is precisely the uncritical application of such notions and the noetic models from which they derived, beyond the domains of science and logic, that is ultimately responsible for the widespread moral skepticism with which at present most of us are afflicted.

I shall attempt, in particular, to show how groundless is the suppostion that there can be objective moral principles only if there is some universal standard or principle of moral right and wrong which is acknowledged as binding by all men of good will. Commitment to the ideal of moral objectivity does not entail the skeptical conclusion that no principle can be regarded as morally valid unless it can be viewed as binding upon every "competent" moral agent; nor does it commit us to the impossible thesis that the fundamental responsibilities and rights of all moral persons must be substantially the same. Quite the contrary. There is no such thing as a competent or incompetent moral agent; indeed, the supposition that there is, is itself a sign of moral immaturity. The ideal of moral objectivity must be adjusted to the possibility of an essential diversity of moral codes and not merely to an accidental diversity of moral opinions. There can be no such thing as "the moral point of view," and if any supposed rule, whether linguistic, legal, or theological, were to serve as a moral principle, it is only we as individual moral agents who could make it do so. If the maxims or precepts that now serve many of us as moral principles should ever come to be understood as definitive principles of morals, then the whole notion of moral agency as it is now understood would simply disappear. But it is only when the implications of this fact have been fully appreciated that we can adjust ourselves to the ordinary notion of moral objectivity whose meaning it is my eventual purpose to explain.

THE ANTIMONY OF MORAL OBJECTIVITY AND FREEDOM

The Presumptive Principles of Moral Objectivity. In principle, it is always proper to inquire of any moral judgment whether it can be objectively sustained. It is proper, also, to ask of most moral principles whether they are objectively valid. But no such judgment or principle can be regarded as objectively valid unless there are certain definitive principles of morals which are binding upon the judgment and conduct of every moral agent. It does not suffice, as Kant at times seems to imply, that every moral agent must be ready to treat the maxim of his judgment as the principle of a universal legislation, for this plainly leaves open the possibility that conscientious men could consistently differ on all matters of moral principle. Objective moral principles are possible only if there is at least one universal principle of morals to which every moral judge and agent is beholden in justifying particular moral judgments and lower-order principles. Since one of its essential functions is to guide our conduct in our interpersonal dealings with one another, morality cannot be regarded as a positive science; so much may be conceded with impunity to those so-called "non-cognitivists" who mistakenly deny that moral judgments are true or false statements. However, this does not imply that in ethics anything goes, or that there is no such thing as a *discipline* of morals, by appeal to whose rules it can in principle always be decided whether any moral judgment is true or false. Like positive science, morality must be understood as a universal discipline to which every moralist must submit. And it is for this reason that we may speak, in ethics as in science, of "qualified observers."

For the sake of clarity, it is well to point out certain consequences of these principles which moral objectivists usually fail to acknowledge. Morality, as we have seen, must be regarded as a discipline. However, every featherless biped must decide for himself whether he should submit to such a discipline. In this respect, morality may be likened to a game. That is to say, any man must act in accordance with the rules of the moral "game" if he is to "do" morals at all. But there can be no moral rule which makes it necessary for every human being to play the game of morals, or if there were, then it would be up to every individual to decide for himself whether he wishes to be regarded as a "human being." Most of us are forced by the circumstances of social life to submit to the discipline of morals, or at least to give the appearance of doing so. But other ways of handling one's personal relations are clearly conceivable. And if an individual is willing to risk being unpopular with the moralists, he is free not to play, or, having played for a term, to play no longer.

There are other consequences of the principles of moral objectivity which many will find more agreeable. For one thing, if there are certain universal and necessary principles of morals, then in principle every contingent moral disagreement can be rationally resolved. Accordingly, every such disagreement may be properly understood as merely a disagreement in opinion rather than a disagreement in principle. Owing to the intrusion of such subjective factors as self-interest, stupidity, and ignorance, such disagreements may be in practice extremely difficult to settle. Nevertheless, we must assume that there is at least a tendency toward agreement on the part of conscientious moralists as the facts come more fully into view and as they become more fully aware of the nature of their commitments as moral beings. In short, underlying every substantive moral disensus there is a basic consensus which ensures the possibility of a rational resolution of any moral disagreement that may arise.

It should be added that when moralists pass beyond a certain point in their disagreements, the issue between them becomes a concealed verbal dispute over the meaning of the concept of morals itself. This fact helps to explain why, in certain instances, the controversialists tend to go round and round without being able to compose their differences. When such situations arise an objective solution may still be reached, but only by appealing to the rules governing the common use and application of the concept of morals itself. Should doubts persist past this point, then the reply must be that they involve a skepticism about the language of conduct generally which can hardly be sustained apart from a skepticism about the rules of ordinary language as a whole. But in that case, the issue has already passed outside the domain of moral philosophy into a sphere where the very notion of an objective disagreement is largely meaningless.

The Presumptive Principles of Moral Autonomy or Freedom. According to the preceding conception of morals, the principles of morals, like the rules of a game, are only hypothetically binding upon the individual person: if anyone elects to do morals, then, as a moralist, he must conform to its disciplinary principles. In such a view, accordingly, the individual acquits himself morally so long as his actions accord with such principles, regardless of his personal reasons for conforming to them. In other words, as a moral being anyone is ultimately responsible only to the principles of morals, not to his own conscience. To be sure, a man may be excused from responsibility for wrong actions if he conscientiously performs them in the belief that they are right; but such an excuse makes sense only if (*a*) the moral agent has (mistakenly) judged that his action is, on the evidence, the objectively right thing to do and (*b*) there is in the situation an objectively right thing to be done which others may know as well as, or better than, he.

This view of morals is incompatible with the principles of moral autonomy or freedom. According to these principles it is not enough that the moral agent should be capable of making mistakes, nor is it enough that he should be free to violate the moral law. As a moral being he must, also, in principle, decide absolutely for himself what that law really is. As we sometimes loosely and misleadingly say, every genuine moral agent must be regarded as a "law unto himself." That is to say, no man is morally responsible for actions unless they are performed for the sake of principles which he cannot in conscience disavow. Here we do not just excuse a man who acts on principles which, as we may think, are objectively wrong. On the contrary, if he sticks to his principles "though the heavens fall," he is entitled to our respect and perhaps even to our admiration. It is for this reason that morally sensitive men not only forgive those who conscientiously oppose them on the ground that the latter "know not what they do"; when the issue between them is a matter of principle, they generously, if also tragically, honor them for exhibiting a moral integrity as great as any to which they themselves may aspire. A more sensitive Antigone would understand that she cannot totally condemn Creon without at the same time condemning herself.

The fundamental point is that morality cannot properly be regarded either as a form of law, as a book of rules, or as a set of socially authoritative commands. It does not suffice, as the objectivists maintain, that a man may be excused or forgiven if he happens unintentionally to do what is objectively wrong. For who is entitled to excuse him and who is in a position to grant him forgiveness? In morals there is and can be nothing to do save to follow the principles to which, upon reflection, one finds oneself committed. Such principles present themselves in conscience as categorical imperatives, not as laws, rules, or commands which are binding upon us *if* we are pleased to do the moral thing. But just because of this it makes no sense, in the moral sphere, to speak of a discipline of morals or of *the* principles of morals; here, indeed, we can speak only of "my principles," "our principles," "his principles," or "their principles." And the ordinary language of morals must and does accommodate itself to this fact.

In the domain of science and logic, where we can speak with a straight face about disciplinary principles or rules, situations often arise in which we properly defer to the authority of observers whom we recognize to be more competent or qualified than ourselves. And it is because of this that, without qualms, we accept certain statements as objectively true even though we ourselves do not fully see why they are so. But in morals such situations can hardly arise. For just as no one can live by another's principles, so no one can be expected to conform his judgment and his will to certain allegedly objective principles which he has not in conscience made absolutely his own. Nor is this situation altered by the fact that some men take their principles from some "authority." For that authority can make no moral claims upon anyone who does not adopt it as *his* authority. In short, while a man may adopt as his moral principle, "Always act in such a way as would meet with the approval of (say) the church," that principle is no less a personal precept than the principle of utility or the principle of veracity.

The principle of moral autonomy can now be restated in the following way: Every moral principle must be regarded as nothing more than a first-personal precept. To be sure, such precepts may be either singular or plural. But no matter how extensive may be the community which commits itself to a particular moral practice or principle, it is morally binding only upon the members of that community. The principle of moral autonomy is thus incompatible with the very notion of a universal discipline of morals to which the conscience of every moral person is objectively beholden. Hence, so far at least as the concept of objectivity depends in principle upon the idea of an underlying consensus of "competent" or "qualified" moral judges, it has no application within ethics. To that extent there can be no such thing as a principle of moral objectivity. Moral discipline is merely a personal regimen, or way of life, whose character is definable only in terms of those precepts to which the individual moral agent holds himself responsible.

By the same token there can be no paradigm cases of a moral principle which every person who understands the language of morals is bound to accept. For if there were such a principle, then every moral agent would automatically have to regard it as binding upon his own judgment and conduct. But the principle of moral autonomy itself precludes such a possibility, even in the case of the principle of compassion itself. In rejecting the principle of compassion, Nietzsche, for example, did not thereby declare himself to be going beyond moral good and evil but only to be "transvaluing" the principles of what he considered to be a "slave morality." Those who really go beyond moral good and evil do so for one reason only: because for them the whole idea of moral obligation—like the idea of God for some others—is simply "dead."

It follows from the principle of moral autonomy that meaningful disagreement is possible only among the members of a particular moral community. So-called "cross cultural" moral criticism can only be regarded as a kind of propaganda, the main function of which is to reassure those "at home" of their moral rectitude. At this level the distinction between "justifying" and "exciting" reasons has no application. And those who talk, philosophically or theologically, of an objective moral law, natural or otherwise, delude no one but themselves.

In the light of these remarks we begin to see the use to which the autonomist is likely to put Moore's "open question" argument. In conscience we are morally free to question any alleged principle of morals. In order to assert our autonomy as moral beings we may even be obliged, in certain circumstances, to defy it. This, so far as I can see, is the principal point concealed in Nietzsche's "transvaluation of values." Its significance lies not so much in the fact that it rejects the principle of compassion, but that it asserts the right of autonomous moral agents to reject any principle when it is presented authoritatively as the principle of morals. In short, from the standpoint of the principle of moral autonomy, ethical naturalism in any form and on any level is *morally* subversive.

TOWARD A RESOLUTION
OF THE FOREGOING ANTINOMY

Let us now examine, somewhat dialectically, certain internal weaknesses in each of the preceding views. For convenience I shall henceforth refer to them as "objectivism" and "autonomism." As we proceed we will also consider reformulations of them designed to remove such weaknesses. In so doing it is my aim to show how we are driven at last to a conception of moral objectivity radically different from that to which objectivism itself appears to commit us. This conception, as I believe, is entirely compatible with at least one form of the doctrine of moral autonomy. But first we must overhaul that doctrine itself.

Now a thoughtful objectivist may point out that autonomism, as it stands, is internally inconsistent and that in removing this inconsistency the autonomist must acknowledge the basic minimal claim of objectivism itself. But when this claim is admitted the case for autonomism is radically weakened, since there are other principles whose claim to be regarded as definitive of morality is prior to that of moral autonomy. This may be seen in the following way: The autonomist asserts that there can be no definitive principles of morals, since, if there were, no moral agent could be regarded, as he must be, as a law unto himself. But if ever moral agent must be regarded as a law unto himself, then the principles of moral autonomy must be themselves viewed as disciplinary principles of morals. In that case the autonomist must admit on principle that there is at least one principle by appeal to which particular moral judgments and principles may be objectively verified (or falsified).

The autonomist may reply to this simply by taking the bull by the horns. He may agree that his position, as previously stated, is inconsistent, and what he should have claimed is that since the principles of moral autonomy are definitive principles of morals there can, by the nature of the case, be no other such principles. The principles of moral autonomy are, so to say, principles to end all ideas of morality which dispose us to treat our moral precepts as objective laws or rules of conduct. These principles are not only a guarantee against moral presumption, but an absolute charter of moral freedom. Such a view—let us call it "essentialistic autonomism"—obviously commits its proponent to a definitive closing of the open question so far as the concept of *morals* is concerned. But this (so it may be said) is no cause for alarm since what it closes is only the question concerning the nature of *moral* judgment or of *moral* right and wrong. As such it does not in the least run afoul of Moore's naturalistic fallacy argument which holds—so far as it does hold—only against descriptive definitions of such words as "good," "right," and "ought."

It may be questioned, however, even with respect to the concept of morals, whether the open question can be closed without violence, or if it can be, whether the autonomist himself is in a position to close it. For the sake of argument let us assume that in principle it can be closed. But definitive principles of morals should be able to meet the test of counter-instances. This, it may be argued, the principles of moral autonomy cannot do. It is very easy to imagine a seri-

ous person who would disallow any alleged obligation as a
moral obligation if its fulfillment involved the performance of
an unjust act, regardless of the fact that it was performed
in accordance with precepts conscientiously avowed by the
agent himself. Of course, a sufficiently resolute autonomist
might deny that such an example provides a true counter-
instance. His only mistake, in that case, would be to suppose
that he thereby secures his own position. For in thus privileg-
ing the principles of moral autonomy he thereby automatically converts them into a statement of the conditions under
which alone he himself is prepared to judge an act as morally
obligatory. In one sense, such a statement may be regarded as
a definition. But what it defines is merely a particular style
of moral judgment. It leaves the concept of morals itself untouched.

Suppose, now, that the autonomist sees that his doctrine
cannot plausibly be defended in its essentialistic form. That
is to say he at last realizes that the principles of moral autonomy can be regarded as formal principles only in the sense
that they define what he himself accepts as a standard of
"good form" in matters of moral judgment. He also sensibly
acknowledges that the only reason he can disallow his critic's
supposed counter-instance is that it really functions in effect
only as an *exemplary* counter-principle. In a word, the autonomist now frankly regards the principles of moral autonomy themselves as first-personal precepts which serve to define only his own moral point of view. What they prescribe,
so far as he is concerned, is that the conscientious judgment
of every moral agent *ought* (not must) absolutely to be respected and that no action performed for the sake of the
principles embodied in such judgments is morally censur-
able.

Such a position—let us call it "preceptive autonomism"—
is perhaps not inconceivable, however hard it may be in
practice consistently to maintain it. There are, however, a
great many *prima facie* duties which ordinary men, including most autonomists, do not question in their dealings
with their fellows. The principles of moral autonomy re-

quire the autonomist to respect such duties in others; within
the limits of such respect they permit him to acknowledge
such duties for himself. But they provide no standard for
judging which duties are to take precedence when they conflict with one another. And they provide but one principle
for making the legitimate exceptions which, in practice, virtually every moral principle is subject to. In practice, I suppose, most men would hold that a promise may properly be
broken if keeping it involved a great deal of suffering to
innocent people. But the principle of moral autonomy itself
entitles us to break a promise only when the keeping of it
infringes the moral freedom of others. Many men would
probably agree also that it is proper to tell a lie in order to
give comfort to a person at the end of his tether. But the
principle of moral autonomy provides no basis whatever for
making such proper exceptions to the principle of veracity.
In short, while the principles of moral autonomy provide a
final restraint in judging the conduct of others, and a minimal basis for making exceptions in the case of our own *prima
facie* duties, they otherwise leave individual conscience completely without guidance.

It is precisely at this point that the objectivist has another
inning. For the autonomist, like anyone else, has the problem of deciding what he really ought to do when a conflict
of duties occurs within the limits set by the principles of
moral autonomy. How is such a conflict to be resolved? It is
entirely possible, moreover, that a particular duty, such as
compassion, may oblige him to press beyond those limits.
What then? Since the principle of moral autonomy is itself
merely a precept, on what basis is the autonomist to decide
to adhere to the principle of autonomy rather than to
follow the obligations of compassion? He may reply that he
needs no basis for deciding, since, for him, the question is
already settled. But then he must admit that his decision is
completely arbitrary and that, in good conscience, it might
just as well have gone the other way. Next week he may find
that it does go the other way; he will then have just as much
or just as little reason for the line he takes. But the situation

is even worse than this. Suppose that the autonomist sticks to his principles absolutely and without exception. For him there is no moral conflict between the principles of moral autonomy and other principles since the latter simply give way whenever the limits imposed by the former have been reached. But what are those limits, and how are they to be found? It should be borne in mind, as Aristotle long ago reminded us, that ethical concepts have not the same exactitude as those employed in logic or science. Here *judgment* is required if they are sensibly to be applied. But what shall guide the autonomist's judgment when he has to decide whether a *prima facie* duty has trespassed upon the moral autonomy of other persons? Indeed, it may be argued that the very admission of the necessity of judgment in applying the principles of moral autonomy involves another principle more absolute than autonomy itself. But even if the autonomist refuses this gambit, the problem of boundaries remains a source, not just of theoretical perplexity, but of constant practical moral doubt. For the frontiers of moral autonomy are nowhere clearly marked, and the petitions of supposedly lower-order principles for satisfaction of their claims are bound to be an everyday occurrence. Beyond such commonplace harassments there also remain more general problems of application to which the principles of moral autonomy themselves provide no clue. For example, does the principle of autonomy entail respect for those individuals who profess no moral principles and whose lives are dedicated exclusively to their "work" or to their own pleasures? Does it entail respect for those whose only conscientious aim is to subvert the whole enterprise of morality? Do the principles of moral autonomy permit us to attempt the reeducation of those who are not themselves autonomists, or does the respect we owe to moral persons require that we accept every such person once and for all just as we find him? Above all, who shall count as a "moral person," and when does he attain his majority? These problems are not external problems pressed upon the autonomist from a different moral point of view. They are wholly internal to autonomism itself, and pending the answers that are to be made to them, autonomism remains, morally, a merely abstract entity. From the depths of the autonomist's own conscience there comes the demand for some way of knowing what autonomism really is, what it really commits him to.

In another domain this is precisely the predicament of Descartes, whose invocation of the principle of intellectual autonomy forced him at the same time to look within his own consciousness for a way to distinguish subjective appearances from objective reality. "But surely," the objectivist will reply, "this is just what cannot be done. Nothing will come of nothing, and if Descartes claims absolute freedom to think for himself, then whatever rules of method he finally adopts can be nothing but subjective precepts. The 'reality' which he claims to discover by their application remains a merely subjective reality." It is here that the objectivist may hope to make his stand. But let us now have a look at the internal problems in which his own position is involved.

In the first place, as the autonomist will quickly point out, the very difficulties which we observed in the case of essentialistic autonomism also beset every objectivist at every turn. For no matter what principles of morals the objectivist comes up with, he must submit his theory to the test of counter-instances. If, when a counter-instance is seriously proposed he refuses to accept it as a counter-instance, then he shows by that very fact that his principles are definitive, not of morality as such, but only of his own style of moral judgment. But if he accepts it, his theory is overturned. Is there any such theory that remains beyond the reach of counter-instances? Or, how are we finally to determine just what the principles of morals really are? The question is exigent since, unless actual principles of morals can be supplied, objectivism is merely a vacuous possibility. In a word, objectivism can be shown to be possible only by confronting us with the unassailable fact of definitive principles of morals to which no one who understands what is being said can seriously make objection. This is a tall order.

There are only two alternatives. One way is for the objectivist himself simply to take the bull by the horns and to tell us, without ado, what really are the principles of morals. But this venture will not do, unless every moralist, without exception, acknowledges that every action prescribed by the principles in question *must* be *morally* right. None of the traditional forms of objectivism has managed to meet so stringent a test. We have already observed the difficulties in which the objective autonomist finds himself. Counter-instances—if that is what they are—have been proposed to every known form of theological objectivism. The only theory known to me which seems to stand a chance of survival is that form of humanitarian ethics which claims that what we mean by a morally right act is one which by intention is compassionate, i.e., which seeks, so far as possible, to relieve suffering. The difficulties involved in such a view are notorious. For example, there are many conscientious moralists who would accept acts of compassion as morally right only if their performance does not violate the personal integrity of the individuals involved. At best, the compassionist may argue that no act is morally right which involves unnecessary or needless suffering. But, what is to count as "needless suffering," and who shall decide? There are also moral obligations which, as such, have nothing to do with questions of suffering at all: for example, the obligation to be fair in one's dealings with others, the obligation to tell the truth, or the obligation to keep promises sincerely made. Here the principle of compassion itself works primarily as a principle of exception which, by that very fact, presupposes that there are, in principle, forms of *moral* obligation which are non-compassionate.

It may be argued, however, that we have hitherto failed to distinguish sharply enough between material or substantive moral principles and formal or definitive principles of morals. But where is the razor's edge which divides them? The principle of compassion, let us agree, is a substantive principle like the principles of autonomy. But then, if we are objectively to resolve disagreements about the commitments which these principles enjoin, there must be certain *other* principles which really do define what is meant by a "morally right action," and which, because of this, state what every moral agent or judge must consider in trying to decide whether adherence to such substantive principles is morally right. What *are* these purely formal principles?

It is at this point that the other alternative open to the objectivist appears most appealing. He may now suggest that our difficulties have been due precisely to the failure of the older objectivists to be sufficiently abstract. Suppose, however, that the very concept of objectivity itself is viewed as a formal standard of moral right and wrong. In short, what if it were argued simply that all and only those acts are morally right which would be approved by anyone who views them objectively? What is wanted is a definitive statement of the characteristics of an objective observer.

MORAL OBJECTIVITY AND THE "IDEAL OBSERVER"

Now it turns out that this alternative has already been carefully explored by Professor Roderick Firth in his essay, "Ethical Absolutism and the Ideal Observer." [1] Accordingly, by examining it in some detail, we may, I think, take the final measure of objectivism in its most rigoristic form.

As Firth is aware, his analysis is not entirely without precedent. Read in one way, it may indeed be viewed as an attempt to clarify the doctrine of a disinterested or impartial spectator which, in one form or another, is to be found in the writings of Hutcheson, Hume, Adam Smith, and Kant. Firth takes these writers to be arguing, in effect, that an ethical judgment is in essence a statement about how an "ideal observer" would react to a certain state of affairs or, variously, how any observer would react to a certain state of affairs under "ideal" conditions. This is an exceedingly plausible reading of them. And although I now take a somewhat different view of Hume's "intentions," I myself so construed

[1] In *Philosophy and Phenomenological Research*, Vol. XIII, No. 3 (March 1952).

him in the introduction to my edition of Hume's moral and political philosophy.[2] In that work I described Hume's position, as it appears in the *Treatise*, in the following terms: "(*a*) . . . Moral judgments are not merely *expressions* of our approval or disapproval; they have descriptive meaning and are capable of truth and falsity; nevertheless, they are empirical and hence corrigible. (*b*) Moral distinctions have a certain objectivity and universality in the sense that they refer to what an impartial and benevolent spectator *would* approve, and not necessarily to what most of us in fact do approve. . . ."[3] What distinguishes Firth's analysis is the care with which he analyzes characteristics of omniscience, omnipercipience, disinterestedness, dispassionateness, and consistency which he takes to be the fundamental hallmarks of the ideal spectator whose reactions we allegedly have in mind in trying to decide what is morally right or wrong.

Whether this particular list of characteristics—which notably does not include Hume's "benevolence" or any term usually associated with a particular moral attitude—is really necessary and sufficient we may leave it to the absolute objectivists to debte among themselves. But on any such list the concept of distinterestedness would doubtless be prominently displayed. Moreover, Firth's analysis of it is typical of his treatment of most of the others. For these reasons we may treat his definition of disinterestedness as a test case for the success or failure of his theory as a whole. If it can be shown that any such definition, whose whole point must be to eliminate all reference to sentiments or principles antecedently acknowledged as *moral*, fails to meet the test of plausible counter-instances, then, by a kind of intuitive induction we may conclude that no supposedly formal principle of objectivity can serve as a definitive principle of moral right and wrong.

According to Firth's account, any observer is "disinter-

---

[2] *Hume's Moral and Political Philosophy*, edited by H. D. Aiken (New York: Hafner Publishing Company, 1948).

[3] Ibid., p. xxxvi.

ested" if, and only if, he is totally lacking in "particular interests," where the phrase "particular interests" is taken to
refer to any interest whose object cannot be defined without
the use of proper names and such egocentric particulars as
"I," "here," "now," and "this." [4] Now it is no part of my purpose to deny that such a definition might do for certain
senses of the term; the only question here is whether it
suffices for what we have in mind when we employ the term
in moral contexts. Imagine, then, an observer who is devoid
of "particular" interests, in Firth's sense, but so single-minded
in his devotion to the pursuit of knowledge that he always
reacts with pleasure to any proposal that would increase
it, regardless of its consequences. Among such consequences,
we may easily suppose, would be a certain amount of unavoidable mutilation of young children, at least some confes-
sions obtained by torture, and a few instances of scientific
eavesdropping on persons at religious confession. Or, again,
imagine a great artist, also devoid of particular interests, who
is so dedicated to the art of painting that he always ignores
even the most elementary claims of veracity, kindness, or
loyalty when they interfere with the demands of the art. Now
I suppose that from a certain standpoint such individuals
may be regarded as "disinterested," perhaps even admira-
bly so. But if so, it is a form of disinterestedness which, as
such, has nothing to do with morals; on the contrary, it involves forms of behavior which most of us would regard as
prime examples of moral obtuseness, if not flagrant immorality. More important, we would probably also agree
that such individuals displayed a singular lack of the sort of
disinterestedness required in moral situations.

But, for the sake of argument, let us assume that Firth's
definition of disinterestedness can, in principle, be amended
so as to rule out all such offending non-particular interests.
Accordingly, our formula will be that any person may be said
to be morally disinterested if, and only if (*a*) he is devoid
of particular interests (in the sense defined above), and (*b*)
he is devoid of any non-particular interests of type *G*. But

[4] Firth, op. cit., pp. 338-9.

how, pray, is this type to be defined? The suggestion which may occur to some moralists is that it should include all non-particular interests, professional, artistic, or institutional, which would dispose one to be indifferent to the suffering of other persons.[5] But aside from the difficulty that the concept of a person is itself by no means a neutral term in moral contexts, it seems evident that we are now attempting to write a particular moral principle into the very definition of moral disinterestedness. In that case, however, the concept of disinterestedness so far loses whatever virtue it may have had as a critical standard to which appeal could be made in trying to decide, among other things, whether that moral principle itself is objectively to be preferred to all others, or whether, in certain circumstances, it should be subject to exception.

The situation seems to be this: The concept of moral disinterestedness, and hence of moral objectivity, cannot be successfully defined wholly without reference to principles antecedently acknowledged as moral. But neither can it be defined in terms of any particular moral principle without at once losing its use as an independent standard of objective moral appraisal. Firth's analysis avoids the latter difficulty; its weakness is that it countenances forms of "interest" which many moralists would regard as obviously partial and which some would regard as immoral on the face of it, whether partial or otherwise. Nor does there seem to be any way of amending Firth's definition which would remove that weakness without at the same time destroying the very feature which originally appeared to commend it.

For the moment, however, let us waive the difficulty that from a moral point of view many non-particular interests seem, ethically, as partial as any particular ones. What we have now to consider is the more delicate problem whether, so far as morality as such is concerned, anyone saliently affected by particular interests of any sort is to that extent lacking in moral disinterestedness and objectivity. In brief, *must* we suppose that a principled concern for "one's own"

[5] Firth, I assume, would have no part of such a suggestion.

is always evidence of partiality and hence of a lack of objectivity? This does not appear to me at all obvious. Consider, for example, a highly conscientious mother who, upon careful reflection, always, and in good conscience, preferred the well-being of the members of her own family to that of any other group in which they happened to be included but which is definable in wholly non-particular terms. Here it is well to bear in mind that Firth's "particular interests" are by no means always self-interested, and that a person such as I have just described may be quite as selfless as any Saint Just who ever dedicated himself to the "universal" principles of liberty, equality, and fraternity. Is such a person, morally, any less disinterested than a Saint Just or, better, a Tom Paine who so appealingly avows that "Wherever there is injustice, there is my country?" On what grounds that are not, at the same time, morally question-begging? She is indifferent to "non-particular" claims that, from the standpoint of her principles, appear impossibly general and abstract; he is indifferent to "particular" claims that, from her point of view, are always overriding. To him she seems insufferably parochial; to her he seems virtually inhuman, a monstrous justice-machine dedicated unfeelingly to mere *names* of virtue. Which, morally, is the more disinterested? Without enlarging our own point of view there is, so far as I can see, no way whatever to decide. One seems as interested-disinterested as the other; the only difference between them is one of moral perspective. Once again, compare a man who is exclusively dedicated to the welfare of the members of his own country with another who is similarly dedicated to the happiness of white protestants, whatever their country. Is the former person, because of his particular interest, any less impartial than the other? Without regard to any other considerations already acknowledged to be morally relevant, I simply do not see how it could be denied that both parties are pretty much in the same boat. Within the range of his principle, each may be completely disinterested; with respect to his principle itself, one seems quite as partial as the other.

It may be replied, of course, that a person may prefer his own to any "outsiders" without being guilty of any partiality, but only on the condition that he is prepared to accept the possibility that everyone else does so as well. In that case his particular interest turns out, innocuously, to be merely an application to his own situation of a non-particular concern for a state of human affairs in which every individual gives the nod to his own when their interests happen to conflict with those of outsiders. This reply is unsatisfactory. It is not hard to imagine a person who would reply, upon reflection, that he simply does not know whether to prefer a world in which everyone gives the nod to his own, whoever they are, but he knows, at any rate, that he ought to prefer "his own" whenever their interests conflict with those of any outside group which he can seriously envisage. Is his "reaction" lacking in *moral* impartiality? But, again, on what non-question-begging grounds? He has not refused the demand to reconsider; he has entertained and then been obliged to suspend judgment concerning the universalistic covering principle in question. Despite this, his original commitment has not been shaken. Once more, I contend, there is no way of convicting him of partiality without introducing other moral principles which he himself has temporarily forgotten, but which, upon further consideration, he is prepared to acknowledge. Apart from them he is no less (and no more) disinterested than any Crito whose dedicated love of Socrates, as it turns out, is merely a disguised interest in the wisest of all men.[6]

From a *morally* disinterested point of view, the question is not whether an interest is particular or otherwise, but only whether, all things considered, it still appears right to realize it. And among the things that saliently require to be considered in such a case are precisely those *prima facie* duties to which one is already conditionally committed.[7]

---

[6] Firth, op. cit., p. 339.

[7] At this point it becomes desirable to remark upon the distinction between lack of objectivity and mere subjectivity. Objectivity is a form of achievement one can miss for a multitude of reasons; such reasons

Consider another problem which often presents itself to the practicing moralist. From his own point of view he may fail to be objective, not only because he is influenced by extra-moral interests, whether particular or general, but also because of an obsession with moral rights of a particular sort. Thus, for example, he may be overborne by a particular *prima facie* duty to which he blindly refuses to acknowledge exceptions he knows to be legitimate. Or he may give the nod to a principle whose place in his moral scheme of things is entirely subordinate, ignoring superordinate principles of justice or humanity upon which the whole virtue of the principle in question entirely depends. I am inclined to think that failures of moral disinterestedness occur most frequently, not because we are overborne by extra-moral considerations, but because we are temporarily blinded by particular moral sentiments, such as indignation, whose "rights" are extremely limited. The would-be objective moralist is thus always placed in double jeopardy; on the one side he is tempted by a host of non-moral inclinations, both "particular" and general, and on the other by particular[8] duties that, on second thought, have no such absolute claim to fulfillment as he permits himself for the moment to believe.

In this connection it may also be well to mention a type of

---

have nothing necessarily to do with subjective preoccupations. On the other hand, subjectivity itself may serve as a kind of principle which, in certain contexts, functions as a test of one's powers of objective judgment. In short, what causes a man to be non-objective in his decisions and judgments is not simply a preoccupation with matters pertaining essentially to himself, but, rather, those beliefs, attitudes, and interests, whatever their objectives, that deflect him from the ends or prevent him from conforming to the principles characteristic of the activity in question. No doubt there are forms of activity with respect to which any subjective concern is evidence of a lack of objectivity. But there are others with respect to which lack of objectivity may be owing to persistent intrusion of completely selfless general concerns that confuse or corrupt one's sense of what is relevant to the form of activity in question. Thus, for example, a Ricardian "economic man" loses objectivity, not when he becomes completely preoccupied with his own greatest material good, but when he allows sentimental "moral" considerations to deflect him from the rational pursuit of that good itself.

[8] Here the term "particular" is used in its ordinary, non-technical sense.

moral problem which is frequently misconceived by moral philosophers. Now it is true that in attempting to reach an objective decision most moralists believe they have some obligation to listen to the considered opinions of other judges. But this obligation, like any other, may itself become obsessive so that the moralist, ignoring other exigent demands which his conscience makes upon him, loses objectivity through the very attempt to achieve it. An individual may well believe that he is morally obliged to suspend judgment, for the time being at least, when he finds that there is a strong consensus of moral opinion against him. But that obligation is one among many. And if he is overwhelmed by it he may be as much incapacitated for objective judgment as when he responds too promptly to his sense of indignation. Contrary to the prevailing view in philosophy there is, in general, no necessary connection between objectivity of judgment and intersubjective agreement. Nor do we automatically establish the objectivity of a judgment merely by multiplying subjective opinions or attitudes. Intersubjective agreement, however extensive, remains nothing more than that; it becomes a test of objective validity only when, as in science, the very form of the activity demands it. There are many forms of activity in which such agreement is not required and where it exists does nothing to increase the likelihood of objective certainty. In such cases, too much concern for the opinions of others may well be the greatest handicap to objective judgment. This is obviously true in the case of literary and art criticism; it is true in the domain of religious belief; it is true also in the sphere of moral judgment where the demands of conscience may require one to stand completely alone.

What has been said above about the concept of moral disinterestedness applies, by analogy, to other "characteristics," such as dispassionateness, of an ideally objective observer. Therefore, I shall not pause to make detailed criticisms of Firth's treatment of them. It is time to make a more general point. Now the common notion of moral objectivity (of whose use I have already given some intimations) has no

tendency to breed a general "philosophical" skepticism about
the validity of moral judgments and principles. However,
Firth's absolute objectivism, when pressed, gradually forces
us back upon a principled moral agnosticism which, if taken
seriously, would result in the destruction of our ordinary
sense of right and wrong or, what comes to the same thing,
the complete paralysis of our moral will. "Judge not!" now
becomes not just an exemplary counsel of moral humility
but, in effect, the defining principle of morals itself. In a
word, if the traits of an "ideally" objective observer are taken
as providing *the* definitive principle of morals, then moral
right and wrong become vacuous conceptions, the use of
which answers to no conscientious human concern. This
point can be shown in a variety of ways. As we have already seen, Firth's analysis of disinterestedness fails to meet
the test of counter-instances. But the attempt to amend it
in a way which at the same time avoids reference to principles antecedently acknowledged as moral, leads us first
into a blind search for a way to eliminate offending non-
particular interests, next to the admission that particular interests are not necessarily less disinterested than any others,
until finally we begin to wonder whether all "interests"—
including even the obligation to respect the judgments of
other persons—must not be eliminated before we can secure
that pure and perfect disinterestedness which (by hypothesis) is involved in the very meaning of moral right and
wrong. Disinterestedness thus becomes a kind of "hidden
God" which, just to the extent that the concept of morals is
made to depend upon it, forces us to question more and
more grimly whether that concept has any intelligible meaning. In another way, the search for an ideal observer whose
attitudes and opinions are *merely* objective leads eventually to the conception of a being who has no favorable or
unfavorable reactions at all. We are reminded at this point
of Job, who, as he comes to realize that his notions of justice
provide no measure of God's justice, is forced to admit that
although he must be a sinner in God's eyes, he can never
know how or why. To this the reply must be that though

moral understanding is a pearl of great price it loses all value if we make the price so high that it cannot possibly be paid.

THE NATURE OF MORAL OBJECTIVITY

The merit of the ideal spectator theory is that it enables us to see just what absolute ethical objectivism comes to when we try to formulate definitive principles of moral judgment, or something called "*the* moral point of view," in total abstraction from any substantive principles and practices to which, in the ordinary course, moral agents find themselves committed. Is such a point of view consistent with the ideal of moral autonomy, to which, within limits, most moralists are committed? It is impossible to say. Who knows how an absolutely objective spectator, bereft of moral principles, would in practice react to any situation? In effect, the spectator theory would replace all of the little perplexities that beset us when we worry about the objectivity of particular moral judgments with one big perplexity about the nature and reactions of the ideal spectator himself. Unhappily, the more we contemplate this big perplexity the more we wonder whether the idea of morality itself may not be a conceptual monster, a mere idea of reason, to which no definite meaning can be assigned. These doubts can be removed, not by further logical analysis, but only by returning, conscientiously, to the world of work-a-day moral problems and judgments. In that world the problem of moral objectivity is mainly a problem of piecemeal mutual adjustment of acknowledged commitments within a loose framework of precepts and practices, none of which is ever permanently earmarked as an absolutely first principle and each of which is subject to a list of exceptions that can never be exhaustively stated. In practice, moral error is due not so much to our lack of omniscience about matters of fact as to philosophical misconceptions about the drift of the terms of our discourse and to our inveterate tendency to adhere inflexibly to particular principles in the face of other loyalties whose claims upon us are equally compelling. What is wanted is not a better understanding of the hypothetical reactions of a perfectly objective somebody-else, but that conscientious second thought which enables us to take a more general view of our own existing responsibilities. Such a general view provides no definition of moral right and wrong; it does not require us to ignore "our own" when we find that their claims upon us cannot conscientiously be universalized; it does not demand that we treat "everybody," whoever they may be, as moral persons; nor does it commit us to some supposed consensus of moral opinion which all other "competent" moral agents must be presumed to share. In brief, there is and can be no absolute or universal vantage point from which conscientious moralists, regardless of their sentiments, may make an objective appraisal of their particular moral decision and principles. Morally, we are always in the middle of things, confronted with eternally exceptionable precepts which, until such exceptions have been made, still lay presumptive claims upon us that we cannot in conscience disavow. What provides the basis for such exceptions? Nothing save other particular principles which, in turn, we are forever driven to qualify in the light of still other principles. And when we come temporarily to the end of a line of qualifications what then do we find? To our dismay, nothing but the very "first-level" duties with which we began.

The ordinary principle of moral objectivity thus prescribes, not that we look beyond the moral life itself for a ground of criticism, but only that we search within it for the soberest and steadiest judgment of which, in the light of all relevant obligations, we are capable. When a question arises concerning the objectivity of a particular moral judgment or principle, our task is always and only to look beyond it to the other relevant commitments which we ourselves acknowledge. And if this answer seems inadequate, then the reply must be that there is, in conscience, nothing else to go on. In the moral sphere it is always, finally, up to us; nor is there anyone to whose steadier shoulders our burden of moral judgment can be shifted. That is the agony of the moral life; it is also its peculiar glory.

The principle of objectivity in morals is, then, essentially a principle of reconsideration. What it demands, when a question about the objectivity of a particular judgment or principle arises, is that we consider whether such a judgment or principle, as it stands, can be consistently upheld in the face of whatever other moral considerations might be thought, in conscience, to defeat it. What do such considerations include? It is beyond the scope of this essay to attempt a codification, even if such were possible, of all of the sorts of consideration that might, in principle, serve to defeat or falsify a moral proposition. It must suffice here to indicate in very general terms a few of the main factors involved, and for the rest to remove certain prevailing misconceptions.

In many situations the objectivity of a particular moral judgment is sufficiently established simply by bringing it under an appropriate covering principle which, in effect, simply classifies the action in question as an act of a certain sort, the performance of which, other things equal, is a moral duty. As a rule we determine at once that feature of an action which enables us to classify it as an act of a certain sort, the performance or non-performance of which is at once required by a relevant covering principle. What creates a problem for us are other features of the situation not covered by the principle appealed to and which make of the action in question something more, or less, than merely an act of a certain sort. A certain line of action involves us, say, in the act of telling a lie, and the telling of lies, other things equal, is proscribed. But it may be that what is proposed, the action to be performed, is more than an act of lying; perhaps it may also be viewed as an act of kindness. In that case, it falls under another principle which, other things equal, provides the basis of a second obligation. In such a situation it is commonly supposed either that there is a clear order of precedence among such principles—that is, an obvious principle of hierarchy—or else that both principles are merely summary applications of some more fundamental principle, such as the principle of utility, by which both such "first-order" principles are justified and from which both are ultimately derived. It is also commonly supposed that such principles define certain distinct "practices," each of which can be criticized only as a whole in the light of some "second-order" principle, such as "justice" or "utility," which alone provides an objective standard of appraisal. Such facile descriptions of the ways out of our moral perplexities usually will not do.

In the first place, moral principles cannot be arranged in a flat hierarchical order. For example, we cannot say without qualification that the principle of kindness takes absolute precedence over the principle of veracity; we cannot say without qualification that promises may be broken when the consequences of keeping a promise are more unpleasant for the people involved than those of breaking it. It all depends upon how much unpleasantness is involved in keeping the promise or how much unkindness is involved in telling the truth; conversely, it also depends upon our considered views of the importance of telling the truth and of keeping promises. For most of us, these practices are important commitments in their own right which are not to be evaluated simply by reckoning the amount of discomfort (or unkindness) that keeping or breaking a promise, telling or not telling the truth, would involve. They are, in short, independent sources of moral excellence which require no justification on merely utilitarian grounds. Secondly, it is a mistake to suppose that what we call the practice of promising, for example, can be understood in complete abstraction from the principles of exception which, on occasion, justify the breaking of a promise. Part of what we understand by the practice of promising is the recognition that promises may, under certain conditions, be broken and that no promise is absolutely inviolate. Not only is every principle subject to exceptions, but the fact that such exceptions are allowable belongs to the very concept of a practice itself. In short, there is no such thing as the practice of promising, the practice of veracity, or the practice of justice independent of the principles of exception which qualify such practices. This means that the principles which form the parts of a moral code can be understood only in relation to a network of such principles, no one of which can be evaluated in isolation from the rest. Nor is there any unqualifiable "second-order" principle so absolute and so impervious to exceptions that it provides a unique and final basis for objective criticism of the rest. Objective criticism of moral principles is mainly a matter of piecemeal qualification of particular practices with a view to their greater coherence within a moral system. Thus the only test of objectivity, so far as principles and practices are concerned, is their ability to survive without further qualification by the other principles or practices with which they may conflict. When qualification is required, nothing provides an objective basis for decisions save the other practices with which, by mutual adjustment, any particular practice must be reconciled.

But there is a feature of the moral predicament still more basic than any hitherto mentioned. Most philosophers hold that what distinguishes moral from merely expedient action is the fact that moral actions are performed not only on the basis of, but also for the sake of, a principle. What is right in one case is morally right only if it is so in cases of a similar sort. Yet this approximate truth must accommodate itself to another, no less fundamental. No action is exhaustively definable simply as an act of a certain sort any more than an individual substance is exhaustively definable as a member of a certain species. It may exhibit morally significant aspects beyond any that have been covered by our prevailing system of moral acts. For this reason it is always possible to maintain that a *particular* line of action ought to be followed even though its performance goes against every principle in the book. In other terms, one may be more certain that a line of action ought to be carried out than of any principle that might be thought to justify or to condemn it. In that case, the action becomes, as it were, a principle unto itself and at the same time establishes the basis for the introduction of a new moral principle.

It is essential that I not be misunderstood in this. It is theoretically possible to say of a particular moral judgment that it is objectively defensible even though it cannot be justified by appeal to any hitherto existing principles of justification or exception. But there is a world of difference between a judgment which is sustained after a full and impartial review of the whole moral situation, including the principles that appear to be applicable to it, and one for which certainty is claimed in advance of inquiry. I am making no defense of moral dogmatism; on the contrary, I maintain that the principle of objectivity may require reconsideration of any judgment. But this applies no less to principles themselves. It is quite as dogmatic and unobjective to maintain a moral principle regardless of the judgments which, upon second thought, may disallow it as to insist upon a particular judgment without regard to the principles which might be thought to invalidate it.

In summary, there is and can be no definitive criterion of moral objectivity and, hence, no definitive principle of moral right and wrong. When a serious question about the objectivity of a particular moral judgment or principle arises, there is simply the further *moral* obligation to re-examine it in the light of the other obligations and duties that have a bearing upon it. If it should be replied that objective reconsideration requires, also, an endless search for new facts which, if known, might alter our notions of our obligations and duties themselves, the answer must be that such a search would defeat the very purpose of moral reflection, which is *judgment*. The principle of objectivity requires only that we take account of any hitherto unconsidered facts to which we may reasonably be expected to have access. But in that case, what is reasonable? There is no formula for answering such a question; our judgment can be formed only by weighing the obligation to look for relevant facts against other obligations. The principle of moral objectivity can neither supply the materials for moral judgment nor tell us where to go in search of them. If we have no time to search for further possibly relevant facts, the principle of objectivity will provide us with not one moment more; if we are otherwise lacking in moral sensibility, it will not make good our de-

ficiency by so much as a single obligation. What it can do—
and it can do no more—is to dispose us to review our decisions so that we may neglect no pertinent fact that is available to us in the time we have, and that we may neglect no
obligation which deserves to be considered. Primarily, therefore, it functions as a principle of falsification, and what consistently survives the general scrutiny which it demands may
pass as objectively valid or true.

A NOTE ON MORAL TRUTH

This last remark provides, in essence, our final answer to
objectivism. But so profound are prevailing misconceptions
that a further word about moral truth is required before
we bring this essay to a close. Now all contemporary moral
philosophers, regardless of school, take it for granted that
there is an intimate connection between the concepts of objectivity and truth. They may believe, as do the emotivists,
that neither concept has a moral application; or they may
hold, with the naturalists, that the conditions of moral objectivity and truth are no different from those of empirical
science. But they all agree that the connection between the
concepts is analytic. They all assume, moveover, that
truth, which they tend to restrict to statements verifiable by
the procedures of science or of formal logic, is logically the
more fundamental concept. On these points the following
statement of Professor Bernard Mayo is typical: "The deepest issue, and the most violent controversy, in contemporary
moral philosophy is between those who assert, and those
who deny, that moral judgments can be true or false. This
difference can indeed be taken as the simplest way of defining the meaning of the pair of correlative terms 'objective' and 'subjective.' What is objective is capable of being
true or false, of being a statement, a belief or opinion; what
is subjective is not capable of a truth-value, but is an expression of some psychological state." [9] Mayo's own view is

[9] Bernard Mayo, *Ethics and the Moral Life* (New York: St Martin's
Press, 1958), p. 69.

that moral assertions, although subject to "criteria of correctness" are not verifiable by procedures akin to those employed in science; he concludes, therefore, that they cannot be true or false and hence that they cannot be regarded as objective statements at all.[1] Professor Kurt Baier, who takes virtually the same position as Mayo toward the relations of truth to objectivity, comes to precisely the opposite conclusion. Accordingly, although he, like Mayo, holds that moral judgments are essentially guides to conduct, he pulls and hauls in order to show that by his definitions moral appraisals are also empirically verifiable and hence that they may be regarded as objective statements.[2] It seems not to occur to either writer that verifiability (or falsifiability) is not a concept for which empirical science alone has a use, and that in certain domains questions of truth are settled entirely by the conclusions of objective judgment itself.

Such at any rate, is the position of this essay: So far at least as morals are concerned, the concept of objectivity is logically more primitive than that of truth, and the verification of a moral proposition occurs when, and only when, we judge objectively that it survives rescrutiny. The plausibility of such an analysis is very great. We have already shown that moral objectivity does not depend upon the possibility that moral judgments are statements of fact, verifiable by procedures analogous to those employed in empirical science. We have shown, indeed, that moral objectivity does not even presuppose that there are definitive principles of morals of any sort. This, however, does not in the least imply that

[1] It should be observed here that Mayo's analysis is inconsistent on this point. Since he regards "objective" and "subjective" as correlative terms, it would seem to follow that he regards ethical assertions, even though subject to "criteria of correctness," as mere expressions of psychological states. However, he goes so far at one point as to say that "What we call objectivity in the former case [that is, of visual perception] we call impartiality in the latter [that is, the case of moral judgment], and impartiality is what justifies us in saying that morality too can be objective." Op. cit., p. 88. The incoherence of Mayo's analysis, in fact, is beyond my powers to describe.

[2] Kurt Baier, *The Moral Point of View* (Ithaca, N.Y.: Cornell University Press, 1958), p. 77 ff.

moral propositions are not statements. In its familiar applications, the term "statement" is by no means limited to empirical descriptions and predictions. Thus, even if it were granted that only statements can be true or false, this leaves us with a very wide range of possibly true or false utterances. In addition to statements of (empirical) fact, there are statements of intentions, statements of policy, statements of principle, bank statements, and a hundred and one other forms of statement, almost as various in their logical functions as discourse itself. I do not, of course, claim that all statements are objective and true or false. I claim only that the use of the concept of a statement is no more the exclusive prerogative of the empirical scientist and the logician than is that of objectivity, and that from the premise that a statement is non-factual, in the empirical sense, nothing whatever can be inferred about the possibility of its being verifiable. The only fundamental question, so far as verifiability is concerned, is whether the statement in question is corrigible, and whether, when we affirm it, we are in any meaningful sense subject to correction. In the case of morals, I contend that possibility is guaranteed by (and only by) the possibility of objective judgment itself.[3]

To say, then, that a moral statement is true is simply: (*a*) to reaffirm it and (*b*) to avow that it meets whatever tests of objectivity are deemed proper by the moral judge himself. He who affirms that a moral proposition is true when it will not abide such tests, speaks falsely. No moral judge, in affirming the truth of a particular judgment or principle, supposes that anyone else must agree with him regardless of his own moral obligations. For in morals there can be no guarantee that all objective judges will acknowledge the same principles of moral obligation.

This means that rational disagreements in morals cannot range beyond an implicit framework of common principles and practices shared, in conscience, by the disagreeing parties. Similarly, meaningful interpersonal discussions of

---

[3] I believe that the situation is much the same in many other spheres of discourse. However, I am arguing here only the case of moral truth.

the truth of a particular moral judgment presuppose the existence of a moral community to which, in conscience, both discussants are committed. This does not preclude the possibility that moral judges may contradict one another; it precludes only the possibility that contradiction can occur outside the limits of a particular moral community. To the extent that moral communities differ fundamentally in regard to their moral precepts and practices, it is pointless to speak of their judgments as logically contradictory. For in that case it is also pointless to talk of an objective settlement of their differences. At such a point, what is wanted is not argument, but education; not the appeal to non-existent principles of morals, but companionship and love.

God and Evil:
A Study of Some Relations
Between Faith and Morals

THE CONTEXT OF THE PROBLEM OF EVIL

To outsiders, there has always been a grim fascination in the
fact that Western monotheism, which arrogates to its God
exclusive power to redeem us from evil, should itself be so
bedeviled by the apparently simple yet evident proposition
that something *is* evil. But even such comparative insiders as
Augustine and Dostoevski have been obsessed by the irony
implicit in the fact that, having hopefully begun by justifying
themselves to God, they must end despairingly by having to
find excuses for him. Between man's justice and God's Justice, as Abraham and Job discovered, there falls a shadow
whose darkness becomes only the more inscrutable as the
light of human reason is trained upon it. This enigma, or
paradox, which marks the profoundest crisis of faith and
morals that the monotheist knows, is usually referred to as
"the problem of evil." It might, with more propriety, be
labeled "the problem of faith and conscience." Compared
with it, the metaphysical perplexities inherent in the notions
of a *causa sui* or a necessary being are, in Locke's sense,
trifling. The latter belong to an episode in the history of a
rationalistic theology whose connection with the faith of the

prophets, the apostles, and the fathers of the church remains problematic. The problem of evil is of a different order. What it concerns is the ultimate consistency of a form of life, and what it threatens is the faith animating that form of life. No solution to it would extend by a hair's breadth either our grasp of relations of ideas or our knowledge concerning matters of fact. It would be more appropriate, indeed, to speak, not of solutions to the problem of evil, but of modes of absolution from it.

In these gay and gaudy days of existentialism and neo-orthodoxy, such remarks may seem merely to underline the dangers of consecutive thinking about religious and ethical problems. Such was not their intention. A problem does not transcend logic merely because we can call it practical or existential. The inconsistency between the faith and the conscience of the traditional monotheist cannot be removed, certainly, by the methods available to empirical science, mathematics, or linguistic philosophy. But the very fact that it can be stated with some precision ought to be sufficient evidence that religious utterances, as well as moral judgments, occasionally have ponderable implications. And our recognition that it is an inconsistency is at the same time an implicit acknowledgment of the rational demand that it be removed.

There is nothing very devastating in these truisms save for those who are tempted to protect their faith by talking nonsense about their God. "If you make up a self-contradictory sentence," Professor Anthony Flew has observed, "it won't miraculously become sense just because you have put the word 'God' as its subject." It should be added that obscurity and obfuscation do not suddenly become edifying when transposed into a theological key. Opinions may differ as to the regenerative value of continual preoccupation with matters of ultimate concern. But there should be no room for doubt that ultimate concerns which cannot be consistently formulated are offenses against reason and hence offenses against the human spirit itself.

A more serious question is whether, within the existential

context of faith, the problem of evil may not be unreal. It has been said that the question of whether God exists has no meaning for the unconverted, but that for the converted it does not arise. It has likewise been argued that the question of whether God's will is good has no significance, since for men of faith his will is, as we say, "good by definition," whereas for unbelievers, who deny that there is a God, any question concerning the merits of his will is meaningless. Within the context of religious faith, which is the only context where such matters could be discussed, there is, in brief, no such thing as the problem of evil. Outside that context it is only a formal dilemma which has no interest save as an exercise in elementary logic.

Before replying to this objection, it is worth remarking that it is not merely atheists and skeptics who have posed the problem of evil. It is already present in Job, and it is expressed with great eloquence by Augustine and by Dostoevski. Such an *ad hominem* is, however, formally question-begging, and, formally, I stake nothing on it. It is more germane to inquire whether conversion has any meaning apart from the possibility of apostasy or, as I say, "deconversion." (The proper word, "perversion," has lost its usefulness in this connection.) It is also necessary to point out in this connection that what we call "faith" is, in most instances, merely an aspiration in that direction. If "outsiders" cannot meaningfully question the existence or the goodness of God, then, since all of us are virtual outsiders, who is in a position to assert this? Limiting questions occur to every man, and every man, "meaningfully" or not, has doubts about the goodness of God and, through them, about His existence. Existentially, deconversion, or loss of faith, is a constant threat which any person can, at best, only hope to overcome. Even those like Nietzsche, who announce that "God is dead," may be said to know whereof they speak. Animals may lack the power to understand religious concepts but, if so, this is not owing to any lack of faith on their part. On the contrary, lack of faith is, logically, as sound evidence of understanding as faith itself.

We tend, I think, to confuse the issue by not bearing in mind the distinction between faith and creed. No problem about God's goodness or existence is explicitly acknowledged by those entrusted with the formulation of a creed. Why should it be? It does not follow from this, however, that such problems have no meaning for those who profess the creed. For a Dostoevski, the problem of evil is not so much the problem of Christianity as it is *his* problem. The creed is a formula which is acceptable or not, depending upon his ability to satisfy the joint demands of faith, conscience, and reason. These are not, as it were, the demands of self-activating and dissociated spheres of activity which are impervious to what transpires in the rest of life. They are the interlocking demands of individual men or groups of men. There is a sense in which we may perhaps agree that the heart has reasons which the intellect knows not of; but they are reasons nonetheless, and what does not satisfy the hearts (and minds) of many men is the possibility that anything can be evil if there is an almighty God who is also perfectly good.

A STATEMENT OF THE PROBLEM

It is not my intention in this essay to offer any particular form of relief from the problem of evil. My present interest in the problem is philosophical: I desire merely to consider what sort of problem it is and to determine the significance of the various theological or ethical moves that have been made in coping with it. This investigation belongs less to theology, which is itself a form of religious discourse, than to the philosophy of religion and of morals—to the logical analysis, that is, of religious and moral utterances and of the forms of life of which they are at once a manifestation and a part.

There are many ways of stating the problem of evil, depending upon the precise nature of the faith in question and the particular evils, natural or moral, whose existence is acknowledged. Because of its comparative brevity, it will be convenient to present here a modified restatement of the problem as Philo formulates it in Part X of Hume's *Dialogues*. It is to be understood that no claims are made here for the merits of the theology involved; from this point of view, my exposition will be as neutral as I can make it. In short, I adopt this formulation for purposes of analysis and only, therefore, as a working model. Many refinements might easily be introduced into it, but I am convinced that they would merely complicate our discussion without increasing our understanding of the concepts and the propositions involved.

As here understood, the problem of evil tends to arise whenever there is a disposition on the part of anyone to assent to both of the following propositions: (*a*) there is an almighty and omniscient being who is a perfectly good person and who alone is God; and (*b*) there is something in the finite universe created by that being which is evil. For purposes of discussion, they may be referred to respectively as (*a*) the theological thesis, and (*b*) the ethical thesis. Their inconsistency may be seen in the following way: By hypothesis, an almighty and omniscient being can do whatever it wills. But any perfectly good person, so far as he can, will do good and prevent evil. Now, if there is a being that is at once almighty, omniscient, and perfectly good, it will be both able and willing to prevent evil. On the other hand, if something is evil, it must be concluded that there is no such being, since a perfectly good person would prevent it if he could, and an almighty and omniscient being could prevent it if it would. Either, then, there is no such being or nothing is evil. But since, by hypothesis, only such a being is God, we are forced to conclude either that there is no God or else that there is nothing which is evil.

This dilemma, however, is a serious problem only for the believer who accepts or aspires to accept both the theological and the ethical theses. His predicament may be expressed in the following way: Both propositions seem to him to be certain; the theological thesis is certified by faith, the ethical thesis by conscience. If he abides by the deliverances of

conscience his faith is imperiled; but if he accepts the faith
to which he aspires, he must evidently disavow what, in
conscience, he knows to be evil. How can he deny what
his conscience tells him to be evil? Yet how can he deny
what by faith he believes to be God? Does his conscience
delude him, or is his faith somehow a mistaken or even a
wicked faith? What can he do? In principle, he may modify
his conception of God; he may change his attitude toward
what he has considered to be evil; he may try to find excuses
for God under the auspices of theodicy; or, finally, he may
try to live with his contradiction as an honest man who de-
spairs of his soul's integrity. Whatever he does, his way of
life will never be quite the same again, for something that
has hitherto been a cornerstone of that way of life has now
been shaken to its foundations.

THE MEANING OF THE THEOLOGICAL THESIS

Before examining the moves that may be made in order to
relieve the problem of evil, it will be necessary to give some
attention to the theses themselves. For our understanding of
the problem and the moves themselves will depend entirely upon what we take the propositions that give rise to it
to mean.

The theological thesis has several parts which are not always clearly distinguished. It is not to be supposed that,
taken as a whole, the thesis explicates the meaning of "God,"
even for the monotheist himself. The fundamental reason
why God has no essence is that no essence can exhaust the
idea of the holy or the worshipful. In theology, as in ethics,
definitions are commonly misleading. Where they occur, they
serve not as explications of the use of expressions, but as
devices for the focusing and directing of sentiments or attitudes. They explain nothing, but signify much, and what
they signify is not something about the nature of things in
themselves but rather the drift of our own sense of what is
holy or worshipful. It is in this way, I take it, that we must
understand how such theologians as Aquinas can argue that

God has no essence, while at the same time discoursing at length about his inherent power, personality, and goodness.

The first part of the theological thesis may be called the metaphysical claim. What it asserts is that there is an almighty and omniscient being. Now the metaphysical attributes of omniscience and omnipotence are not, of course, entirely free from internal difficulties of their own. It has been argued that no consistent idea of them can be formed at all, and that when we stretch the notions of potency or power and knowledge to infinity and undertake to conceive them in absolute or unconditional terms we always land in paradox and confusion. I myself am inclined to think that any terms which have a persistent and common use also have or gradually acquire a meaning, and that if we bear in mind the context in which they are characteristically employed, we will usually find an idea which is neither vacuous nor inconsistent. I intend this, however, less as a "theory" than as a heuristic principle of interpretation to which we are free to admit exceptions in particular cases.

As R. B. Perry has remarked:

> God conceived as perfection reflects man's experience of imperfection. Practicing and suffering injustice, man dreams of perfect justice; being both hateful and the victim of hate, he dreams of utter and universal love; being ignorant, he conceives of omniscience; amidst the ugliness and drabness of life, he fancies a perfection of beauty; from his unhappiness there springs a vision of perfect and uninterrupted bliss.[1]

The point is that "omniscience" primarily represents the overcoming of our own deprivation of knowledge or, rather, the ideal overcoming of this deprivation. As such it signifies an ideal of knowledgeability to which we ourselves conceivably may aspire and which we may endlessly approach. Similarly, "omnipotence" represents an ideal of power or puissance, of ability to do and to accomplish whatever one may will, without external interferences of any kind.

[1] Ralph Barton Perry, *Realms of Value* (Cambridge: Harvard University Press, 1954), p. 483.

Both characteristics are ascribed to God as inverse symbols and measures of our own imperfections and limitations.

Some hold that the metaphysical attributes must be ascribed to God in a merely analogical sense, on the ground that God is a being so utterly unlike ourselves. To me this seems problematic, since God, conceived as a "Thou," cannot be absolutely unlike ourselves. Such attributions merely tend to be regarded as analogical when we re-emphasize the distance between ourselves and God. Briefly, whether such attributions are to be regarded as analogical or not depends precisely upon how we ourselves conceive of God, upon how near or far, like or unlike, he appears to us to be. But this will depend, in every case, upon the particular stresses to which the religious life itself happens to be subject. It is my contention that one primary motive for insisting upon the "merely" analogical or even metaphorical character of all such attributions as "omnipotence" to God is the felt necessity to overcome the inconsistencies involved in the problem of evil. For in regarding his "power" as merely analogical or metaphorical we seem, at least, to relieve ourselves of the necessity of treating him as an agent, like ourselves, who does things and who is therefore responsible, in the ordinary way, for what he does.

Be this as it may, God is presented, throughout the biblical literature, as one who acts and as one who *is* only in the manner of an active being. Might is ascribed to him as one who performs prodigious acts and who does deeds of inestimable importance for mankind. Might itself is essentially the power to do something, and someone is mighty in so far as he has the power to do and to act. Thus, in speaking of God as "almighty," one is saying that the object of worship, the holy one, possesses unlimited might or power, that it has power over all, especially over ourselves, and that nothing has power over it. And in asserting that there is an almighty or omnipotent being one is saying that there is something whose nature it is to act and whose power is unrestricted.

As for the attribute of omniscience, it is surely a radical error to restrict its meaning within the religious context in accordance with the preconceptions of some special theory of knowledge such as empiricism or rationalism. The term had a use before philosophers undertook to solve their epistemological puzzles and before they attempted to establish specific criteria of knowability. So far as religion is concerned, I think it suffices to say that an omniscient being would know whatever there is to know, and that just as Omnipotence is not expected by sensible men to do the impossible, so Omniscience is not expected to know more about the impossible than that it is such. What is logically unknowable could not be known even by an omniscient being. Such a being would not know how to square the circle; on the contrary, it would know with blinding clarity that the circle cannot be squared. Hence, if anyone should claim that an omniscient being would understand how injustice can be just or how evil can be good our best recourse would be simply to stare him out of countenance. Should a question be raised as to God's ability to know everything that will happen in the future, we have only to consider whether anyone can properly be said to know that something will happen in the future. An omniscient being will know whatever there is to know about the future; and if it should be that the future cannot be known, then not even an omniscient being could be supposed to know it. How omniscience might be come by is an interesting question, but I think we do not have to consider it. It is hardly for us to ask how the deity may have got into his line of work. Nor need we consider here whether there is an omniscient and omnipotent being. For in dealing with the problem of evil, we are concerned with a situation in which certain propositions have already been premissed and which, for those involved in it, are accepted on faith.

THE MORAL CLAIM OF THE THEOLOGICAL THESIS

The second part of the theological thesis may be called the moral claim. What it asserts is that there is an almighty and omniscient being which is also a perfectly good person.

More specifically, it asserts that such a being is both a person and good—good in the way that a person is so. For present purposes, it will be unnecessary to consider the many other ways in which God may be good, since they are not directly involved in the problem of evil. Many people, no doubt, will wish to say that God is good not only in the way that persons may be good but also in the way that beautiful things are good. There are conceptions of deity, such as that of Plotinus, which are more aesthetic than moral. But traditional theism, while it has its aesthetic aspect, is more fundamentally concerned with God's justice and benevolence than with his radiance.

Now, there is no logical connection between the metaphysical attributes and the moral attributes. Logically, there is no reason why an almighty and omniscient being might not be a perfect stinker. Nor is it logically impossible that such a being might be worshipped as God, even if it were denied the attributes of a good person. The notion of a God of pure power is not attractive, but it is conceivable. But from Genesis on, the goodness of the almighty being is constantly reiterated, and even the imponderable "I am that I am" plainly implies by the presence of the first-person pronoun that whatever else it is, "the being" is not to be conceived as a mere thing. It is not difficult to attenuate God's personality, and those who would relieve him of responsibility for evil are likely to be attracted to this way out of their perplexities. But they do so at a price which is greater than traditional monotheism has usually been willing to pay.

The term "good," as everyone now knows, is a general term of commendation and praise. In using it, we normally perform what Professor John Austin calls an "illocutionary act." That is, in saying that something is good, we are doing something with words, and in this case what we are doing is to praise or to commend the thing in question in some way. Ordinary commendations, of course, are always qualified and, in context, they presuppose some standard in relation to which the commendation is made. We have here to do only with moral goodness, and hence with moral praise or commendation, for we are considering God only as one who acts and whose merits are those of a good person.

The notion of personality, what it is to be a person, is more elusive and more ambiguous than that of goodness, and contemporary philosophers have devoted far less attention to its analysis. We are not here concerned with "personality" in the sense in which that term is used by empirical psychologists, such as Professor Allport, when they talk about the "psychology of personality"—the psychology, that is, of individual character and temperament. As employed in ethics and in theology, personality is not an empirical characteristic like green or hot; nor is it exhaustively definable in terms of empirical characteristics. Being a person, like being a work of art, is a functional conception which has to do with a characteristic way of treating or dealing with the thing in question. This fact is most easily seen in the following way: It is always proper to speak of "treating a person as such" or of "treating a work of art as such," and there is always a point, at once understood, in saying that something should be treated as a work of art or that someone should be treated as a person. But were it asserted that a mountain, a thunderstorm, or a green object should be treated as such, or if someone should speak of "treating a mountain as such," the point of the remark would not be readily understood and we would be obliged to ask the speaker what in the world he meant by it. It is not that mountains cannot be treated in various ways. On the contrary, that is just the trouble: mountains can be treated or dealt with in innumerable ways according to our own interest or pleasure. But just because of this there is no way of treating them as such, no characteristic way that the being of a mountain as such requires.

In the sense in question, then, ascriptions of personality differ radically from descriptions of the empirical characteristics of things. In speaking of someone as a person, we are assigning to him a certain function, role, or status and conferring upon him the title of personality which goes with that function, role, or status. And in addressing someone as a person, we are thereby dealing with him in that role, and are entering into those relations with him that such a role may prescribe. In this sense, a personal relationship consists, not in the innumerable *ad hoc* dealings which individual persons happen to have with one another, but, rather, in the restricted class of dealings that are prescribed by the role and which may affect the status of the individuals involved as persons.

A personal relationship may be properly said to fail when the parties to it are correctly charged with failing in their mutual responsibilities as persons. If it fails absolutely, then, so far at least as the individuals themselves are concerned, their very existence as persons is placed in jeopardy. As in other spheres, repudiation of the role means abandoning the responsibilities that go with the role, and vice versa. It is thus no idle question whether someone is a person or whether we ourselves stand in a personal relationship to him. For upon the answer to it depends the validity of the ascription to him of a whole system of rights and responsibilities. The denial of a personal relationship does not involve the cessation of all dealings on the part of the individuals involved. But it amounts to the active repudiation of specific commitments to deal and to be dealt with in certain characteristic ways. In short, there is already built into the notion of personality a characteristic normative function which prescribes a certain comportment toward those to whom personality is ascribed and which at the same time imputes to them certain inescapable liabilities and responsibilities.

There are, of course, many kinds of personality, each carrying with it a distinctive role and status. Juridical persons are thus distinguishable from moral persons essentially by the different prerogatives and liabilities that go with their respective roles. The rights and responsibilities of juridical persons are defined by law, and may be altered as the law requires. The rights and responsibilities associated with moral persons pertain to moral agency as such, and they will change in accordance with modifications in our conception of the moral agent. In our system they include, above all, the right to independent judgment and choice, and the reciprocal responsibility to judge disinterestedly and to choose in accordance with principles of right action that are equally binding upon all persons.

Every moral person is liable to moral praise and blame. In fact, anyone for whom moral personality is claimed is *ipso facto* subject to moral praise and blame as a "good" or "bad" person, since such praise or blame is equivalent to the assertion that he has fulfilled or failed in his responsibilities as a person. Anyone who acquits himself of his moral responsibilities thereby deserves to be praised as a good person, and anyone who fails to do so thereby deserves to be censured as a bad person. Should it be argued that a certain person is not, in principle, subject to moral criticism, this would amount to saying that he cannot be charged with moral responsibilities. By the same token, to remove an individual altogether from the sphere of possible moral reprobation is so far to cease to regard him as a moral agent and hence as a moral personality.

If this is so, it would appear to be impossible to speak of an almighty and omniscient being as a good person without in some degree treating it as a moral agent and hence as, in principle, subject to the blame to which moral agents are liable. And to the extent that we address such a being as a person or as a "thou" we automatically treat it as an agent to whom certain obligations are due and from whom the fulfilment of corresponding obligations may be expected. There may be reason to deny that such a being can reasonably be regarded in this way. Thus it might be argued that it would be pointless to address an almighty being as one would address ordinary mortals who are subject to our censure as moral agents. How, it may be asked, can we reasonably think of such a being as beholden to us in any way? It is not my purpose here to assess the merits of such arguments and questions. I contend only that if, for whatever reason, we should seek to place such a being altogether beyond moral good and evil, the effect would be, so far as we ourselves are concerned, to relieve it of certain attributes of personality and so to make it impossible to address the being, with a straight face, as a "thou." Hence, just to the extent that we are impelled to say that the "justice" of such a being has nothing to do with our standards of justice or are moved to stress the "mere" analogy between its "goodness" and that which we ascribe to ordinary mortals when we consider them as moral agents, we thereby radically attenuate its status as a person and jeopardize any moral claims that it might be alleged to impose upon ourselves. On the other hand, we may speak, if we will or must, of "the almighty to whom all praise is due"; but if we do so in a sense that has any ethical significance, we render it possible also to speak of "the almighty to whom all blame is due."

A "holy person" does not mean the same thing as a "moral person." A holy person is one who is entitled, as such, to religious devotion or regard, and for whom the status of holiness is claimed. A moral person becomes a religious person and the moral "thou" becomes a religious "Thou" just to the extent that the former is regarded as something which is to be treated reverentially—just to the extent, that is to say, that his principles, his conduct, and his volitions are not merely praiseworthy, in the moral sense, but also holy or divine. Certain persons, such as Jesus, are thought to be morally exemplary by many who would not dream of regarding them as divine.

On the other hand, it is conceivable that something might be treated as a holy person without at the same time being regarded as a good person in the moral sense. It is also logically possible that ascriptions of moral personality might be defeated without thereby entailing the defeat of ascriptions of holiness or divinity. In the case of ethical religions such as Western monotheism the relations of religious personality to moral personality are far from simple. A certain tension between the holy personality and the moral personality of God is bound to occur in so far as one is obliged to treat, as holy, principles or actions which, on their own account, may appear to be reprehensible. No doubt the moral personality of God is to be conceived as deriving from or as dependent upon his holy personality. But because of this, the holy personality of God is placed in jeopardy when his perfection as a moral person is impugned.

It is therefore entirely understandable that certain monotheistic theologians should have sought to treat the holiness of almighty God as something which absolutely transcends his moral personality. Yet a too emphatic emphasis upon the absolute transcendence of God's holy self is bound to result in a tendency toward the secularization of the moral and hence in a radical circumscription of the domain of the religious itself. Such tendencies are plainly discernible in Kierkegaard and even, at times, in Martin Buber. On the other hand, identification of God's holiness with his justice and his law may result in the defeat of the faith in him as a divine being, when the validity of his justice and his law has been placed in question. If his divinity may provide the guaranty for his wisdom, so, in turn, the authenticity of his wisdom tends to become a criterion of his divinity. This hazard is inherent in every ethical religion, and no amount of purely dialectical maneuvering will permanently remove it.

THE RELIGIOUS CLAIM OF THE THEOLOGICAL THESIS

The most crucial part of the theological thesis is that which asserts that the one almighty, omniscient, and perfectly good person is God. I shall call this the religious claim. The most important thing to be said about it is that the word "God" functions at once as a holy name and as a title which serves to deify that upon which it is conferred. The active verb "to deify" is illuminating in this connection precisely because it brings out the point that in calling something "God" we are *giving* it a holy name and *conferring* upon it the status of divinity. Or, to put the matter in another way, in speaking of something as "God" we are using a name which at the same time invests the being with the prerogatives, responsibilities, and claims upon ourselves to which that name entitles it.

The apparent circularity in this analysis is removed when it is observed that in deifying something we are treating it as an object which is holy, worthy of our worship and reverence. If any being is God, then by definition it is worthy to be worshipped and ought to be worshipped. Because of this, those who do not worship that being which is God are *ipso facto* reprehensible or blameworthy. It is also for this reason that atheism is not generally regarded by the pious as one philosophical or theological position among many, but as a wicked or sinful attitude. Atheism is not the same thing as the denial that there is an almighty being. One is an atheist, in the strict sense, only if he asserts that there is no God, which is to say, no being that is holy or worthy of worship.

In order to reinforce the validity of this analysis, let me call attention to the essential difference between the meaning of "God" and that of "god." The word "god" is not at all a holy name, and its application to any being carries with it no titular claims whatever. It may be used by anyone without the slightest suggestion of blasphemy or impiety. It is, in fact, impossible to take the name "god" in vain, for it is not a name at all, but, like "cat" or "tree," a mere common noun. There is nothing blameworthy in denying the existence of a god or in refusing to worship a god, for there is nothing intrinsically worshipful about the being of a god.

THE MONOTHEISTIC "SYNDROME"

We have now to consider the theological thesis as a whole. If I am right, there is no logical contradiction in accepting any one of the three main claims embodied in the thesis while denying the rest. One may accept the metaphysical claim without accepting the moral or the religious claim; and one may accept the metaphysical and moral claims without necessarily accepting the religious claim. In principle, it would also be possible to accept the purely religious claim that God exists or that there is a being that is God without thereby accepting either the metaphysical or the moral claims. In brief, it is not logically necessary that God should be almighty and omniscient or even a perfectly good person, and it is not necessary that an almighty being or even a perfectly good person should be God. For the ordinary monotheist, nevertheless, such logical possibilities are not theologically conceivable, or at any rate they seem not to be so until the problem of evil is confronted. So regarded, the theological thesis may be called "the monotheistic syndrome." Given this syndrome, God "must" be viewed as an almighty, omniscient, and perfectly good person, and conversely, if there is an almighty, omniscient, and perfectly good person, that person is alone entitled to be called God.

What, logically, is the import of this syndrome? It is certainly not an analytic truth. Nor is it as such an ordinary statement of fact. It is more illuminating to compare its function with that of moral principles. Now, as everyone knows, it is always logically possible to question whether happiness and pleasure are good. The ordinary usage of "good" allows for the possibility of such a question, and those who speak of "good" and "happiness" or "pleasure" as synonyms are simply mistaken. For the ethical hedonist, however, it is, in effect, not morally possible to ask whether pleasure alone is good. For him, although "pleasure" and "good" do not mean the same thing, pleasure is still held to be the only intrinsic good, the only thing, therefore, which ought to be desired for its own sake.

It is not very helpful to speak of ethical principles as *a priori* synthetic. Were we so to speak of them, it would be only in order to emphasize the point that it is a mistake to treat them either as tautologies or as contingent ascriptions of value. For those who accept it, the greatest-happiness principle is not at all analytic; nor could its validity be established by inspection of the meaning of the phrases in question. Taken as a principle, it serves, rather, to prescribe the standard of right action which is to be used in justifying particular maxims of conduct. When it is accepted, the contingency that a particular pleasure may not be intrinsically good is excluded, as we say, on principle, and the moral possibility that a right action would not conduce to the greatest happiness is precluded *a priori* from one's moral reckonings.

Such a conception of moral principles provides a useful analogy, I think, for interpreting the monotheistic syndrome.

For the monotheist it functions, in effect, as a religious principle which pre-empts the holy name and title of "God" for the almighty, omniscient, and perfect being. I think this explains the grain of truth implicit in R. M. Hare's view that theological theses are not falsifiable. To put it bluntly, they are not falsifiable just because they are so treated; because, that is to say, the person who accepts them refuses, on principle, to consider seriously any other alternative and because he refuses to allow for the contingency that they might turn out to be false.

But now I shall appear to contradict myself. For I wish to say that while the convinced monotheist regards the theological thesis as a principle which is not falsifiable, still it is not, in practice, absolutely beyond question, even for him. Here, I confess, I find myself in need of words. But it is necessary to press the point, even at the risk of apparent contradiction, for it takes us, as I believe, to the very heart of the spiritual perplexities with which we here have to do.

It is significant, in this connection, that we do not so naturally say that a theological thesis is proved or disproved as that particular individuals have faith or lose it, and are subject to conversion and apostasy. And it is relative to our faith or lack of it, our conversion to or deconversion from a theological thesis, that we may say that the thesis is, in some sense, religiously defeasible. At any rate, in speaking here of the defeasibility of a theological thesis, I will mean that with respect to it we are subject to conversion or deconversion, and that our faith in it, despite the fact that we may hold it beyond all doubt, may in fact be defeated by considerations which, as Mill would say, are capable of influencing the mind.

It is sometimes thought that faith and conversion, while subject to causes, are impervious to reasons; and that while they may have, so to say, a psycho-logic they have no logic. This is simply not true. Pascal, the arch-fideist, claimed that the heart has reasons that the intellect knows not of, but he still claimed, significantly, that the heart has reasons, not that it is subject to causes. I should prefer to say that faith, although it may perhaps have no reasons, is nevertheless subject to reasons, and that it may be weakened or else defeated by reasons, as well as strengthened or confirmed by them. I think it is in this light that the proofs for the existence of God are to be understood from a religious point of view: they are not really proofs at all but, for those who accept them, confirming evidences of a faith which might still be sustained without them.

Although, despite Spinoza, there are thus no *Q.E.D*'s in the domain of religion, there still are reasons, and reasons may as well prepare the way to a conversion as may a mystic experience, a dose of laughing gas, or a series of responsive readings from *The Brothers Karamazov*. The process of conversion would be irrational were the monotheistic syndrome acquired solely as an effect of a mystic experience or a reading of Dostoevski, just as deconversion from the syndrome would be irrational if, one fine morning, one simply woke up without it. A rational deconversion occurs in consequence of careful reflection upon the practical reasons that are found inescapably to militate against it.

In this connection there can be no thought of necessary or sufficient reasons, but only of good reasons which religious persons find themselves bound to take into account. What is to count as a good reason is not something which could be codified for us by theologians. In common practice it is something which is recognized by ordinary reflective persons, within a common tradition, to be relevant. Apart from a common, traditional form of life which is accepted as normative by most persons within a culture, the notion of a good reason would have no meaning. But apart from such a tradition it is doubtful whether the notion of reason in any sense would have any significance.

Taken as a whole, the monotheistic syndrome cannot be understood as a speculative hypothesis; it is not a "theory" in the scientific sense or even in the metaphysical sense. Such possibilities are precluded by the presence within it of the moral claim which asserts that the almighty and omniscient being is a perfectly good person. But they are also precluded by the religious claim itself. In avowing the theological thesis, as I should like to put it, we are not so much asserting something about the nature of *things* as expressing certain regulative attitudes toward the *nature* of things. More briefly, we are testifying to a way of life or to the foundational commitment of a way of life. Similarly, to reject the theological thesis is not simply to deny a metaphysical hypothesis about the origins of things but, more saliently, to disavow the way of life which the monotheistic syndrome prescribes. The theological thesis is thus a practical proposition, and commitment to it is a practical commitment whose consequences for the person who accepts or rejects it are incalculably great.

THE SIGNIFICANCE OF PROPOSED SOLUTIONS
TO THE PROBLEM OF EVIL

We are now in a position to consider the significance of solutions to the problem of evil. In turning to them, we must re-emphasize here that what we have to do with is a practical, or existential, problem of faith and morals which is only secondarily concerned with matters of fact. The inconsistency between the theological thesis and the ethical thesis represents a conflict of attitudes toward reality and the conduct of life rather than a contradiction in our beliefs about the nature of what exists. Hence the question of removing such an inconsistency concerns essentially the possibility of a consistent system of religious and moral sentiments rather than the possibility of a consistent theory about the nature of things.

In principle, there are many ways of seeking relief from the problem of evil. Some of them involve primarily some modification of the theological thesis. Others involve a modification of the ethical thesis. Whichever way is taken, the inevitable result will be a modification of the way of life of the person involved. Let us first consider those forms of relief which do not entail a direct rejection of the ethical thesis. Some of them involve a radical deconversion from the monotheistic syndrome and hence the adoption of a very different attitude in regard to the object of religious faith; others involve changes of a more limited sort.

The least radical way of relieving the problem of evil is to find, or make, some excuse for the existence of evil which modifies God's responsibility for it. But if this way is preferable, since it seems to leave the monotheistic syndrome fairly intact, it is also much more difficult to render convincing precisely because of the claims regarding the nature of God. It should also be borne in mind that it is one thing to propose an excuse and another to accept it. No such proposal functions as an excuse unless someone is prepared to accept it. A proposed excuse is no excuse at all, any more than a mere hypothesis is a statement of fact. Moreover, finding an excuse is a very different sort of thing from finding a ten-dollar bill or a cure for cancer. It does not involve looking in a certain place, nor is it like making a lucky guess concerning causal correlations which may happen to be confirmed by observation. Rather, it is to give a counter practical reason which defeats or extenuates or removes a charge of responsibility. To excuse is to perform a distinctive act which is correlated with acts of moral praise and blame. Where there is no question of praise or blame, there can be no question of making or finding excuses. And where there is a question of excuses, there is also the question of praise and blame. A valid or acceptable excuse serves to impugn the legitimacy of blame or to sustain the legitimacy of praise. Invalid excuses formally leave open the question whether the praise or blame is justified. In most situations, however, there are not many plausible excuses to be made, and it frequently happens that there is either one excuse or none at all.

There are, I think, four main ways of making excuses for a person: (*a*) by showing that the act in question was unavoidable; (*b*) by showing that, although the act was avoidable, it is justified in view of its consequences; (*c*) by shifting responsibility, in whole or in part, to someone else; and (*d*) by making an exception of the person in question.

Now, given the assumptions of the theological thesis, it is
hard to see how a plausible excuse of the first sort could be
made for God. Apparently he cannot be excused on grounds
of ignorance or inability. If such an excuse is made either
through some qualification of the concept of omniscience or
of the concept of might, then the conception of the holy or
worshipful itself already begins to undergo a sea-change with
consequences that may well be devastating to the delicately
balanced conception of man's religious and moral relationship to God. For example, it might be argued, in the manner
of Leibniz, that any universe created by God must be the best
of all possible worlds and that for whatever evils that exist
there must be, *a priori*, a sufficient extenuating reason. Logically, and perhaps metaphysically, God could have created
some other state of affairs, but since he is a perfect being, it
is theologically impossible that he should create any other
universe than the one which exists. In short, if God exists, his
act in creating this universe is unavoidable. The effect of
such an excuse, however, is simply to reaffirm the absolute
benevolence of God—which is the very point at issue. It
clarifies the aspiration of the monotheist, but it does not necessarily remove his moral qualms that the world is ethically
out of joint. If, like Pangloss, he does manage to accept the
excuse, he must now view the evils of the world in such a
fundamentally different light that his whole conscientious attitude toward them is virtually transformed. That is to say,
if he is consistent, he is bound to accept in advance whatever
happens to exist as something which is at once unavoidable
and good. I shall not here remark upon the merits of the
quietism and optimism implicit in such a view. But it is
doubtful whether anyone deeply involved in the problem of
evil will find it easily acceptable.

Initially, the second sort of excuse may seem more promising, particularly if we restrict ourselves to the question of
moral evil. Thus, it might be argued that, although God may
have a certain collateral responsibility for moral evil, since
he granted freedom to man knowing in advance what use
man would probably make of it, moral freedom is neverthe-

less a good so great that it outweighs any possible evils that may attend it. In short, God's goodness is saved by claiming that God's act, in creating man as morally free, has good consequences that outweigh all admittedly evil consequences, and that although he shares, in one sense, responsibility for moral evil, his goodness as a person is not thereby to be impugned. This excuse is of interest because it commits him who offers it not only to the intrinsic worth of moral freedom but also, comparatively speaking, to the insignificance of happiness, aesthetic values, and, indeed, all the goods that are usually classified under the heading of "welfare." But again, it is a question whether men of ordinary good conscience will be able to make this commitment. If they do, another profound shift will doubtless occur in their scheme of values. It should be noted, however, that such an excuse does not touch the question of natural evil, including the involuntary ills that innocent persons are made to suffer in consequence of the evil acts of others. Here, one can imagine, those afflicted with a sense of estrangement or forsakeness (My God, my God, why hast thou forsaken me?) or outraged at the "inexcusable" sufferings of their loved ones are not likely to be edified by any attempt to show the greater good inherent in the consequences of these evils.

Doubtless there are some who would hold such a justification of moral evil to be defective precisely because, although it removes God from blame, it does not entirely remove him from responsibility. From this point of view, so long as God is held to be responsible in any way at all for moral evil, our faith in him is imperfect and our own sense of freedom and moral responsibility is incomplete and immature. Thus it may be argued that we ourselves must share the total burden of responsibility and guilt for our acts, and that God's act, in making us free, has nothing to do with our evil choices.

What is the spiritual significance of such a view? Now, in ordinary circumstances, when a person is relieved entirely of responsibility for a particular act, his ethical connection with it ceases, and any question of praise or blame of him so far disappears. Ethically, so to say, he becomes irrelevant to it. If, then, we alone are to be held responsible for our actions, if our responsibility cannot be shared, then not only any blame but also any praise is ours alone. How could we consistently praise God for saving us from moral evil, if we cannot share with him the blame when we do evil things? If he has no hand in the evil, how then could he be said consistently to have a hand in the good? When we commit murder, the sin is ours. But then, when we are loving, kind, or just, must not the credit and the praise be ours as well? In that case, however, any reciprocal ethical relationship between ourselves and God would tend to disappear. Correspondingly, it becomes increasingly hard to see how he could still be addressed as a "Thou" to whom we are in any way morally beholden.

The most radical way of excusing God from responsibility for evil is simply to make an exception of him. This sort of thing is done in ordinary life when someone is pardoned for a wrong act which he has committed. A man is also sometimes excused, whether properly or not, for acts involving a moral fault if, for example, he is acting in some publicly acknowledged capacity which carries with it non-moral responsibilities that, in the circumstances, are thought to be overriding. In the latter case, the excuse simply places the individual, for the nonce, beyond moral good and evil. Were such an excuse made, for whatever reason, in the case of God, it would undoubtedly involve a modification of the monotheistic syndrome and with it a modification of the sense in which monotheism could still be considered an ethical religion. As for pardoning or forgiving God, perhaps it is possible that we might try to do this, but not without impairing God's value to us as an ethically exemplary being, and not, therefore, without diminishing our sense of responsibility to him. Normally, it has been supposed that the relation of forgiveness should go the other way around: we are to forgive one another, even as God forgives us.

In general, any form of theodicy, the aim of which is to justify God's ways to man, is bound to appear implausible to anyone who has an overwhelming sense of the natural evils that abound in the world; and at best, it only serves to extenuate God's responsibility for moral evil. Even so, the consequence of having to make excuses for God—to "save his face," as it were—is to jeopardize our own sense of obligation to him and to render his goodness inoperative as a *moral* ideal. Religiously, the almighty being might still be conceived as God, but he would no longer be looked to as the source of moral goodness and as the being to whom, in the moral sense, "all praise is due." Briefly, theodicy nearly always increases the sense of the distance between man and God, and the remoteness of the moral life from the life of religious worship. In some people it *may* also reinforce a sense of complacency, resignation, inevitability; but they are precisely those who are least likely to be affected by the problem of evil. Conversely, those who are affected by the problem are most likely to be repelled by theodicial excuses. In so far as they do accept them, their excuses for God serve to reinforce the sense of personal guilt which may, in the end, become so overwhelming that nothing is left of their sense of personal dignity save the bare freedom—to go on sinning.

Several other ways of relieving God of responsibility for evil remain, but they are all more drastic, since they involve a more radical modification in the conception of God's nature and hence in the attitudes that are possible toward him. All such ways of overcoming the problem of evil involve a fundamental breakdown of the monotheistic syndrome or, what comes to the same thing, a fundamental attenuation of the traditional monotheistic faith. Nor can they be effected without in some measure incurring a liability to deconversion from monetheism.

The most radical, but in some ways easiest, way out is to renounce one or more of the attributes ascribed to God by the metaphysical claim. One may cease to hold that God is almighty or that he is omniscient, or may cease to regard omnipotence or omniscience as necessary attributes of holiness, of that which is worthy of piety or worship. In so doing, the problem of evil is automatically relieved, since a God who is not almighty or who is not omniscient need incur no responsibility for evils that he may not have anticipated or could do nothing to prevent. Giving up the metaphysical claim, however, does not require renunciation of faith in God's goodness; nor does it preclude us from still worshipping him as the holy of holies. But it does affect our attitudes and acts of faith in other important ways. For while God may still be worshipped, claims can no longer be intelligibly addressed to him and, at least in one sense, praying to him becomes correspondingly pointless. Likewise, it becomes increasingly difficult to view the whole of creation in a religious spirit as the providential work of deity. But, most seriously, the sense of absolute dependence upon God tends to disappear and, as one realizes that the amelioration of one's lot depends, not upon Grace alone, but upon one's own efforts, God ceases to appear in the guise of an all-powerful father, and becomes rather a kind of outsized brother who has his own troubles with evil, even as you and I.

I, for one, respect those contemporary theologians who candidly accept the notion of a finite God. If such finitistic theologies are still involved in grave metaphysical difficulties, they at least enable the believer to preserve his moral integrity and his religious devotion to a God who can be regarded with a straight face as a good person. They are possible, however, only to men of great emotional maturity and stability for whom, so to say, the trauma of birth has in some measure been overcome. They are not appealing to those for whom religious piety is possible only to the degree that the needs of emotional dependency are satisfied.

Another way of relieving the problem of evil is to qualify or else to give up altogether the moral claim concerning the goodness of God. To some, for whom religion means ethical religion, such a possibility may appear repugnant; but logically there is nothing to oppose it. There is no logical connection between the metaphysical and the moral claims of the theological thesis, and it is entirely possible to regard an omniscient and almighty being as God without investing him with the attributes of a perfectly good person. But if one does accept this alternative, God automatically loses his moral significance, and the autonomy of the moral life must now become a reality. Thus, while God's "commandments" may still be obeyed, one's obedience to them is no longer a consequence of one's faith, or, to say the same thing in other words, they are obeyed not because God commands them but because they are deemed right and good on their own account, regardless of the fact that he commands them. From this standpoint, the religious life now detaches itself altogether from the ethical life, with consequences which are incalculable to both. The appeal to God's will can no longer be used in justification of a moral principle or in extenuation of a practice which, on other grounds, might seem wicked or nefarious. It must be confessed, moreover, that the deification of the metaphysical attributes as such is likely to appear repugnant to an ordinary moral consciousness, and that once God's goodness as a person has been effectively challenged, the whole interest in his metaphysical attributes is likely to collapse.

The most drastic way out of the problem of evil is to give up altogether the belief in God—the belief, that is, that there is anything worthy of worship. But this way of putting the matter is ambiguous. For one may renounce the belief that any actual thing is worthy of worship, without ceasing to have attitudes which may be deemed religious. Thus, for example, philosophers like Comte or Dewey appear to have thought that while no actual thing is worthy of worship the moral ideal is itself worshipful. This is not the place to enter into detailed discussion of the concepts of existence, actuality, and being. There is, however, a quite proper sense in which one might be able to say that there is something worthy of worship, or even that something is God, without at the same time implying by this that there is a thing or a person that is God. The term "something" does not mean "some thing," and the contention that something is worthy of worship or that something is God does not entail that there is a thing, a substance, an actual entity which is worshipful or God. It is owing entirely to the exigencies of our own

Western religious tradition, and to the monotheistic syndrome which goes with it, that we would consider it misleading to claim that there is a God, an object worthy of
worship, while at the same time denying that there is any
thing or any person that is worshipful and toward which our
piety is due. And it is merely because of this that it has not
been customary for naturalists, materialists, or positivists to
say that they believe in God or that God exists. This is perhaps nothing more than a sign of the parochial limitations
of Western theology which, all too frequently, mistakes the
meaning of the so-called "atheistic" religions of the East.
From a logical point of view, there is nothing whatever to
preclude the possibility of a person sincerely affirming his belief in God while at the same time denying that God is a
person, a substance, or a thing.

This possibility suggests a way of modifying the monotheistic syndrome itself in such a way as to solve, once for
all, the problem of evil. Thus, one might adopt the view that
God, as such, is completely unknowable, and that as such no
positive attributes may validly be imputed to him. From
this standpoint, God's nature becomes a complete mystery,
and the worship of "him" as an "other," not ourselves, ceases
altogether to be the worship of an almighty or good person
who creates the universe out of his infinite goodness and
who gives to man the commandments by which he is to live.
This is the move which has been taken, now and then, by
"pure" mystics and by men of "pure" faith. But it is a form
of adoration or worship which is virtually devoid of content
and which, at last, merely battens upon its own subjective
intensity. Saying nothing, it commits us to nothing; affirming
nothing about God, it divests God of any significance for the
conduct of life. It solves the problem of evil, but only
by removing the religious life altogether from contact with,
and hence possible contamination by, the moral life. Precisely because it views God as utterly transcendent or, as
some theologians put it, as sheer "transcendence" itself, it
loses all relevance to the ordinary problems of human action.
Such, I take it, is at bottom the theological position of

Kierkegaard. But the spiritual remedies which it proposes are desperate remedies which ordinary persons are not likely to be able to accept. What remains of monotheism when it is accepted is anybody's guess—indeed, it is not for nothing that Kierkegaard himself has been sometimes called an "atheist." No doubt some precedent for the view can be found in the biblical literature. But surely the drift of what most people think of as biblical monotheism is incompatible with it, and surely it is not the view of God which is normally entertained in our churches and our synagogues.

FURTHER SOLUTIONS

All of the foregoing ways of relieving the problem of evil involve some tampering with the theological thesis and hence some degree of deconversion from the monotheistic syndrome. Traditionally, however, relief has frequently been sought through a modification of the attitudes expressed by the ethical thesis that something in the created universe is evil. It is this way out which most obviously shows how morals and religion may come into conflict and how, in turn, moral sentiments may be modified to meet the exigencies of religious faith.

The most drastic, if also the most implausible, way of dealing with the problem of evil from this standpoint is simply to deny the ethical thesis altogether. On this view, which most men would regard as highly immoral, there simply is no evil, and when someone says that something is evil he speaks falsely: evil, that is to say, is merely apparent, and the common view that such things as earthquakes, insanity, and cancer are evils is illusory. This, we have been told, is the position taken by Christian Scientists, but I do not vouch for it. In any case, it is hard for an outsider to see how such a point of view could be consistently maintained in practice. No doubt a sufficiently resolute optimist might say, for the nonce, that God's in his heaven and all's really well with the world. But it is not something which can seriously be asserted by anyone who takes a dim view of pain, loneliness, and cruelty. No ordinary Jew or Christian, so far as I can see, could entertain it for more than a moment, for it makes nonsense of the moral life. If nothing is evil, choice is pointless, and responsibility has no meaning.

A subtler view involves a persuasive redefinition of evil which conceives it as merely a privation of being. According to this view, whatever is created by God is good and hence worthy of praise. Evil, no doubt, is a necessary consequence of finite or created being, but only of its finitude, not of its being. Thus, so far as they *are*, pain, suffering, and guilt are good. The evil in them is only that of a limitation or privation.

At this point, it is easy to become entangled in a web of words. We are interested here only in the moral significance of such a view, that is to say, in its bearing upon our spiritual attitudes toward the world and toward the conduct of life.

Formally, everything seems to remain just as it was before, since, in one sense, it is still possible to say that something is evil. But materially, a complete sea-change comes over the moral life. Thus, for example, so far as pain or suffering are positive facts of experience, they are to be approved of as good, as something, that is to say, which ought to exist and which should be affectionately endured or, more strictly, rejoiced in. To that extent, the will to remove suffering and to root out pain, as well as the conviction that, simply per se, pain ought not to exist, must be regarded as forms of impiety. The man who worships God as good and accepts His creation as part of His divine providence, must so far acclaim pain and suffering as intrinsically good. It is only in so far as pain indicates some privation of being, some privation of a higher perfection which is potentially ours, that it can be regarded, albeit misleadingly, as evil. Strictly, it is merely an indication or sign of evil; what is evil is simply the accompanying privation.

To many moralists the quietism implicit in this view has seemed obvious. It is not my purpose here to evaluate it either from a moral or from a religious viewpoint. It is undoubtedly the view of many so-called saints, and those who are taken with saintliness will undoubtedly be attracted to it.

My point is that it is not an ethically neutral position, and that it does not leave our ordinary moral attitudes just where it found them. Moreover, strictly speaking, it cannot be regarded as a final solution of the problem of evil. For it still countenances the assertion that something, namely, privation of being, is evil. Indeed, from the point of view of those who are faced with the problem of evil, the privation theory merely forces the issue onto another plane. The problem, now, is to justify creation itself, which reopens the question of theodicy in its most radical form. It may be argued that it was always possible for God to choose not to create anything at all, and that if he could create something only by bringing evil—or privation—into the world he should not have created anything. Here we find the problem of evil in perhaps its most poignant and intractable form. For even if the individual can make his peace with pain and the sense of moral guilt, he may still find existence itself stale, flat, and unprofitable, and he may still be torn between his desire to love God and his unqualified loathing of the world which God has created.

Here we face the very issues implicit in Professor Tillich's discussion of what he calls "the courage to be." It is essential to bear in mind, however, that the courage to be is not something which can be required by theological pronouncements. For those who lack this sort of courage, the problem of evil is not remotely relieved by pointing out that evil is a necessary consequence of finitude, and hence of all created being, for it is the very evil of creation itself which is now in question. Why should anything exist? Such a limiting question is not meaningless, but it cannot be answered by the ploys of theodicy. It can be answered, if at all, only by a change of heart. But who shall say to another that such a change of heart is good? Even so, recovery of the courage to be does not necessarily involve a reconciliation of faith and morals, since it is entirely possible that, in recovering, a man might still, in his heart, condemn as evil many positive features of created being, with the consequence that his faith in the goodness of God continues to conflict with his conviction that at least some of God's works ought not to be at all.

Up to this point, I have proceeded on the tacit assumption that the problem of evil is itself an unmitigated evil, that it is something which, at least from a logical point of view, is intolerable. I have assumed, that is to say, that the acceptance of an inconsistency, and especially a practical inconsistency, is wrong and that it ought to be overcome. In effect, this means that, like most moral philosophers, I have taken it for granted that self-consistency and integrity in the spiritual domain is the consummation most devoutly to be wished. But is it? Why should the demand for consistency be regarded as categorical or as taking precedence over every other requirement of the moral or religious life? Within the moral sphere itself, we are frequently faced with conflicts of principle which can be removed only by subordinating one principle to another and which, therefore, can be removed only by disavowing some hitherto fundamental moral commitment. In such a case, is it reasonable to insist that an individual ought to modify his principles? Without begging the question, what sort of reason could be given that would at the same time satisfy the requirements of logic and those of conscience?

Suppose, then, that someone found himself faced with the problem of evil and that even after the most deliberate and painstaking reflection he still found no answer to it. Suppose also that he found that he could bring himself to reject or qualify neither the theological thesis nor the ethical thesis. No doubt, such a person would find that his religious aspirations and his moral intuitions cannot be reconciled and hence that at the very heart of what is deepest and most sincere in him as a person, there remains an insuperable and unremitting tragedy of spiritual self-division. Shall he be told to fish or cut bait? But from what standpoint could such a request significantly be made? If we appeal to the principle of consistency or integrity, we are evidently appealing to something which, even if he is sensible of its proper claims, requires him to renounce his profoundest loyalties—to cease, that is, to be the very person he is. To reply to him, as Professor C. I. Lewis might, that if he continues self-divided he will be sorry, is not to tell him something he does not already know. Of course he will be sorry; he is already sorry. But what, in the name of goodness and of God, is he to do?

In saying this, I do not wish to be misunderstood. I have been trying only to illustrate certain approaches to the problem of evil in order to see what their existential or practical import really is—not, on my own, to advocate one solution above another. Study of the problem of evil is instructive in many ways. It helps us to see, in the first place, how questions of logic may arise within the moral and religious life as well as within science or mathematics. The very possibility of a problem of evil makes plain the fact that questions of consistency are not impossible in the domains of religion and morals. Such questions, I have argued, are, at bottom, practical, and the reasons that may be offered in attempting to answer them must provide motives to influence the will, or heart, or they are nothing. Any arguments in this sphere have a point only in so far as they effectually dispose us to modify our active religious or moral commitments. Any religious or moral dialectic must be, in Hegel's phrase, a "logic of passion."

In the second place, the problem of evil makes us forcibly aware that philosophical theories which insist upon the necessary "autonomy" of moral and religious principles cannot be sustained. This is not to say that it is logically impossible to divorce morals from religion and to separate questions concerning what is right or good from questions concerning what is worshipful or holy. It seems evident to the humanist that questions of right and wrong are answerable without recourse to the will of God. What is good is good, and the fact that God wills it cannot make it more so. What he forgets is that, for the theist, God's will alone certifies that anything

is good at all. Here, however, is no mere problem of analysis which closer inquiry into the meanings of moral and
religious expressions might be thought to solve.

Too often such a problem is presented as an external conflict between two distinct ways of life. But for anyone involved with the problem of evil it is an internal problem,
since in affirming the ethical thesis in the teeth of the theological thesis he is so far acting as a moral autonomist who
accepts as final the deliverances of his conscience, whereas
in affirming the theological thesis (which itself involves a
moral claim) he is accepting the will of God, whatever it is,
as that which alone makes good things good. Such a person
is caught within himself in a practical conflict of religion
and morals. But it would be more accurate to say that he
is caught in a conflict between ethical independence and
ethical dependence, between a conscience which presumes
to judge for itself what is good or evil and an ethical faith
which depends upon the will of God to authorize what is
to be believed in the moral sphere.

The study of the problem of evil is instructive, finally, in
that it enables us to see with great clarity what it can be to
question the existence of God and how, within the religious
context itself, such a question is bound to arise. I have never
doubted that the word "God" gets its primary meaning from
the part it plays in religious discourse. And I not only accept but insist upon the thesis that religious speech and literature provide the paradigmatic uses of the term which it
is the business of the philosopher to explain. But religious
discourse is not the discourse of angels who do not know the
meaning of doubt, but of men for whom doubt is a condition of life. To ask whether there is a God constitutes the
fundamental trauma of the religious life itself, just as the
question whether anything is good is the great night-
mare of the moral life. In the case of our own traditional
forms of monotheism, this trauma is brought on directly by
the problem of evil. Pending resolution of the problem, or
our absolution from it, the possibility of answering "No" to
the question of God's existence hangs immediately in the

balance. Religious faith is not necessarily dependent upon the confirming evidences of reason. But it may be impugned by contrary evidences which reason recognizes to be incompatible with it. Although it is perhaps possible that men of faith believe or wish to believe that the theological thesis is true, it is as certain as the proposition that two plus two equals four that the thesis is falsifiable. What makes it certain is Augustine's ancient question: "Whence, then, is evil?"

PART TWO

[X]

Commonsense Ethics
and Ordinary Language

"ORDINARY LANGUAGE" AND LIMITING QUESTIONS

Future historians of ideas may well come to regard the first of the twentieth century as "The Age of Symbol." As applied to the fine arts, to literature, to psychology and psychiatry, and to social studies in general, this epithet connotes a refusal to accept appearances at face value, an insistence upon interpretation, indirection, complexity, and depth. As applied to philosophy, however, it will probably suggest to some minds that ours is "The Age of Superficiality" *par excellence*, a period that has witnessed the possibly final abandonment of philosophy's ancient quest for understanding and assurance concerning the nature of things. But to those who begin to discern the ulterior ramifications of the study of signs, I. A. Richards will scarcely seem to be exaggerating when he says that it is "the most fundamental and extensive of all inquiries," and not a mere "preliminary or preparation for other profounder studies." For them, philosophy, conceived as the analysis of symbols, is for the first time coming into its own. No longer required to provide the poor man's science or the intellectual's substitute for religion, it is finally free to fulfill the tasks of logical analysis which are proper to it.

There are however, various ways of approaching the analysis of signs. And at the present time there are several schools of "philosophical analysis," each as bitterly opposed to the others' conceptions of its aims as all are jointly disapproving of traditional metaphysics. One influential group, deriving primarily from the earlier works of Bertrand Russell and Ludwig Wittgenstein, includes most of the logical positivists. This group is mainly interested in mathematical logic, in the methodology of exact science, and in the formulation of codified "ideal languages" from which all vagueness, ambiguity, and reference to unobserved entities have been eliminated. For them the absence of clearly stipulated definitions and the presence not only of multiple meanings but, worse, of multiple modes of meaning, make natural languages inadequate vehicles for the precise communication of logically coherent descriptions of fact. On the whole this school has been indifferent to the noncognitive, non-scientific uses of language. And it has tended, somewhat indiscriminately, to consign moral, poetic, religious, and "philosophical" discourse to the semantic dustbin of "expression" or "emotive meaning."

Meanwhile, particularly at Cambridge and Oxford, another school has arisen to challenge the methods of the positivists. Sometimes referred to as the "philosophy of ordinary language," its somewhat discredited godfather is G. E. Moore, whose powerful dialectic and passionate devotion to "common sense" provided the initial incitement to the general revolt which has taken place in England against the obscurity, the jargon, and the artificial technicalities of the classical metaphysical systems. Moore not only stimulated a renewed interest in and respect for ordinary language, but also showed by his own example the possibility of conducting subtle and exact analyses without ever resorting to a logical apparatus beyond that afforded by natural language itself. More recently, it has been the stimulating informal discussions of the later Wittgenstein and the writings of such followers as John Wisdom and Gilbert Ryle that have steered the philosophy of ordinary language into its present course. Moore was not hostile to metaphysics as such, and in his own ethics he was quite capable of asserting the existence of unanalyzable "non-natural" qualities and intuitively necessary moral truths. But Wittgenstein and his friends are as suspicious of metaphysical "double-talk" as are the positivists, although for somewhat different reasons. Thus, for example, in his brilliant *The Concept of Mind*,[1] Ryle patiently attempts to uncover the categorial confusions which, as he believes, lie at the heart of such hoary philosophical issues as "the mind-body problem." Moore had often been content simply to bellow, "Of course I know I had my breakfast this morning," or "Certainly, this is a hand; who could doubt it?" His younger contemporaries are more interested in revealing the sources of the linguistic confusion that give rise to such "queer" philosophical doubts than in asserting the obvious commonsensical truths which should dispose of them.

On one point the later Wittgenstein and his group violently part company with the other school of analysts. They respect and defend ordinary language, but, as Max Black has recently pointed out, they also regard those who are preoccupied with the construction of "ideal languages" as guilty of the fundamental philosophical blunder of "treating language like a calculus." Aware of the great richness and complexity of ordinary language, and perhaps because of their more adequate training in the humanities, they realize that modes of meaning other than the logical or scientific may have their own implicit standards of precision and relevance. And what is more important, they have tended to supplant Moore's question "What does it mean?" with such questions as "What is its function or role?" and "What are the distinctive criteria for judging the success or failure of symbols in the very different roles which they are called upon to play?"

Such an approach to the study of symbolic forms is, in my judgment, a stimulating and fruitful way of considering them. But it has its own limitations, and in the hands of its more pedestrian advocates, it can be exceedingly stuffy and often vague. Especially is this so when, somewhat in the manner of Dr. Johnson, all violations of ordinary usage are condemned out of hand on the sole ground that ordinary usage is the correct usage. There is no *a priori* reason why

[1] G. Ryle, *The Concept of Mind* (London: Hutchinson, 1949).

ordinary language should invariably be capable of adequately expressing what we may wish to say when we pass beyond the middle-sized problems with which it is designed to deal.

Be this as it may, the philosophy of ordinary language has shown how easily and, in many instances, how unnecessarily we can pass into paradox and pseudo-problems when we mix up our categories or misconceive the different roles of words in common speech. Mr. Stephen Toulmin's recent *An Examination of the Place of Reason in Ethics*[2] is an impressive example in the sphere of moral philosophy of how, by shifting the question, the philosopher of ordinary language may help to remove the "mental cramps" that for a generation have prevented subtle and careful thinkers from resolving the issues which divide them.

Concentrating exclusively on the "meaning" of such terms as "ought" and "good," most moral philosophers continue to debate interminably the question of whether they refer to objective qualities or are subjective expressions of approval or disapproval. Mr. Toulmin asks, in effect, that this question be deferred, and that we consider instead the kinds of "reasons" that are ordinarily regarded as relevant or acceptable in arguing a moral question. In the end, he maintains, we may perhaps better understand the meanings of moral judgments by following this course than by attacking this latter problem head on, without regard to the special role played by such judgments in the larger system of activities of which they are a part.

In the first part of his book, Toulmin explains what he believes to be the fatal flaws implicit in each of the three main traditional approaches to ethics. The first, which he calls "the objective approach," is vitiated from the outset by an uncritical assumption that when we assert that something is "right" we are simply ascribing to it an objective property in the same way as when we assert that it is "yellow" or "cold." But in fact ethical terms just do not function in this way. And so the objectivist is forced to assume an entire battery of special

[2] Stephen Toulmin, *An Examination of the Place of Reason in Ethics* (Cambridge, Eng.: Cambridge University Press, 1953).

categories such as "non-natural" qualities and *a priori* synthetic propositions, and special "faculties" of "moral intuition"
and "practical reason," in order to account, even in principle,
for the distinctive features of moral discourse. Even so, his
whole elaborate construction in the end falls to the ground
when we ask the simple question, "What *is* the distinctive
quality 'goodness' which is supposed to be common to humility, pleasure, friendship, and promise keeping?" For when
we look, even with the "eye" of the mind, this quality always
eludes us.

The basic error in this approach, Toulmin believes, is the
logical blunder of assuming that when one person asks another whether a given course of action is right, he is inquiring about a property, when in fact what he really wants is a
reason for deciding what to do. In moral discourse we do not
expect merely to be believed when we inform someone that
an act he is about to perform is wrong; we expect also, if our
statement goes unchallenged, that we will be construed as
providing a valid reason for not performing the act. And if
someone tells us that he doesn't know what rightness is, we
don't accuse him of not knowing the meaning of a word;
rather do we expect him to break his promises, or to lie, or
steal. Toulmin points out that in so doing we implicitly recognize that what is meant by "knowing what rightness is" is
very different from "knowing what redness and hardness
are."

Disillusioned with an approach that invariably lands us in
Queer Street, many philosophers have taken the "subjective
approach." In this view, the sharp distinction, between
values and such subjective relations as "desired" or "approved," which is insisted upon by the subjectivists, is
denied. Despite obvious weaknesses, which in their turn the
objectivists have not failed to indicate, the subjective approach has its points. For one thing, it stresses the obviously
close connection between "desirable" and "desire," and between "value" and "satisfaction." For another, it also appears
to provide an intelligible account of the genuine variations in
the ethical judgments and standards of persons who are in

other respects equally well-informed. Nevertheless, it has its
own fatal flaw, for it is incapable of accounting for what we
actually mean by a "good reason" for desiring or approving
something as distinct from a "reason" which merely causes us
to desire or approve it. In a word, the subjectivist inevitably
blurs the distinctions between obligation and inclination and
between what Hutcheson called "justifying" and "exciting"
reasons.

We are left, therefore, with our central question still unanswered: "What makes an evaluative inference valid or invalid, relevant or irrelevant?" Both the objectivist and the
subjectivist fail to provide an answer because they both assume that ethical judgments can only contradict each other if
they refer to an objective property of the object in question,
and that unless they do refer to such a property, they must
express some psychological state of the speaker, in which
case no significant contradiction can possibly arise. But why
should we assume that these are the only alternatives? It is
just this assumption which is challenged by the "imperative
approach." In this view ethical judgments are essentially disguised commands, and they oppose one another simply as
conflicting prods to action. Like the other approaches, however, the imperativist accepts without question the thesis
that there can be no question of validity which is not strictly
factual or, in the narrow sense, "logical." Accordingly he
regards the whole question of "justification" in ethics as
senseless. Commands cannot be logically derived from statements of fact; nor can they be intelligibly said to be verifiable as true or false. Hence the only "reasons" which can be
given for obeying them are purely "exciting reasons."

The flaw in this approach is that it fails utterly to comprehend that, whereas in the case of ordinary commands arguments *are* logically irrelevant, this is not so in the case of
particular moral judgments. In the latter case, it is always
"reasonable" to ask why we ought to do what they prescribe.
And what we want is not just any answer that will "do the
trick" of causing us to agree with the speaker, but a real reason for agreeing even when we do not agree.

Toulmin himself is a pluralist in the sense that he believes (as I think, correctly) that the sense of ethical terms tends to shift with its context. There are occasions when "Good!" may mean little more than "Hurrah!" But, especially when we are pressed for an explanation or justification, the sense of ethical terms gradually shifts to something which is more "objective" or impersonal.

The conclusion which Toulmin reaches in the course of an ingenious and frequently convincing analysis is that while there are important analogies between the functions of reason in science and in ethics, there are also some significant differences, which indicate essential differences in the functions of the two types of discourse. Both are concerned, in some sense, to distinguish between appearance and reality; but what counts as "real" is very different in the two spheres. In ethics, the purpose of judgment is not to correct our mistaken identifications and expectations but to alter our sentiments and to correct our behavior. So far Toulmin roughly agrees with the imperativists. But he also recognizes, as the latter do not, that something of which we express our approval may not be "really good."

There are two ways in ethics, according to Toulmin, of showing another person why, as we say, we really should not perform a certain act: (*a*) we may explain that the act contravenes some part of the customary moral code of the community to which he belongs; or if this fails, we may (*b*) further explain that the consequences of the act would be likely to cause other members of the community some serious inconvenience or suffering. These types of "reason," says Toulmin, simply "cry out" to be called "moral." And surely he is right. Notice, however, that he is not saying that "good" is descriptively synonymous with "approved by the community" or "conducive to happiness." Rather he is asserting that when we attempt to provide a relevant reason for a particular moral judgment only two main types of supporting argument are regarded as ethically valid.

In this view, an immoral person is primarily and literally an outlaw. To advocate, as Nietzsche prescribed, living be-

yond "good" and "evil" is simply to declare oneself in effect
impervious to the kinds of reason which morality acknowledges. In principle, one might be none the less kind or benevolent for all that. But Toulmin also recognizes that, at
least in "open" societies, there is a legitimate ethical procedure for criticizing the moral code of the community itself.
And he sees that breaking the moral code must be sharply
distinguished from disinterested moral disapproval of it. It is
important to recognize, however, that when one questions
whether an act which is in fact prescribed by the prevailing
moral code is really right, one is going outside the normal
ethical universe of discourse of one's community. In such a
case one is challenging not the propriety of some particular
act, but the whole moral code itself.

Even though this sort of challenge is morally permissible,
at any rate in open societies, there are clearly limits to the
questions which may be validly asked about the right and
the good. Thus if someone should ask as a matter of principle, "Why should I be moral?" there just is no valid answer to
the question. As Toulmin says, there is simply no room
within ethics for it. It resembles nothing so much as the com-
pulsive "Why?" of a child, who will accept no valid explanation that we can give. For this reason, Toulmin thinks that
"philosophical" attempts to justify morality as a whole by
referring it to some ulterior metaphysical "ground" are bound
to be pseudo-explanations. Like attempts to justify our belief
in the external world or in the existence of other selves, they
invariably pass beyond the bounds of sense, precisely because we have no notion of the kind of reason which would
constitute a valid answer.

And yet Toulmin, in the manner typical of the younger
members of his school, does acknowledge the importance of
what he calls "limiting questions," irritating and misleading
as they often are. Psychologically they help us to adjust to
the world, just as the explanations of science help us to
understand it. He recognizes, in short, that there are profoundly important human problems which pass understanding.

ON SAYING WHAT CAN'T BE SAID IN ETHICS

Just at this point, however, certain general doubts about the adequacy of Toulmin's analysis begin to obtrude. If he is right, then limiting questions about the merits of morality as a whole or about the correctness of moral reasoning as a whole necessarily involve an abuse of the ordinary language of conduct. Hence, while he grants them a certain psychological significance, he is obliged also to regard both the questions and the answers we may make to them as lacking in any literal, rational sense. That is to say, they make sense, according to him, only in the way a tic or a fetish makes sense to a scientific observer who understands it as a symptom of some psychological ailment. But they make no sense as ethical questions and answers, since, on Toulmin's account, they seek to say what can't be said. As it happens, they involve the use of words, but they do not employ the words in question as words, just as eating peas with a knife involves the use of a knife, but not the use of it as a knife.

I am convinced that such a view of the matter cannot be sustained, either as a theory of moral discourse or as a partial theory of the common language of which moral expressions are a part. Let us first consider the latter point. Now we may agree that when philosophers become involved in general category mistakes, as they do when they treat ethical predicates like "good" as names of perceptual qualities like "warm" or "yellow," they systematically misconceive and misrepresent the linguistic function of moral judgments. But it is not at all clear that such mistakes are involved when we ask limiting questions. In such cases, it seems rather that we are merely extending the application of such terms as "good" and "right" beyond certain contexts in which they are familiarly employed. What is involved here is not so much the confusion of expressions of one logical type with those of another, but rather the application of terms of a certain type in circumstances for which there are, or appear to be, no well-defined precedents. Now it may be granted that in stretching the application of a term in this way we may temporarily lose our logical bearings. And when this fact is pointed out we may find that we no longer are so ready to press our questions to the limit. But this is not inevitable. Toulmin's theory of language evidently assumes that the rules governing the use of ordinary expression are normally both clear cut and consistent. It does not reckon with the facts that such words as "good" are, as Stevenson has reminded us, exceedingly flexible and vague (that indeed is their merit), and that although in context we may give them as much precision as is necessary for particular practical purposes, the general rules governing their uses are entirely permissive in this regard. In short, while we may contextually reduce the vagueness of "right" or "good" for purposes of discussion, we may also, if we so wish, avail ourselves of that very vagueness in order to say certain very big or even sublime things with respect to which it is perfectly appropriate. Limiting questions are vague no doubt, but it does not follow from this that they make no literal or rational sense. But even if they make no literal sense, it still would not follow that they make no sort of linguistic sense or that there can be no discursive reason to ask them. For taking our ordinary language as a whole, the rule is not that we must always speak literally or that we must always remain well within the bounds of our commonsensical applications of words, but, on the contrary, that we may, by analogical and metaphorical extension, press them into use in order to say many things of which common sense may not approve and of which normal, literal-minded people, as it happens, have no reason to speak.

The fact is that the great talk of poets, moralists, divines, and philosophers is nearly always abnormal in some respect. It is intended, however, not necessarily for abnormal persons who have lost their minds, but for normal persons in those outsized circumstances in which both language and every other human resource are put on the stretch. Nietzsche said that God is dead. Now I can well imagine that a common-sense, ordinary-language theologian of Toulmin's stripe might reply that since, by definition, God is eternal, Nietzsche's utterance transcends the bounds of proper theological discourse and hence makes no literal, rational sense. Yet we all do understand Nietzsche, and, what is more important, we also understand him to be saying something of profound interest and importance for our culture. There is, of course, a sense in which his remark is paradoxical, but just because of this it conveys the point Nietzsche wished to make more poignantly and powerfully than a dozen pages of careful, literal discussion of the atrophy of traditional religion.

I am not suggesting that it is impossible to talk sheer nonsense. If I should say that the square-root of minus blue is a close friend of my mother, I would be talking gibberish, if only to prove a point. Nor am I denying that there may be an important philosophical point in saying that statements of a certain sort are nonsensical, even when with some ingenuity we might find a small logical needle in the linguistic haystack. A good deal of metaphysical discourse, although not gibberish, says obscurely and portentously what is hardly worth saying when we boil it down. And the same is true of much "philosophical" ethics which merely tells us in an elaborate, roundabout way that on the whole honesty is the best policy or that those who ignore their obligations may come to grief. But not all of it is so. When Kierkegaard talks of "suspending the ethical" he is saying something which I find it necessary to construe, but whether or not in the end I am prepared to follow him in this regard, it is plain to me that he raises a profoundly important question which I cannot ignore and which I am bound to try to answer. The trouble with Toulmin's philosophy of language, it seems to me, is that, while it admits that we can ask limiting questions, it apologizes for and hence downgrades them in advance by making them appear to be, strictly and "rationally" speaking, meaningless. In so doing it ironically creates a contempt both for ordinary language and for reason, which is precisely the opposite of its own intention. It seeks to protect our work-a-day ethical establishment by throwing over it a cloak of built-in linguistic and logical respectability which no morally well-spoken person can wish to tear asunder. It succeeds, however, only in disposing moral "outlaws," like Nietzsche, to go beyond good and evil and to abandon all pretense to coherent, rational criticism.

ON THE MEANINGS OF "ETHICAL" AND "MORAL"

This brings me to certain questions about the adequacy of Toulmin's account of the use of the language of morals in more ordinary contexts. One such doubt concerns his delimitation of the logical use of the words "ethical" and "moral" as applied to judgment. According to him, the function of an ethical judgment—what it is that makes us call it "ethical"—"is the fact that it is used to harmonize people's actions. . . ." [3] But this is surely false, even on his own account. For he admits that there are at least two levels on which ethical judgments are made: (*a*) the level on which we judge the rightness of particular actions which fall naturally under some rule prescribed by our moral code; and (*b*) the level on which we judge the merits of the social practices of which such rules are the leading parts. On the first level, we are normally precluded, according to Toulmin, from asking directly whether a particular action as such would increase social harmony so long as there is an appropriate covering rule which prescribes the action as a moral duty and so long as its performance does not involve us in a conflict of duties. [4] In short, many, perhaps most, ethical judgments are regarded simply as straightforward rule-determined assertions about the rightness of particular actions, which, on Toulmin's account, are commonly supported merely by properly classifying the action as of a sort that the moral code prescribes as a duty. With respect to them there need be—indeed, if he is right, there *can* be—no thought on the part of the judge about the tranquillizing effects either of his judgment itself or of the action whose rightness is in question. But even when we turn to moral judgments concerning general social practices, it does not appear at all obvious that such judg-

[3] Ibid., p. 145.
[4] Ibid., p. 146.

ments must always be made with a view to increasing social harmony. On the contrary, it seems entirely possible to judge ethically that, on the whole, a certain practice should be kept intact even though its modification would reduce social conflict, on the ground that the practice itself has such great intrinsic value that it overrides any inconvenience or disharmony resulting from its observance. Moreover, it is also proper to judge ethically that a certain practice should be modified, not because the practice as it stands makes for conflict and disharmony, but simply because it is unfair or because it unnecessarily restricts the freedom of its practitioners. In a word, while social harmony is, for most of us, an important moral good, it by no means provides the only criterion for all moral judgments, much less the definitive one.

Unless I am mistaken, Toulmin is attempting, unwittingly, to write his own utilitarian standards of ethical propriety into the very use of such expressions as "ethical judgment" and "moral judgment." To this extent he himself is confusing a question of usage with a question of morals, or, better, he is confusing a question of common or ordinary usage with a question of proper or correct usage which itself can only be settled on moral grounds. On those grounds, however, there is little to be said for his view. For, to put the point in the bluntest possible way, to convert utilitarianism from a substantive moral philosophy, as Mill envisaged it to be, into a semi-logical truth even about moral reasoning concerning social practices would be at once to trivialize utilitarianism and radically to constrict the area within which substantive moral reasoning may occur. For my part, I would not, even if I could, write my own moral convictions into the very language of morals precisely because this would reduce my own subsequent freedom as a moral critic and agent. Toulmin, in effect, is trying to make the rules that govern the usage of ethical expressions do his own moral chores for him. To this extent he is also trying to reduce the area of his own responsibility as a moral judge. I believe he cannot succeed; but if he could, I would deplore the result, if for no other reason than simply that it would convert his own moral life into a kind of game. Where morality is thought of, as it sometimes is, as a matter of "playing the game," immorality automatically becomes a matter not of conscience but of taste, and those whose tastes run in other directions are then at liberty to play an entirely different sort of game, or else to play as they please according to no rules at all.

Here we come within sight of a fundamental error in Toulmin's analysis which is reflected in his facile tendency to equate the terms "ethical" and "moral" as applied to such things as judgments, codes, arguments, and practices. It is a tendency, I may add which is none the less mistaken because of its prevalence among contemporary moral philosophers.[5] Now it need not be denied that in certain contexts, the meanings of the words "ethical" and "moral" overlap in such a way as to make it extremely difficult to distinguish them. Nonetheless, each has distinctive connotations, more clearly apparent in other contexts, the confusion of which can lead only to radical misconceptions of the language of morals.

Suppose, for example, that we were asked by a novice in the use of ordinary language for a clear case of an ethical code. One perfectly natural answer, I think, would be to mention the traditional professional code of physicians embodied in the Hippocratic oath. Suppose then that our novice went on to ask whether that code is also to be called a moral code. To this it is entirely possible, or even likely, that we would say yes, since many of the rules embodied in the Hippocratic oath are similar to, and may even appear as mere corollaries of, certain moral principles which we ourselves accept. Suppose, however, that we were also asked for a clear case of a moral code. Now I admit that we might be tempted to reply by citing once more the Hippocratic oath. Nevertheless, the temptation should be resisted. For while, at least in one sense, there may be clear, paradigm cases of ethical codes, there can be, at best, only exemplary instances of moral codes, since nothing makes any rule of conduct a moral principle save the conscientious belief of its adherent

[5] In other essays, I am frequently guilty of this error.

that he himself ought to live by it. The obvious reason why ethical codes are so commonly confused with moral codes is that the former often serve also as moral principles for certain individuals who hold themselves personally responsible to their demands and who therefore feel a sense of personal guilt when they violate such codes. The moral consciences of organization men seem largely preoccupied with the performance of duties imposed upon them as functionaries of the institutions of which they are members. But few men are, morally, merely organization men. And even within societies as well-organized and institutionalized as our own there may be men, such as Thoreau, who refuse on principle to regard themselves as categorically bound by such duties while at the same time having very high standards of personal conduct. Such standards, by hypothesis, are the rules of no ethical code; if there are such things as "moral principles," these are moral principles *par excellence*.

Now Toulmin's characterization of ethical codes and hence of purely ethical reasoning, so far as it goes, is not far from the mark. It does well enough, that is to say, as a general description of those rules which define what is regarded as "ethical behavior" among particular classes of men who are organized for certain particular purposes and who accept such rules as a condition of class membership. It also provides a description of the codes that determine what is to count as proper or good conduct in the various professions, in service organizations, and in such institutions as the family, the state, or the schools. But it does not adequately describe those distinctively *moral* codes which we have in mind when we speak of "personal morality." Such codes, even when they overlap the codes of various groups to which we may belong, are not, as such, systems of rules which we *must* accept as the members of any group, including the society of moral agents. For there is no such society, and there is no general code of morality to which every moral agent is beholden. A *moral* community, as distinct from any formally organized society, is merely a group of like-minded moral persons, each of whom is responsible to the principles of the group only insofar as his own conscience permits. In a word, no moral agent can be an agent of morality, and no mere agent of morality, if such there were, could possibly qualify as a moral agent.

However, the issue here goes beyond the verbal question of whether, without violating ordinary usage, we can speak of a general code of morality for the critique of social practice which by definition is binding upon every moral agent simply as such. It is whether such a code, even if it were possible, is, in the sense of the term with which we were concerned in the above remarks, morally binding upon us. For in *that* sense, no rule can be a moral principle and no code of "morality" can be a moral code unless the individual persons who adopt it believe, for their part, that they ought to live by it. Thus even if there were no linguistic oddity in speaking of a general code of morality, it would still be an entirely open question whether I or anyone else really ought to accept its rules. In other words, as individual moral judges and agents, we would still have to face the problem of deciding whether we ought to regard ourselves as functionaries of that public institution which some may call "morality." For us, what they call "morality" seems hardly a form of morality at all. And in saying this, we are testifying to a fundamental fact about the linguistic behavior of the word "moral" and its cognates.

Thus are we brought back, once more, to the "limiting question" of whether we ought to be moral. In one sense, which is not Toulmin's, that question may well be senseless, as Bradley long ago pointed out. But in Toulmin's sense, as it turns out, the question may not be so very limiting after all for anyone but that Golem of contemporary sociology, "the organization man." So choice a spirit as Thoreau would not have thought it so; for, like Kierkegaard's Abraham, he had long since "suspended the ethical" so that he might at last hear the small, still voice of his own conscience.

In conclusion, let me say a word about Toulmin's thesis regarding the alleged independence of morals and religion. As he puts it, "Where there is a good moral reason for choosing one course of action rather than another, morality is not to be contradicted by religion. Ethics provides the *reasons* for choosing the 'right' course: religion helps us to put our *hearts* into it. There is no more need for religion to compete with ethics on its own ground than with science on its: all three have their hands full doing their own jobs without poaching." [6] This point, Toulmin continues, "is sometimes expressed by saying, 'We believe God's will to be good, not because it happens to be *His* will, but because it *is* good'; and it only reflects the difference between the functions of ethics and religion. If an action were not right, it would not be 'God's will' that we should do it. Or again, if an action were not right, it would not be for religion to make us feel like doing it." [7] It must suffice here to say that the last telltale sentence of the preceding quotation clearly shows how far Toulmin is either from a sympathetic understanding of religious discourse or from a comprehensive grasp of its functions. To the man who believes in God, his religion does not simply make him "feel like doing" what he antecedently and independently knows to be right. Indeed, he may not recognize it to be right at all apart from the fact that his God prescribes it. Toulmin's own morality, like that of Mill, is plainly secularistic. And such a morality, despite the Church, is plainly possible. The interesting consequence of his view, however, is that it requires him to think both of morals and of religion in terms of specialized "jobs of work," which men of God and many conscientious moralists would consider merely ludicrous. There are some religious mystics, for example, for whom religion has nothing whatever to do with morals, not even in the secondary "backing up" role which Toulmin assigns to it. For them we do not even come within range of the religious life until the ethical life has been completely transcended. There are also many others for whom the "will of God" defines, in the practical sense of the term, what is to be accepted as morally right and proper. For

[6] Op. cit., p. 219.
[7] Ibid., p. 220. For a more extended discussion of this issue, see my essay IX, pp. 171-205.

them, it is quite true that if an action were not right, it would not, of course, be "God's will" that we should do it, but then, in their eyes the only reason for regarding any act as right is that God himself has willed it.

Once again, as it seems to me, Toulmin makes the mistake of confusing his own settled attitudes toward morality and religion with the ordinary rules that govern the usage of moral and religious expressions. It also mistakes the proper moral autonomy of persons for the illusory logical autonomy of something he calls "ethics" and "religion." What some of Toulmin's secularistic readers may not see is that the autonomy he offers them as agents of morality is a mess of pottage which "frees" them from bondage to an authoritarian God or church only in order to subject them to a system of supposed linguistic rules which they can escape, if he is right, only by following Nietzsche beyond the horizon of moral good and evil.

A New Defense
of Ethical Realism

The seemingly naïve title of Professor E. W. Hall's new work is both accurate and misleading.[1] It correctly reflects the author's unquestioning assumption that in some sense there are *values*. Indeed, Hall writes almost as though the emotive theory had never been conceived. Yet any prospective reader who supposes from this that Hall merely rings the changes on traditional ethical realism will be in for something of a shock before he finishes the book. Hall agrees that from one standpoint "value" is unanalyzable, and that value judgments are irreducible. But he takes this to mean something quite different from what Moore, for example, appears to have understood by it. Hall rejects even the formal model of descriptive sentences as a basis for understanding value judgments. According to him the latter have a concealed syntax which is different in kind from that of factual statements. They are also subject to distinctive validating conditions.

Hall admittedly never succeeds in defining the difference between fact and value. In his view this is not due merely to his own philosophical limitations, for in the end, he believes, the difference cannot be directly stated at all. The only alternative open to him, as an analytical philosopher, therefore, is to try to *expose*, as it were, the distinctive nature of value through a series of critical studies of other objectivistic theo-

[1] E. W. Hall, *What Is Value? An Essay in Philosophical Analysis* (London: Routledge and Kegan Paul, 1952).

ries. Criticism is thus an essential adjunct of Hall's method of analysis. Without it any attempt to characterize value as a unique ontological category, co-ordinate with fact, would be frustrated from the outset. By what might be called the technique of successively less misleading approximation, at each stage of which still another, more subtle categorical confusion is revealed, Hall seeks gradually to "induce" in the reader a firmer grasp of the delicate and complex difference between value predications and other forms of rational utterance.

The essential puzzle involved in the analysis of value arises from the fact that although value judgments do not assert any matter of fact, they somehow include an unasserted reference to fact, which is revealed in the locution "ought to exist." Strictly speaking, the answer to the question "What is value?" cannot be expressed in a correct language. Indeed, the very question itself, which Hall thinks "so eminently basic and eminently sensible," seems inevitably to mislead us into an implicit yet fatal blurring of the distinction between what is and what ought to be. Thus the dilemma. In a correct language, there is no answer to the question. The only possible answers must be formulated in ordinary language which invariably lands us in paradox. Yet the question still persists.

According to Hall, the difficulty arises not from the lack of an adequate vocabulary, but rather from the nature of value and fact, which are irreducible but indefinable features not only of the logical syntax of language but also of what there really is.

The resemblance between Hall's point of view in this regard and that of the early Wittgenstein is not at all coincidental. It is in full view throughout the latter sections of the book. However, I myself was rather more struck by the unanticipated affinity, which Hall himself appears not to notice, between many of his characterizations of moral discourse and corresponding views of certain recent neo-Wittgensteinian analysts in England. This similarity is all the more striking in that Hall regards the departure of the later Wittgenstein and his followers from what may be called the linguistic idealism and ontologism of the *Tractatus* as philosophically retrograde.

Let me try to make this affinity a bit more explicit. In so doing, I may better succeed in characterizing Hall's own position, which is a difficult one to try to summarize in a significant way. Since Toulmin has given us the most well-known statement of the point of view of the English school, I will use his work as a basis for comparison. First of all, then, ethical naturalism is not a live theoretical option for either writer. Yet there is a common rejection, based upon similar arguments, of ordinary objectivistic approaches which conceive value as a property. In effect, they both hold Moore to be right in what he denied, but wrong in what he asserted. There is a common sense also of the theoretical futility of trying to state precisely what the *meaning* of "value" is. Yet neither of them is prepared to follow the emotivists in concluding from this that value is a pseudo-concept. Neither thinks that value judgments can be properly explained as disguised forms of first-personal imperatives (though Hall toys with the idea that imperatives may be disguised forms of "normatives"). Both writers insist upon a sharp distinction between "psychological" questions concerning the causes that may induce us to accept a moral judgment and the "logical" question concerning its validity or legitimacy. There is a plain sense, they believe, clearly reflected in the procedures of ordinary ethical language, in which value judgments are "objective" and hence justifiable by an appeal to rules. This means that they reject Stevenson's psychologistic account of "disagreement in attitude" as an adequate account of ethical disagreement on its logical side.[2] It means also that there is common agreement that the notion of a "logic" of valuation is meaningful. Such a logic, moreover, is held by both writers to be fundamentally different in character from the ordinary deductive logic of the books.

But there is still another, deeper likeness which is as central as it is elusive. It consists in—how shall I put it?—a

[2] Hall himself has elsewhere given a searching criticism of Stevenson's analysis of disagreements in attitude.

covert anti-intellectualism which is at the same time committed to the defense of valuation as a form of rational discourse. Or better, and perhaps still more darkly, there is a
common underlying conviction that the defense of rationality
and objectivity in ethics must go together with a rejection of
any formal identification of factual and value sentences. For
at the end of the road of intellectualism and descriptivism in
ethics, however sophisticated it may be, lies moral irrationalism—and this whether the intellectualism be naturalistic or
non-naturalistic.

These remarks are not intended to detract from the originality of Hall's analysis. Quite the contrary. They are intended rather to place it in relation to other contemporary
discussions of the problems of ethics. I am all the more impressed by this wide area of agreement precisely because
there is so much difference between the respective writers on
more ultimate questions. In my judgment it is this area of
agreement which will provide the focal point for further
analysis on the part of analytical moral philosophers in the
decade ahead. It is veritably the new thing under the sun
which offers a plausible way out from the impasse of the
emotivist-descriptivist controversies of recent years. For this
reason, despite several serious reservations on specific points,
I am prepared to say that careful reading of Hall's book is
mandatory on the part of all philosophers interested in the
progress of ethical theory.

I will now mention one or two aspects of Hall's later analyses which bear upon some of my own basic doubts about his
position. One of the most suggestive and provocative parts of
the book is the section in which he discusses the possibility
that "value," like truth, may be a semantical predicate. In
this section there is an especially acute analysis of R. B.
Perry's interest theory of value which Hall interprets, by
deliberately stretching a point, as a kind of precursor of the
semantical predicate theory. This interpretation requires that
"interest" be construed as referring not to an organic behavior pattern, but rather to a distinctive referential aspect of
symbols themselves. So construed, the "object" of interest,

which is so puzzling in Perry's own account, is interpreted not as the potential *terminus ad quem* of such a pattern, but, somehow, as the referent of a certain unique mode of designation.

Such an interpretation, if it could be carried through, would have advantages even for Perry himself. In the first place, it enables us to make more sense of Perry's insistent reiteration that value is a relation into which things of any ontological status whatever may enter with interested subjects. It enables us better to understand how there can in some sense be value even when the *object* of interest, which is not the mediating *act* of expectation but its cognitive content, is never realized at all. And, since interest is distinguishable from cognition, it makes it possible to preserve in semantical terms, as a purely behavioral interpretation cannot do, a formal distinction between value and fact. For if Hall's interpretation be accepted, fact becomes the reference to a cognitive or descriptive sentence, while value is the designatum of a different sort of sentence which Hall calls, for purposes of contrast, an "interest" or "value" sentence. (This is not to be confused with Perry's own "interest judgment" which is purely factual.) [3] But at the same time, since every interest contains an implicit interest judgment, every value sentence, on this interpretation, would include an unasserted reference to fact. This would be advantageous since, if Hall is right, every value judgment asserts that something ought to exist.

Hall recognizes that such an interpretation is incompatible with many other things that Perry says. Above all it is incompatible with the latter's view that although "mediating" interest-judgments may be mistaken, interest as a whole is never so. For every interest, in Perry's view, there is a corresponding fact. This renders it impossible to say strictly that any interest or, to adopt Hall's new way of putting the matter, that any "value sentence" is in error. One presumably could say this, however, if Hall's interpretation were

[3] By "interest judgment" Perry means any mediating judgment which locates, identifies, or characterizes the object in which interest is taken.

adopted, although it is unfortunately still unclear, even so, as to just what the validating conditions of such a sentence might conceivably be.

In order to resolve this difficulty, Hall examines similarly reinterpreted versions of Ewing's view that value is the "fittingness" of an attitude to its object, and Brentano's neglected but suggestive view that value is the being of an object of a right love. In the end, however, he feels compelled to reject such views, even when interpreted as holding that value is a semantical predicate, precisely because of the fact, as he reluctantly admits, that in ordinary discourse words such as "good" are ascribed not merely to sentences but to things. If "x is good" is essentially an elliptical semantical sentence like "x is true," then it cannot be directly applied to the extralinguistic world. Such a limitation, Hall thinks, is fatal. And in order to overcome it, he tentatively adopts the position that there are "zero-level" value sentences which, however, are not true or false, but legitimate or illegitimate. "X is good" thus remains strictly irreducible and unanalyzable, but we can now also say, by analogy with Tarski's famous condition for any definition of truth, that "X is good" is legitimate if and only if X is good. The semantical term is thus "legitimate" rather than "good" itself. "Good" remains a term in the object language.

Here, however, a curious difficulty arises. All along Hall has seemed to hold, as against theories which treat "good" as a property, that the grammatical form "x is good" is logically misleading, and that properly interpreted it is an elliptical way of saying "It ought to be the case that A is xyz." It is this interpretation also which appears to substantiate Hall's rather obscure view, reaffirmed on several occasions, that value judgments contain an unasserted reference to existence. Now I am not sure that I clearly understand what references to existence are, whether asserted or unasserted. But so far as I do understand it, I confess that I do not see how Hall's translation of "x is good" contains either an implicit or an explicit reference to what there is. Or if it does, I should then like to know whether Hall could produce a declarative sentence of any sort which does not contain such a reference. More important, however, I fail to see how one can at once hold that "good" is a term applying to nonlinguistic entities and that "*x* is good" is an imprecise and misleading way of saying that "it ought to be the case that *A* is *xyz*." For this translation surely does seem to convert "ought," the word which now does the work of evaluation, into an explicit semantical predicate which ranges, not over nonlinguistic existences, but rather over statements of the form "*A* is *xyz*." This point is clinched, I think, when we observe that the sense of "it ought to be the case that. . . ." is itself very close in meaning to "it is good that. . . ."

Let me put the matter now in more summary terms. I do not see how "good" can be a term in the object language if "ought" is a term which ranges only over statements. On the other hand, it does not seem to me at all obvious that the term "ought" itself ranges only over statements. At the intuitive level, certainly, it is predicated not only of statements, but also, like "good" itself, of actions and persons. When I say that a certain action ought not to have been performed, clearly I am saying something about the action itself, and when I say that a certain person ought to do something, I am just as clearly saying something about him. Here, it seems to me that Hall's tortuous "categorial" analysis raises more questions than it appears to solve, and obscures as many points about ordinary moral discourse as it pretends to illuminate.

This point is related to another of even greater importance. Hall is never content merely to explicate the uses of expressions. Like the early Wittgenstein he is impelled also to invest their uses with a portentous power of ontological illumination, so that when we have unpacked the meaning of a form of words we have also disclosed at the same time an objective or categorial trait of being. The assumption is that forms of words are logical pictures which present the underlying structure of things in themselves and that if we wish to understand clearly what that structure is we must reduce our form of words to some basic standard forms of expression which are themselves irreducible. As Wittgenstein himself later came to see, this gambit is completely misdirected. Outside the Bible, language is not a means of revelation. Nor are there any forms of expression which are logically primitive in any absolute sense or which present the facts more perspicuously than all the rest. Linguistically and logically, we are always in the middle of things, and this being so, there is just no way whatever to proceed to the fringe which uniquely and unassailably mirrors reality. The aim of analysis is indeed to make us understand our ideas more clearly. But this understanding comes mainly to an ability to handle them more adeptly in doing the jobs of work for which they are fitted. Knowing clearly what an expression means is, at bottom, knowing how to use it correctly, and knowing how to use it correctly is not so much a matter of "seeing" or "perceiving" something but of being able to do something in a certain preferred way. In short, sentences are not pictures of any sort, but utterances which we make, either to ourselves or others, in order to get something done. Or, to vary the figure, the word pictures which they provide are not photographs or x-rays which copy reality but compositions, arrangements, forms of artifice, which we ourselves make in order to accomplish our own ends. And if the reply is now made that one such end may be simply to copy or mirror reality, then my rejoinder is that this largely misses the point. For making all allowances for the metaphors involved, it still remains a question whether a particular expression actually does serve the purpose of a copy and whether what it mirrors is anything more than the face that looks into it. In his later years Wittgenstein was apparently fond of saying that forms of words are and reflect forms of life. And this dictum seems to me to contain a profound insight. But its value is not so much ontological as sociological, not so much cosmological as, in the widest sense, personal and moral. No doubt the language of valuation reveals something. But, in my opinion, what it reveals is not a distinctive category of being, but a form of action and behavior. Or if it reveals a category of being, then we must completely revise our notions concerning the nature of ontology. For then ontology becomes a study of the forms of human existence—or conduct.

Thus, although I am sympathetic to the views which, rightly or wrongly, I seem to find Hall sharing in common with some of the younger English ethicists, I have grave doubts precisely at the point where he goes beyond them to say what he calls "the philosophical thing"—not that I have anything against philosophical things as such. In particular, I find the whole attempt to derive metaphysical categories from an exposure of "the" structure of human discourse not only a hazardous but an essentially wrong-headed venture. Here, if anywhere, is the quintessence of the ontological fallacy. To my mind, there is something essentially "queer" and paradoxical in locutions such as "there are particulars," "there are states of affairs," "there are properties," and—in Hall's sense—"there are values." It isn't that I wish to deny them. It is rather that I can't get the hang of them. I just don't know what sort of thing to *say* in reply to the question "Are there particulars?" It is like the embarrassment I feel when my young daughter asks "silly questions." I don't know how to answer the question, because I do not understand what sort of question is being asked. Perhaps all the ethical realist wishes to assert in the end is that valuative discourse is, in some sense, rational and objective, and that one can make significant mistakes in one's moral judgments. With this I agree. But if this is what he is saying he goes about saying it in a very odd and misleading way.

Hall evidently refuses to take the emotive theory seriously because it is incompatible with the objectivity which he rightly assigns to value judgments. Yet the whole tenor of his analysis implies that there is not merely a substantive but also a formal difference between factual and value sentences. For him, value sentences do not in any sense describe the facts of life; they are neither true nor false; their underlying syntax, if not unique, is at least very different from that of factual assertions. He strongly suggests also that whereas declarative sentences express beliefs, value sentences may

be thought of as "normatives," and that this amounts not
to a difference in what they refer to but in the very nature
of the way in which they "refer." He talks, indeed, as though
there were "modes" of reference, in much the same way that
other analysts now talk about "modes" of meaning. But
precisely because "referring" is ordinarily thought of as applying only to the terms of factual sentences, Hall appears
to be faced with a strange dilemma: Either evaluative expressions strictly do refer, in which case, despite his protestations to the contrary, he has in the end assimilated value
judgments to statements of fact; or they do not refer, in
which case all the talk about the peculiar kind of reference
involved in value judgments is simply a misleading way of
saying that their mode of meaning is nondescriptive, even
perhaps, in the narrower sense in which that term is now
used, "noncognitive." I submit, however, that one may defend
the objectivity of moral judgments without supposing that
its key terms must be construed as "referring" to anything at
all. The issue is no longer cognitivism versus the emotive
theory. Indeed, Hall himself suggests how "normatives" may
be construed as having a syntax and a logic without reducing
them to statements which are factually true or false. In this
way he helps to show how value judgments may be properly
said to be objectively validated without implying from this
that their primary function is referential.

One final comment. Now, as I have already admitted,
there is a sense in which every moral philosopher who seeks
to understand rather than merely to reconstruct the language
of valuation must begin as a "realist." That is to say, what
Hall calls "value sentences" are used to make statements about
matters about which plain men constantly raise questions of
validity and even of truth. Men do say things *are* good or
right, just as they say that things *are* green or hot or pleasant,
and when they do other persons frequently raise questions, which are not in the least odd, about the truth, validity,
or correctness of such claims. These ordinary, common-sense
features of evaluative discourse become linguistic anomolies
when such statements are regarded merely as alternative,

disguised ways of issuing commands or orders. We may go further: our sense of linguistic propriety is in no way strained by remarks about "the moral facts of the situation" or even by statements which assert that particular judgments do not "correspond" to such facts. These features of evaluative discourse demand explanation, and we must be grateful to the intuitionists for calling our attention to them year in and year out in the face of the prevailing tendency of the so-called non-cognitivists to ignore them or else to explain them away. I myself have also called attention to them, over and over, in my criticisms of the emotive theory and the imperative theory of ethics. But to call attention to something is not to explain it. And the "realism" to which it commits us in this case, although essential, is nevertheless pre-analytic. In the same way, the so-called correspondence theory of truth, although unexceptionable when taken pre-analytically, is simply useless and redundant when offered in explanation of the nature of truth. Of course true propositions must correspond to the facts, whatever they are; the question remains what it is to say this.

Fundamentally, then, I find Hall's analysis unilluminating. It serves to reinforce pre-analytic convictions or habits of speech, but it merely gives the illusion of explaining their import. In effect, it tells us only that when we say that something is good we really mean to say that it is good and that when we say this sincerely we do believe it to be a fact. It reiterates without clarifying the by now obvious point that in asserting that something is good we are talking *about* something, though what we are saying about it is also very different from what we say when we assert that it is heavy or big. Hall is free to say, if he likes, that what is involved here is a peculiar mode of reference. But this is not instructive. For now one has still to ask what reference in this or any other mode actually comes to. I can of course "refer" to colors, people, numbers, mythical heros, theories, and values, and I use words in order to make such references. The only interesting question, it seems to me, is what I am *doing* in making them. Once this question is raised, however,

it becomes immediately evident that in using words we are
not always making references. Referring is one important
"illocutionary" act, as Professor John Austin calls it, but it is
not the only one. Nor is it logically or linguistically more
fundamental than any other. It seems plain to me that
what I am doing when I commend something as good or
prescribe something as obligatory is not essentially "making
references": I am simply commending it or prescribing it. I
may also say, if I please, that in commending or prescribing a
thing I am "implicitly" making references to its goodness or
obligatoriness. But this gets us further and further off the
track and at the same time misleads us into supposing that
commendations, after all, must be nothing essentially but
references to queerish non-empirical entities.

Here, I think, the followers of the later Wittgenstein, as
well as some Oxford philosophers who profess not to follow
him, ask better and more helpful questions than the realist
Hall. Actually their questions are not particularly new.
Berkeley, Hume, and Kant asked some of them many generations ago. And, more recently, the pragmatists have turned
such questions into a veritable method of philosophical analysis. If I correctly understand them, both Peirce and James
insisted that if we want to answer questions concerning the
"meaning" of our ideas and if we want to give clear, decidable
answers to them, we must stop trying to inspect the "essences" to which our ideas or words presumably refer, and
observe what we normally do in trying to confirm or sustain
the propositions in which they occur. This does not imply
that the meaning of an expression is, in the sense in which
the positivists understood that phrase, its "method of verification." It does mean, however, that language is first of all
a form of *speech*, and that the only clues we have as to the
forms of actions which we perform in speaking and thinking
with words are the various activities and operations that
are involved in carrying them through. Like all realists who
cleave to their realism in attempting to make their ideas
clear, Hall leaves even their points of reference themselves
ultimately obscure. In fact he makes of reference itself an

ultimate mystery and the "objects" referred to in value sentences something beyond the power of human discourse to illuminate.

In the end, then, it strikes me that although the logic of Hall's own analysis forces him in spite of himself away from the descriptivistic reductivism which so seriously handicapped analytical moral philosophy in the twenties and thirties, he is still unable to enter the philosophical promised land to which his own suggestive study so plainly points the way.

A Revival
of Ethical Naturalism

Those for whom the life of reason is still an essential part
of what should be meant by "the human condition" will find
encouragement and refreshment in Philip Rice's distinguished book.[1] It should also produce a certain amount of
static in the ears of those fair-weather rationalists who have
been beguiled by the angel voices that are again calling
from reason's backyard. Rice is one unrepentant son of the
Enlightenment who has managed to remain loyal to its ideals
without in the least blinking the fact that on this side of
Paradise life can be very real and very earnest indeed. In
him the truly perennial philosophy, which Mill called the
philosophy of experience, has found another powerful exemplar and advocate. In these jittery days of existentialism,
neo-orthodoxy, and public philosophy, this very fact is an
intellectual and moral event of some significance. It should
help to dispel the prevailing illusion that seriousness and
intelligence are sworn enemies.

The biblical allusion in Rice's title is not accidental. He
underlines its point in his fine opening commentary upon the
ambiguities of the archetypal Genesis story; what follows
thereafter is, in one sense, merely an elaborate meditation
upon its underlying meaning. So to have conceived his subject was a stroke of genius that makes clearer than a hundred

[1] Philip Blair Rice, *On the Knowledge of Good and Evil* (New
York: Random House, 1955).

pages of apologetics the essential continuity of analytical ethics with the hoariest traditions of Western ethical reflection. This is Rice's lie direct to those opponents of philosophical analysis who would have us believe that "meta-ethics" is a frivolous game of words, played only for the laughs by rocking-chair linguists who have turned their backs upon the ultimate concerns of humankind. The logical analysis of moral discourse, as Rice conceives it, is a serious and exacting business. It is, in truth, only a more careful endeavor to answer questions about ethics that reflective men have been raising ever since Adam and his wife left Eden. To see such questions as, in part, questions about language is not thereby to dissociate them from the moral life, but to view morality, more accurately, as the primary symbolic form of social deliberation. Forms of words, said Wittgenstein, are forms of life. But if this is so, then anyone who is seriously concerned with the latter cannot be indifferent to the former. It was because he wished to know on what terms he must live and act that Rice was compelled to make inquiry into the nature and efficacy of moral notions.

Rice's point of view is plainly incompatible with that of the self-acclaimed disciples of Edmund Burke who yearn impossibly for a golden age of custom before sophists had taught the classes to mouth sceptical questions about the meanings of good and evil. These gentlemen regard themselves as realists. But the notion of a purely customary morality, untroubled by naughty questions about its own validity, belongs to the same limbo of philosophical and theological fictions that is inhabited by progress, the philosopher king, and original sin. Since Adam, ours has always been an open or reflective morality. Because of this, we have never really been able, even when we have been willing, to let Somebody Else decide for us what good and evil are. And because of this, we have never for long succeeded in avoiding the dialectical or, as they are now called, analytical questions about the meanings of goodness and moral obligation. The only serious question to be asked regarding any moral philosopher, therefore, is not whether he is engaged or whether the object of his affection is virtuous, but whether he has illuminated his subject and whether he speaks the truth. It is easy to become engaged; it is not hard to engage oneself to Virtue; the difficult problem is to understand why Virtue is so called.

But Rice's book provides a more eloquent defense of philosophical analysis than I can give. The only thing to say to those traditionalists and obscurantists who prefer conformity and commitment at any price to understanding is simply that it is better to be a Socrates, however unhappy, than a contented cow that chews its cud in accordance with something called Natural Law. It may do better to forestall another line of criticism which may come from some of Rice's own brothers of the more immaculate conception. Rice turned to the problems of analytical ethics, not because he was diverted from his proper vocation as a moralist, but in order to fulfill that vocation more adequately. Meta-ethics remained for him a means; his end, like that of Aristotle, was to live well. This conception of the function of ethical theory is not shared by all analysts, many of whom, unfortunately, have transformed a necessary distinction between the use and the mention of words into a pernicious bifurcation between human practice and philosophical theory. In doing this, they have also done the home-work of the firing-line philosophers for them.

Rice does not blur the distinction between use and mention. But he is aware, as some analysts are not, of the feedback, the effect, that is, of talking about his talk upon the talking animal. An excellent example of this phenomenon has lately been provided us by Walter Lippmann, the well-known public philosopher. Mr. Lippmann is not the most meticulous analyst of his age, but he has very strong convictions about the nature of good and evil and the source of the moral authority. His meta-ethics, for the most part, is a somewhat attenuated version of the doctrine of natural law which Locke inherited through Thomas Aquinas from the Stoics. What is significant, however, is not so much the question whether that doctrine will bear scrutiny. That question may have been settled by Hume in the Third Part of his *Treatise*. More important is the fact that Lippmann uses the theory as a prop for his own highly conservative ideal of "civility" and his anti-utilitarian conception of the whole duty of man. But Lippmann is not the only philosopher whose feed-back has been working overtime. The same is true of the followers of Bentham and Mill, whose intended reforms in the theory of morals and legislation merely had the effect of determining the practice of liberal moralists for over a century and a half.

In short, theories of practical reason invariably turn out to be something more than diagnoses of moral discourse. They are, also, willy-nilly, reconstructions of second-level attitudes which govern the actual validation and justification of moral judgments. No doubt they sometimes contain their grains of truth; in that event, they can tell us something important about ourselves that we ought to know. But they have a strange way of making themselves come true, just to the extent that we take them as models of propriety for practical reasoning. There is nothing mysterious about this. Everything, we have been told, is what it is and not another thing. But it is also true, on occasion, that things turn out to be what they seem. A rose is a rose; it only needs to be. But we, it happens, are not roses. We fancy ourselves to be creatures of a certain sort, and then fashion ourselves accordingly; or else we imagine that we have a certain nature and destiny and then conspire against destiny in order to prove that we have no nature. In saying this, I should not wish to give more comfort than necessary to the existentialists. Like the rose, man also has a nature of sorts, but it is mainly an acquired characteristic which we impose through our talk upon one another. Whether the images of man that Freud, Jung, and Marx have created bear much resemblance to their original is, as we say, a nice question. Meanwhile, the rest of us have been helping them out by taking on an Id, a racial unconscious, and even membership in one of the social classes. It was for just this reason, as I remember, that Plato thought it undesirable that the truth about man should get around.

Rice's constant attention to the relations holding between
methods employed in the study of moral ideas and those
that are used in practical deliberation is the source of many
of his most searching criticisms of such opposing theories of
ethics as intuitionism. He does not believe that there is any
evidence for the supposedly simple and "non-natural" quality
which G. E. Moore, the father of twentieth-century intuitionism in ethics, identifies with moral goodness. But his
more serious objection to intuitionism is that it employs a
method of analysis which makes for dogmatism and mystifi-
cation in the conduct of life. Bad methods of analysis
produce mistaken theories, and mistaken theories result,
one way or another, in bad practice. Actually, there is an
interesting parallel in this respect between Rice's position
and that of Moore himself. It was from Moore that most of us
have learned the importance of distinguishing questions
about the meaning of goodness from those concerning the
things that in fact are good. But Moore distinguished these
questions because he believed that only if the former are correctly answered can the foundations of practical moral
science be securely laid. The trouble with erroneous theories
of "good" and "evil," such as hedonism, is that they invariably
result in faulty deliberation, bad judgment, and, hence, wrong
action. By mistakenly identifying goodness with pleasure, the
hedonists commit the "naturalistic fallacy" of confusing the
property of goodness with something else which may be common to the things that are intrinsically good. More important,
however, they thereby are prevented from raising the entirely rational question whether pleasure alone is really good.
It may turn out upon reflection, of course, that pleasure is
the only thing to which we can justifiably ascribe intrinsic
value. But even if this were so, it is still, for reasonable men,
an open question, and its answer should not be settled by
definition in advance of inquiry. In short, questions of definition are, particularly in the domain of ethics, questions of
the utmost practical importance. Taken at its own word,
analytical hedonism makes the open question appear silly by

converting the principle, "The only intrinsic good is pleasure and the avoidance of pain," into an apparently vacuous tautology. In the same way, according to Moore, those metaphysical ethicists who identify goodness with Being or Reality at the same time renounce the moral right and duty to ask seriously of anything that is, whether, really, it ought to be. And because of this, theoretical errors on the part of metaphysicians, from Augustine to Hegel, have been paid for heavily in each case in terms of spiritual confusion and disorder.

Rice, the naturalist, and Moore, the intuitionist, are thus both preoccupied with questions of method, precisely because they are aware that methods of analysis in ethics powerfully affect our basic attitudes toward moral deliberation itself. Each in his own way seeks to understand the nature, conditions, and limits of ethical justification in order that he may think more clearly about the problems of conduct with which they are both faced as human beings. Moore opposes naturalism because he thinks it deprives us of the ability to raise seriously the essential critical question, "But is it, after all, good?" Rice opposes intuitionism because it makes a mystery of the property of goodness and because it thereby removes moral judgment and deliberation from the sphere in which publicly observable evidence can be requested or given. In this way, despite Moore's intentions, intuitionism provides others with an escape into dogmatism and hence into irrationalism. For even if its "insights" turn out to be true, it has no way of showing why they are so. Rice's own rationalism, however, is not hypertrophied. He *believes in* reason, but he has no illusions about the reality of the surds of human existence. His only aim is to keep them from multiplying beyond necessity. The moral life, he is quite aware, is not wholly encompassed by the magic word "rational." It also has its non-rational dimensions of emotion and decision. The problem is to keep them from becoming confused, as Pascal and Rousseau confused them, with reason and knowledge.

Although he had an instinct for system which is in evidence throughout the book, Rice has not left us a fully worked-out system of philosophy. It is necessary, therefore, to reconstruct his views upon the larger questions of metaphysics and theory of knowledge from brief passages that are to be found in *On the Knowledge of Good and Evil*. But his moral philosophy is consciously formulated as the part and function of an inclusive world-view, and it is worked out in the light of a rigorous methodology. Rice's basic philosophy is broadly empirical in method and naturalistic, but not materialistic, in ontology. (It should be pointed out, in this connection, that Rice's ontological naturalism should not be confused with his "naturalism" in ethics. The two are consistent, but neither entails the other. The latter, as Rice understands it, is simply the view that ethical judgments sometimes contain factual information which can be verified by ordinary scientific methods, and hence that there are, in context, empirically discernible characteristics that function as the "Conferring" or "Identifying" properties of value.) As a metaphysical naturalist, Rice believes that what we call "nature" is a self-contained system of phenomena that operates according to immanent laws without miraculous intrusions from any supernatural realm outside it. As an empiricist, he is committed to the "method of experience," as he calls it, reminiscently of Mill. For him, all justifiable beliefs, whether in ethics or in any other sphere of knowledge, rest, directly or indirectly, upon observation. However, these theses are not held by Rice as unarguable dogmas. He arrived at them, painfully, only after prolonged study of their major alternatives. Even when, in the end, he could not accept them as they stand, he strove to discover their underlying rationale and to utilize what concealed truths they might contain.

Rice's method and ontology were stern task-masters. They permitted him no easy recourse beyond experience in order to justify his conviction that there is knowledge of good and evil. His results are all the more impressive, in fact, precisely because of this. Since his findings do not depend upon the disclosures of a special faculty of intuition or insight, others may verify his findings, at their leisure, by garden-variety methods that should be accessible to any person who is willing to use his headpiece. And because he does not claim privileged access to the revelation of a supernatural authority, it is not necessary to undergo a conversion in order to agree with him.

As a naturalist in ethics, Rice has a much tougher job on his hands than did his predecessors. It scarcely occurred to John Dewey or to R. B. Perry, perhaps the two most distinguished of the older naturalists in this country, that the search for definitions of "good" and "ought" might come to nothing more, finally, than the conclusion that these words are not terms of knowledge at all. Apart from intramural disputes regarding the particular empirical property with which good or value is to be identified, the older naturalists had nothing more to contend with, or so they supposed, than the accursed intuitionists with their everlasting open question, "But is it good?" But what if there is no property of goodness, and what if "good" literally designates nothing at all? Since Hume, naturalists and intuitionists alike have been puzzled by the nature of the relation between the "ought" and the "is"; but perhaps the difficulty does not lie in anything more recondite than the fact that judgments of value and obligation are not statements of any sort, but are merely expressions of emotion. In short, what if there is no such thing as the knowledge of good and evil, and if moral discourse is merely a highly stylized device for venting and irrigating our attitudes?

When Rice himself first began to write on the theory of value, such questions as these had not been seriously considered by most moral philosophers in this country. His own earlier papers, which appeared intermittently in the professional journals for nearly a score of years, reflected the then prevailing assumption that there is an objective property of value, the only serious theoretical problem being to define it correctly. In recent years, however, this problem has been found to be egregiously question-begging. Advanced discussion, therefore, has shifted radically from the ancient debate between the naturalists and intuitionists over the definability of "good" to a new and far more crucial argument between the "cognitivists" or "descriptivists," who continue to believe that there is a property of goodness, and the "emotivists" who hold that "good" is not a descriptive term and that value judgments have a merely expressive and incitive function. Rice himself remains a cognitivist, but with a vital difference. He still believes that there are ethical beliefs as well as ethical attitudes, and that ethical propositions are empirically verifiable. But he now faces head-on, with no lingering trace of question-begging, the challenge of the emotive theory. Because of this, his own naturalistic or quasi-naturalistic moral philosophy has been immeasurably strengthened.

Rice is a skillful strategist. Realizing the essential elements of truth implicit in the emotive theory, he very wisely prefers to lose the opening battle in order to win the final campaign. He acknowledges from the outset, therefore, that what he calls the "matrix meaning" of ethical terms is non-cognitive. The primordial common role of "ought" and "good," which he refers to, suggestively, as their "trigger function," is not that of describing the character of an act or of its result, but rather that of expressing the fact that a decision has been reached or of signalling the release of a contemplated line of action. No emotivist has described more carefully this performative dimension of moral discourse, and none has explained more clearly why it cannot be reduced without remainder to the descriptive dimension.

However, there are pervasive differences between moral judgments that prescribe what we ought to do and simple first-personal imperatives that tell us, without ado, to perform an act. In clarifying them, Rice already shows how far removed is his theory from the cruder forms of emotivism. In the first place, moral judgments are expressed, as a rule, with a characteristic tone or accent which is at once deliberate and judicial. Reflecting upon this, we are made to think at once, not of someone giving orders, but more of a judge instructing the jury or delivering a sentence after the verdict. The point is that in moving from the simple imperative to the moral judgment, we are aware, so to say, of a shift in "voice." In the former case, we speak to someone for ourselves and on our own authority; in the latter, we speak more impersonally, and the fact that it is we, Stan Spatz or Joe Doakes, who happen to voice the judgment is felt to be irrelevant. The language of morals enables us to voice claims that are taken by both parties to be "objectively" binding upon all moral agents. There are also tell-tale grammatical and syntactical differences between moral judgments and ordinary commands. Commands are expressed, characteristically, in the imperative mood, whereas ethical discourse employs the indicative. For this reason it is nonsense to inquire about the truth of "Pass the cigars," but entirely natural and proper to ask whether "Pleasure is the only intrinsic good" is true. It is no accident that generations of moral philosophers, however mistakenly, have adopted the model of factual statement in analysing the meaning of moral judgments. For if these grammatical and apparently logical features of moral judgment make no difference, at bottom, to what is asserted through them, why then should they exist? Were such judgments merely concealed imperatives, moral discourse could be eliminated without serious loss. In that case, one would suppose, it should be eliminated, since it serves only to mislead not only philosophers, but even ordinary men, as to what is being said. In short, the emotive theory makes of moral discourse a linguistic anomaly, at least for those who accept the sensible principle of analysis that natural languages do not, in general, multiply forms of words beyond necessity. Surely, then, the heavy burden of proof rests with those who hold, despite all this, that the language of morals is essentially the same in meaning and function as that of imperatives.

Rice thus contends that the grammatical aspects of moral discourse are evidence of its distinctive role within the wider domain of practical discourse which also includes commands, requests, invitations, oaths, blessings, and the thousand and one other special ways of doing things with words.

This role is distinctive, besides, in at least two fundamental respects, one of them having to do with the sorts of attitudes which moral discourse expresses or evokes, the other having to do with the mediating cognitive sets which it releases. As we have just seen, the attitudes incited through moral judgment are not those of immediate, unreflective compliance, but rather those of impartial scrutiny and deliberation. The conclusion to a train of moral reasoning is expressed in the form of a judgment, not of a decision or demand. To say that an act ought to be performed is by implication to vouch for it, impersonally, as worthy of performance on the part of any man. Indeed, this is the feature of moral discourse which Kant, who himself is responsible for confusing moral judgments with imperatives, so clearly understood, and it was for this reason that he could speak of judgments of moral obligation as rational, while insisting on an absolute distinction between pure speculative and practical reason.

But if ethical terms function as triggers of a certain sort, they are not merely triggers, but also sights. In this fact Rice locates the possibility of an unPickwickian knowledge of good and evil. By itself, as he says, the matrix meaning is empty and blind; it tells us to go or to be ready to go, but not where to go or how. It serves to prescribe, yet leaves unanswered the all-important question as to the characteristics that an act should have if it is properly to be prescribed as right or obligatory. But how are such characteristics to be identified? In Rice's opinion, they are to be found, in the first instance, in the ordinary lower-level ethical maxims which supply our conventional standards of right and wrong. These criteria are not explicitly mentioned in particular moral judgments, and unless some issue is raised concerning the rightness of a particular act, they remain implicit. The fact that they are there becomes clear only when the request for a justification is made and answered. Now if the emotive theory were correct, then anything that happens to set off the trigger of ethical terms could properly be said to justify our doing what moral judgments prescribe. With such a view, in which the connection between an ethical judgment and its supporting "reasons" is seen as entirely psychological, it is hard to see how it could be denied that if "All camels have two humps" caused you to agree that you ought to keep your promise, it would be as good a reason as any other. In practice, however, the justification of moral judgments is not so wildly open-textured as this. Not just anything that we may happen to say about an act is considered relevant in answering the question, "What features of a right act make it right?" Some characteristics of acts, as we think, make them right or bear essentially upon their rightness; others plainly do not. But how can this be, unless implicit in the very use of "right" are criteria that, in context, restrict its range of application?

Here is the crux of the matter, and in answering this question Rice seeks to make good his claim that, in addition to their distinctive matrix meaning, ethical terms also have a meaning which may properly be called "cognitive" or "descriptive." For if there are prevailing, interpersonal standards that govern the application of evaluative terms in particular contexts, so that in such contexts these standards are normally part of what is understood when the terms are used, it is not implausible to say that they are part of the very meaning of the terms themselves. Consider, for example, the use of "good" as applied to poetry. If the emotive theory were true, then anything we might say about a particular poem could properly be called a reason for regarding it as a good poem. But this is plainly belied by the common practice of literary criticism. The fact that a poem happens to express desirable political or theological sentiments does not, as we say, make it a good poem. And if some benighted critic should call it a good poem for such a reason he would be regarded as incompetent. The "as we say," here, is essential. What it suggests is that when applied in a literary context, "good" is ordinarily understood to have a very limited range of application. This range of application, in turn, presupposes a built-in standard of merit for literary works which is quite different from those standards by which we judge social policies or submarines. Such qualifying adjec-

tives as "aesthetic" owe their use precisely to the fact that
they serve to render explicit a frame of reference that is
already tacitly supposed, in the literary context, in the use
of "good" itself. Where there are such standard contexts,
although "good" functions as a trigger, it also functions as
a sight. Thus, although "good" is a term of praise or commendation, it also serves, in normal circumstances, to focus
our attention upon certain characteristics that are expected
and required of things so commended.

How such criteria have been acquired or modified is
another question. It is easy at this point, to confuse questions
of meaning or validity with questions of origin. Although
Rice is at times sorely tempted to justify certain validating
standards on what would appear to be essentially psychological grounds, on the whole he keeps genetic and logical
issues reasonably distinct. But, again, a distinction is one
thing; a bifurcation is another. Standards are not written up
in heaven; they are acquired, one way or another, by men,
and they are adhered to or broken for reasons that function,
psychologically, as causes. If a reason for doing something did
not in the least dispose us to do it, we would be hard put
to understand what might be meant in calling it a "reason"
at all. Because they wholly ignore questions of genesis, the
intuitionists are led, without knowing how or why, to talk
of "objective" standards of right action. Likewise the proponents of natural law tell us that there are certain "self-
evident" rights and duties that are universally binding upon
all rational agents; yet they leave utterly unexplained how
they are so, thereby permitting the skeptic, who happens for
the moment not to feel their moving-appeal, to deny the very
meaningfulness of such expressions. In Rice's view, the presence, within the language of morals, of contextual standards
for the application of ethical terms reflects certain prelinguis-
tic valuational habits that can be explained only in socio-
psychological terms. Such habits exist, but they are not
acquired at random. They are adopted, for the most part unconsciously, in accordance with empirical laws of learning
and motivation that describe the formation and modification

of human wants. Rice is an environmentalist. But in an interesting chapter, which he calls "The Appeal to Human Nature," he speculates upon the possibility of a congenital or, as he calls it, a "structural" *a priori*, which lies behind and gives efficacy to our linguistic-conceptual *a prioris*. In any case, whether there actually are certain built-in regulative principles of human thought and action as Kant believed, or it is just that we think them to be such because they have become second nature to us through social conditioning, the fact is that our maxims and principles are not bolts from the blue but the articulation of psychological dispositions to think and act.

Rice has many illuminating or suggestive things to say about the genesis and mutation of value-standards. His unusual command of contemporary psychological and social theory is in evidence throughout this part of the book, and it gives a decent firmness to reflections upon the nature of man that, in most other philosophers, tend to become impossibly speculative. Nowhere does he permit himself to go very far beyond the empirical evidence in the interests of theoretical order or for the sake of a unified explanation of the human tendencies which lie behind our ethical standards and principles. Above all, he refuses to succumb to the temptation, which has overwhelmed so many psychologists and social scientists these days, to convert a description of human practices into a moral law or to derive a justification of moral universals from a theory of underlying similarities in the social customs of different peoples. For Rice, as for Mill before him, the logical derivation of practical principles from theories of man or of society is always illicit. Rice's "naturalism" in ethics is thus always qualified by his recognition of the generic difference between statements about interest and expressions of interest, and between descriptions of human tendencies and the ethical prescriptions that are designed to guide or correct them. The "appeal" to human nature is of importance if what you want is an explanation of how standards are acquired or changed; it will not do, if your aim is to validate them.

Perhaps the most important feature of Rice's lengthy analysis of moral justification is the distinction he draws between the "good-making" characteristics which confer value of a certain sort upon a particular class of things and those identifying properties which, as he thinks, are "common to all things or acts of which any normative term, such as 'intrinsically good' or 'morally obligatory,' can be asserted." In an older philosophical tradition, the former were usually referred to as "virtues"; Rice calls them "Conferring Properties." The rules through which these properties are specified are to be found in the innumerable maxims, formulas, and grading schemes by which we regulate the assortment of practices and activities that answer to our special common interests. To list all of the Conferring Properties, or the rules that define them, would be an endless and unprofitable task. For what we would have, when we were done, would be nothing more than a catalogue of the innumerable ways in which things may be suitable or satisfactory to us. It would provide no illumination of the problems of valuation which confront us when excellence competes with excellence or when various virtues clamor for preferment. Nor does it shed light on the question of what we are to do when it becomes necessary to modify a whole grading system or an entire technique of conventional commendation.

The question arises, therefore, whether there are any interpersonal and super-ordinate principles of justification to which appeal can be made "objectively" when it becomes necessary to decide between rules or when particular procedures require modification. Rice is not content to settle, as some of his contemporaries have done, for the pluralism implicit in the job-lot of Conferring Properties. Nor does he admit that with them we reach the limits of objectivity and cognitive meaningfulness in the use of ethical terms. Beyond them there are certain justifying principles of intrinsic value to which appeal is made in justifying or criticizing the rules through which the Conferring Properties are specified. The characteristics defined or stipulated by such principles as essential to anything worthy to be called "intrinsically valuable" are called by Rice "Identifying Properties." It is in the discussion of them that one finds the closest tie to his earlier work and through this to the older tradition of ethical naturalism in this country.

For Rice, the fundamental problem regarding Identifying Properties is whether, finally, they are one or many. After much detailed analysis, which cannot be adequately represented here, Rice eventually concludes that there is only one such property. Following C. I. Lewis, who has greatly influenced Rice's thinking at this point, he holds that the basic normative category, intrinsic value, applies only within experience itself ("things" are only extrinsically good). He also agrees with Lewis that the feature which is common to all experiences that we would be willing to commend as intrinsically good is that "dimension-like mode" or range of feeling which we more or less inadequately designate by such terms as "pleasure" and "enjoyment." It is important to a correct understanding of Rice's theory, however, that the Identifying Property not be simply defined as pleasure. For none of the ordinary feeling words in English covers the entire mode or dimension of experience which is here in question. For Rice, every pleasure is a case of intrinsic goodness, but not every experience which exemplifies the Identifying Property would normally be spoken of as "pleasant" or as "a pleasure." When we try to make the word "pleasure" answer for the whole dimension, as the older hedonists have done, we stretch it unmercifully beyond its normal range of application. The result is the inevitable misunderstanding that has attended such forms of hedonism as Epicureanism and Utilitarianism.

Whether Rice's doctrine is classified as hedonistic is not important. It is very far, in any case, from those forms of "naturalistic" hedonism which regard "good" and "pleasure" as virtual synonyms. Nor is Rice's analysis, whatever its other faults may be, open to any of the customary objections that have been made, again and again, to the textbook varieties of hedonism. Rice never asserts that "good" is identical in meaning with any ordinary feeling word such as "pleasure," "enjoyment," "delight," or "satisfaction." "Good" always has a distinctive matrix meaning not possessed by any of these terms. And beyond this, none of them, as it stands, conveys all of what is meant by the "Identifying Property" of intrinsic value.

In his book Rice has become at once more sensitive to and more respectful of the proprieties of ordinary language than he was in his earlier papers, with the result that his whole analysis is now vastly more subtle and far more adequate to its subject. He is no longer tempted to cut Gordian knots by arbitrary stipulation or definition, and because of this he now rarely, if ever, misleads either himself or his reader by what are only apparent "clarifications" of the concepts whose meanings he seeks to understand. Most important of all, he now sees with far greater clarity the logical force of the arguments that have been raised against earlier hedonistic theories of valuation, including even that of Lewis. Rice's new respect for ordinary language indicates, I believe, an increasing influence of recent Oxford philosophy upon his thinking during his last years. This influence, I also believe, was wholly benign, and perhaps it was greater than Rice himself fully realized. The arresting parallels between Rice's theory of justification and those of such younger Englishmen as Toulmin and Hare are not accidental. Yet it is equally important to observe the points of difference between them. In the first place, Rice is far more tenaciously systematic in his thinking about the problems of ethics than are most of the philosophers of ordinary language. He does his proper share of detailed, piecemeal analysis in the book, but in the end he aspires to give us a comprehensive theory of valuation which will fit such analyses into an intelligible pattern of inter-locking hypotheses. Moreover, while he respects ordinary language he does not regard it as a symbolic paragon incapable of modification or improvement. As in the case of the Identifying Property of intrinsic value, ordinary language may not happen to provide terms of sufficient generality and clarity for the jobs of work that philosophers want performed. In that case, it is necessary to resort to jargon or stipulation if what one wants to say is to be said at all. Finally, Rice finds the somewhat easy-going pluralism of such writers as Toulmin, Hampshire, and, if I may say so, myself, essentially unphilosophical. And just as he will not rest with a plurality of basic principles of intrinsic value, so he refuses to accept the idea that there are peculiar rules of inference within the domain of ethical reasoning. The logic of morals, according to him, is no different from that of ordinary deductive and inductive inference; only its terms and the function of its principles and conclusions differ from those of factual or scientific discourse. Moral principles are not rules of inference, but premises of arguments. When so regarded, the supposed need for a "third logic" of ethics to cover the passage from factual premises to ethical conclusions entirely disappears.

It should not be inferred from this that Rice is unaware of the margins of vagueness and uncertainty that are inherent in all moral deliberation and criticism. He likes things to be as tidy as possible, but he is aware of Aristotle's wisdom in saying that in the ethical domain things are true "only for the most part." He believes that there is only one supreme principle of intrinsic value, and he thinks that it can be given a vindication of sorts. Yet he knows that moral principles, unlike stars, are not born but made, that their guidance is uncertain, and that they do not automatically apply themselves to particular cases. The guidance they offer for the conduct of life, when all is said, is hardly more than that of a basic orientation toward the solution of practical problems. They are not recipes for ethical cookery or doctor's prescriptions for what ails you. The philosopher, in Rice's view, "*cannot be finally convinced that the domain of values is chaotic,* that it will ultimately resist his passion for finding or making intellectual order." [2] But Rice does not blink the difficulties that stand in the way of moral order. Nor does he suppose that any particular philosopher or school of philosophy has managed, once and for all, to triangulate the good. His tentativeness, throughout the book,

[2] Italics in the text.

is only one more evidence of his own intellectual discipline and civility.

I, for my part, greatly, if also somewhat ruefully, admire the systematic unity and constructive power of Rice's moral philosophy. These are qualities that are all too rare in contemporary philosophical writing. Yet I would also be less than candid if I did not say that I do not always find Rice's own system wholly convincing as it stands. In one of the later chapters he argues at length against my own irreducible plurality of ethical principles. It has seemed to me that the principles of liberty and of justice impose demands upon us which sometimes conflict with those of the principles of least suffering and greatest happiness. Hence I have been unable, in recent years, to accept the thesis that there is only one Identifying Property which is essentially common to all cases of intrinsic value. And I have offered certain "hard cases" which are intended to show this. The tactics of Rice's reply are sound enough. He argues, first of all, that the notions of liberty and justice are not so clear as to enable one to be quite certain, in particular cases, that the principles of liberty and justice really do make demands which conflict with those of least suffering and happiness. This is true, but perfect clarity, in this sphere, is something which I, no more than Rice, aspire to. Vague as they undoubtedly are, the principles of liberty and justice express orientations toward social relations and individual life that have involved men of good conscience in fundamental conflict with the principle which he would have us accept as *the* principle of moral justification. What are we, in conscience, to do? Rice's whole theory of Conferring and Identifying Properties of value requires us to accept as given those standards which are interpersonally recognized and invoked by men within a common culture. Any appeal beyond them must of necessity be to individual conscience or interest. At that point, however, we pass, in one sense, quite beyond the bounds of "rational" justification to something else which can only be called personal or existential concern. If this is lacking, or is otherwise motivated, the appeal, rational or otherwise, is simply defeated. More bluntly, it becomes an apostrophe.

The issue here is fundamental, but it must not be misunderstood. Such conflicts of principle as I have mentioned are not external conflicts between competing systems of morals. They are not analogous, for example, to the conflicts which arise, at fundamental points, between Catholics and Protestants or between Fascists and Liberals. Rather are they internal conflicts that occur within a common semi-system, the one, as I think, with which most of us, including Rice, must try to reconcile our actions. If this semi-system constitutes for us what is to be understood by "rationality" in the sphere of conduct, I simply do not see how Rice can demand more unity and order than it provides in the name of "reason." If the philosopher cannot, in the face of this, restrain his passion for making order, then let him make it, but at this point he will have passed beyond the bounds of mere analysis or understanding, and, like Bentham, will have adopted the role of a legislator's legislator. He is free to do so. But he cannot then reasonably complain if the rest of us do not choose to ride down the king's highway on his hobby-horse.

It will have been observed that I am not denying that Rice's principle of intrinsic value is a valid principle. Nor do I contend that the principles of liberty and justice take precedence over it. What I am objecting to is merely the thesis that the dimension of "affective tone," as Rice sometimes calls it, is to be regarded as the only Identifying Property of intrinsic value. I say that we live in an ethical pluriverse, not a universe, and that as long as we remain as we are, Rice's Identifying Property will not be the only one to which "intrinsic good" is the trigger.

Rice's concluding chapter is called "Naturalism and the Tragic Sense." No other contemporary philosopher, naturalistic or otherwise, has better understood or faced more unflinchingly the inescapable tragedy of human existence. Like the great tragic poets, upon whom he discourses in his last pages with so much sensitivity, he finds in tragedy both a metaphysical and an ethical dimension. The metaphysical tragedy, if you like, is the extinction of life; the ethical tragedy arises from man's incurable finitude and the consequent waste of good. However, there is one aspect of Sophoclean tragedy which, as it seems to me, Rice does not adequately explain. In fact, I do not see how he could explain it, given his doctrine of intrinsic value. The tragedy of *Antigone,* in its ethical aspect, is not, at bottom, a tragedy of conflicting maxims that might perhaps have been removed, had Antigone or Creon been wiser, more selfless, or more restrained. Here, as Hegel pointed out, is the tragedy of spiritual self-division within the moral life which cannot be removed by an appeal to some higher principle of adjustment or harmony. In the case of *Antigone,* we are not faced with a case of routine wasted good or sacrificed virtue. Neither is it a case, such as we find sometimes in Aeschylus or in Shakespeare, of the universe being out of joint, so that man's deepest cry for justice, liberty, or mercy goes unheeded by the natural or, if it exists, the supernatural order. Nor, finally, is it a tragedy which can be fully comprehended in terms of Aristotelian flaws. All of these forms of tragedy are real enough, God knows. But beyond them there is that special and supremely poignant form in which the individual or the society is confronted with an internal conflict of principle for which the moral order provides no solution.

What this sort of tragedy teaches us is that while there is wisdom in the search for moral as well as intellectual order, there is also a kind of wisdom and integrity that comes from the recognition of the surds of the ethical life. The myth of Genesis embodies a second great archetypal situation in which Western culture has always been involved. Before the Fall, man lived innocently, in joy and peace, but without freedom and without dignity. In the one case, he was supremely happy, but lacked all sense of what it means to be a person; in the other, he acquired personality and the rights of conscience, and with them guilt and responsibility.

From the standpoint of the greatest happiness principle, the price that he has paid for these human prerogatives must seem exorbitant. From this standpoint, it is hard to see how the conclusion is to be avoided that, if he had the chance, man ought to return to Eden. But it is a conclusion which dies on our lips. For we would not buy felicity, for ourselves or others, if it required us to forego altogether the rights and responsibilities of freedom and justice. In another way, while we yearn for love, we demand respect, and if love is offered in place of respect, it is a sinful love which we must reluctantly oppose.

There are one or two other aspects of Rice's theory about which I also have certain reservations, but I must deal with them, now, very briefly. After several rereadings, I am still not wholly satisfied by his account of the relations between Conferring and Identifying Properties. In the first place, it does not appear to me that the relation between them is, as Rice himself suggests, a relation of the less to the more general. The difference between the properties that make things of a certain sort good in their kind and those which have to do with right action is of another order. Rice does not make as sharp a distinction as I could wish between those virtues of things which answer merely to specific interests such as gardening, fly-casting, and the selection of judges, and the standards which, even provisionally, prescribe what we think of as moral duties. There is, in brief, a functional difference between, on the one hand, forms of grading which establish the criteria for evaluating or commending things that answer to particular wants and needs and, on the other hand, the maxims which we call "moral," the role of which is to prescribe, in our dealings with other persons, our special duties or obligations to them. In justifying the latter, we do undoubtedly appeal to higher level ethical principles of intrinsic value. But it is not clear to me that such principles are relevant when questions are raised about the standards that are used for grading dry-flies or garden-hoses. It is only when we have to decide whether we ought to cast flies or to garden that questions of moral principle and hence of intrinsic value need arise. The grading of tools and the appraisal of specific "goods" are normally tied to particular activities and concerns which, as such, do not raise questions of conduct. It is for this reason, so far as I can see, that it is necessary to distinguish between ethics proper and the general theory of valuation. Certainly, Rice himself has recognized this distinction in his previous writings. I am inclined to think that he, like Perry, has drawn it in the wrong way.

XIII

History, Morals,
and the Open Society

In the year 1909, Thorstein Veblen summed up the method which at long last would transform the "sciences of man" from essays in ideal social mechanics or mere empirical agglomerations of "facts" into genuine sciences capable of arriving at laws of social behavior and development.

> In so far as modern science inquires into the phenomena of life, whether inanimate, brute, or human, it is occupied about questions of genesis and cumulative change, and it converges upon a theoretical formulation in the shape of a life-history drawn in causal terms. In so far as it is a science in the current sense of the term, any science, such as economics, which has to do with human conduct, becomes a genetic inquiry into the human scheme of life; and where, as in economics, the subject of inquiry is the conduct of man in his dealings with the material means of life, the science is necessarily an inquiry into the life-history of material civilization, on a more or less extended or restricted plan. . . . Like all human culture this material civilization is a scheme of institutions—institutional fabric and institutional growth.[1]

Here are the key concepts—"genesis," "cumulative change," "life-history drawn in causal terms"—the application of which,

[1] "The Limitations of Marginal Utility," 1909. In *What Veblen Taught*, edited by W. C. Mitchell (New York: Viking Press, 1945), pp. 162-3.

in the view of Veblen and his contemporaries, was to raise inquiries into human behavior from the "taxonomic" stage to that of "evolutionary science." Yet not four decades later, this same method, under the epithet "historicism," has become the flogging horse of advanced critics who regard it as a prime reason for the failure of social theory to achieve the status of genuine science. With the appearance of Professor Karl Popper's book, *The Open Society and Its Enemies*,[2] this revolt against "the historical method" enters into the stage of a full-blown war against all attempts to understand man and his institutions in terms of the "laws" of their historical development. But the enemy is no longer limited to latter-day historicists. Nearly the whole first volume of Popper's book is devoted to tracing in Plato's dialogues—and especially in the *Republic*—the reactionary moral and social theories in which germinated the central ideas of an "evolutionary science" of political and social change.

Unlike Professor John Wild, who has found in Plato's *Republic* the perfect anagram of the "good"—that is, the democratic, classless—society, Popper discovers there the perfect prototype of tribalistic collectivism. For Wild, Plato was the first to discern the true, rational, and natural order of things, the inversion of which leads to all the ills, spiritual and material, that flesh is heir to. For Popper, Plato's "Reason" is a reversion to the methods of "insight" and "prophecy" which are characteristic of pre-rational mythological modes of thought. Yet, ironically, both Wild and Popper, in their respective defense of and attack on Plato, regard themselves as defenders of the faith in free and rational society.

This antithetical partisanship reaches its climax in their contradictory interpretations of the "ideal" of the philosopher king. For Wild, this conception is but an idealization of that rule of reason and virtue which is the aim of all true democracy. For Popper, the doctrine of the philosopher king is a not too subtly disguised bit of propaganda on Plato's part for his own claim to kingly power in Athens.

In a polemical age it is perhaps not permissible simply to

2 4th edition (London: Routledge and Kegan Paul, Ltd., 1962).

sit on the sidelines and cheer. Let me say, then, albeit reluctantly, that Popper's caricature seems to me somewhat more recognizable than Wild's. For my part, however, I should prefer to remember the great dualist who gives us "the free interplay of ideas," each of which embodies a part, but only a part, of the truth. It is this Socratic Plato, for whom the polar ideals of order *and* freedom, unity *and* difference, personal integrity *and* collective security, individual conscience *and* public opinion, quality *and* quantity, all have their inviolable rights in any adequate social order. This Plato, I believe, would have seen Popper's antithesis of "open" and "closed" societies represent not simply a conflict of light with darkness, of good with evil, of tribalism with human dignity, but the complementary sides of one economy of values, which must include them both as counterpoises.

The liberal mind, in my opinion, has nothing to do with such inordinate and partisan zeal as Popper so frequently displays in his book. His method can only stultify the understanding of our intellectual heritage. Its aim is not merely to criticize and correct what are considered to be the lawful errors of one's fallible predecessors, but also to discredit them *in toto* by inference and innuendo. They are treated, not as "the loyal opposition," but, in many instances, as men ridden with ambition, as sycophants and mystagogues. Their doctrines are construed not as honest attempts at evaluation and understanding, but as deliberate obscurantism and intellectual chicanery. This is true of Popper's treatment of Plato and Aristotle. It reaches its climax in his treatment of Hegel, whom he regards, following Schopenhauer, not merely as an intellectual clown, but as a paid mercenary of the King of Prussia. Only Marx, of the major figures discussed, is recognizable as something other than an "enemy" in the literal sense. Marx was, Popper concedes, an honest man, a genuine scientist, and a true humanitarian. He was simply misled, by his addiction to "historicism," into unscientific formulations of laws of social development and ungrounded prophecies concerning the future of democracy and capitalism.

ECONOMIC PLANNING AND
FREEDOM OF CONSUMPTION

In the remainder of this essay I will concern myself no further with Popper's interpretations of the great historical figures mentioned above, since it is not with them but with the ideas they represent that the more interesting portions of Popper's book are concerned. I will discuss, instead, several of Popper's own theses which seem to me of great importance to contemporary social philosophy.

At the outset, it is well to call attention to an openly avowed relationship which is important for a correct understanding of Popper's whole point of view in social philosophy. This is his connection with Friedrich von Hayek, many of whose ideas find a close parallel in Popper's work. Popper acknowledges his indebtedness to Hayek in the "Acknowledgments,"—"without his interest and support the book would not have been published." It is not hard to see, I think, why Popper should have found Hayek such a determined supporter. Popper's objections to what he calls "Utopian engineering" are even more extensive than Hayek's criticisms of centralized or collectivist planning. Popper refers approvingly to Hayek's criticisms of such forms of planning on the ground that they "eliminate from economic life some of the most important functions of the individual, namely, his function as a chooser of the product, as a free consumer." [3] Popper's own criticisms in part also follow this line.

Nowhere, however, is there any sustained analysis of the alleged "technological impossibility" of a planned system of production in which there also would be "freedom of consumption." Popper ignores the point which many economic collectivists regard as essential, namely, that without organized and planned distribution of commodities the masses, in such countries as India and China, are often powerless to procure even the basic necessities of life. He also forgets that even in a "free economy" effective choice is often limited

[3] Popper, op. cit., Vol. I, p. 242.

to a selection of alternative labels rather than different types of product. Popper comments on money as a "symbol" of the open society.[4] Money, according to him, is "part of the institution of the [partially] *free market*, which gives the consumer some measure of control over production." [5] But he does not seriously consider the means by which a "free" economic system can secure a more equitable distribution of money so that the people may effectively and continually exercise the freedom of choice about which he is so much concerned. It is true that the Marxists fail to realize "the danger inherent in a policy of increasing the power of the state." [6] But Popper too easily passes from the idea of collective planning to that of a totalitarian or closed society. Moreover, when it suits his purpose he is quite capable of arguing, as he does here, in terms of the "essentials" and "inherent characteristics" which he finds so objectionable when employed by his opponents, whether Aristotelian or Cantabrigian.

THE CRITIQUE OF HISTORICISM

The central concept of the book is something called "historicism." Indeed, it is the exploration of the many-sided consequences of this idea which provides the book with whatever unity it possesses; and Popper's most serious objections to the major historical figures discussed [7] are based on their adherence to "historicist" principles.

The critique of historicism actually proceeds on three main levels: (*a*) an analysis of the effects of historicist assumptions upon the social philosophies of Plato, Hegel, and Marx; (*b*) an analysis of the usefulness of the historicist method as a means of deriving laws of historical development from the observation of social phenomena; (*c*) a discussion of the implications of historicism with respect to the

---

[4] Ibid., Vol. I, p. 266.
[5] Ibid.
[6] Ibid., Vol. II, p. 121.
[7] That is, Plato, Hegel, and Marx.

possibility of social planning and control. According to Popper, if we accepted the fatalism implicit in the historicist theory of laws of social development, we would logically be driven to deny the possibility of human choice and hence of the piecemeal planning and control of social forces in which, according to him, lies the salvation of mankind.

Historicism appears in its earlier (as well as some later) forms in the guise of the myth of the chosen people, selected by fate to inherit the earth, or to lead mankind to the classless utopia. Later it is transformed into the "scientific doctrine" that laws of historical development can be determined which will enable us to predict the future course of social change. Popper rejects both theistic fatalism and the later "scientific" historical determinism. Sweeping historical prophecies, he maintains, "are entirely beyond the scope of scientific method." [8] "The future," he insists over and over again, "depends on ourselves, and we do not depend on any historical necessity." [9] What Popper advocates is a type of social engineering which asks no questions about historical tendencies and human destiny. He believes that "man is the master of his own destiny, and that in accordance with our aims, we can influence or change the history of man just as we have changed the face of the earth." [1]

Here we may perhaps discern a certain ambivalence in Popper's position: We are the masters of our destiny, but only so long as we radically limit our conception of what that destiny is to be; we can predict and control in a limited way what will happen *next*, but we can not predict or control long-range social developments. In this way, as it turns out, there is a sense in which the historicist "utopian engineer," believing as he does in the possibility of long-range predictions and the desirability of long-range blueprints for distant objectives, has a more complete faith in man's mastery of his destiny than Popper has.

In what, precisely, does the basic error of historicism

[8] Popper, op. cit., Vol. I, p. 3.
[9] Ibid.
[1] Op. cit., Vol. I, p. 17.

consist? In order to make this clear, it is necessary to refer briefly to Popper's conception of causal explanation and prediction in the "generalizing sciences such as physics and biology." Causal explanation involves the framing of general hypotheses (universal laws) which, together with certain specific (or singular) statements of the initial conditions which pertain to the special circumstances of a given case, enable us to deduce a statement (prognosis) of what will happen to the case in question. The initial conditions are regarded as the "cause" of the event, and the deduced results are the "effect." Thus we can only speak of an event as a "cause" relatively to some universal law; when the predicted event is observed actually to occur, the theory itself is then said to be tested or confirmed. Now the pure generalizing sciences are not interested in the prognosis as such. They are concerned with it only as a test of some law or principle. In the case of applied science, however, the interest is in the prognosis itself. Hence the difference between "pure" and "applied" generalizing sciences is primarily a difference in *interest*. "Whether we use a theory for the purpose of explanation . . . or of testing, depends on our interest, and on what propositions we take as given or assumed." [2] It follows from this that applied generalizing sciences are concerned to predict specific or particular events.[3] It would seem to follow also that the interest of such sciences is, in part at least, historical, since according to Popper the so-called historical sciences are interested "in specific events and in their explanation." [4] Nonetheless, and this is the puzzling point, Popper tells us that "the sciences which have this interest . . . may, in contradistinction to the generalizing sciences, be called the *historical sciences*." [5] But how is this statement to be reconciled with his preceding remarks about *applied* generalizing sciences? To me, at least, the answer remains obscure.

[2] Op. cit., Vol. II, p. 250.
[3] Ibid.
[4] Op. cit., Vol. II, p. 251.
[5] Ibid.

He goes on, at any rate, to say that "from our point of view, there can be no historical laws." [6] Generalization simply belongs to a different line of interest. This seems to be the sole basis of Popper's criticisms of Professor M. G. White, whom he criticizes for neglecting "what has been described here in the text as *the distinction between historical and generalizing sciences,* and their specific problems and methods." [7] But such an exclusion, purely by definition, of "historical laws" is simply verbal. It sheds no light whatever on the employment of the historical method or the possibility of laws of development which apply to historical processes. It is also misleading, since it has nothing to do with other, more serious difficulties which Popper raises with respect to the *use* of history for the purposes of generalization and prediction. However, the two are constantly run together and confused in Popper's exposition.

In order, therefore, to distinguish between Popper's real and his merely verbal objections to historical laws, we must distinguish, as Popper unfortunately does not in any clear way, three different questions: (a) whether historical data can be trusted for evidence for social laws, historical or otherwise; (b) whether there are verifiable laws of development upon the basis of which we may predict future events (and confirm our laws); and (c) whether there can be what may be called laws of "unrestrictive scope" in terms of which all social processes may be explained. The denial of c does not entail the denial of b nor of a, nor does it render b trivial, as Popper suggests. On the other hand, the denial of a would, as we shall see, render a positive answer to both b and c impossible. But Popper's emphasis on the uniqueness, unrepeatability, and uncontrollability of historical data suggests, at the very least, that they cannot be trusted, and hence, as we shall see, that there can be no trustworthy social theories whatever. This despite the fact that he raises no doubts at all about the possibility of sociological,

[6] Op. cit., Vol. II, p. 251.
[7] Op. cit., Vol. II, p. 344. Cf. M. G. White, "Historical Explanation," *Mind,* Vol. 52, 1943, pp. 212 ff.

economic, or political laws, but only about laws of historical development.

(*a*) To answer the first question, it should first be pointed out that Popper nowhere denies that social theories can be successfully used by the historian in validating records and in ascertaining the reliability of historical data. Granted that the margin of error is always very considerable, it would seem that if they can be used at all, they can be used for the confirmation of "historical" or any other type of social theory. The trouble with such data is of three sorts: they can not be varied or repeated at will; they are always a very limited selection of all possible relevant data and are based upon the "preconceived" interests or theories of those who select them; and since no further facts are available, the testing of theories "will not, as a rule, be possible." [8]

These are serious charges, and I am sure most historians and social scientists would agree that they present very important obstacles to the verification of social hypothesis. But are they any more serious for historical theories than for merely social theories in economics, sociology, or politics? If "the so-called 'sources' of history only record such facts as appeared sufficiently interesting to record, so that the sources will on the whole contain only facts that fit in with a preconceived theory," and if "since no further facts are available, it will not, as a rule, be possible to test that or any other subsequent theory," [9] are not the consequences of this quite as devastating for one type of social hypothesis as for another? The charge of circularity in the case of historical theories would, if we agree with Popper, apply also in the case of sociological and economic theories.

According to Popper the facts in science are always collected with an eye upon the theory, but they confirm the theory "only if they are the results of unsuccessful attempts to overthrow its predictions, and therefore a telling testimony in its favor." [1] It is, he insists, "the possibility of over-

[8] Popper, op. cit., Vol. II, p. 252.
[9] Ibid.
[1] Op. cit., Vol. II, p. 247.

throwing it, or its falsifiability, that constitutes the possibility of testing it, and therefore the scientific character of a theory." [2] Popper does not deny that such possibilities are in fact open to the social scientist, despite his disparagement of the historical source material upon which all social sciences depend. Yet he regards this as a conclusive argument against historical laws.

(b) The second question, whether there can be laws of development, must, I think, be answered in the affirmative by anyone who admits that there are dynamic laws of society, i.e., laws of succession rather than coexistence. Whether such laws are called "historical" or "sociological" is a question of terminology. If such laws are, as they must be, largely based on historical data, and if they are used for the explanation or prognosis of other historical events, future or otherwise, then it seems not inappropriate to speak of them as historical as well as sociological. Popper himself explicitly admits that there can be sociological laws, even ones pertaining to the problem of progress.[3] But if this is so, then to argue that "we should better not speak of *historical laws* at all" merely on the ground that when we are confined to one unique process there can be no law of nature, or that history is interested in specific events rather than general laws,[4] is to quibble (inconsistently, as we have seen) about the use of a word. Why should it be assumed that all historical events are unique (i.e., absolutely different from all other events) or that the interest in generalizations and their employment in explaining historical events is beyond the scope of the historian? Such assumptions are clearly in flagrant inconsistency with what the historians have found and done. If Popper argues that it is not within the scope of the historian, as historian, to concern himself with such matters, then I reply that he himself is taking the "essentialist" position which he has so brilliantly criticized elsewhere in his book.

[2] Ibid.
[3] Op. cit., Vol. II, p. 306.
[4] Ibid.

(c) The third question, whether there can be a "universal point of view for history," can easily be answered in the negative. But it does not follow from this that the laws of society, historical or sociological, are not quite general. Popper seems to me to confuse the generality or universality of a proposition with its scope. For example, any proposition is general if it asserts that all of the members of one class are members of a second: "All men are mortal" is quite general, even though there are many things to which it does not apply. Such a proposition is limited in its scope in the sense that there are many things not explained by it simply because they do not belong to the class of men.

The "infinite subject-matter of history" doubtless renders it impossible to obtain hypotheses which are not of limited scope. Therefore, as Popper says, we cannot avoid a limited point of view in history; we must, that is to say, limit ourselves to "economic" laws of history, "political" laws of history, "military" laws of history, etc. (Popper himself is very partial to political laws, especially those which assert a universal tendency to the abuse of power.) To this most of us would undoubtedly agree. Those writers such as Hegel, Marx, Spengler, and perhaps Toynbee, who have attempted to formulate general social laws of unrestricted scope, in terms of which every historical event is to be explained, are deserving of Popper's strictures against them. But not all historicists have attempted anything so grotesquely speculative. Nor does the failure to achieve a universal point of view for the universe itself impugn the importance of laws of historical change, any more than the failure to achieve a universal point of view for the universe itself impugns the importance of the laws of physics. Triviality is not necessarily commensurate with limited scope.

We may then agree with Popper that Mill was probably wrong in supposing that we can "find the law according to which any state of society produces the state which succeeds it, and takes its place." [5] But the implications of this

[5] Quoted by Popper, op. cit., Vol. II, p. 83.

are surely as momentous—and as trivial—for one science of society as for another. They are surely no more so for history than for economics.

It would seem, then, that Popper's wholesale indictment of "historicism" begins, after a while, to wear the aspect of an intellectual witch-hunt, rather than a merely objective criticism of *presumptuous* hypothesizing and ungrounded large-scale prognostications about what "must" happen in the future.

To return, now, to Popper's contrast between Utopian and piecemeal engineering, we may agree that large-scale planning for distant objectives is likely to be both unscientific and difficult to implement. It is safer and easier always to plan on a limited scale. But without long-range objectives, the hope for organized and ordered social change must give place to *ad hoc* remedies for specific immediate ills. Whether such remedies are desirable, however, in the light of more general social purposes, would, if Popper is right, be impossible to determine. Actually the effect of Popper's analysis is to discredit the practical use of our rational faculties when applied to anything but the simplest and most immediate of results. Its social consequence, I fear, is a deep conservatism and an opposition on principle to bold policy-making of any sort in the interest of the people as a whole.

The fact is, however, that we cannot escape making large-scale predictions and plans. The reasonable procedure seems, then, not to renounce any attempt at prognosis concerning the future development of society, but to try to deduce the margin of error in such prognoses as much as possible by constantly improving our interpretations of history. By denying them the title "scientific" we might inculcate a proper humility and scepticism with respect to our guesses. But we must also remember that there is an enormous difference between crystal-ball gazing and responsible interpretation. In the end the task of the critic of social theory is not to persuade men to forswear long-range planning, but to make them conscious of its extreme difficulties, and the urgent necessity of keeping plans flexible enough to accommodate the unanticipated changes which they may have to face.

There are certain other aspects of Popper's attack on historicism, however, with which I am in somewhat closer agreement, especially as it applies to the problems of ethics, although even here Popper strikes me as being at once doctrinaire and misleading. Now, according to the historicist point of view, moral categories are wholly relative to particular historical situations. Is it "right" to keep one's promises? To this question one can only reply: Yes and no; yes, if you are speaking from the standpoint of a certain particular society or period; but no, if you generalize with respect to mankind in general. Any moral system applies only within a cultural-historical epoch, society, or class.

The interesting point about Popper's rejection of moral relativism, however, is that it goes with an insistent rejection of (a) the possibility of a scientific ethics, and (b) the verifiability of normative statements of any sort. The grounds of his rejection of a system of ethical norms constructed on a scientific basis are of considerable interest. In the first place, "if it could be achieved, it would destroy all personal responsibility and therefore all ethics," [6] this despite the fact that science has nothing to do with determinism. Secondly, only "a scandalmonger" would be interested in such judgments as applied to other people; "'judge not' appears to some of us one of the fundamental and much too little appreciated laws of humanitarian ethics." [7] Thirdly, the attempt to base an ethics on "human nature" leads nowhere, since all actions are founded upon human nature, so that the moral problem invariably becomes the question: "which elements in human nature I ought to follow and to develop, and which sides I ought to suppress or to control." [8] Fourthly,

[6] Popper, op. cit., Vol. I, p. 207.
[7] Ibid.
[8] Ibid.

any analysis of the word "good" would fail to answer the
question: "Why ought I to concern myself with *that?*"

He concludes that all discussion about definitions of good
are useless. Indeed, even the attempt to determine stable
cognitive meanings, and hence verifiable ethical judgments,
is an escape from the realities of the moral life; i.e., our
moral responsibilities. But, of course, the question remains:
"What *are* our moral responsibilities?" Is it possible to "know"
them? And if I elect to ignore them ("Why should this concern me?"), then what? It is all very well for Popper to
deny the possibility of objective ethical *judgments,* but then
he must, it seems to me, eschew talk about moral escapism,
evasions of responsibilities, and the evils of the closed
society. Is he simply blowing off steam, or trying to goad us
into agreement with him? After all, why *should* we agree?
In his view, is it even possible to make *sense* of this question?

Popper devotes a whole chapter (Chapter V) to a discussion of the distinction between natural laws and normative laws or rules of conduct. The distinction is for him
"fundamental." He contrasts the "naive monism" of the proponents of the closed society with the "critical dualism" of
the proponents of the open society. The former makes no
distinction between natural and moral law. The latter, which
accompanies the breakdown of magic tribalism, sees that
human laws are "*made* by men." Norms are "man-made" in
the sense that we "must" (*sic*) blame nobody but ourselves
for them. They are not necessarily "arbitrary"; they can be
improved; some are "better than others." [9] But in saying this
we are in no sense stating a fact.

Now Popper is obviously right in insisting upon the importance of the distinction between natural laws and man-
made laws. In fact it is nearly incredible that anyone should
have been confused on this point merely because of the historical accident that the word "law" is employed ambiguously
in referring both to well-established scientific theories and
to the positive laws of politically organized societies. But it

[9] Op. cit., pp. 51-2.

is no less astonishing that anyone should be confused by the historical accident that the term is also employed ambiguously in speaking both of positive laws and of the principles or precepts that serve as guides to personal moral judgments and decisions. What certain philosophers, ecclesiastical dignitaries, and holiday orators call "the moral law which stands above the laws of men" is certainly not a law of nature, and the whole "natural law" tradition in moral and legal theory was exploded the moment Hume unpacked the logical confusion on which it rests. But it does not follow from this that moral principles are to be classified, along with positive laws, as man-made. Nor is this confusion mitigated by the fact that neither moral principles nor positive laws are falsifiable or testable by the procedures of empirical science. A great many forms of utterance, including most philosophical theses, works of literary art, many interpretations of history, and religious creeds are not testable by such procedures. But what else do they share in common? Here, as it seems to me, we are faced with the age-old tendency of the rationalistic tradition to lump together indiscriminately any and all propositions which happen not to convey testable information about something which is called, in some privileged sense, "reality." [1] The reason for this, I am convinced, is not that the representatives of this tradition are in possession of sounder, logically more coherent theories of meaning and knowledge which enables them to strip these other forms of discourse of their false or misleading pretensions, but rather that the rationalists are not really interested in any proposition which does not purport to increase our knowledge of "reality." They are, in effect, "gnostics" who consider any form of theoretical activity unrespectable for which no "cognitive" claims can be made. And it is for this reason that they are so obsessed with what Popper elsewhere calls "the problems of demarcation": the problem of finding a general criterion by means of which we can distinguish between propositions which convey knowledge of reality and those

[1] The great question here, from a logical point of view, is whether they are entitled to their privileges.

which do not. Any other problems of demarcation simply
do not interest them. In this respect, at least, Plato and
Popper are identical twins! Popper calls it the problem of
demarcation; Plato calls it the problem of the "divided line."
Once this problem has been solved to their satisfaction, their
interest in analyzing what lies *on the other side of* the divided
line simply disappears. And they are both content with
catch-as-catch-can remarks about the "non-cognitive" discourse of poets, politicians, lawyers, divines, and moralists.
Plato regards them, in effect, as liars and pretenders. Popper
is more discreet. But the difference between them is less
logical than rhetorical.

What Popper fails to see is that the very "critical dualism"
of which he makes so much is itself largely responsible for the
tendency of many who reject the notion that moral principles are "man-made" to reassimilate moral principles to the
"laws of nature." For example, Plato, whom Popper classifies as a "monist," understood quite as well as Popper the
difference between man-made laws and the laws of natural
science. It was indeed this very difference which formed the
basis of his harsh criticisms of the Sophists, for whom Popper
has such a tender regard. Plato correctly perceived the error
involved in classifying moral principles, as the Sophists had
done, as forms of man-made law, but as a critical dualist
he was forced to conclude that they must therefore be a kind
of natural law which conveys information about some trans-
empirical realm of being. His error is precisely a mirror-
image of Popper's own. As a critical dualist, Popper's problem is no different from Plato's, but perceiving the equally
profound error of classifying moral principles as laws of
nature, he, like the Sophists, is obliged to regard them as a
kind of man-made law. And because he so treats them, he,
like the Sophists, makes it appear that his own libertarian
moral convictions are no less arbitrary and no less conventional than those professed by the proponents of the closed
society. At the same time he seems to undercut any clear,
logical basis for a moral critique of positive law itself,
thereby disposing his critics to think that the difference be-

tween the closed society and the open society is merely a difference in regard to the conventional forms of justice which in each society determine what is lawful.

Here it strikes me that the intuitionists, whom Popper so much abhors, show a nicer sense of discrimination. Whatever their other faults, their fidelity to the familiar forms of moral discourse saves them from the logical confusions which Popper's own legalism and decisionism involve. They observe, quite properly, that without committing a solecism we cannot speak of "making" our moral principles any more than we can speak of making the laws of nature. They point out also that we do not ordinarily speak of "deciding" what principles we ought to live by, but rather of believing or knowing that we should live by them. Popper's analysis of morals makes it appear to be a sheer verbal anomaly that, whereas it makes no sense to ask whether a positive law, a social convention, or indeed any "man-made" rule which rests upon a decision, is true or false, it is considered proper, in the moral sphere, to speak of true or false judgments, of knowing what is right and good, and of discovering certain moral truths which one did not know before. The intuitionists, on the other hand, accept these linguistic facts as indicative of interesting and important logical characteristics of moral discourse which any adequate moral theory must at least try to explain. In season and out, they insist upon the meaningfulness of our ordinary questions concerning the objectivity of moral judgments and the validity of the justifications we offer in their defense. Not only does Popper offer no explanation of these features of moral discourse, his radical non-cognitivism and subjectivism forces him systematically to discount them in effect as so many evidences that ordinary moral thought, as reflected in our prevailing language of morals, is nothing more than the hangover of a tribalistic verbal magic which clear-headed scientific philosophers will have nothing to do with. They are, of course, entirely free to do so, just as they are also free to renounce theology or any form of discourse other than those of empirical science and mathematics. But then they can hardly

expect to escape rebuke from the theologians or moralists
when they take a holiday from their scientific labors in
order to play at linguistic games whose rules they despise.

These remarks are by no means intended to imply that I
agree with intuitionistic explanations of the meanings of
ethical terms and judgments. Far from it. As I have explained elsewhere, the intuitionists are themselves radically
misled by gratuitous assumptions concerning the nature of
meaning, truth, and definition into the construction of hypostatic ontologies and epistemological mythologies which I, like
Popper, want no part of. However, I want no part of them
because they are, in my opinion, *completely unnecessary.*
What I do contend is that, at what may be called the phenomenological level, they describe the forms of moral
thought and judgment far more truly and accurately than
Popper. Popper's own uncritical version of critical dualism
precluded him from making good sense of the very forms of
words which, in practice, enable ordinary men to preserve a
clear and radical distinction between moral principles and
man-made laws or decisions, between questions of moral
justification and those which are addressed to matters of
conventional propriety and good taste. Let me say also that
no more than Popper do I regard ordinary language as a holy
of holies. I am saying only that before its rules are amended
they should be correctly understood, and that Popper, like
most other scientific philosophers of our age, has simply not
taken the trouble to study them with any care. Because of
this, he casually and uncritically adopts the makeshift di-
chotomies of "critical dualism" which prevent him not only
from clearly articulating his philosophical disagreements
with Plato and other proponents of the closed society but also
from making clear to his readers what are the fundamental
moral bases of his own defense of the open society. Thus he
makes it appear, tragically, that the man-made morality of
the open society is just as arbitrary, just as willful, just as
subjective, and, at bottom, just as much a matter of individual
taste as that of the totalitarians.

By a strange irony, Popper's moral theory thus leads him

to the verge of another mistake which is also analogous to one which he ascribes to Plato. In pointing out this error, I should like to emphasize that I am merely following Popper's own practice of tracing undesirable moral stances to philosophical theories about morals which, apparently, belong to a completely different level of discourse. I do not object to this practice, so long as one does not confuse the intention with the effect of a theory and so long as one bears constantly in mind that in judging the "consequences" of the theory one should not uncritically beg the very point at issue. In this sphere it is not easy to say where questions of "logic" leave off and questions of "ethics" begin; that, indeed, is just the point. Popper's error, like Plato's, is "global," depending as it does upon a complex of logico-ethical beliefs which are hard to disentangle from one another and whose "formal" implications, therefore, are next to impossible to determine.

Now it seems to me that Popper shows great insight in pointing out the moral and political aestheticism which stems from Plato's reduction of all moral and social questons to questions about what appears most harmonious, "just," and "fitting" to a detached, impersonal observer who, fortunately for himself, doesn't have to live in the picture whose elegance and unity he so greatly admires. This aestheticism, as Popper shows, is closely related to the views that moral and political issues are essentially problems of knowledge, that in knowing something one's love of it is consummated, and that knowing anything, including the good, is essentially a matter of impersonal contemplation or intuition of its ideal form. To adopt a convenient phrase of Professor Gilbert Ryle, Plato is thus involved in a series of monumental "category mistakes" which lead him ineluctably to judge social systems, not from the moral standpoint of human rights and sufferings, but from the aesthetico-cognitive point of view of harmony, coherence, and clarity. Thus also Plato is led to construct his ideal republic as if he were composing a picture or proving a theorem, rather than helping his fellows to find a way out of the land of Egypt, out of the house of bondage. And it is for this reason that the Hebrew prophets are in the end morally and politically so much *wiser* and so much more *moral* than he.

Here, it must be understood, we have to do with questions not only of substantive precept but of underlying method, not only of judgment but of the whole philosophy which animates and guides that judgment. So it is in Popper's case as well. Popper will have nothing to do with the "logical" thesis that morality is a form of natural law. Strictly speaking, moral principles are not falsifiable, and, accordingly, are neither true nor false. Moral laws belong to the class of man-made laws, and in making a law the fundamental problem is to determine what one really likes. But this surely suggests—if indeed it does not imply—that every fundamental question of ethics is a question of taste. And, as everyone knows, about tastes there is simply no disputing. Popper's own moral taste, as it turns out, is not for orderly, well-proportioned social structures in which there is a place for every part and every part keeps its proper place. Rather does it resemble that of a romantic artist who, disdaining contemplation, is interested only in doing and making something which expresses his own heart's desire. If it happens not to look well to a disinterested observer or critic, why so much the worse for him. What has the art of morals to do with agreeable proportions and harmonies? "True" morality is not a matter of judgment but of action, not a matter of knowledge but of decision, not a matter of perception and understanding but of feeling.

There is a further aspect of Popper's conception of morality which remains to be mentioned. It is not unrelated to his attack upon historicism, I think. Now it is characteristic of many historicists, such as Hegel, to emphasize the extent to which the consciousness of individual persons reflect and are determined by the historical institutions of the societies to which they belong. Accordingly, they tend to view morality not so much as a matter of the independent, critical judgments of individual men who have managed to break out of the social womb in which they have been nurtured, but rather as a code of traditional precepts which tie the individual umbilically to forms of activity whose authority is completely impersonal and customary. For them, morality tends to be viewed as part of the "constituton" of an "objective" social system, the criticism of which amounts in effect to a revolutionary rejection of the system itself. It thus becomes increasingly difficult for them to distinguish between moral criticism and legal outlawry or between righteousness and conformity to the requiements of the traditional code of society. Popper, on the other hand, begins, a-historically, with an idea of morality as a matter of man-made laws and decisions. And he concludes accordingly that what man hath made he can also unmake, and what others have decided, every individual is free to decide against. Hence his opposition to historical determinism. From such a standpoint, the historicist is made to appear as the advocate of a closed society and his opponent as the advocate of the open society.

Of course, there is no purely logical reason why an advocate of Popper's ethical theory should not decide for himself that conformity is always the best policy and that slavish adherence to the traditional constitution is the only right thing to do; indeed, so far as the sheer logic of the matter is concerned, there is no reason why a critical dualist like Popper should not decide for a completely closed society within which no person, including himself, would henceforth know the difference between conformity and conscience or between criticism and revolution. On the other hand, there is no reason in logic why an historicist, if he can extricate himself from the influence of traditional ways, should not conclude in conscience that they are evil ways, and hence that the moral constitution of the community ought to be abrogated. The historicist is also free to observe that in some cultures "openness" is itself traditional, and that in upholding the sacredness of the constitution of an open society one may help to make it certain that self-appointed lawmakers will not decide to introduce new laws which will henceforth make it illegal to think and speak as a free man.

My point is this: Just as proponents of the doctrine of

natural law may be found at any given time in the camps of reaction, liberality, or revolution, both proponents of historicism and proponents of Popper's critical dualism may be found there also. The real differences between them, so far as morality, politics, and law are concerned, are on a different level. The proponent of natural law, ignoring the historical differences among men and institutions, is likely to talk formalistically of certain abstract natural rights of men without regard to their changing needs and individual capacities. Thus, he is likely to be *unwise* and arbitrary in his defense of principles which in one certain historical situation are morally necessary but in another are morally impossible. The doctrine of natural law tends to make men dogmatic, inflexible, and peremptory in their moral judgments and deliberation. Analogous weaknesses are implicit in Popper's own position. Abstract natural rights and a-historical man-made decisions are in fact two sides of the same coin. Both ignore the existential context in which every moralist finds himself and which no moralist may with impunity ignore. The proponent of natural law declines to make a truce with contingency; Popper, in the name of freedom, refuses to make a truce with necessity. Both are blind. The one is the philosophical progenitor of the paper-constitutions which loudly but ineffectually proclaim "the rights of man," the other of libertarian platforms and statutes which are incapable of implementation or enforcement. By comparison, it seems to me, there is something to be said for the historicists. The historicists' dull "grey on grey" is not inspiring: sometimes it leads to the indecisive and indiscriminate blurring of moral distinctions which Popper rightly deplores. But it also saves them from the flat moralistic and legalistic blacks and whites which obscure the practical problem of relating discussions of moral rights and responsibilities to the concrete historical conditions which determine whether any right may realistically be claimed or any responsibility may sensibly be assumed.

But Popper is not all of one piece, any more than is Plato or Hegel. In other ways one finds strange parallels between some of his own substantive moral views and those of the very historicists whom he excoriates. For example, one of the fundamental lessons of Hegel is the futility as well as the provinciality of most abstract retrospective moral criticism which spends itself in brooding judgment of crimes committed against the abstract name of "justice," rather than in responsible deliberations which have in view the removal of existing inequalities and injustices acknowledged by the constitution of the community within which one lives. This corresponds quite closely to Popper's own insistent claim that moral judgment should always begin at home and that the fundamental business of the moralist is to determine what he himself ought to do rather than with what others ought to have done. Again, Popper is opposed to essentialistic theories of human nature which conceal an implicit and uncritical normative claim within a pretentious "real" definition that relieves the individual of all responsibility in deciding what sort of person he ought to become. But surely it was the great historicists of the nineteenth century who prepared the way for Popper's position by insisting that man, *the only being with a history,* is therefore alone the being without an essence. And surely it was the historical idealism of Fichte and Hegel which first insisted that man's existence as a moral being begins with the recognition that no law, whether physical, logical, or even historical, can determine what any spiritual being is to do or what it is to become. Unlike Marx, Hegel did not profess to be able to predict, through his dialectic, the next spiritual development of man. And he did not do so precisely because there exists a domain of "absolute" spirit, which is also a domain of absolute freedom and responsibility, within which everything turns on what the self at last recognizes itself to be. Here nothing is, or can be, preordained, for here the spirit enters (or re-enters) history of its own accord, and by its judgment determines what *shall* be. The language, of course, is not Popper's, but it can be translated, without too much difficulty, into a doctrine not so very different from his own. And the fact that in his old age Hegel's own absolute spirit turned out to be a functionary of

the Prussian state no more blurs this philosophical agreement
than does Popper's libertarian antipathy to the aged Hegel.
In essence, both preach a moral gospel of continent *self*-
determination which has nothing to do either with the laws
of nature or the laws of men.

From Popper's point of view the historicist is an equivoca-
tor who is misled by a false logic into a nerveless and cynical
acquiescence in things as they are. But there is another
side of the picture of historicism which Popper wholly ignores and which, more sympathetically described, is not so
very different from his own best view. For example, it is
characteristic of the historicist to urge great restraint in judging "lesser breeds without the law," both on the ground that
objective historical facts about human actions are hard to
come by and on the ground that judgments which assign
responsibilities without regard to the principles avowed by
the lesser breeds themselves not only beg a point which may
be at issue (what really *is* right?) but also, and more important, violate the principle that no man shall be judged morally save by a company of his peers. It is indeed worse than
pointless to blame men for the performance of actions of
which we disapprove on principle but which, on their principles, are either permissible or even proper; it is itself, from
our own point of view, immoral. Any significant *moral* disagreement presupposes some sort of underlying spiritual
consensus. In its absence, we simply debase the currency
of moral discourse when we charge others with obligations
and responsibilities which their own principles do not permit them to assume. The point here is not that, since every
one in fact views moral problems from a certain historical
perspective, we can never truly say that anything is either
right or wrong; it is rather that the freedom proper to any
moral agent entitles him to act on his own principles, and
that when we blame him for actions that run afoul of principles which he does not share, we ourselves may properly be
blamed for an insensitivity in the use of the language of
morals which itself amounts to a kind of moral fault. It appears to me that, as he makes it, Popper's own principle,

"Judge not!", which he does not always consistently honor, has much the same point in view. The trouble is that it is made to depend upon a supposedly logical theory that there *can be* no such thing as moral objectivity. Since for him, as for the positivists, there is no conceivable methodology for their justification or verification, every moral judgment can only be understood as an expression of some subjective sentiment or attitude, with respect to which questions of propriety and validity cannot even arise. One wonders therefore whether the "moral" freedom which Popper preaches is itself anything more than a logical consequence of a meta-ethical subjectivism which, in viewing all moral judgments and principles as "man-made," converts the principle, "Judge not!" into a kind of truncated logical truth. On this score, one may again prefer the position of the historicists who at any rate still regard self-righteousness as a moral rather than a merely logical fault.

The most important philosophical use of the "historical consciousness," of which Hegel made so much, is not only that it serves to sharpen one's wits—on this score, any comparative study of cultures may do as well—but also that, by enlarging one's sympathies, it helps to make one less parochial in one's judgments and more disposed to respect the dignity and integrity of "lesser breeds" who, however benighted their customs may seem to us, follow them as seriously, as loyally, and as tragically as we do our own. Understanding the historical conditions which provide the context within which all moral sentiments are acquired, one is gradually made aware of the pointlessness of efforts at moral reform which do not reckon with all of the complex circumstances which affect moral education and re-education. Aristotle wisely said that knowledge of the good is impossible without a sound moral training. In one way, the historicists reaffirm and amplify that insight by showing how rare are the conditions which make for such training and hence for such knowledge. In so doing they also show us how futile is that nostalgia for the golden ages of virtue, when the knowledge of good and evil was securely possessed by simple, dutiful, god-fearing men. Living at the end of history, the education of the historicist, like his moral problems, is bound to be more complex. For while he may appreciate the moral grandeur of the Prophets or the wise men of Greece, he also knows that such simplicity and such unity of feeling are not for him. Perhaps he may still regard the Ten Commandments as exemplary, but for him their proper meaning and application are no longer self-evident. He sees why it is no good simply to mumble over to oneself the First Commandment when one feels in one's heart that God is dead, and why it is no good saying to oneself that one should honor one's parents when one no longer has a spiritual home. In a word, the lesson of both Hegel and Nietzsche is that if one lives at the end of history, that very fact is a fundamental condition of one's moral consciousness or existence, which makes it necessary to face the bitter remoteness of all ancestral moralities. Hence again the "grey on grey," and hence also the necessity of a philosophical-ethical reconstruction which is made all the more difficult by the fact that the parts out of which the reconstruction has to be made tend maddeningly to go to pieces in one's hands.

One should face facts, moral as well as otherwise. But I at least cannot follow Popper in his wholesale condemnation of the historicists since I myself share many of the moral ambiguities and perplexities which afflicted them. No more than anyone else can I "make" a moral law for myself, as Popper has evidently tried to do, and this for the reason that I find all talk of such laws is as dead as the God in whose name they have historically been proclaimed. For me, also, it is not a question of deciding what to do, but of first discovering morally what I am and what *my* principles really are. Many of Popper's own libertarian precepts strike a responsive chord in my own conscience. But the sound is muffled, for I hear also the cries of those for whom the only fundamental moral reality is estrangement. How then shall I condemn all of the ideals of the closed society in the names of liberty and equality, so long as the ideals of the open society neglect the demands of community and fraternity? And how shall I condemn all of the tribal "magic" of the institutions of community when, in its absence, what I find is an aggregation of moral atoms, each as lonely as it is autonomous, and equal in nothing but its sense of isolation? Popper still lives spiritually in the aftermath of the American and French revolutions. He is a true son of Paine and Jefferson and the French *philosophs*, and, up to a point, I honor him for it. But their world, alas, is not my world, any more than it is the world of Marx or Nietzsche or Freud. And it is for this reason that however much I may deplore or even loathe the moral standards of the totalitarians, I cannot so unqualifiedly give my allegiance to the "open" society as Popper has described it. For what he neglects is the history of the nineteenth century which, for profoundly important reasons, could no longer simply reiterate the ideals of the Enlightenment.

There is one final aspect of Popper's moral philosophy which requires some comment. As I have already remarked, although Popper is a philosophical analyst who takes very seriously the study of the logic of scientific inquiry, he deplores the "useless" preoccupation of other analysts with the problems of defining ethical terms. The fact is, however, that his own conviction that all discussions about definitions of such terms as "good" and "right" are useless itself presupposes an analysis of their meaning or use which precludes the possibility of defining them in terms that are used to describe the objective, empirical characteristics of things. Popper thus agrees with the intuitionists that any attempt to construct an empirical science of ethics is doomed from the outset by the impossibility of giving its basic concepts a genuinely empirical meaning. Let us agree to this. Let us also agree with him (and Moore), for the sake of argument, that all attempts to define goodness have proved futile. It still does not follow that they are useless, since it was only after repeated attempts to define goodness that anyone was disposed to explain why it is indefinable. What I object to is Popper's assumption that since the truth about ethics has been proclaimed, it is idle for *anyone else* to raise questions concerning the meanings of ethical terms, and that hence-

forth the logical analysis of moral discourse is an escape from
the realities of the moral life. Indeed, he is not even consistent, for a great part of his own critique of historicism is
predicated on the thesis that incorrect analyses of moral
thought have momentous practical consequences and that
a sound analysis, such as his own, is a corrective to many of
the spiritual confusions to which the proponents of the
closed society are heir.

What I fundamentally object to in all this is what I also
complain of in the case of the positivists, from whom Popper
differs technically but not ideologically, namely, the traditional philosophical rationalism which assumes that what is
not a problem of knowledge (as rationalism elects to define
knowledge) is not a problem at all, and that since morality
is not (in the preferred sense in question) verifiable, every
moral issue is resolvable only by a decision. The odd consequence is that, although the processes of reasoning by
which the two schools arrive at their conclusions seem so
widely different, the rationalists are led, slowly but inevitably, to the existentialist conclusion that at bottom morality, like religion, is intellectually absurd. Thus, to the precept,
"Judge not!" we may add another: "Don't stand there; do
something!" But what if one decides, absurdly, that the thing
to do is to think a little more about the nature of morality itself?

POSTSCRIPT ON SOCIALISM

In conclusion let me briefly summarize what seems to me
good and bad in Popper's general position. In the first place,
in some ultimate sense, I am inclined to side with his *generic
point of view,* from which stems much of his antipathy to
Plato, Hegel, and, in part, Marx. So far as it goes, this point
of view may be characterized positively as (*a*) scientific
and naturalistic, but not narrowly positivistic, in historical
methodology; (*b*) humanitarian and liberal in morals and
in politics. Negatively it is (*a*) anti-intuitionistic in logic and
in philosophy; (*b*) anti-authoritarian in ethics, and (*c*) anti-

totalitarian in politics and ideology. All this I associate with sanity and good will. *But,* I see no reason simply because of this to reject limited, gradualistic, *democratic* socialism. Nowhere does Popper show that free society is incompatible with social organization of modes of production or even distribution, provided that constitutional government, due process of law, and the preservation of essential civil liberties, including freedom of press and speech, are rigorously adhered to. In countries like Great Britain, the basic constitutional and political structures may survive profound changes, involving greatly increased state control of social and economic institutions, without jeopardy to the basic democratic political controls which insure society against willful and unchecked abuses of governmental authority.

Finally, Popper seems to me to have evaded the problem which in two-thirds of the world is most pressing today: What shall be done by the men of good will who confront entrenched tribalistic closed societies in their own countries? Piecemeal social engineering is all very well for democratic countries which are already partially "open." But such a choice is not open to the people of many countries. It would be refreshing, at any rate, to find in Popper any echo of Thomas Jefferson's affirmation of the eternal *right* of a people to revolution against tyranny and oppression.

It is not without significance that the emphasis in Popper's book is upon a maintenance of present institutions in the "democratic countries" rather than upon the radical changes which many of us believe are essential in non-democratic countries. Again and again he praises the improvements (which Marx fully admitted) that have occurred in the condition of the working classes under capitalism. He points out the high standard of living prevailing in the United States, due to the free-enterprise system. He does not mention the misery, wretchedness, and grinding poverty that also exist; nor does he point out that many of the improvements are due to the organization of labor and the increasingly effective use of its economic power. He praises those who "emphasize the tremendous benefit to be derived from the mechanism of free markets, and who conclude from this that a truly free labor market would be of the greatest benefit to all concerned." [2] He forgets that a "truly" (essentially?) free labor market has in the past often resulted in exploitation and "economic terrorism." The point is that it is impossible to remedy the ills of *laissez-faire* without limiting *someone's* freedom. Either you increase the power of government to interfere in economic arrangements and so impede the free private use of economic power (by capital *and* labor), in which case you approach socialism in fact, whatever you call it in name, or you allow the "free" use of economic power, in which case you get large-scale monopoly capitalism *and* a *closed* labor market.

In the end Popper is merely equivocal. A more candid facing up to the problem of power and the inescapable necessity of its increased and responsible use by the state, if the social and economic conflicts of modern civilization are to be resolved, would have led him to assume a far different position from that which he adopts in this book. He would then have seen, perhaps, that some of the apparent enemies of the "open" society whom he so bitterly excoriates are its real friends in a common pursuit of "the wisest" and "the best."

[2] Popper, op. cit., Vol. II, p. 116.

XIV

Utilitarianism and Liberty: John Stuart Mill's Defense of Freedom

MILL AND THE ESSAY "ON SOCIAL FREEDOM"

In 1941 there appeared a volume bearing the title *On Social Freedom*, the authorship of which was unequivocally attributed by its editor, Miss Dorothy Fosdick, to John Stuart Mill. The work had originally appeared in 1907 in the *Oxford and Cambridge Review*, the original manuscript having been found after Mill's death among his other papers. More recently, Mr. J. C. Rees has argued convincingly that Mill cannot be the author of the essay, and I gladly accept his verdict. The whole style of the work, with its rather heavy-handed jocosity, its poor organization, and its close affinities with the schools of intuitionism and idealism, always made it a rather puzzling document for those who, like myself, had no reason to question Miss Fosdick's account of the matter. Had I been disposed to doubt Mill's authorship on the basis of internal evidence, the editor's acknowledgment to Professor R. M. MacIver for his "encouragement and advice," together with the fact that the volume was published by the Columbia University Press, would have sufficed to reassure me. But no such doubts occurred to me, nor did I ever hear any expressed, until it was pointed out to me, after the general subject of this paper had already been proposed, that Mr. Rees had established beyond peradventure that my easy assurances were without foundation.

Mill is an interesting person, and any work ascribed to him must be taken seriously, even by one who, like myself, has been primarily interested in his ideas themselves, rather than in his advocacy of them. The issues raised in the essay "On Social Freedom" were, and are, serious ones. This essay, which I accepted as Mill's, forced me to re-examine his treatment of the issues in the essay "On Liberty," and to discover in consequence how little I could agree with his defense of social liberty. The fact that "On Social Freedom" does not do full justice to some of its own implicit criticisms of Mill made it all the more desirable that others should seek to do so. Let me present the situation in the bluntest possible terms: nearly everyone, at least in this country, pays lip service to the depth of Mill's feeling in the essay "On Liberty"; yet nearly everyone acknowledges his argument to be defective. What, then, is there left in the essay to commend? It is not unfair, I think, to say that the predicament of most contemporary moral and social philosophers in regard to the essay "On Liberty" is similar to the position of many contemporary theologians in regard to Christianity; that is to say, they try, albeit unsuccessfully, to swallow Mill's argument for the sake of its sentiment, yet, because of their unavoidable doubts about the argument, they cannot help being secretly doubtful of the justifiability of the sentiment itself. And it is precisely for this reason that contemporary liberalism, caught between a commitment to the absolute value of liberty and a utilitarian belief that all liberties can be justified only by an appeal to something called "the general happiness" or "the general welfare," pass uneasily back and forth between a last-ditch defense of liberties whose general utility remains unproved and an over-ready acceptance of their curtailment in the supposed interest of the common good.

My own view is that we must fish or cut bait: if Mill's

conception of liberty as well as his defense of it will not
stand, as the author of the essay "On Social Freedom" implies, then we must ask whether his libertarian sentiments
should not be rejected, as the Marxists, neo-Thomists, and
idealists maintain. If, on the other hand, we regard those
sentiments as among the most precious of the attitudes
which compose our so-called way of life, then we must
question whether the principle of utility, as their covering
principle of moral and social justification, must not be flatly
given up. In that case, we will have moved away not only
from one of the positions of the essay "On Social Freedom,"
which may be no great loss, but from the position of the
essay "On Liberty" as well. My taste is to take the latter alternative, even if it involves a break with the Benthamite
tradition of philosophical radicalism as sharp as the break
of the philosophical radicals with the doctrines of natural
law and the social contract. Mill himself was unable to make
such a break and it is precisely because of this that an impartial rereading of "On Liberty" is such a disillusioning experience.

The merit of the essay "On Social Freedom" is that it
forces us at once to reconsider Mill's whole individualistic
conception of liberty, to which it is opposed, and to question the general utilitarian defense of social freedom, which
it accepts. Let me be more explicit. In the first place, by
taking a more consistently utilitarian stand in regard to the
appraisal of liberty, the author of that essay is able to show
without too much difficulty how far, on such grounds, the
defense of individualism is compromised from the outset.
From such a point of view, the liberty of individual persons
cannot be regarded, as Mill tends at times to do, as an end
in itself. For the utilitarian, liberty is, at best, a means, not
an end, and the defense of any particular liberty must be
solely on the ground of its social utility. Mill himself had
argued for the principle that "the sole end for which mankind are warranted, individually or collectively, in interfering
with the liberty of action of any of their number, is self-

protection." [1] This may be an admirable precept, but the
case for it, on purely utilitarian grounds, is extremely dubious. On such grounds, indeed, there can be no theoretical
limit whatever to the restrictions of individual freedom of
thought and action. And if, in practice, as Mill himself admits at times, the majority of mankind is neither very wise
nor very prudent, then it may be necessary for their wiser
and more public-spirited utilitarian leaders rigorously to regulate their activities both for their own sakes as well as for
the common good. But in the second place, as the essay "On
Social Freedom" implies, Mill's theoretical consistency is
hardly less defective than his sense of fact. No sharp distinctions can be made, as Mill supposes, between spheres of
private activity within which the individual person is alone
concerned and a sphere of public interest which is the
exclusive interest of something called "society." In one way
or another, virtually every human activity is other-regarding,
just as, in one way or another, it is also other-affecting. If,
then, the defense of privacy rests on nothing more certain
than the thesis that there are affairs of men which are essentially non-social and in which, therefore, society as a whole
has no legitimate interest, then not even the affairs of the
toilet can be properly regarded as matters of exclusively
private concern. Virtually every human activity, not only in
the cultural but also in the material and economic sphere,
depends upon the active cooperation of others, in many cases
not merely as individuals but also as groups. To that extent, every human activity affects the interests of others,
and, as such, is a matter of public concern. Hence, if the defense of non-interference in a sphere of activity is simply
that the activity is self-interested, then nowhere can, and
perhaps nowhere should, that defense succeed. If, on the
other hand, its defense depends upon the supposition that
a sphere of activity does not involve the well-being of others,
and it therefore is of no proper concern to them, the defense equally fails. In either case, Mill's case for liberty

[1] J. S. Mill, *On Liberty* (London: J. M. Dent & Sons, 1944), pp.
72-3.

is doomed. To be sure, the author of the essay "On Social Freedom" does not quite manage to make this point; yet he says enough to allow others to draw the inference for themselves. And if somehow we remain unconvinced by such an argument, then it is not so much because we really believe the facts to be otherwise, but because we realize at last that the premises of the utilitarian ethic must be disallowed. Unfortunately, however, this is precisely what Mill, who explicitly rejects the Lockean view of liberty as an "abstract right, as a thing independent of utility," [2] is unable to do. As he still forces himself to say, even in the essay "On Liberty" itself, "I regard utility as the ultimate appeal on all ethical questions." [3] The flatness of this commitment is, to be sure, seriously qualified by the proviso that "utility" is to be construed "in the largest sense, grounded on the permanent interests of a man as a progressive being." [4] But this means merely that Mill himself can accept the principle of utility only if he is allowed to define what should be meant by "the public welfare," or, better, the individual interests in terms of which the public welfare is to be constituted. How far such normative qualifications are removed from the concept of "the greatest happiness of the greatest number," as understood by Jeremy Bentham, the founder of utilitarianism, needs no emphasis. Neither Mill nor the author of "On Social Freedom" is remotely a Benthamite. Yet the latter, whatever his qualifications of the original utilitarian standard may come to, really does mean to judge liberties solely by their social consequences; nor is he in the least dismayed by the strenuously limiting judgments which he is obliged to make. Mill, on the other hand, both loosens the utilitarian standard itself and overhauls the facts of long-run private and public interest so as to guarantee in advance that, at any cost, the standard will be left intact. He is immensely imaginative, not to say fanciful, in construing individual liberties as public benefits. He is incredibly dull when it is a matter of search-

2 Ibid., p. 74.
3 Ibid.
4 Ibid.

ing out, impartially, reasons to limit liberties whose exercise, on his own grounds, may result in public misfortune.

We must, then, be grateful to the author of the essay "On Social Freedom" for forcing us to reconsider the whole basis of the modern liberal defense of liberty. And if he leaves us in the lurch at all crucial points, he at any rate says enough to show that any true disciple of Mill has his work cut out for him. In what follows, I shall first discuss critically in some detail certain important similarities and differences between the essays "On Liberty" and "On Social Freedom." In the concluding part of this paper, I shall offer in summary form the sketch of a very different view of liberty than is to be found in either of these essays. Briefly, I consider the case for liberty, either on strict utilitarian or on idealist-utilitarian grounds, very shaky indeed. At one point or another, both of these points of view betray the cause of liberty; in the case of the idealists, the betrayal was more or less explicit; in the case of the utilitarians, it remained for the most part implicit, and, as in the case of Mill, recognition of the fact was forestalled only by muddle-headedness and inconsistency. Unfortunately, I am not much attracted to those aspects of Mill's own defense of liberty which, as many critics have observed, verge away from utilitarianism. In my opinion, they add confusion without appreciably increasing the strength of his position. Specifically, I am not impressed by the thesis that, for most men, liberty forms the great part of happiness. Erich Fromm, among others, has shown how dubious is this thesis as a general proposition. Still less am I persuaded that much of a case can be made for liberty on the ground that it is the condition of individuality. Individuality is a variable commodity of whose value Mill made a fetish. Nonetheless, liberty itself is a great good, so great in fact, that it ought not to be jeopardized by such precarious defenses as these.

SIMILARITIES BETWEEN "ON LIBERTY" AND "ON SOCIAL FREEDOM"

It will be convenient first to discuss critically certain points of similarity between the two essays, and then to consider some of their differences.

As to their similarities, it is important to remark at the outset that although both essays are ostensibly limited to the topic of social liberty or freedom, neither entirely succeeds in confining itself within these limits. The essay "On Liberty" contains an elaborate discussion of the ethical ideal of individuality, much of which is only indirectly related to the problem of social freedom. The essay "On Social Freedom" contains remarks upon the general question of liberty and necessity and some closing comments upon the doctrine of motives, including the concept of "higher" and "lower" motives, whose bearing upon the problem of social freedom is not made apparent. The proper implication to be drawn, however, is that the question of social freedom is not an isolatable topic; proper discussion of it as we shall see raises virtually every question that can be raised concerning the doctrine of liberty or freedom. Nevertheless, the manner in which it is discussed precludes adequate treatment of certain important topics, and for this reason it is necessary to remark upon the formal limits which both authors set for themselves. By social liberty or freedom both of them understand pretty much the same thing: that is, the liberty of individual men in relation to the constraining power of something called "society." And what interests them are the nature and limits of the constraining power legitimately exercised by society over the individual, and, conversely, the proper limitations upon individual freedom by society. Mill is more interested in the limitations of social control; the author of "On Social Freedom" is more interested in the limitations upon individual freedom; but the difference is mainly a matter of emphasis. The important thing is that neither writer is much concerned with the freedom of particular societies in relation to other societies, or the freedom of societies in relation to the restraining power of individuals. Neither carefully considers liberty as a freedom from environmental necessitations and determinations of behavior of which political compulsion and legal constraints are merely particular forms. Both formally acknowledge that other such constraints exist, and the author of the essay "On Social Freedom" tells us in effect that power of law may be useful as a way of offsetting other forms of social constraint. But neither discusses in any detail the ways in which nonpolitical forms of organization may serve to protect the individual against the encroachments of government and to assist the individual in removing burdensome laws or in changing the law with a view to more effective forms of social action which, in practice, may serve to guarantee social rights. More significantly, perhaps, neither discusses the many ways in which, as the idealists were fond of pointing out, nonpolitical as well as political institutions constrict the area within which individual freedom is exercised—by formal education, by moral training, and, in general, by the various informal social determinants of character. Thus neither considers, for example, whether parents should be free to determine the character and attitudes of their children which, even after the latter come to the age of maturity, still effectively limit the range of their deliberations and choices in many important spheres. In the essay "On Liberty," Mill expressly says that his doctrine only concerns mature persons who "have attained the capacity of being guided to their own improvement by conviction or persuasion." [5] In fact, so far in this direction does he go that he argues that "Despotism is a legitimate mode of government in dealing with barbarians. . . ." [6] But what if men like to be "barbarians" and want to train their offspring to prefer barbarian habits and customs?

These problems become even more exigent when we ask directly about the limits of moral freedom. Given certain

[5] Ibid., p. 73.
[6] Ibid.

notions of religion, it may perhaps be argued that the religious life concerns nothing more than a man's relations to his own God, a matter which, to that extent, has no direct bearing upon the common good. But every form of morality, utilitarian or otherwise, is concerned with the rights and responsibilities of men toward other men. On the other hand, there is no morality unless men are free not only to do as they please but also as they think they ought. Where morality takes the form of law, whether it be in the name either of the greatest happiness or of a so-called law of nature, moral autonomy so far disappears. In that case, even if our remaining liberties amount virtually to license, freedom of conscience—as distinct from freedom in the pursuit of scientific truth and freedom of worship—no longer exists. Now up to a point, of course, Mill himself defends moral freedom, but only as part of that freedom of thought whose aim is the pursuit of objective truth or as part of what is involved in self-development. Nowhere, so far as I can see, is moral freedom discussed on its own grounds as the condition of a form of life whose value to us derives from no other source whatever.

In the second place, neither essay gives much attention to the concept of society. However, it is evident upon analysis that what is meant in both essays by "society" is, on the whole, a politically organized society of the sort exemplified by a modern nation-state. For neither author is a form of non-political association such as a trade union, an international social class, or humanity as a whole considered a form of society—or, perhaps more important, as a social institution. This point is of importance in a number of ways. For example, Mill admits, more or less in passing, that individuals may be constrained not only when their actions would be harmful to others, but also in some cases when the performance of the act is a positive benefit, or the non-performance an injury, to them. Thus, a man may be rightfully compelled to give evidence in a court of law, bear his fair share in the common defense, or "in any other joint work necessary to the interest of the society of which he enjoys the protection." [7] But of course such forms of constraint mean one thing if one is talking about a nation-state, another if one is talking about some other form of social organization. A Marxist, for example, might well argue that forms of compulsion which Mill countenances without batting an eye are in the highest degree arbitrary and illegitimate interference with the social freedom of the international working classes. Or a Christian might argue that compulsory armed service for the defense of an un-Christian state is a form of tyranny which ought to be resisted. The fact that Mill and the author of "On Social Freedom" tend to identify society as such with the nation-state thus unconsciously puts a premium upon forms of coercion that are necessary to the preservation of welfare of nation-states. Liberties and restraints, and hence rights and duties, that cut cleanly across political and legal boundaries are thus scarcely acknowledged to exist. To be sure, both essays acknowledge such forms of restraint as may arise from the pressure of custom and public opinion, and the author of "On Social Freedom," at least, is aware of some of the ways in which economic sanctions may affect the use of government and law as ways of protecting the individual against the coercive and restrictive power of non-political organizations within a politically organized society. Yet neither he nor Mill sees how the countervailing power of non-legal associations and nonpolitical institutions, both within and without the boundaries of nation-states, may serve as shields for the defense of common social liberties against the abuses of state power and the many subtle forms of oppression that are so often sanctified in the name of law.

In the modern world, it is frequently not the defense of individual liberties against the state which needs arguing, but the principle of institutional autonomy. Most liberals accept Holmes's dictum that individual civil liberties should be qualified or sacrificed only in the case of a "clear and present danger"; they are also prone to extend it to some, although not all, forms of cultural organizations such as education and the church. It should be borne in mind, however, that

[7] Ibid., p. 74.

such a view still accepts clear and present dangers to the nation-state as primary. Such a position may be defensible when one is arguing, as Holmes was, simply as a judge and jurist. In that context, no doubt, the position may pass as "liberal." It becomes far more dubious when treated, as most liberals do, as a moral principle. For, so construed, it in effect places the state in a position of peremptory privilege, and, in times of political crisis, requires not only the sacrifice of the civil liberties of individuals but also the social freedom or autonomy of other, perhaps higher institutions. Mill's position unconsciously anticipates that of the followers of Holmes. And it does so precisely because the only ultimate form of liberty which he acknowledges is the liberty of individuals and because the only form of society which he seriously contemplates is that of the nation-state. Had he conceived of the concept of liberty as applying not only to individuals, but, without reduction, to groups, and had he conceived society in other than purely legal and political terms, he might well have seen many of the problems of social freedom in an entirely different light. And it is because of this, I fear, that the defense of the utilitarian ideal of the general happiness as well as that of social liberty or freedom has passed, for so many decades, from his followers to men whose conception of the good life, in the end, is very remote from Mill's own.

DIFFERENCES BETWEEN THE ESSAYS

Let me now examine certain major differences between the two essays which will enable me to underline the moral which I subsequently wish to draw from this discussion.

In the essay "On Liberty," Mill adopts a conception of self-interest and of the individual's power to satisfy it which differs only in degree from that of Locke. And he tends to think of the collective interest or "welfare" of society as an aggregation of the self-interests of its members. Finally, although he rejects the Lockean theory of the social contract, he, like Locke, nevertheless tends to think of civil society and its institutions as existing solely in order to protect the self-interested activities of individuals from interferences due to the self-interested activities of other individuals or groups. The plain implication is that to the extent that an individual is capable of satisfying his self-interest by his own efforts he should not be restrained by "society" except in so far as his actions interfere with the actions of others in their own behalf. From this standpoint, the virtue of collective action is mainly the negative one of protecting the individual from overt harm due to other individuals and to prevent him, in turn, from harming others in the pursuit of their own self-interested activities. As in the case of Locke, Mill also explicitly rejects the view that an individual can "rightfully be compelled to do or forebear because it will be better for him to do so, because it will make him happier, because, in the opinions of others, to do so would be wise, or even right." [8]

The essay "On Social Freedom" represents, on the whole, a quite different point of view. Partly because of its brevity, it does not press its argument very far; but there can be no doubt that it regards the basis of Mill's distinction between the domains of private and public interest as untenable. In the earlier essay, private interest is largely taken to coincide with "self-interest," and "public interest" simply with the aggregation of self-interests of the members of a society. As the author of "On Social Freedom" argues, however, self-interest is frequently not limited to what we commonly regard as the domain of private activity. What a man does in private life is largely determined by his view of what other people will think of him. The love of money, the love of property, is as much affected by the social passion for emulation as by the interest in personal security. In short, what men aim at, in their own interest, are not merely the "necessities of life," but social position, power over their fellows, and, in general, the goods represented by the term "status."

But the matter goes still deeper than this. Now in *Utilitarianism* Mill himself had made a great point of the

[8] Ibid., p. 73.

role of social feeling in the moral life. But he did so mainly in order to provide a basis for the principle of utility other than the prudential self-interest which, for the elder utilitarians, had provided the fundamental motive for altruistic action. In short, Mill introduces social feeling or sympathy partly in order to protect utilitarianism against the charge, which Butler had earlier leveled against Hobbes, that it reduces the whole moral life to a calculus of pleasures or interests whose principles or laws are nothing more than summary prudential rules which at once lose their authority when the conditions of personal well-being are altered. Nowhere, however, does Mill lay much stress upon the more positive roles of the non-moral fraternal and communal impulses in human nature. On the contrary, so far as he attends to them at all, he tends to view them primarily as tendencies toward conformity which inhibit the individual's capacity for free self-development. And it is significant, I think, that his whole approach presupposes that he views what may be called the socialization process as a factor which merely serves to constrict the individual's freedom to develop his own personality. But is this so? Is it not true, rather, that for many men spiritual self-development means, in effect, submersion of the private self in some great collective enterprise or work? And for them may it not be the freedom of collective interests and actions against the hampering activities of egoistic individualists that constitutes the most serious problem of social freedom?

I mention this possibility not because I delight to contemplate it, but because it is necessary to underline the point that Mill, like most men, is really interested only in a certain kind of self-development, rather than in self-development as such, and because he so little appreciates the view, represented by the idealists, that if self-development is the primary element of man's spiritual well-being, then social life cannot, in general, be regarded simply as a threat to individual freedom. On this score, at least, the author of "On Social Freedom" comes somewhat closer to seeing that, from a moral point of view, the essential problem may be

not whether society as such has fairly got the better of individuality, but rather what sort of individuality is worth
cultivating, and whether a particular social institution or
system puts that sort of individuality in jeopardy.

There is one important respect in which, surprisingly
enough, the argument of the essay "On Social Freedom" is
more characteristically utilitarian than that of the essay "On
Liberty" itself. In the latter, Mill sometimes speaks as though
the very idea or feeling of being unconstrained is itself an
intrinsic part of individual happiness and hence of the
general welfare. If I correctly interpret him, he maintains
that not merely is doing what you please to do a good, but
the idea that you can do whatever you might please to do
and the sense of spontaneity are also positive goods in their
own right. In this sense they are essential ingredients or
parts of the general welfare which the principle of utility
envisages as its end and which it is the primary business of
society and government to protect. The author of the essay
"On Social Freedom" appears to reject such a view. He is
concerned with the values neither of spontaneity nor of the
idea of liberty. For him, I gather, liberty is in every sense
merely a means to an end. Liberty is desirable, when it is so,
merely because without it some particular good would be
unrealizable. From his point of view, the general principle
that every man ought to be at liberty is, as it stands, absurd.
Again, there is no liberty that is not a liberty to do or not to
do something in particular. It is worth defending or imple-
menting only if the end of which it is a condition is antecedently desirable. Therefore, liberty, forms no essential part
of the general welfare conceived as an end. It is desirable,
when it is so, only as a condition of the end, and then only in
so far as that end is itself desirable.

Here, as it seems to me, Mill is partly right, but for the
wrong reasons. I have no doubt that the idea of being able
to do as one pleases is, for many men, a great good. But
that idea is not itself a form of freedom. Likewise, the sheer
feeling of being unconstrained or the sense that one is acting spontaneously, as Hume had earlier pointed out, is, as

such, not a form of liberty. On the contrary, it may easily be present in forms of behavior in which the individual is acting, without thought or choice, merely at the behest of another person. If it is a good, and I do not doubt that it is, it is only one good among many. Nor is there any clear evidence that it will occur more frequently in an individualistic society than in a collectivistic society.

For my part, however, it is not the idea of being free or the sense of being free, but freedom itself that principally matters when we talk of rights and responsibilities. A man ought to be at liberty, even though in being so he may have a smaller share of the feeling of unconstraint than have men who live in a smoothly functioning, planned society.

I also think that Mill supposes there to be a far more intimate connection between political and social liberty and individuality than in fact exists. In our country there is considerable political liberty, but far less individuality than in many countries in which there is a greater amount of political constraint. But I do not believe that this fact, if such it be, would provide a good reason for curtailing or minimizing the value of the liberties we presently possess. If individuality is a good, it must be cultivated by other means. Mill, the son of a highly tyrannical father and the victim of one of the most remorseless educations to which a precocious youth has ever been submitted, could only conceive of freedom as a sphere of private activity within which the individual can simply "be himself." On this score, the author of the essay "On Social Freedom" occupies a firmer position. He quite properly attacks the whole strategy of those liberals who seek at the same time to confine men's legitimate aspirations toward freedom within a Chinese wall of individualistic private activity which corresponds neither to the social and political liberties to which most men aspire nor to the long-range happiness of society itself. And he sees also that if liberty is a good, it is a good for conformists and nonconformists alike. What he does not see so clearly is that, regardless of the sphere within which it is exercised, and regardless of its effects upon the general welfare, the liberty of men is an intrinsic moral good. No human good, whether it be liberty or life itself, can be defended without qualification. But a beginning in the right direction can be made only by the firm adoption of the principle that every person, simply as such, has a right to be at liberty.

This brings me to a final but striking theoretical difference between the two essays. In the essay "On Liberty," Mill has nothing at all to say abut the so-called metaphysical problem of freedom versus determinism. I presume that the reason he did not discuss it in that work is that, like Hume, he felt that it forms no part of the problem of moral or social freedom. We know from his other works, however, that as a philosopher of science and of history Mill was a strict determinist. On the other hand, the author of the essay "On Social Freedom," in marked contrast to Mill, opens his analysis with a perfunctory but none the less definite rejection of determinism. Unlike Mill, he regards indeterminism as an essential condition of a morally free will. He also appears to think that the doctrine of determinism is incompatible with any "practical assertion of the existence of individual freedom."

Now when I first read this discussion, I was impressed only by the slackness of the analysis, which seemed to me to confuse a metaphysical or logical problem, if indeed such a problem exists, with a purely moral and social problem. From the time of Hume on, liberal moral and political philosophers have generally insisted that the question of determinism and the question of moral and social freedom have nothing whatever to do with one another. I am now convinced that the matter cannot be so simply disposed of, and that, however inadequately he argues the case, the author of the essay "On Social Freedom" was right in maintaining that there is a genuine practical connection between the metaphysical doctrine of determinism and the problem of social freedom. Unfortunately, I must here state my case in his defense in terms that are too brief and too dogmatic to make it immediately convincing to every reader. Let me emphasize once more that in my judgment most metaphysical questions, including most so-called ontological ones, have a practical and ideological as well as a purely logical aspect.

Now the doctrine of determinism forms no part of the positive content of any science or of any scientific description of what there is. Positive science seeks only to formulate verifiable hypotheses and theories about the behavior of classes of phenomena under certain conditions. The cash value of the metaphysical doctrine of determinism, I believe, is simply that of a procedural resolution to search unceasingly for more and more adequate explanations of phenomena and for more and more reliable hypotheses for prediction. Suppose, however, that a given society is committed morally and legally to a conception of spheres of free activity within which not only no scientific experimentation but also no scientific observation is permitted. Suppose, also, that the society systematically and effectively succeeds in preventing men from putting into effect the policies and procedures that, in science, are necessary for the acquisition of certain kinds of information concerning phenomena, and in particular concerning human phenomena. My contention is that in such a society commitment to a deterministic philosophy would be not so much false as pointless, and that for all practical purposes acceptance of a certain element of irreducible indeterminacy in the sphere of human activity would be the only sensible attitude to take. Let me make the point even more strongly: Suppose that the members of the scientific community are themselves opposed on moral grounds to certain forms of experimentation with and observation of human behavior. Are they not on principle thereby committed to proceed as though there were certain unavoidable restrictions upon the very freedom of scientific inquiry and hence of the pursuit of knowledge and truth? And because of this are they not correspondingly committed in practice to assume that a certain indeterminacy in human conduct ought on principle to be acknowledged? Indeed, does not this obligation, together with the corresponding right, imply in effect that a certain commitment to indeterminism may be part of any effective doctrine of social freedom which, morally and legally, vouchsafes to the individual a certain area of private activity within which no inquiring mind shall be permitted to trespass? On the other hand, would not an effective and consistent commitment to the doctrine of determinism commit anyone who accepted it to reject any hampering restrictions upon the free pursuit of knowledge and, by a kind of irony, to the belief that the only sort of liberty that ought to be defended is the freedom of inquiry which Mill himself extols with such vigor? These questions are complex. Nor do I have the answers to them all. I raise them only in order to show how problems of morals and metaphysics may intersect and how shallow is the prevailing libertarian acceptance of metaphysical or scientific determinism.

THE MORAL FOUNDATIONS OF LIBERTY

From what has now been said, it will be clear that I believe that the utilitarian defense of liberty, like its defense of justice, is doomed. Morally, as Mill himself is constantly forced in practice to admit, the problem seems always to be not whether to grant or to extend a liberty as a right but whether to disallow or to limit it. And this suggests to us that the utilitarians have fundamentally misconceived the ethical role of the principle of utility itself. They have endeavored to treat it as a supreme principle of justification for other supposedly lower-order practices and principles. From such a point of view, neither liberty nor justice or even individual acts of kindness have any intrinsic merit. Nor can they independently form the basis of any moral right or obligation. I maintain, on the contrary, that the principle of utility, in whatever form one may choose to state it, is at best to be viewed as a principle for the making of exceptions to other principles that are themselves independently binding. Liberty is not a moral good only because it may conduce to the general happiness, nor even because, by an extension of the original meaning of that idea, it may form a part of the happiness of most men. Such a defense is wholly problematic and leads those who employ it into unreal distinctions and imponderable estimations. The moral foundation of liberty, I contend, is nothing other than the right to be at liberty itself. In short, the fountainhead of freedom (if the phrase may be allowed) is not utility but simply and solely the principle that every person has a right to be at liberty. This principle, I contend, requires justification by no other principle whatever. Nor does it require the support or sanction of any higher authority, institutional or otherwise. It is no more to be viewed as God-given, as a law of nature, or as a dictate of pure practical reason than the principle of utility itself. What authenticates it is merely our own conscientious avowal of it. In the language of Kant, the principle of liberty is categorically imperative.

However, one or two possible sources of misconceptions must be removed. In saying that every person ought to be at liberty, I do not, like Mill, mean to restrict the principle to every adult person, every reasonable person, or every knowledgeable person; nor do I suppose that every person must prove his right to be at liberty by proving his moral competence, his humanity, his submission to the law of the land, or his readiness to fight in the defense of freedom. I make no such limitations of its application, and I deny that any such limitations can conveniently be made. I mean just what I say: "every person has a right to be at liberty." I use the word "person" advisedly and deliberately. In the moral sense, "every person" does not mean "every man," "every human being," "every sentient being," or simply "everybody." Nor does it mean "every individual." Morally, as well as legally, groups as well as individuals may be regarded or treated as "persons." In the moral sense, the term "person" may properly be applied to any individual (or group of individuals) toward whom a moral responsibility is due and who is therefore in a position to claim a moral right. In short, the term "person" is not an ontological but a functional concept; in saying that someone is a moral person we are merely asserting that he may lay a certain claim upon us and that we acknowledge a responsibility to or for him. In some degree

children may be persons, lunatics may be persons, animals
may be persons, associations and societies may be persons,
and divinities, if any there be, may be persons. It is, in my
judgment, one of the fundamental faults of the traditional
liberal philosophy to misconceive the use of the concept of a
person and, quite without reason, either in logic, metaphysics, or morals, to restrict the application of the term person
to individual featherless bipeds.

The second main point to be made is that liberty is not
confined merely to overt actions of a deliberate or voluntary
sort. A person ought to be free to think, to deliberate, and to
choose, as well as to act. Indeed, he ought to be free in any
respect in which it makes sense to speak of him as confined,
hampered, or restricted. Nor does it appear to be at all obvious that any one such mode of freedom is more fundamental
than any other. It is persons who should be free, and their
liberties are all their own. There are some who would argue
that thought should be free, but only because thought is
for the sake of action. This strikes me as fallacious. For it
assumes that a particular form of freedom requires defense
or justification. Thought should be free to the extent that
persons think, and to the extent that it makes sense to speak
of a person's thoughts as controlled, confined, or hampered. If
a man's thoughts are not subject to control, then his thought
cannot be free, either. But, manifestly, there is a sense in
which what a man thinks can be controlled, and a sense
therefore in which a person can be confined or hampered
through the determination of his thoughts. Again, although
freedom of choice should not be restricted, it is not true, as
Hume and others have argued, that the concept of freedom
begins only with choice and has no application to what lies
behind it. To restrict the freedom of persons to their choices,
especially if one limits the application of the concept of a person to adults, may well be, in many cases, to countenance by
implication perhaps the worst of all forms of oppressors—the
over-zealous guardian or parent, such as the utilitarian, James
Mill. If children are persons, then there is always a *prima
facie* case against disciplining them in any way. This is not

to say, of course, that discipline is always unjustified; it is to say that *it must always be justified,* whereas the right to be at liberty need not be.

Thirdly, neither the concept of liberty nor the principle of liberty has any necessary or even any very close connection with such other notions as self-interest, private interest, or individuality. As I have already said, the author of the essay "On Social Freedom" wisely pointed out that no sharp distinction can be drawn in practice between private and public interests, and he quite properly insisted upon the fact that most forms of private and self-interested activity involve social relations of the greatest importance both to the individual himself and to his fellows. In any case, the problem of liberty itself does not turn on such questions as these. To my mind to defend a liberty only on the ground that its exercise is merely of concern to the individual person himself or on the ground that it serves his own self-development is to compromise it from the start. Moreover, other-regarding impulses, I should have thought, have quite as much right to be unhampered as self-regarding ones. No doubt busybodies are a nuisance, and no doubt most of us rather like to help ourselves so far as we are able. And the fact that busybodies are a nuisance may well be a reason to restrict their other-regarding activities in certain directions. But the liberty of a busybody, if he is a person, is as much a liberty as that of the hermit; as such, it is as worthy of respect as that of anyone else who is concerned only with his so-called private affairs. Again, the liberty of altruistic organizations to conduct their activities is not something which needs justification on the ground that it conduces to the general welfare or on the ground that it makes possible a greater freedom of action for those whom they benefit. Liberty, once more, does not require to prove its case. What wants proving is the case for its limitations.

Fourthly and finally, it is no part of my intention to argue that the principle of liberty should replace the principle of utility as the great covering law of moral and social action. There are no moral laws, and none of them is completely

covering. All persons have a right to be at liberty. But principles of justice or fair play, of security, of truth, and of
promise-keeping also impose independent responsibilities
upon us. One fundamental error of Mill's essay is that it
sometimes suggests that the only reason why a liberty of one
person may be restricted or curtailed is to protect the liberty
of another. To my mind, this is absurd. Which of the several
primary moral principles by which we live should take
precedence? I think that no general answer can be made to
such a question. It has always seemed to me that the most
artificial as well as the most uninteresting part of Plato's
moral philosophy is his tendency, in the *Philebus* and elsewhere, to arrange abstract goods or virtues in an absolute
hierarchical order of merit without regard to the particular
circumstances within which any good must be actualized or
any obligation fulfilled. What we ought to do in a particular
situation is not always determinable by mechanical resort
to obvious covering principles which tell us that justice
should be done or liberties defended. In practice, every
moral principle contains within itself an unwritten "unless
clause" which provides a basis for the making of exceptions.
The principle of utility provides one basis, though certainly
not the only one, for making exceptions to particular moral
principles. In that case, however, it cannot be used, as Mill
and the author of the essay "On Social Freedom" use it, as a
supposedly higher-order principle for the justification, as well
as the qualification and correction, of all particular moral
practices. And not conceivably does it provide a definition, as Stephen Toulmin and others have in effect regarded
it, of what we mean by a genuinely moral practice.

George Santayana: Natural Historian of Symbolic Forms

SANTAYANA'S PHILOSOPHICAL INTENTIONS

The death of George Santayana has not been the occasion for any searching reappraisal of his work. He is ignored by the philosophical *cognoscenti*. Nor are his more serious works widely read as literature. Why this is so is not difficult to understand, even when one believes, as I do, that he is one of the few great philosophers of our age. The times are out of joint. In the older and larger sense, Santayana remained a moral philosopher, a seeker after wisdom in a period whose more influential minds have been preoccupied with exact logic and the methodology of science. Recalling Bergson and Whitehead, Alexander and Heidegger, it is possible to claim that there has also been a strong undertow of metaphysical interest, and perhaps a place may be claimed for Santayana in their company. Yet the comparison is unilluminating, for even as a metaphysician Santayana remains apart from such as these. The controlling and never forgotten interest of his metaphysics is always moral. Like the ancient Stoics and Epicureans, he was animated not by a driving curiosity concerning the nature of things, but rather by a search for the underpinnings of the rational life. Fundamentally, his materialism is hardly a theory at all. It was intended neither as a scientific cosmology, as was the evolutionary materialism of Herbert Spencer, nor as the necessary outcome of a logical analysis of the basic categories of being, as is that of contemporary naturalism. Santayana's doctrine of substance, for example, is in reality a sort of linguistic ritual in terms of which he pays homage to the factuality—or mystery—of existence. To call it "material" is hardly more, for him, than to evince one's natural piety before it, to signify, as it were, that one bows to its royal unconcern for the affairs of the spirit. Thus conceived, materialism provides no further description of the natural world which could conceivably add anything to what the physicist may tell us about it. Its "truth" is dramatic rather than logical or empirical. To regard it otherwise is to misconceive its function and to reify the very symbols by which it is expressed.

If Santayana is right, however, all metaphysical systems are to be read in this way. Perhaps this is not the only way to view them, but it might well serve to rekindle interest in metaphysics in quarters where that subject is currently regarded as the graveyard of meaningless linguistic confusions. So construed, it may be argued that Plato, Spinoza, and even Hegel at least make sense, as unquestionably they do not if one tries, as some do, to read them as super-scientists who have their own more esoteric methods for discovering what there really is. Perhaps, indeed, the "real" itself is at bottom a term of appraisal, by means of which we serve notice of what most profoundly concerns us. Thus, though metaphysics may have nothing to say to us as scientists, it may still say much that is vital to us as men. If so, metaphysicians will have to regard the poets and the prophets, rather than the scientists, as their natural allies. Nor can they expect to interest those victims of "scientism" who are prepared to consign to the limbo of "emotive meaning" every form of human utterance that cannot be confirmed by the procedures of experimental science.

Nearly everyone pays lip service to Santayana's powers as a stylist. Yet to many, by no means all of them analytical philosophers, his manner of writing has seemed essentially unsuitable to its genre. Under the present dispensation, philosophical discourse is not regarded as a branch of literary art. And its inclusion by university administrators under the rubric of the humanities is resented almost as much by the philosophers themselves as it is by professors of literature. Its aim, more properly conceived, is said to be the logical analysis of concepts and the clarification of propositions. For such a purpose, evidently, what is wanted is a style like that of Bertrand Russell, stripped of hyperbole and embellishment, and exhibiting at once to the analytic eye the bony structure of its argument. Clarity, economy, and objectivity are its sole standards of perfection; ambiguity, vagueness, and rhetoric its mortal enemies. Now in the hands of a Russell such a style, at its best, may possess great elegance and charm. When employed by a Spinoza its very austerity and impersonality may also be powerfully expressive of a noble mind that is able to view all reality under the form of eternity. But whatever its uses, it is not a style which was possible to Santayana. On occasion, Santayana could cut like a master to the heart of a logical confusion, though he does so intuitively rather than by a process of discursive thought. Something of this power may be witnessed in such little masterpieces as "Some Meanings of the Word 'Is'," or in the devastating "Hypostatic Ethics," which sufficed to convince Russell himself of the confusions involved in an ethics that reduces goodness to a simple quality. Yet such efforts were sporadic, and we have Santayana's own word for it that dialectics went much against the grain. His more natural manner is dialectical only in the free, ironical way of Socrates in the earlier dialogues of Plato. Like that of Socrates, his dialectic always wears the aspect of a half-playful improvisation, to be forgotten once its moral point is understood. Santayana's writing is also clogged with imagery and laden with all the tropes that are so maddening to a literal mind. It represents, or so it is said, the mind of a poet who for some perverse reason insists on dealing with subjects inherently alien to the poetic imagination.

Santayana himself, of course, violently opposed the poetics implicit in such a view as this. Indeed one of his major contributions to contemporary critical theory was to dispose of the myth that there is such a thing as a poetic idiom or subject-matter. In his own case, at any rate, the style is surely the icon of a mind which was incorrigibly concrete and an imagination which was incurably pictorial. As I shall presently try to show, these qualities served Santayana's philosophical purposes very well, but they have plainly blocked the way to a better appreciation of his work on the part of some, at least, who like himself have found in the study of symbolic forms a powerful clue to the understanding of man.

Moreover, even among those who still respect the name of wisdom, Santayana largely remains unhonored. Here, it must be confessed, the grounds for indifference appear somewhat stronger. It cannot be denied that, as Russell once put it, Santayana was a "cold fish." Unlike Dewey, or Russell himself for that matter, Santayana was not deeply engaged by the great issues of our lives. He remained untouched by the terrible anxieties of his generation, and aloof from its profounder loyalties and betrayals. His own commentary, rich and racy as it so often is, seems at times to belong rather to the domain of natural history than to moral philosophy. He defines with apparently equal relish the lineaments of slaves and freemen, or of romantic barbarians and rationalistic liberals, always subtly intimating that all are worshiping false gods. Yet his basic motivation is always clear. Distraction, on all levels, remained Santayana's special devil; and on all levels distraction is the special curse of modern life. In America, he thought, it reached its final apotheosis when, in pragmatism, distraction finally achieved the status of an official philosophy. He found here every spontaneity and freedom save that for which alone he yearned, the freedom of the spirit to behold, without attachment or care, the realm of essence. Santayana's only cure for sick souls is inward removal to the life of contemplation, but for such a cure there is no political prescription.

What Santayana preaches, in so far as he can be said to preach anything at all, is a personal ethics for the undistracted individual whom, for the nonce, nature permits to loll in some quiet backwater of existence. Such an ethics can have little meaning save for cultivated men of leisure who have no serious mortal attachments. What it seeks is pure vision. In Santayana's case, however, its special objects were the forms and patterns of human culture. What he most delighted to contemplate were the ideal stages of human progress, removed from their accidental historical embodiments. Compared to this, the aestheticism of a Pater or a Berenson remains meagre and half-hearted. For unlike Santayana, the latter required the continual stimulus of individual works or movements of art. But as Santayana himself acknowledges, works of art did not in the end suffice to satisfy his poetic imagination. They tied him down to the perspectives and emphases of the particular artist; they imprisoned his spirit within the limits of alien forms and compelled his mind to attend to matters which were not of his own choosing. Santayana preferred a wider perspective than any poet affords and a freer deployment of his imaginative powers than any decent work of art could possibly permit. In short, he wished to be unhampered by all adventitious material integuments whatever, so that he might follow in his own way the ideal fulfillment of any individual or collective purpose that happened to take his fancy. What he sought was the internal rationale underlying any cohesive domination or power, and when he found it he could usually manage to call it good. He had a predilection for order and solidity, and it was this no doubt which caused him to prefer aristocratic hierarchy to democratic confusion and disorder. But his vision, at least, was catholic. The only lesson here, if such it be, is that the manifest form of any great collective aim or destiny, when witnessed sympathetically at a sufficient distance, may serve to delight an imagination to which nothing human is finally alien.

Whatever its faults, such an aestheticism as Santayana's has certain obvious merits. Within limits, it tends to breed consideration, tolerance, and urbanity. And certainly these traits are among the more attractive by-products of Santayana's point of view. He is never parochial, never fanatical, never unfeeling, so long at least as the object of his sympathy is willing to keep its distance and asserts no claims. The egoism, if you like, is profound. But it is not cruel or self-assertive. It is possible to prefer it to the harm which many better men have done.

It is not, however, my desire here to defend Santayana's aestheticism as a way of life; my concern will be rather with the qualities of his defects, and with the products of those qualities. For if the truth be told, although Santayana is often accounted wise, I cannot deeply believe it. In what sense, finally, can this hardly human detachment be wisdom at all? Or if it be such, then it is of no sort of which such harassed and bedeviled creatures as ourselves can make much use. By a strange irony, which Santayana himself might have relished, his own way of life is for us very little more at bottom than a beguiling pose, the apparent form of an alien purpose which for the time being we are willing to contemplate because its possessor expresses himself so well. But at last we are compelled to say that any wisdom so imperturbably indifferent to the more exigent needs of men is, if not a contradiction in terms, then at any rate the product of a fantastic inversion of human functions, the ultimate proof, if such were needed, of the absolute plenitude of being.

SANTAYANA'S CONTRIBUTIONS TO THE STUDY OF SYMBOLIC FORMS

Yet the very qualities that repel us, when we view them morally, made possible a unique and original contribution to what may well turn out to be the major intellectual achievement of our age, the philosophy of symbolic forms. Precisely because of his hypertrophied disinterestedness and his strange lack of ordinary human commitments, Santayana was left free, while still living within our civilization, to examine its controlling symbols and myths. His attitude toward them, if not his method, is almost that of a scientist. There is a profound difference, however, between the equipment required of the natural scientist and that necessary to the student of symbolic form. In the latter case the principal data are not external material events observable by all who have the eyes to see. Here the data are meanings, the point or significance of which cannot be understood without the guidance of sympathetic intuition. To grasp the full import of the idea of Christ in the Gospels, for example, it will not suffice simply to observe the external behavior of Christian believers. One must also be able to experience, as only a Christian may do, the unique suasion of that many-sided idea. Only so can one become fully aware of what the data for the study of the Christian myth really are. Meanings, no doubt, are human responses; but if one remains unresponsive oneself, the character of any meaning will remain obscure. For successful criticism one must also be a primary interpreter.

Because of his peculiar background, Santayana was exposed from early age to many winds of doctrine. And so he acquired at the outset a sensitivity to their inward significance which an outsider can achieve only by long years of loving and laborious study, if at all. At the same time, however, circumstances prevented him from ever settling into a single cultural mold. He spoke English like a native, yet English was not his native tongue. His familial influences were mainly Catholic, yet a true believer he could never become. Thus by second nature he was destined to remain an ever-sympathetic observer rather than a committed participator in the complex cultural life about him. By good fortune he knew at first hand the suasive powers of the symbols in terms of which the members of our civilization express, commend, protect, and order their values. Yet he remained sufficiently aloof from their spell never to confuse his own primary interpretations of them with his philosophical gloss. He could both reify the symbol or its function and accurately note the fact; he could personify when the myth required, yet clinically observe the personification; he could project his emotions at an artist's or a prophet's bidding, and still know the projection for what it is.

These faculties of second nature would not have served for Santayana's special purpose, however, without the poet's special sensitivity to the ways of words. This gift freed him forever from the temptation to worship paraphrase. Literalmindedness has its uses; but it is the bane of those who would grasp the sense of the life-symbols of art, morality, or religion. Because he was a poet, Santayana knew intuitively the volatility of words, their constitutional powers of association, their subtle affinities and mutual aversion. Language, for him, was not and could never be a calculus. He understood, as only the poet can, that vagueness, ambiguity, and metaphor are not diseases of language, and that in the hidden meanings of a word may lie its chief glory.

But even this rich and varied endowment would still have left Santayana inadequately prepared for his special vocation. This required also a philosopher's special powers of abstraction, by means of which he might accurately discern in some particular trope the paradigm of a more general symbolic form.

In this respect also Santayana was peculiarly fortunate. For the same power, in another, sometimes blinds him to the very features of symbols to which Santayana was naturally so sensitive. Santayana probably had less command of mathematics and natural science than any other first-rank philosopher since Hume. His education was overwhelmingly humanistic and literary. In a philosopher with the primary interests of a Russell or even a Whitehead this incompetence might well have blocked the way to any lasting constructive effort. But in Santayana's case it merely freed him once and for all from that fatal worship of science and mathematics as the models of perfect communication, which until very recently has impaired the philosophical study of other dimensions of human discourse. The fact that Santayana not only spoke the common tongue but could speak no other immunized him, as it were, from the syntactical virus of descriptivism in all its forms. Unlike Russell, Santayana was never tempted to regard ordinary language as merely an unconscious repository of outmoded metaphysics; and unlike the logical positivists it never occurred to him that ordinary language might be no more than an obsolescent progenitor of some ideal language of science. Thus he did not need to relearn the lesson, as so many philosophers have had to do, that the special qualities of an ideal language, if such a thing could be constructed at all, would radically unfit it for every other occasion for which men use symbols. As it was, he saw very early that the languages of poetry, religion, and morals may possess a distinct theoretical interest not only for the anthropologist or clinical psychologist, but also for the philosopher of symbolic forms. The net result was that Santayana was equipped as perhaps no one else in our time has been for the philosophic study of the spiritual symbols of western culture. In this respect only Cassirer, who possessed a profounder erudition but lacked Santayana's sensitivity, can be compared with him.

HIS INTERPRETATION OF RATIONALITY

Perhaps the most distinctive feature of Santayana's portrayal of the cultural symbols of art, morality, and religion is his placement of them within the life of reason without at the same time forcing them into the molds which alone count as rational in formal logic or empirical science. There are, he contends, standards of adequacy and relevance, and hence of reasonableness, for the criticism of the former which in no way depend upon the assumption that works of art are logical systems or that religious myths are scientific hypotheses. Rationality is a wider concept than logical deducibility or scientific verifiability. Its core meaning involves the notion of order; as applied to human activities in any sphere, it primarily connotes fitness, propriety, and adjustability. Wherever there are proprieties, there also, at least implicitly, are standards of reasonableness and unreasonableness. Given them, we can provide a rationale for judgment in any domain; without them judgment lapses into an expression of arbitrary preference or animal faith. This means, of course, that any rational art or morality must be traditional, for without tradition standards of propriety would have no meaning. An art that was all individual talent would be an art to which rational criticism would be irrelevant, just as a world of experience in which every item were unique would be a world in which the principles of rational understanding could gain no purchase.

Rationality, then, is the regulation and coordination of activity by ordering principles or rules. As in the case of natural languages, these may be largely tacit and implicit. But where they operate, there is nevertheless a usage which defines what it means to be rational and, hence, irrational. Irrationalism in the domain of knowledge implies precisely the setting up of individual judgment or intuition against established canons of right thinking and evidence; in religion it means a rampant protestantism which has no standard of integrity beyond the intensity of personal feeling and commitment; in art it means a restless romanticism which places novelty above style, and holds originality in self-expression to be an end itself; and in politics it means contempt for law, treaty, and diplomacy. In each of these spheres Santayana himself was a traditionalist, but what this meant to him fundamentally was devotion to the life of reason. If he fears democracy, then this is because he views democracy as Socrates doubtless viewed it at his trial, as the epitome of lawlessness and unreason. If his customary urbanity is temporarily in abeyance when he is criticizing Fichte or Hegel, then this is because he regards their philosophies as the embodiment of an unbridled wilfulness inflated to cosmic propositions. Hegel may call his system rational, but in the misuse of that term he is, for Santayana, committing a double crime against reason.

However, Santayana's preference for the life of reason does not prevent him from seeing the importance of understanding and sympathizing with irrationality. Here we come upon another distinctive feature of his analysis. I have said that Santayana approaches the study of symbols somewhat in the spirit of a scientist. In this connection it would be more illuminating to compare him to some logician who found the study of fallacies and illogic as absorbing and, in its way, as illuminating as the formulation of the principles of valid inference. In logic or in science such an interest would have no point. The logician sometimes desultorily catalogues a few types of fallacy, but only in order to put us on our guard against their commission. As such, fallacies have little importance for logical theory. When an inference has been shown to be invalid, the logician forthwith dismisses it. Similarly once a scientific hypothesis has been shown to be false, it retains interest only for the historian or pathologist of human thought. But in the case of other symbolic forms such indifference to the invalid and irrational is not always justified. Just as ambiguity and vagueness have their uses for the poet if not for the scientist or logician, so in morals or religion irrationality may have a function which is vital to the ethical or spiritual development of mankind. If they did nothing else, the irrationalists would still hold before us a kind of inverted mirror in which we may more truly see our parochial and custom-ridden selves. By going outside the rules they force us to re-evaluate our habitual adherence to them and so to decide for ourselves whether, as it stands, it may be worth while to continue playing the moral game. Thus they may also compel us to see the need to modify the rules in order to make room for new values. In this way, indirectly, they may even strengthen a moral order which has become inflexible and hence is weakened by every vital interest which cannot find a place within it. As Santayana shows us, in effect, the life of reason itself has its uses for irrationality which reasonable men do well to acknowledge. For only when we occasionally look beyond the limits of reason can we reasonably decide whether its boundaries have been well drawn.

In this way Santayana absolves himself of any charge of rationalistic formalism. Discipline is as essential to rational art or rational religion as it is to rational morality. But all of these activities are more than disciplines, and they serve needs which are more vital than any interest in order for its own sake can ever be. We play games in accordance with rules, but—unless we are mad—not for the rules' own sake. Within art, morality, or religion there is always a post-rational aspect which reasserts itself for the sake of delight, or passion, or ecstasy. Yet even the post-rational itself may gradually be rationalized as reason extends its bounds in order to become more hospitable and more humane. Thus, most broadly conceived, the ideal of reason itself may be envisaged, without fatuity, as a gentle, encompassing order which is coterminous with joy. Since no need would ever arise to be aware of them, such an order would know no bounds, but they would still be there, doing their silent work of civilizing our passions and domesticating the urgencies that we call will.

No doubt such a vision of the ideal of reason is fanciful. But it, or something like it, nevertheless keeps the mundane life of reason open at its further end, so that the stream of post-rational aspirations and values may gradually filter through. In this way we learn to preserve our sanity while at the same time continually enlarging its scope. Madness is always the counterpart of a rigid rationality faced with a world beyond itself which it cannot comprehend. Stated in another way, every healthy and adequate symbolism must have its symbols of self-transcendence, boundlessness, and inexpressibility. By learning thus to say what cannot be said, we manage by the art of paradox to reduce the margin of terror and to give sanity even to madness itself. There are no questions, finally, which have no answers. This is the final commitment of the life of reason.

On its more ordinary planes, as Santayana conceives it, the life of reason is any life which, at the respective levels of common sense, science, art, morality, or religion knows how to guide and correct its attitudes and beliefs in the light of certain ordering principles. These in turn reflect, at a distance, the respective communal demands in response to which they themselves were instituted. In any of these domains, criticism is saved from being a merely *ad hoc* symptom of first-personal preference or prejudice by the invocation, as it were, of a social rite, in relation to which the individual critic functions as a spokesman and mediator. Rational criticism requires the giving of reasons, and reason-giving presupposes relevant procedures in accordance with which, in each case, we make the moves of a solemn game. Only in this way do we ever become aware of the meaning, within any sphere of human life, of the distinctions between appearance and reality, or between irrationality and rationality.

REASON IN CRITICISM

It is with *The Sense of Beauty* that aesthetics may be said to have come of age in America. That work has already become a classic; it is doubtful, indeed, whether its leading ideas have since been greatly clarified or improved upon by the aestheticians. Its limitations are serious, but it is Santayana himself who in his own later writings shows the way to a more adequate philosophy of art. *The Sense of Beauty* is not, plainly, a work by which its author sets much store. For it still moves within a traditional framework of artificial concepts which he subsequently found to have generated false issues completely remote from the interests of art or criticism. In the end the whole subject of aesthetics became distasteful to him, and its problems came to be viewed as the irrelvant consequence of a series of accidents in the history of ideas. Later, whenever he had occasion to speak of it or its practitioners, Santayana did so condescendingly and disparagingly.

It is essential to our present purpose to inquire into the philosophical causes of this disenchantment. In this way we may somewhat better comprehend with what serious intent, in *The Life of Reason*, Santayana wrote of reason in art, or why, in *Three Philosophical Poets*, he regarded such a work as *De Rerum Natura* as a great poem and not merely as a derivative philosophical treatise that happened to be written in verse. When the reasons behind these views are brought to light, it becomes startlingly clear how profound was Santayana's opposition to prevailing philosophical conceptions of the so-called aesthetic attitude. What he really proposed, in effect, was a revolution in critical theory, the full significance of which we only just now begin to comprehend. For by insisting, both as a theorist and as a practicing critic, upon the relevance of the full symbolic content of a work of art to our appreciation and appraisal of it, he was virtually maintaining the irrelevance of so-called aesthetic analysis and judgment.

How, then, did it happen that after what seemed such an auspicious beginning, in a subject for which he was apparently so eminently qualified, he thenceforth resolutely turned his back upon aesthetics? One clue may be found in the essay "What is Aesthetics?" which is included in the volume *Obiter Scripta*. What he there describes is not an organic discipline at all, but a factitious medley of history, psychology, morals, and bad philosophy. It is a subject which altogether lacks any unifying concept that could bring into clearer focus the full range of what we hold intrinsically valuable in art. The term "aesthetic" itself, at any rate as it is currently understood, is pre-eminently unsuitable for such a unifying purpose, especially as applied to the symbolic arts of poetry and painting. It actually diverts attention away from nearly everything in a work of art which gives it significance and value. Taken seriously, it forces us to regard the complex beauty of *The Divine Comedy* as hardly more than a witless swill of pleasant sensation, or the myriadic levels of significance in *Hamlet* as sheer unaesthetic irrelevance. How could such a concept provide the basis for serious interpretation and criticism?

Santayana's attitude on this point is easily misunderstood. It must not be forgotten that in his case, unlike that of so many philosophers and critics in the recent past, this disparagement of the aesthetic was in no way attended by a corresponding revulsion against contemplative values. On the contrary, he reacted, as we have seen, ever more intensely against the pragmatic spirit of the age in which he lived. Indeed, viewed in one way, his entire later work is a continuing protest against the distracted obsession of the age with the instrumentalities of social and political organization and against its theoretical and moral glorification of activity. *Realms of Being* may turn out yet to be Santayana's masterpiece; but it can scarcely fail to appear anachronistic, both in attitude and in doctrine, in a period of ascendent pragmatism and operationalism. What do the activistic psychologies and theories of knowledge engendered by this mentality have to do with such notions as essence and contemplation? If the former are taken seriously, then the latter become correspondingly obscure or meaningless. In *Realms of Being* a whole province is inhabited by nothing save essences, and in *The Realm of Spirit*, possibly the most affecting of all his works, Santayana devotes his finest prose to the delineation and praise of the contemplative life. He did not thereby renounce empiricism and naturalism; but in *Realms of Being* what we find are an empiricism and a naturalism very remote from the prevailing philosophies which share these names.

Because of this proliferation of "realms" in his later work, some of Santayana's critics have suggested that his ontology acutely suffers from a problem of overpopulation. This is mistaken, as a glance at the above-mentioned essay, "Some Meanings of the Word 'Is'," may suffice to indicate. To explain this would require a full chapter in a comprehensive study of Santayana's philosophy of language. Be this as it may, it is notable that nowhere in all his realms of being does the notion of the aesthetic find any place or purchase. For sensation and for sensations there lie ready at hand more appropriate and less misleading terms; so also for awareness, attention, and pleasure, the other concepts frequently associated with the aesthetic. As now used, this misbegotten term is intolerably ambiguous, and its use results merely in theoretical and critical confusion. On the one hand it appears to refer to the intrinsic interest or satisfaction we may take in the contemplation of any object; on the other to the apprehension of what Prall calls "sensuous surface" and Northrop the "aesthetic continuum." Mixed together, as is usually the case, these completely different notions yield the useless theory of aesthetic experience as a delightful but thoughtless arrest of attention in sensation.

What conceivably could be the use of such a concept either for our understanding of the arts or for our more normal apprehension of them? The one it empties of all pregnancy and expression; upon the other it saddles a misplaced notion of the epistemological "given" that was conceived originally for an utterly different theoretical purpose. It does not even provide a helpful semi-technical gloss upon the normal meanings of "beautiful." For when, beneath its sensuous charm (which there is no intention here of disparaging), we discern in a work of art some intimation of its fitness to a human purpose, or some larger sense of order and design, or some poignant articulation of the life-values of a culture, or, finally, some intensification of our awareness of what it means to be human, then we do not hesitate to credit that work with a richness or quality of beauty beyond that usually ascribed to the sensuous surfaces of images. It is this many-leveled beauty of the symbolic forms of art which creates his problem for the critic and calls forth his special resources as an interpreter. When, as in our own age, a sometimes "penitent art," as Santayana calls it, renounces all meaning and representational form in the name of something called "aesthetic purity," the result, however interesting it may be in itself, is an art which has gratuitously forsaken its heritage for the sake of a confused slogan whose very meaning can scarcely be rendered intelligible. Santayana's protest here is not against the sensuous, but against a theory of aesthetics which has nothing to do with our normal transactions with works of art. Works of art are symbolic forms, and only when they are so conceived can we begin to grasp the richness of their moving appeal or their place among the high intrinsic values of our lives.

In maintaining that not merely does the literary dress or the incidental play of imagery in Lucretius' poem, but also its imaginative philosophic content, belong inherently to it as poetry, Santayana's profounder intention, of course, is to restore to the life of contemplation the full range of meaning and significance from which our modern empiricist theories of knowledge have tended to divest it. It has become a dogma of latter-day empiricism, in short, that contemplation —or acquaintance, as James and Russell used to call it—can have no object save what is "given" in sense perception. However useful this doctrine may have been in directing attention to the crucial role of observation in the enterprise of knowledge, it had also the incidental effect of reducing the contemplative values traditionally associated with art, as well as with philosophy and religion, to the level of sensation and feeling. It thereby renounced exclusively to science the whole domain of thought and meaning. The result was a tremendous cultural calamity. The impressive thing about Santayana is that he could reasonably claim membership in the empirical tradition in philosophy while at the same time seeking to restore to the true contemplative interest in art all of the levels of meaning which most other empiricist aestheticians in our time have denied it.

At such a point it is easy to go too far and claim for the poet a primarily cognitive intention. Santayana, however, does not do this. Indeed, it is precisely to free the philosophy of symbolic forms from its preoccupation with the role of symbols in the communication of knowledge and truth that he offered his elaborate interpretations of western poetry and religion. The "idea" of Christ in the Gospels, as Santayana portrays it, is not a vehicle of knowledge in the ordinary sense. Its primary function is quite different. So also in the case of poetry: the poet's basic intention is expressive and imaginative. Ideas are used in poetry, but they do not exist there for the sake of information. "The poet's art," he tells us, "is to a great extent the art of intensifying emotions by assembling the scattered objects that naturally arouse them." In most cases these objects are perceptions or their conceptual counterparts and surrogates. But for the poet their role is to provide a correlative object in which our emotions and feelings may be projected; through its perception alone are they focused and intensified. To accomplish this result the poet uses, or is free to use, every symbolic resource of which nature and convention can avail. The difference between the poet and the scientist is not so much a difference in the sorts of symbols which each employs; it lies rather in the different uses and kinds of total response made by each to their symbols.

Just as Santayana finds himself unembarrassed in ascribing conceptual meaning to art, so also he is not fazed by speaking of art as "rational." In a lesser philosopher, this would doubtless signalize an attempt to "reduce" the arts to science or to logic and hence to impose upon criticism a rationale fundamentally alien to it. In Santayana's case, however, this is precisely what was not intended. His contention, at bottom, is merely that great art exhibits certain characteristic features of order, coherence, and unity which alone entitle us to call it "rational" in the generic sense of that term. From our awareness of these characteristics we gradually acquire implicit standards of artistic relevance and cohesion which we then apply in judging works of art and, when challenged, in the justification of our judgments. The unfitness or unrelatedness which we discern and condemn in inferior works is not a matter of logical incoherence or invalidity; the unity of a work of art is a unity of style, feeling, and mood. But why, if they are the products of orderly adjustment, and if, at the same time, they communicate to a manifold of impressions, thoughts, and images a real sense of interrelatedness and relevance, should works of art be denied the title to rationality?

The symbols of great poetry, then, reveal to us a world unified, orderly, and serene. For the time being at least, this world is no less objective and no less real than those of rational common sense or science. Indeed, the very fact that poetry reveals a world to us suffices to guarantee its rationality. For what we mean by the rational, fundamentally, is by definition to be distinguished from chaos, confusion, and irrelevance. Great art is never a phantasmagoria. Even the *Walpurgisnacht* of Goethe, for example, is in no sense a manifestation of disorder. On the contrary, it is a powerfully wrought creation of a profoundly ordered poetic imagination. As such it is a product of rational art. In the older and deeper sense of the term, every great poem is a design. But just as the older theologians sought in the argument from design to demonstrate the overarching rationality of the universe itself, so the critic in pointing out the design of a work of art is thereby testifying to the rationality of a system of symbolic forms. Logic presents us with one type of order among symbols and is rational because it does so. The arts, at their best, present us with another type of order among symbols, and this too may be regarded as rational, although in a different sense.

Here, curiously, may be discerned an echo of old Kant who perhaps alone among the classical philosophers of art understood how the beautiful may imbue us with a sense of purposiveness and objectivity, and hence of rationality, without at the same time transforming the object contemplated into an instrumentality of action. It is an echo, I submit, which deserves to be heard again and again in the sphere of art criticism and interpretation.

REASON, MORALITY, AND TRUTH

Now as I have already observed, Santayana's whole philosophy is, in the broadest sense, a moral philosophy. Perhaps this explains why he never bothered to write an independent treatise on ethics. However, there may also be another reason for this omission, not unlike the reasons which lay behind his increasing contempt for the academic discipline of "aesthetics." In the course of a very funny reply to Professor Stephen Pepper's essay on "Santayana's Theory of Value," Santayana makes the following interesting statement:

> . . . Pepper finds my "theory of value" ambiguous. It is so ambiguous that, under that name, I was not aware that I had one. I certainly have a doctrine concerning the good, borrowed from Socrates and his school: a doctrine rather than a theory, since it professes to be a judgment rather than the description of a fact. And it concerns the good, the object of desire, rather than

"value." Value is an economic and secondary term like "use."
Things have or acquire value in different connections from different points of view; and a universal history of ethics and economics would no doubt contain a theory or description of values,
which might be abstracted from the total picture. But I confess
that when Pepper goes on to distinguish various literal theories
of value, I hardly know what he is talking about.[1]

Some critics have inferred from such remarks as these that
Santayana was wholly interested in substantive ethical questions and that he was indifferent to the linguistic and logical
problems of so-called meta-ethics. But they are mistaken, and,
as I shall show in a moment, it is not difficult to piece together the outlines of a fairly coherent and always interesting *theory* of moral discourse from various chapters in his
works from *The Life of Reason* through *Winds of Doctrine*
to *The Realm of Truth*. The fact is rather that, given Santayana's own conception of moral judgments and their justifications, he could not but think that whole enterprise of
value theory, as conceived by such writers as R. B. Perry
and Pepper, is fundamentally misdirected. For them the only
interest in answering questions about the meaning of such
terms as "value" and "good" is to provide descriptive definitions of them which will provide a comprehensive conceptual
scheme for a general science or theory of value. From Santayana's point of view, such a program mistakenly assumes
that so-called ethical expressions are terms of objective empirical reference and that all value judgments, including
moral judgments, are, with a little pulling and hauling, logically reducible to ordinary statements of fact. For him this
mistake is fundamental. How, then, could anyone speak of
his "theory of value" when he denied the basic premise underlying such a theory? And how could any just critic point
out ambiguities in his theory of value when indeed no such
theory existed in which ambiguities might be found?

But these questions, after all, are a trifle disingenuous. For

---

[1] "Apologia Pro Mente Sua," *The Philosophy of George Santayana*,
ed. by Paul Schilpp; Vol. II in The Library of Living Philosophers
(Menasha, Wis.: George Banta Publishing Company, 1940), p. 577.

at the beginning of *The Sense of Beauty*, for example, Santayana himself boldly asserts that "the philosophy of beauty
is a theory of values," just as he also says that "A definition
that should really define must be nothing less than the exposition of the origin, place, and elements of beauty as an
object of human experience." [2] He also says other things in
that work which may give the impression, not unnaturally,
that he actually meant to equate the meaning of "the good"
or "the desirable" simply with "the desired" as such. Thus he
remarks, "We may therefore at once assert this axiom, important for all moral philosophy and fatal to certain stubborn
incoherences of thought, that there is no value apart from
some appreciation of it, and no good apart from some preference of it before its absence or its opposite. In appreciation, in preference, lie the root and essence of all excellence.
Or, as Spinoza clearly expresses it, we desire nothing because
it is good, but it is good only because we desire it." [3] Of
course it is just a little ominous, particularly in a writer so
inexact as Santayana, that as late as the *Apologia,* in the very
passage which I quoted above (pp. 333-4), he could speak
quite comfortably of "the good, the object of desire" in the
same breath that he emphatically distinguishes a "doctrine"
or "judgment" concerning the good from "the description of
a fact." But it is also true that in *The Sense of Beauty,* in the
paragraph immediately following that in which the reference
to Spinoza is made, he goes on to say, "It is true that in the
absence of an instinctive reaction we can still apply these
epithets by an appeal to usage. We may agree that an action
is bad or a building good, because we recognize in them a
character which we have learned to designate by that adjective; but unless there is in us some trace of passionate reprobation or of sensible delight, there is no moral or aesthetic *judgment*. It is all a question of propriety of speech,
and of the empty titles of things. The verbal and mechanical
proposition, that passes for *judgment* of worth, is the great

---

[2] *The Sense of Beauty* (New York: Charles Scribner's Sons, 1936),
p. 13.
[3] Ibid., p. 16.

cloak of ineptitude in these matters. . . . Verbal judgments
are often useful instruments of thought, but it is not by them
that worth can ultimately be determined." [4] Whatever else
this fascinating and prophetic passage may seem to imply, it
surely does not suggest that judgments of value are conceived by Santayana as ordinary empirical statements of fact.
On the contrary. Although, as he says, we may agree that an
action is bad because we recognize in it some character
which we have learned to designate by that adjective, this
does not amount to a moral judgment on our part unless our
agreement involves an expression of our own positive approval. When our own approval is not involved our agreement amounts to a "verbal and mechanical" proposition in
which, so far as we are concerned, the word "bad," conceived as a moral term, is merely idling. Spinoza himself
said that we call things good *because* we desire them; but it
does not follow that in so calling them we are merely re-
porting our belief that they are, for ourselves or others, objects of desire.

It seems reasonable, then, to say that even as early as *The
Sense of Beauty* Santayana never meant to lend support to
any program, such as Perry's, which would reduce all judgments of value, including moral judgments, to ordinary empirical statements about objects of interest, their causes, effects, and interrelations. Interests, or, as he later preferred
to say, "passions," are no doubt the "source" or "seat" of
values. It is entirely with them and the actions issuing from
them that moral judgments are concerned; it is in order to express or to incite them that such judgments are made; and it
is in order to reinforce them that moral justifications are
provided. In view of their expressive and incitive function, it
is entirely natural that moral judgments should also serve to
inform our listeners or readers of our sentiments and feelings
about things, just as facial expressions and gestures similarly
inform them. In conventional situations, moreover, such
words as "good" and "right" *may* also be used, in a derivative, secondary sense, to inform others that the objects to

[4] Ibid., pp. 16-17. Italics mine.

which they are applied conform to certain conventional standards in which we ourselves may have no great personal stake. Thus the butcher tells us that a certain cut is a very good steak, though he himself detests steak and would, if he could afford to do so, commend it to no one at any price. Likewise the art dealer tells us that a certain picture is a very fine Matisse though he is bored silly by Matisse and sells his paintings only as a convenience to his customers. Yet, if I correctly interpret Santayana's view of the matter, such factual information as these remarks may convey is not what is involved when we employ such words as "good" in making genuine moral or aesthetic judgments. Moreover, even when we assert conventional "propositions" about good beefsteaks and Matisse, a residual element of commendation remains. For the idea of a good steak would not connote a steak which is, say, tender, juicy, and well-aged unless most steak fanciers would be prepared to judge a steak having these characteristics as something worth eating. In fact, it is precisely this logical dependence of what Professor Pepper himself calls "standard value" upon the use of evaluative terms in first-personal *expressions* of interest or satisfaction which in part lies behind Santayana's own claim, in *The Sense of Beauty*, that "all values are in one sense aesthetic." For "aesthetic" judgments are by definition merely expressions of immediate appreciation which articulate our sentiments and feelings, without reference to or thought of the conformity of their objects to any conventional standards whatever. In them, such terms as "good" are used in their logically most primitive and fundamental sense simply to express our liking or favor of any object which we directly contemplate, imagine, or envisage. And it is only because our likings are, for the most part, fairly stable, and hence our expressions of them tolerably uniform, that "good" and "valuable" gradually become associated in particular contexts with certain perceptual characteristics of which our value judgments are presently taken as signs.

Such, it seems to me, is a not-implausible reading of Santayana's so-called "theory of values." However, it might be

argued that, with the benefit of a good deal of hindsight, I
am reading into Santayana's words in *The Sense of Beauty*,
just what I am disposed to find there. A more crucial work
in this connection, therefore, is the essay on "Hypostatic
Ethics," which is included in *Winds of Doctrine*, his devastating critique of Bertrand Russell's early philosophy. It is an
interesting piece, even if, as Santayana remarks somewhat
ironically, his logic in it is "not very accurate or subtle."
Most of Santayana's critics, including Russell and Pepper, remember it chiefly for its attack upon the thesis, which Russell
took over from G. E. Moore, that the term "good" refers to a
unique, unanalyzable, and absolute quality whose presence in
any object can be apprehended only by a special form of
non-empirical, ethical intuition. What they forget is that Santayana completely agreed with Moore and Russell, as against
the ethical "naturalists," that goodness as such is indefinable
and that it is always a mistake to equate it with any characteristic whatever which may be common to the things men
call "good." It is therefore a nice question whether what
Russell admitted to having learned from Santayana's essay
is precisely what Santayana meant to teach. Let us see.

Santayana's statement of his position is so succinct and so
forceful that it would be foolish of me to try to paraphrase it:

> Before proceeding to the expression of concrete ideals, he
> [Russell] thinks it necessary to ask a preliminary and quite
> abstract question, to which his essay is chiefly devoted; namely,
> what is the right definition of the predicate "good," which we
> hope to apply in the sequel to such a variety of things? And he
> answers at once: The predicate "good" is indefinable. This
> answer he shows to be unavoidable, and so evidently unavoid-
> able that we might perhaps have been absolved from asking
> the question; for, as he says, the so-called definition of "good"
> —that it is pleasure, the desired, and so forth—are not defini-
> tions of the predicate "good," but designations of the things to
> which this predicate is applied by different persons. Pleasure,
> and its rivals, are not synonyms for the abstract quality "good,"
> but names for classes of concrete facts that are supposed to
> possess that quality. From this correct, if somewhat trifling,
> observation, however, Mr. Russell, like Mr. Moore before him,

evokes a portentous dogma. Not being able to define good, he hypostasises it. "Good and bad," he says, "are qualities which belong to objects independently of our opinions, just as much as round and square do; and when two people differ as to whether a thing is good, only one of them can be right, though it may be very hard to know which is right." "We cannot maintain that for me a thing ought to exist on its own account, while for you it ought not; that would merely mean that one of us is mistaken, since in fact everything either ought to exist, or ought not." Thus we are asked to believe that good attaches to things for no reason or cause, and according to no principles of distribution; that it must be found there by a sort of receptive exploration in each separate case; in other words, that it is an absolute, not a relative thing, a primary and not a secondary quality.[5]

At this point, unfortunately, Santayana's talk of qualities leads us a bit off the track. He makes it appear momentarily, that the fundamental issue between him and Russell is only whether goodness is an absolute and primary quality which is predicated of things "as they are in themselves," or a relative and secondary quality which is predicated of them only under certain standard, operative conditions. Were this the real issue between them, then it would be hardly necessary to take sides, since the whole distinction between primary and secondary qualities remains notoriously unclear, and since it may plausibly be argued that when any term, relative or absolute, is literally predicated of a subject it really and absolutely is predicated of it, just as it is also true that the use of all predicative terms, whether the "qualities" they represent are secondary or primary, presupposes what may be called "a context of predication." Thus, when we say that something is "heavy" or "sweet" or "good," we are talking about the object, not about our view of it, our sensations of it, or our feelings toward it. And the same is equally true when we say, a trifle more complexly, that something is to the right of something else or even that it causes certain re-

[5] George Santayana, *Winds of Doctrine* (London: J. M. Dent & Sons, 1940), pp. 140-1.

actions in us. But it is also obvious that we would not say
sincerely that it is heavy if, for example, we do not think it so,
if it simply disappears from view whenever we try to weigh
it, or if the situation in which we make the statement is not
one in which it is understood that we are speaking of things
of comparable weight. If one is talking about animals it is
true, absolutely and unconditionally, that elephants are
heavy. But when the talk is about planets, it is not merely
false to say that elephants are heavy, but grotesque, ridicu-
lous, or even senseless. But such remarks as these take us
farther and farther from the real point at issue between Russell and Santayana. For it is no part of Santayana's intention
to deny that when we judge something to be good we really
mean to be saying something about it; nor is it any part of his
purpose to assert that when we judge something to be evil
we mean to say merely that it appears evil to us, though perhaps not to someone else. In sum, I take it that it is *not* his
view that nothing is good or evil but thinking makes it so.[6]
Santayana's own relativism is not in the least Protagorean; it
turns on a different point altogether. But again it is well to
let him speak for himself:

> . . . what suggests this [Russell's] hypostasis of good is rather
> the fact that what others find good, or what we ourselves have
> found good in moods with which we retain no sympathy, is
> sometimes pronounced by us to be bad; and far from inferring
> from this diversity of experience that the present good, like the
> others, corresponds to a particular attitude or interest of ours,
> and is dependent upon it, Mr. Russell and Mr. Moore infer
> instead that the presence of the good must be independent of
> all interests, attitudes, and opinions. . . . To protect the be-
> lated innocence of this state of mind, Mr. Russell, so far as I
> can see, has only one argument, and one analogy. The argu-
> ment is that "if this were not the case, we could not reason with
> a man as to what is right." "We do in fact hold that when one
> man approves of a certain act, while another disapproves, one
> of them is mistaken, which would not be the case with a mere

[6] I myself doubt very much that anyone at all in his right mind ever
meant to maintain precisely this view.

emotion. If one man likes oysters and another dislikes them, we do not say that either of them is mistaken." In other words, we are to maintain our prejudices, however absurd, lest it should become unnecessary to quarrel about them! Truly the debating society has its idols, no less than the cave and the theatre. The analogy that comes to buttress somewhat this singular argument is the analogy between ethical propriety and physical or logical truth. An ethical proposition may be correct or incorrect, in a sense justifying argument, when it touches what is good as a means, that is, when it is not intrinsically ethical, but deals with causes and effects, or with matters of fact or necessity. But to speak of the truth of an ultimate good would be a false collocation of terms; an ultimate good is chosen, found, or aimed at; it is not opined. The ultimate intuitions on which ethics rests are not debatable, for they are not opinions we hazard but preferences we feel; and it can be neither correct nor incorrect to feel them.[7]

Now, making due allowances for the fact that Santayana's idioms are not those of many contemporary analytical philosophers, I think it is plain that the fundamental gist of these remarks is precisely that moral judgments are logically of a sort completely different from statements of fact, whether "natural" or "non-natural"; that they are made in order to express commitments or preferences, not in order to state beliefs or opinions about questions of fact; and that this being so, it is pointless to argue about their "truth" or "correctness," at least when we have passed beyond the point where a sincere consensus of moral sentiments or attitudes may be presupposed. If, past this point, we persist in saying to those with whom we disagree in attitude that our own judgments are "true," we will be doing nothing more than misleadingly reaffirming our loyalty to them. And when we admit, despite our present convictions, that they still may be "false" or "incorrect," this is hardly more than a way of indicating our own willingness to reconsider them if and when it can be shown that in continuing to hold them we would be false to our own true heart of hearts. In a word, to admit the possibility that a "fundamental" moral judgment may be false is only a

[7] Ibid., pp. 143-4.

way of suggesting that it may turn out to be not quite so fundamental or unalterable after all. Making such admissions to those with whom we morally disagree is merely a way of holding out an olive branch, to preserve the peace until we have had time to search out, and perhaps to find, a more ultimate area of agreement within which our present moral differences may gradually be resolved.

Thus, long before the current vogue of so-called "non-cognitive" ethics, Santayana was already saying in substance that morality, conceived as a form of first-personal judgment, is not and can not logically be reduced to a science of any sort, and hence that what we can plausibly mean by such phrases as "rational morality" and "moral truth" must be something quite different from what many philosophers have had in mind in speaking of "scientific ethics" and "the truth about morality." This reading of Santayana becomes indisputable in the intriguing chapter on "Moral Truth" in *The Realm of Truth*.[8] In that work, he grants that the moral commandment, "Love they neighbor as thyself," "purely hortatory as this seems . . . may be almost entirely translated into propositions that would be either true or false."[9] For embedded in the commandment is the knowledge that all living things are ends to themselves as much as we to our own selves. Yet, as he says, this truth "is not, and cannot become, a moral commandment," since "The categorical nerve of every imperative is vital, it expresses an actual movement of the will."[1] For both Santayana and Kant every principle of *practical* reason must contain within itself what Kant calls a "determination of the will," and every moral principle is essentially a practical principle which, as such, can never be translated into any

---

[8] *The Realm of Truth*, in my opinion, is one of Santayana's best and most neglected works.

[9] *Realms of Being*, one-vol. ed. (New York: Charles Scribner's Sons, 1942), p. 475.

[1] Op. cit., p. 476. In this instance, Santayana's idiom, interestingly enough, is very close to that of Kant, which, incidentally, shows how far, despite his formalism and his rationalism in ethics, the great "Chinaman of Konigsberg" really was from what passes nowadays for "cognitivism" in ethics.

purely speculative theory about what purport to be matters of fact.

Santayana also makes a great point of the distinction between morality proper, which is concerned with the articulation of our "actual allegiance in sentiment and action to this or that ideal of life," and the "descriptive science of ethics," as he calls it, which describes "the history of such allegiances, and of the circumstances and effects involved." [2] In fact, it is this distinction, which lies at the root of so many of Santayana's most penetrating, yet always sympathetic, criticisms of the philosophies and theologies of his predecessors. For him, it is the blurring of this distinction which is responsible in large part for the fabulous moral histories of the Jews and Christians, the hypostatic, moralistic metaphysics of the Platonists, the mythic philosophies of history of the Hegelians and the Marxists, and the transcendental philosophies or "sciences" of mind to which so many German philosophers have been addicted since the time of Kant himself. The same confusion is also responsible for the various *ad hoc* epistemologies that philosophers construct out of whole cloth in order to provide at least a verbal account of the meaning and verifiability of propositions whose ambiguous functions are thus systematically run together. As a detached man of the world, Santayana is rarely censorious of the forms of life that are embedded in these doctrines, and so long as they are sincerely avowed he is prepared to respect them for the vital human concerns which they may unconsciously express. What he deplores, as a lover of truth and wisdom, are the comprehensive illusions to which they give rise, the false comfort which they afford to their victims, and the terrible way in which they help to harden natural moral affinities into metaphysical dogmas and theological creeds. Himself an instinctive traditionalist and aristocrat, Sanatayana is always immensely respectful of Plato as a philosophical moralist. He objects only to Plato's tendency to convert his own moral perspectives, by a piece of logical legerdemain, into a mythological cosmology whose peculiar "truth," quite understand-

[2] Ibid., p. 473.

ably, is apprehendable only by a specially trained philosophical elect, whose unique powers of insight extend beyond the
understanding of ordinary scientists and mathematicians and
the lay moral intuitions or sentiments of the ruck of mankind.
Santayana's spiritual catholicism is always put on the stretch
when he discusses anything German. But even German egoism he can understand when conceived as a sincere preoccupation with the affairs of the self. His objection is that the
German idealists, mistaking the nature of the informal moral
dialectic of the soul's discourse with itself, converted it into a
monstrous organon or method for the construction of elaborate *Geisteswissenschaften* which purport to tell us, at one
and the same time, both what there is and what there ought
to be. The always chaster English logicians, although pas-
sionately insisting on the logical distinction between what is
and what ought to be, convert what ought to be into a queer
realm of being populated by strange, unanalyzable qualities,
whose relations it becomes the province of an unnatural science of ethics to describe. And once more, in order that man
may come to know the principles of that science, there is the
tell-tale postulation of a special faculty of ethical intuition
which, independently of all human attitudes and preferences,
is supposed to give us that truth about morals which is also
the moral truth.

For Santayana it was thus the part of wisdom to know our
moral principles for what they are, the all too human expressions of organic passions and sentiments. So conceiving
them, we are no longer tempted to press beyond the congenital "naturalism" of undeceived common sense in order to
postulate moral half-substances which would matter less to
us if we knew them for what they really are. When we know
what we are up against, we are left free candidly to avow
and to defend the way of life embodied in those precepts we
ourselves find most congenial, without dogmatically opposing
others whose principles are affirmed on grounds that are
logically as impeccable as our own. Nor will we then seek that
spurious assurance of all metaphysical moralists who suppose
that the unrighteous would be automatically converted if

only they were required to take a proper course in moral physics.

Here, however, we must make another turn of the linguistic screw. In his later writings, as he perceives more clearly the fundamental logical point of his distinction between morality and the descriptive science of ethics, Santayana is no longer so reluctant to admit that there may be such a thing as moral truth. No longer anxious lest such an admission may seem to countenance a mythical moral physics, he is left free to acknowledge the familiar fact that ordinary men also sometimes claim truth for their moral principles. It is now only a question of explaining correctly what such claims amount to. His suggestion is that although fools, in morals as elsewhere, are always ready to cry, "How true!" to any proposition which is widely held, expressing thereby little more than their own diffused and cowardly wish to belong to the crowd and to share in its sentiments, men of integrity will reserve the title of "moral truth" for considered judgments which they sincerely and steadily profess in the light of the best knowledge of themselves which moral intuition or insight may afford. However, once again he tirelessly reaffirms the point that "This Socratic self-knowledge is not scientific but expressive, not ethical but moral; and here if anywhere, in the discovery of what one ultimately wants and ultimately loves, *moral truth* might be found." [3] And then he at once so wisely adds, "This is no easy discovery; and we must be prepared for surprises in morals, no less than in physics, as investigation and analysis proceed. As the blue vault vanishes under the telescope, so moral conventions might dissolve in an enlightened conscience, and we might be abashed to perceive how disconcerting, how revolutionary, how ascetic the inmost oracle of the heart would prove, if only we had ears to hear it. Perhaps a premonition of this ultimate moral disillusion rendered Socrates so endlessly patient, diffident, and ironical, so impossible to corrupt and so impossible to deceive." [4]

[3] Ibid., p. 480.
[4] Ibid.

The basic error of Socrates, as it is also the error of all dogmatists, is the assumption that human nature is single and immutable and that "the good that glimmered like buried gold in his own heart must lie also in the hearts of others, and only ignorance or sophistry could keep them from seeing it." [5] It is for this reason that Santayana, who opposed any attempt to stretch moral unity "beyond the range of natural organization," considered it the part of wisdom, as well as of logic, to recognize the ultimate diversity of morals. And although "politically, and within the living organism . . . moral dogmatism is morality itself," it remained for him spiritually "a sinister thing, a sin against the spirit elsewhere." Where, we may ask, *is* elsewhere? To this, I suppose that Santayana would reply, that region, secret to every man, in which, like Kierkegaard, he "suspends the ethical" in order that he may achieve a vision of that quiet and serenity which is spiritual liberation. This does not mean that the liberated spirit may not return to the forum or to the battlefield of the moral life where, like everyone else, he is bound at last to speak for a moral truth which he cannot sincerely disown. It means, rather, that he returns in effect as one twice-born, who views the necessity of returning at once tragically and ironically, as a condition which befits a being created in the image of God yet compelled, whether he will or not, to dwell forever in the realm of matter.

There is a final, closely related, error of the sons of Socrates which the philosopher Santayana would remove. Here, curiously enough, he once more comes close to the pragmatists, particularly to William James. James, it will be remembered, spoke of "rationality," the love of order, coherence, and harmony, as a "sentiment." And it was his claim that when this sentiment wars within our breasts for regimen over other passions it must make its own way and prove itself by its own fruits. It has no antecedent metaphysical claim to priority, and if we ourselves say that it ought to prevail, why then we are once more expressing our own submission to it in the face of other claims which we thereby find less exigent. But we

[5] Ibid., p. 481.

may of course deceive ourselves, and there is no natural harmony, written into either nature or the *logos*, which precludes the possibility that we may discover later that at our heart's core, "whirl is king." Similarly, while proclaiming throughout a long life the merits of the life of reason against barbarians and protestants and romantics of all sorts, Santayana also insisted that the truth about morals everywhere does not include the thesis that no principle may count as "moral" which cannot be universalized or which defies the moral principles of concord and consistency. What, when all is said and done, if we find that we prefer discord? And what if our moral passion for equality or freedom refuses to give way, in cases of conflict, to the sentiment of rationality? In that case, by a curious paradox, does not that sentiment itself then become unreasonable in demanding an organization, whether personal or interpersonal, to which our unruly natures will not submit? And do we not then subvert the name of moral truth in proclaiming its universal validity, when we know that we cannot avow it sincerely and with an undivided heart?

Some have misunderstood Santayana at this point. Of all men, he is perhaps the last to preach irrationalism. What he does preach is the cause of self-knowledge and the refusal of true moralists to say, as a certain self-styled Christian platonist and socratist was once overheard to say in a moment of apoplexy, "Jesus is reason!" Reason is a principle or complex of principles, among the most precious, certainly, which a moral philosopher may avow. But it is not, properly, an object of worship, not a surrogate-God, before which all men must bow their heads and bend their knees. Santayana may have worshipped no god, and, as some will think, that was his final limitation or trouble. His great merit as a philosopher consisted in the fact, that at any rate, he worshipped no false gods, including the philosophical god of reason. And this, in my opinion, helped him clear his head for the study of the treacherous symbolic forms which men call "morality."

CONCLUSION

It is my belief, then, that Santayana is best understood as a natural historian and philosopher of symbolic forms. So conceived, his work takes on a relevance for both contemporary philosophical analysis and critical theory which has a significance that this brief study has barely intimated. Still I would not claim too much. When one presses Santayana beyond a certain point for answers, they are often not forthcoming. At the crucial point he is more likely than not to put one off with a flashing metaphor or figure of speech, when what one wants is definition and plain talk. One feels that he is more at home in the middle region between general theory and specific interpretation or judgment. Indeed, this is why in my title I have preferred to call him a natural historian rather than a philosopher of symbolic forms. It is hardly worthwhile, however, to dwell upon his limitations, which are well known to all, when his contributions to the philosophy of meaning are so little known and so poorly understood. He has given us insights, as I have tried to show in the case of aesthetics and ethics, which we have hardly as yet begun to recover. If there were space, much the same could be shown to be true of his theories of religious discourse. If he lacked fundamental warmth, this very fact made possible the detachment which was necessary for his probing studies of the controlling symbols of western culture. If on occasion we are outraged by his fantastic indifference, we may at least be grateful for its fruits. Man, it has been said, is the talking animal. Santayana, through a long life, contributed much to our understanding of the nature of his talk, and therefore to our knowledge of the animal himself. No more can be claimed for any contemporary philosopher.

Philosophical Analysis and the Spiritual Life

A REPLY TO MR. WILLIAM EARLE'S "NOTES ON THE DEATH OF CULTURE"

MR. EARLE'S CRITIQUE OF MODERN CULTURE

Academic philosophers, by the nature of their calling, are menders and preservers. For them, existence is a subject for discussion, and language something to be mentioned but never used. You would never guess from their immaculate publications that doomsday may be in the offing. Western civilization may be cracking up, but no signs of the fact are to be found on the pages of *The Journal of Philosophy* or *Mind*. There, if nowhere else, the *Logos* remains undisturbed; there anxiety is acknowledged only as a concept, and consciousness exists, if at all, only as a phenomenon, like dust, black-spot, or the great bend of the Orinoco. Professor William Earle, that is to say, is something new under the academic sun, at least in America; and his disturbing essay, "Notes on the Death of Culture," [1] would deserve notice if for no reason but the fact that he not only loathes his "subject" but says so in so many words. What is still more impressive, however, is his readiness to generalize; the dreadful predicament of contemporary professional philosophy is, for him, merely a symptom of the dry-rot which is destroying our entire Western culture.

[1] *Noonday I*. New York: The Noonday Press, 1958.

As Mr. Earle himself points out, his theme is not new; for over a century unacademic philosophers, historians, and men of letters have debated the causes of what Matthew Arnold called "this strange disease of modern life." More original and intriguing are Earle's diagnosis of the ailment, and his "private" dream of a new, authentic culture which might conceivably arise from the ashes of our existing pseudo-culture. For him, there is no hope of reviving what pundits call "The Great Tradition." He admires it, somewhat nostalgically, for what it was, but he believes that it is now without a saving remnant, and he boldly calls therefore for a complete and revolutionary break with what has gone before. Like Marx, and unlike Nietzsche and Kierkegaard, Earle conceives of this break as a social and not merely as an individual necessity. But like Nietzsche and Kierkegaard, and unlike Marx, he conceives it in purely spiritual rather than in material terms. What is wanted, in short, is a completely new vision of human destiny in which the activities of religion, art, and philosophy may again be fused, as perhaps they were in biblical times, in one great communal act of cultural creation.

If Mr. Earle's intentions are revolutionary, there is something slightly archaic, at least, about his diction. In our time the concept of culture has been largely appropriated by bacteriologists and social scientists. But Mr. Earle makes it clear from the outset that he is not talking about phenomena of any sort, whether microscopic or macroscopic, whether individual or social; he conceives of culture in a purely ideal sense, as "the whole life of the human spirit in communities." This sounds a bit like Hegel; as we shall see, the idea behind it is also Hegelian. In Earle's philosophy, as in Hegel's, it is the concept of spirit itself which is the operative term. What is spirit? Earle's answer is somewhat muffled, but it provides, nonetheless, the essential clue to his diagnosis of our cultural predicament. It must be understood, in the first place, that the life of the spirit is never "automatic or instinctual": "it must be created by the spirit itself." This means, among other things, that the spirit must be *concerned*, concerned "for itself, for its life" as a "free effort." It means also a striving toward self-consciousness, toward *lucidity* about what it itself is and what other things are. And it means, finally, that the spirit must *manifest* itself to others in works lucidly expressive of its self-concern. Such a conception invites parody. I myself am reminded of a line in one of W. H. Auden's poems about "the high, thin, rare, continuous worship of the self-absorbed." The proper analogy, however, is again with Hegel, whose talk about spirit as something which exists in, for, and through itself is plainly echoed in Earle's very turns of phrase. There are some, I know, who will take this comparison itself as an implied rebuke. It is not so intended. And if the complaint is seriously pressed that Earle has utterly failed to define the essence of spirit, the only and sufficient reply is that spirit, like existence, has no essence. Indeed, the very attempt to define "spirit," like the attempts to define "existence" or "good," is the root of many philosophical evils. The *uses* of such expressions may be explained, but that is another matter. Earle does not attempt this, nor, I suppose, would he consider it a useful philosophical venture.

But there are many ways of clarifying an idea, and Mr. Earle has at any rate managed to specify three characteristic and inalienable "functions" of spirit, as he calls them. And it is precisely in their dissociation that he locates the spiritual derangement of modern culture. In our time, unfortunately, "religion" no longer has anything to do with matters of creed or commitment; like Royce's loyalty to loyalty, it has become, on the contrary, a sheer concern with concern itself. What passes for "philosophy" is no longer a love of wisdom or an attempt to clarify a total vision of human destiny, but an obsession with lucidity as an end in itself. And what we call "the arts" are no longer expressions of human emotion or representations of recognizable forms with which men in real life are deeply concerned; they are, rather, vacuous efforts at "pure" expression or meaningless arrangements of "aesthetic surfaces." In a word, "religion," "philosophy," and "the arts," no longer serve as names for dimensions of an existentially undivided spirit; they have become mere disciplinary titles for sterile academic subjects and professional activities which have lost any vestigial sense of their common spiritual vocation. Meanwhile philosophers analyze, theologians dread, poets howl, painters arrange pieces of wrapping paper, musicians make sounds, and sculptors bend hairpins. All are quite mad, and like madmen, all are spiritually dead. They have nothing to do with culture, and culture has nothing to do with them.

Mr. Earle's diatribe also reminds one of Wyndham Lewis. Unlike Lewis, however, Earle has no personal animus. He is talking more of trends than of the achievements of particular men. He does not make the mistake of denying the specialized talents of the Picassos and Schönbergs, the Russells and Wittgensteins, the Bubers and Tillichs. They are sometimes clever or amusing; they may, for a time, titillate the senses or intrigue the intellect; but in the end, as Mr. Earle sadly confesses, they always become a bore. And boredom, of course, is the final and most terrible enemy of spirit.

THE STATE OF PHILOSOPHY IN
THE AGE OF ANALYSIS

As it stands, such a diagnosis is excessively abstract. It would be improper therefore to criticize it until we have first seen how it is fleshed out in Mr. Earle's more detailed criticisms of what is now happening in philosophy, religion, and the arts. His description of the condition of contemporary philosophy, naturally enough, is the fullest and best informed, and it is to this that I will give closest scrutiny.

Symptomatic of the decline of philosophical culture in our age, according to Earle, is the emergence of the "technical philosopher," a fabulous creature whose sole professional interest in the clarification of ideas has lost all contact with the spiritual ends which alone give point to the demand for lucidity. Earle portrays him, with great gusto, as an intellectual eunuch, obsessed with narrow "analytical" questions of logic, meaning, and method which, by definition, have nothing to do with reality and, because of this, are devoid of content. This frivolous logic-chopper, whose clever little word-games are as immaculate, impersonal, and witless as the computations of a Mark III, is then compared, somewhat to his disadvantage, to that paragon of serious intent, the "traditional" philosopher, a man of large and "edifying" visions who has somehow managed to transcend the ordinary man's unphilosophical concern with such particular evils as sickness, poverty, war, and tyranny in order to meditate without distraction upon the sheer meaning of existence.

Earle names few names, but one of his examples of the analytical school is J. S. Mill, whom Nietzsche contemptuously referred to as a "blockhead" and whom an admirer called, perhaps not inconsistently with Nietzsche, "the Saint of Rationalism." Earle's classification of Mill is not unjust but misleading. Mill did write a famous treatise on logic and scientific method in which he had a great deal to say about the problem of meaning. But, as in his other works, his concern in writing it was philosophical. That is to say, it was part of his life-long campaign against the dogmatism and apriorism which stand in the way of human enlightenment and progress. Mill hated the so-called Reason of the intuitionists and transcendentalists because it short-circuits criticism and fortifies entrenched opinion and habit under the guise of insight. And he respected logic and science because he believed that in them lies our only hope of destroying the idols which have enslaved men's minds since the dawn of history. Earle's complaint against Mill, however, is that he supposed that the suffering of human life may be analyzed into a plurality of specific correctable ills. What Mill failed to see, according to Earle, is that the suffering of life is a problem which "requires for its solution an inner philosophic transformation of our attitude toward life." To this last, however, the only reply is that Earle has evidently forgotten Mill's moving *Autobiography* or such pieces as his fine appreciative essay on the arch-transcendentalist Coleridge. It is true that Mill thought deeply and often effectively about specific remediable miseries; it is not true that he had no conception of the "pathos of human existence," or the necessity of facing it with philosophic fortitude and understanding. Quite the contrary, utilitarianism, in its most extended sense, was for Mill a way of life, as it had been also for Bentham. And if it partially failed in its Benthamite formulation to satisfy all of his spiritual needs, Mill continued to revise and to enlarge it throughout his career.

In Mr. Earle's jaundiced eyes, more recent analysts lack even Mill's diversified interest in human life. They spend their time tracking down metaphysical absurdities which they ascribe exclusively to the misuse of ordinary language. Or else they devote themselves to the construction of unintelligible systems of symbolic logic or to the creation of impossible "ideal languages" of science from which every trace of spiritual meaning has been relentlessly eliminated. In brief, the contemporary analyst of whatever school is a fanatical methodolatrist and logomaniac who no longer remembers, if he ever knew, what existence really means. Bereft of vision and devoid of style, his vacuous little papers on the meaning of meaning are so tedious that not even his own friends can keep awake while they are being read.

What shall we say to all this? I believe that, to begin with, we must acknowledge, with chagrin, its grains of truth. Most professional philosophers, let it be said, are not large-scale dreamers, dedicated, at least in their waking hours, to the pursuit of wisdom and the edification of their fellows; they are, in a word, clods. And this is as true of the professional metaphysicians as it is of the analysts. At our best universities there are numbers of men now writing and teaching something called "philosophy" who would find the craft of the greengrocer taxing and the simple integrity of a virtuous chimney-sweep beyond their powers to emulate. They not only have no vision; they have no ideas. And their inflated academic reputations as "scholars" depend entirely upon their familiarity with the lore and jargon of their profession itself. Such men, I agree, are not practitioners of philosophy, but its scholastic spawn.

So much, and more, needed to be said, and we may be grateful to Mr. Earle for saying it so entertainingly. But when since the morning of the world have things been different? Plato's heaviest ironies were directed at sophists who teach nothing for a price. And the Bishop of Cloyne—himself, as it happens, a first-rate analyst and a profound student of the philosophy of language—directed all his efforts against those "minute philosophers" who first raise a dust of words and then complain that they cannot see. No century has ever produced more than a bare handful of authentic philosophers, and in every century the Spinozas, the Kants, the Mills, and the Russells have had to fight their way against a ruck of academic deadbeats who are always on hand to throw the book of tradition—or culture—at anyone who manages to think for himself. Now it is easy, I know, to exaggerate, just as it is also easy to undervalue, the achievements of one's immediate predecessors and contemporaries. But even if we limit the list to primarily analytical philosophers, it would be hard to deny the term "authentic" to such original thinkers as Russell and Wittgenstein. And by extending somewhat the notion of analysis, we might also include the American pragmatists, Peirce, James, and Dewey. In various ways, all of these thinkers have thought profoundly about the nature of language, thought, and truth. It could be argued, indeed, that they have jointly effected a revolution in our very conception of the life of reason and hence of culture. And most of them have written with as much distinction and style as the philosophers of any age.

Merely to say this, however, is to play Mr. Earle's own game, and I, at least, decline to play it. For, despite Earle, Morton White's phrase, "The Age of Analysis," is not exact as a characterization of the twentieth-century in philosophy; nor does White himself pretend that it is. Such systematic thinkers as Whitehead and Santayana were men of vision in precisely Earle's own sense; they sought through philosophical study and contemplation to find a vision of reality which would provide the basis of a truly philosophic way of life. But unlike Earle they were not hostile to the analysis of concepts, and both of them used their own analytical powers to great effect in clarifying the fundamental concepts and cate-

gories by which contemporary men must try to live. I am also
just a little puzzled by Mr. Earle's reluctance to mention the
phenomenologists and existentialists with whom in the past
his own work has been most closely identified. It cannot be
that he regards the existentialists as analytical philosophers,
for their anti-intellectualism and anti-rationalism is as great
as their manner of writing is inexact. True, it could be argued
that the phenomenologists, in their own odd way, are analysts
who believe that by a special form of inspection or intuition
they can discern certain primordial forms of human experience. And Husserl, one of the founders of the phenomenological school, was certainly interested in problems of logic.
But, as White remarks in *The Age of Analysis*, Husserl believed that his own analytical method could also shed light
on art, religion, law, history, "and all other aspects of culture
and the universe." In short, ours is by no means exclusively
an age of analysis; nor are the analysts as devoid of concern
for the life of the spirit as Earle pretends.

But with the exceptions of Santayana and Whitehead,
there is one fact about contemporary philosophy of all schools
that distinguishes it from the philosophy of earlier times. This
is its inability to construct or, in many cases, its lack of interest in constructing philosophical systems in the grand style of
a Spinoza or a Hegel. And for this no apology need be made.
What remains illuminating in Spinoza's philosophy is not his
rationalistic metaphysics and theology, but his acute and
highly technical analyses of the passions of the soul and the
sources, in them, of human bondage. Likewise what remains
of interest in the ponderous tomes of Hegel is not his deadly
ontologic, which Kierkegaard parodied with such devastating
effect, but his immensely suggestive side-glances at human
institutions and his vivid sense of the mutability of all things
human, including the life of reason itself. Much the same, I
should judge, will turn out to be true of the philosophies of
Whitehead and Santayana. If one thing is dead in contemporary philosophy, it is system.

But there are reasons for this which Mr. Earle fails to consider. In fact, the fundamental weakness of his description of the present philosophical scene is precisely its lack of that sense of dialectical historical development of which Hegel was so acutely aware. Earle wholly ignores the fact that there are compelling historical reasons why philosophers in our age distrust the very idea of system. He also ignores the shifts in perspective which have disposed his contemporaries to question even the intelligibility of those edifying visions which he ascribes, with something less than complete accuracy, to the traditional philosopher. Historically, the gnostic's vision of reality went together with a characteristic theory of knowledge and a metaphysics which seemed to provide its philosophical foundation. This was as true of Plotinus as of Spinoza or Leibniz. To most philosophers since Kant, however, such a theory of knowledge and such a metaphysics are no longer credible. In fact, the whole preoccupation of contemporary philosophers with problems of logical and linguistic analysis is an inevitable consequence of the running critique of traditional ideas of reason and reality initiated by Hume and Kant. Certainly the end is not clear. But anyone who dreams to any purpose of the future of philosophy cannot dismiss a critique of reason which, for over two centuries, has transformed the very notion of the philosophical enterprise itself.

In his own way, Mr. Earle himself recognizes the futility of trying to go back again to the visions of his predecessors. What he must be asked, therefore, is whether his own gnostic conception of wisdom, which is so deeply entangled with traditional rationalistic notions of human knowledge, is any longer viable, even for those who, like himself, reject the view that philosophy consists merely in the logical analysis of concepts. Like many others, Earle believes that the tradition of Western philosophy has come to a dead end. Yet at the same time he yearns toward an ideal of the philosophical quest which lies at the heart of the tradition which he rejects. Now I hope that I understand something of Mr. Earle's fundamental ambivalence; like Nietzsche, I also share it. But we

must cut our losses and accept the fact that there is no longer
a *Logos* at the heart of things. Thenceforth we must go it on
our own.

PHILOSOPHICAL "VISION" AND
THE NATURE OF LANGUAGE

Why are contemporary philosophers unable to believe in the
idea of a *Logos* and hence in the ideal of a philosophical
vision of things which has any noetic significance? The fundamental reason concerns a traditional philosophical conception of language and hence of thought itself which is just now
in its death throes. In order to make this clear, it will be
necessary to say something about that conception itself; only
then will we be in a position to estimate the contribution
which the analytical study of language can make to the understanding and the preservation of our common culture.

It should be emphasized at the outset that, contrary to the
impression conveyed in Earle's "Notes," technicality is nothing new to philosophy. Indeed, from Plato to Spinoza most
traditional philosophers believed that true philosophical vision is itself attainable only through the study of exact science, mathematics, and formal logic. Plato himself assigns to
these disciplines a higher place than poetry and music on the
hierarchy of cultural activities precisely because the forms
which are their objects are closer to the form or idea of the
Good. In short, like all true gnostics, Plato assumed that the
fundamental significance of all cultural acts is noetic, and
hence that the spiritual order of merit is at bottom a cognitive
order. For him, even goodness itself is conceived mainly as an
object of knowledge, and man's own highest good consists in
its sheer apprehension. This doctrine, however, is rooted in
preconceptions concerning the nature of thought and, ultimately, of language which have been fully exposed only in
very recent times.

Here it is necessary to correct another impression conveyed in Mr. Earle's "Notes." He intimates, if he does not
actually state, that the interest of technical philosophers in

the nature of language is something peculiar to our own age. Actually, the philosophical preoccupation with language is at least as old as Plato himself. From his *Cratylus* to Berkeley's astonishingly prophetic *Alciphron,* the problematical relations of language to thought and to the "objects" of thought— "what there is"—have been frequently, if also inconclusively, debated by philosophers of all types and schools. In fact, it has frequently been argued by Bertrand Russell and others that such philosophers as Aristotle took far too seriously the syntax, parts of speech, and terms of *ordinary* language as essential clues to our understanding of the categories of being and even of being itself. In my own opinion, they were, in one sense, right to do so; that is to say, it may be that our knowledge of "what there is" will turn out to be, or at least to depend upon, a clear understanding of what we are doing when we *say* that something exists, that something is good, that there is a God, that there is a number between one and three, or that space is infinitely divisible. But this is plainly very different from what the traditional philosophers seem to have had in mind. In their case, as also in the case of a great many later philosophers including Russell and the early Wittgenstein, it was assumed, in effect, that when language is used meaningfully it provides a kind of relief map of that portion of reality which it is said to represent or signify. And it is largely for this reason that Russell, like Leibniz, regarded the study of the logical grammar or syntax of language as philosophically important. For him, the philosophical analysis of language matters because the grammar of a truly clear language would disclose the underlying metaphysical structure of reality.

This traditional conception of language is closely related to the also common view, most succinctly expressed by Hobbes, that "words are wise men's counters." According to this notion, as it has been developed in more recent times, any proper or healthy language is a kind of calculus whose "transformation rules," as they are called, prescribe the exact logical conditions in accordance with which alone any significant complex statement may be translated (or reduced) into conjunctions of logically basic or simple propositions. The latter propositions, in turn, are held to be meaningful only if their semantical elements or terms each signify, in virtue of an explict "formation rule," some distinct and perspicuous item of experience. Superficially at least, such a theory may seem reasonable enough. But it plainly implies that ordinary language, which has no such rules, and which contains many terms, such as "spirit," whose "objects," if they exist at all, are exceedingly obscure, is necessarily an imperfect vehicle for precise thought or communication. It implies also that such forms of utterance as poetry, which admits of no precise translations or paraphrases, or morals, whose essential terms, such as "right" and "ought," literally signify nothing at all, must be consigned to the semantical ash-can of "pseudo-statements" and "pseudo-concepts," as Rudolf Carnap calls them.

Whether culture, in Mr. Earle's sense, can survive such rough-shod treatment without perversion is very doubtful. And if this is what positivism in its contemporary forms comes to, then I, like him, want none of it. The important point, however, is that it is not his traditional philosophers who provide effective tools for fighting such a rampant scientism but rather the so-called philosophers of "ordinary language," whose preoccupation with the ordinary ways of words Earle, like Bertrand Russell, so deplores. In fact, the traditional philosopher could not effectively oppose positivism, since positivism is itself merely the historical outcome of his own basic misconceptions concerning the nature and function of meaningful discourse. He too was profoundly afflicted with the same philosophical virus of "descriptivism" which leads those who suffer from it to assume that all significant utterances are mere descriptions or signs of what exists in "the real world."

Actually, however, the real philosophical tradition is far more complex than either Mr. Earle or I, up to this point, has suggested. Already in the eighteenth century, "the old happy time" as Nietzsche nostalgically called it, a new conception of language was emerging which in the end was to sound the death knell to the whole rationalistic and gnostic tradition. The first philosopher to oppose the traditional view was the Irishman, George Berkeley. Berkeley, himself a spiritualist and churchman, saw at once that the traditional religions of the West could not survive, were the view ultimately to prevail that meaningful "trains of words" should be treated merely as signs of "trains of ideas" (or perceptions) which in their turn signify the true order of things in the external world. Even if such a view would do, as it will not, as an account of the language of science, it maims every other cultural activity that depends essentially upon the use of language. Accordingly, Berkeley argued in effect that, not only in religion and ethics, but also in mathematics and logic, words do not normally function as "signs" at all. Their meaning, he contended, can never be determined by following *a priori* that prime rule of all "literalists of the imagination," "Hunt the referent!" On the contrary, it can only be found by examining in the contexts of their ordinary uses what we, as speakers, *do* with them.

But it was not only in his conception of language that Berkeley thus anticipated the later thought of Ludwig Wittgenstein, the prime mover of contemporary linguistic philosophy. Berkeley's philosophy of language was conceived primarily as a weapon for the defense of the spiritual life against would-be atheists and materialists. In short, like Wittgenstein and his followers, Berkeley used linguistic analysis "therapeutically." That is to say, he sought by its means to iron out the strange "mental quirks," as Gilbert Ryle calls them, that have landed traditional metaphysicians on philosophical "Queer Street." Much the same is also true of the celebrated "critical philosophy" of Kant, whom Bertrand Russell once spoke of, contemptuously, as "the greatest mistake in the history of philosophy." A large part of Kant's purpose in his *Critique of Pure Reason* was precisely to expose the basic "category mistakes" that were responsible in the past for such philosophical pseudo-sciences as "rational ontology," "rational cosmology," "rational theology," and "rational psychology." At every point Kant's own essentially therapeutic criticism of these mis-

directed "disciplines" amounts to an exposure of the philosophical misues and misapplications of such terms as "cause"
and "substance" and "existence" to "things in themselves." He
argued, accordingly, that there are no real answers to the
questions of traditional speculative metaphysics, but only the
philosophical cure which occurs when we see why such questions have no real meaning. For Kant, the true interest in
metaphysics is moral and religious. And for this reason, he
treated the "transcendent" ideas of freedom, immortality,
and God as principles or "postulates" of "practical reason."

Kant's successors, the great German idealists, continued his
attack upon the traditional tendency to subordinate the practical to the speculative use of reason, and hence, to misapply
its standards of meaning and truth to the so-called "objects"
of religious belief, moral endeavor, and artistic expression.
Properly understood, a large part of their work was directed
to freeing what Hegel called the "symbolic forms" of *Geisteswissenschaft* from their historic subservience to ideals of
lucidity and knowledge that properly hold only in the sphere
of *Naturwissenschaft*. In one way, indeed, Hegel's much-
ridiculed dialectic or "logic of being," which he also called,
significantly, a "logic of passion," is at bottom only a misguided effort to disengage the spiritual activities of art, religion, and philosophy from the stifling hold, not of science
itself, but of the perennial scientism and logicism of the tradition. But Hegel forgot the precautionary lessons of his master, and once again the forms of "logic" were treated as a
virtual map of the forms of being. So far in this direction did
Hegel go, in fact, that for him the dialectic itself became a
law of historical development, and the developing ideals or
aspirations of the human spirit came to be hypostatized,
paradoxically, as successive "moments" in the historical self-
revelation of that obscure substance he called "the absolute."
In short, Hegel once more reduced all affairs of the spirit to
a special form of spiritual knowledge or "science," whose
higher value depended for him entirely upon his own conception of its underlying cognitive significance. Thus, as
Kierkegaard perceived, Hegel remained in the end a gnostic

in spite of himself. And his extreme "panlogism," as it has been called, is perhaps the most extreme example of what a rampant gnosticism can come to. At bottom, however, Hegel's obscure efforts to explain and defend the life of the spirit against the philistines went awry precisely because of his faltering grasp of the drift of the symbolic forms through which that life is articulated.

It is a commonplace that contemporary analytical philosophy arose, in the first instance, primarily as a reaction against the self-discrediting metaphysical paradoxes of idealism and its outlandish claims regarding the nature not only of human history but of the universe as a whole. Whatever their faults and limitations, such philosophers as G. E. Moore and Bertrand Russell attacked idealism primarily in the name of lucidity; what the idealists *said* was confused and even unintelligible. If this is philosophy, then philosophy is an offense against the intellect and therefore against the human spirit itself. The irony is that Russell's fundamental weakness is of the same sort: that is, his contempt as a logician and a philosopher for the ordinary uses of words. But his attempt to establish a truly "scientific" philosophy at any rate rested on an expert knowledge of logical and scientific procedures. Because of this, he did not fall into the trap which proved the undoing of idealism: the representation of art, morality, and religion as vehicles of a higher form of cognition which, by obeying the laws of a peculiar spiritual logic, could give us a knowledge of reality inaccessible to the ordinary scientific understanding. And his celebrated "logical atomism," so far from being a wanton effort to destroy the underlying unity of the spiritual life, was an heroic, if also misdirected, effort to hold it together. It represented merely his hope of discovering those simple, perspicuous forms of thought which, as he believed, represent the same basic ontological patterns which are everywhere embedded in our experience of what there is. Like Plato, Russell believed also that through the study of logic and the "ontology" which it reveals, the philosopher may attain to that contemplative understanding of reality to which rationalists and gnostics of all ages have aspired.

The fact is that Bertrand Russell, the arch-exponent of mathematical logic and conceptual analysis, is merely the latest, and possibly the last, great exemplar of the rationalistic-gnostic tradition which Mr. Earle so much admires and whose decline he so much deplores. Russell is still looking for that logical needle in the ontological haystack, the word which will reveal the Word behind the "word." For him "knowledge by description" is at best a poor sign and necessary substitute—for time-bound men—for that direct acquaintance or intuition which provides a vision of what is really *there*. Russell admits, to be sure, that men do other things with words than formulate the knowledge about reality with which, unhappily, finite minds must make do. But he deplores such other uses of language; nor will he admit that the study of them has anything to do with philosophy. The business of the philosopher, as of the scientist, is exclusively with truth, and the salvation that it offers is that which lies in knowledge of the truth about the nature of things. This is why Russell excludes ethics from philosophy: ethics, as he believes, gives us no knowledge of what exists; it is why he is not interested in aesthetics: art is not a form of knowledge; and it is why he hates traditional theology and religion: they give us no understanding of the nature of things, but on the contrary visit us with illusions which obscure our vision of what there is. In short, no activity is worthy of the name of "philosophy" unless, at the least, it is a substitute for vision; and science is the god of thought because it, and the philosophies that emulate it, alone provide a reliable substitute for and guide to vision. The professed aims of Bertrand Russell and Earle's traditional philosopher are thus very close; their differences are differences only of idiom, detail, and perspective. And I am sure that, by and large, the traditional philosopher would read Russell's *History of Western Philosophy* with fascination and sad approval. "So this," he would say, "is what my vision comes to when it is corrected by the glasses which have been ground for me with the tools of twentieth-century analytical philosophy. The world looks smaller, in a way, but also much clearer. So be it."

Is this what Mr. Earle himself wants? I cannot believe it. I cannot believe that he thinks, like the gnostic, that vision is all, or even the all of philosophy. I cannot believe that like other gnostics, from Plato to Russell, he thinks that the aim of the spiritual life is vision, either literally or metaphorically, either directly or indirectly, by description. Nor can I believe that he thinks that every other cultural activity is subordinate to, if indeed it is not an inferior form of, knowledge, *however "knowledge" may be defined*. But if I am right, then who, really, are his friends and allies? Or better, since it is culture we are talking about, who, among contemporary philosophers, are the true friends of culture? Not, certainly, the time-serving culture-vultures who batten on the carrion of the dead tradition; not the phenomenologists whose analytical and visionary obsessions are devoid of saving grace; and not the existentialists who, for all their concern, are devoid both of reason and of lucidity. Who, then? I submit that they are the much abused philosophers of ordinary language (many of whom write with great wit and charm as well as with clarity) who, following the leads of Berkeley, Kant, and Wittgenstein, have enabled us at last to understand in detail how the forms of discourse which serve as leading parts to the spiritual activities of art, morals, and religion may be fully lucid and in their own way rational even though they describe no matters of fact, provide us with no clear and distinct ideas of the nature of things, and, in short, tell us nothing about the world around us.

To the casual observer, such slogans of the ordinary-language philosophers as "language should not be treated as a calculus," "not all words function as names or signs of objects," "the meanings of words are to be found in their uses," may not appear world-shaking. But it is through their application in the study of moral, religious, and critical ideas that we have begun to see how profoundly our basic cultural activities have been misunderstood and subverted by philosophers throughout Western history. At long last we may understand, for example, why the only alternatives to the traditional view of art as imitation need not be those anti-intellectualistic theories which regard art either as an arrangement of merely sensuous surfaces or as an expression of pure emotion. Similarly, we begin to see why the only alternative to a supposedly scientific ethics which treats moral principles as laws of nature is not an ethics of pure decision which denies any place to reason in moral deliberation and criticism. Morality, like art, provides, in context, its own meaningful standards of propriety, validity, and reasonableness. In use, moral principles function neither as arbitrary expressions of emotion which cannot be criticized without begging the question nor as scientific laws which describe or predict certain supposedly objective features of the moral universe. But there is no way to see this without detailed study of what we actually do with words when we state a moral principle, apply it to a particular case, or dispute its validity. In the same way we may come to understand, in the end, how theology and even metaphysics itself may have significance even though what they may tell us has no validity as an explanation either of mundane or of supermundane realities. The problem, again, is to discern what the theologian and metaphysician are *doing* with language. It has been said that the God of the philosophers is no God at all but a bogus principle of explanation or "ground of being." But, if so, this is primarily because traditional philosophers, ignoring the contexts of its ordinary religious use, have misconceived the meaning of "God" in treating it as a term of transcendent reference. How little such a conception of God has to do with actual religious thought, however, is only just now becoming clear through the analytical study of our talk of God in the familiar circumstances of religious prayer and meditation.

Thus, by directing our attention to the various ways of words in their different authentic vocations, and to the traditional human practices with which they are commonly correlated, the much-abused philosophers of ordinary language are bringing us gradually to recognize that in any sphere lucidity is as lucidity *does*, that "reason" is not the sole prerogative of the scientist and the logician, and that even

what we call "knowledge" need not be assumed in advance
to be a representation of what traditional philosophers understood, or thought they understood, by "existence." In a way,
it may turn out that through a more liberal and relaxed use
of the methods of analysis employed by the ordinary-language
philosophers even the strange-sounding talk of the existentialists may be seen for what it is, not as an obscure or irrational description of what "exists" *in rerum natura,* but as
a faltering but intelligible effort on the part of care-ridden
and anxious men to tell each other what it means to "face
reality" without the illusion of a *Logos.*

LOGICAL ANALYSIS AND THE LOVE OF WISDOM

It is now necessary to place these remarks in a somewhat
different perspective. I have argued that until very recently
technical analytical philosophy itself has belonged in the
direct line of Mr. Earle's gnostic tradition. However, there is,
one salient feature of that tradition which is conspicuously
absent from contemporary technical philosophy of nearly all
types. This is the notion that there is a unique philosophical
mode of salvation of the sort depicted by Spinoza, for example, in the Fifth Part of his Ethics. Mr. Earle regrets it, but I
am bound to say that, to my mind, this is good riddance.
The "visions" of the traditional gnostics and rationalists were
not synoptic but pseudo-visions. There is no esoteric philosophical *gradus ad parnassum* through which we may be led
to a saving glimpse of "the Good" that lies, supposedly, at
the core of being itself. And if such be "wisdom," then we
are better off without the spurious comforts which it affords.
As Socrates knew, but Plato and Spinoza forgot, the philosopher is not by vocation a kind of secular savior; at his best,
he is a midwife whose first function is to clarify and connect
the concepts by which we give focus to the ends that guide
us in the ordinary conduct of life. Philosophy, in short, provides no access to a unique reality which may console us, in
Mr. Earle's words, for our "wrecked lives." On the contrary,
to attempt as the gnostics do, to make philosophy serve as a

natural or lay religion is to pervert its primordial and proper
Socratic function. It is also to destroy religion itself.

This is not to deny to the philosopher his ancient claim to
be a lover of wisdom. Rather it requires a very different view
of the wisdom that he seeks or may command. Now I am
aware that the enigmatic commandment of the Oracle,
"Know thyself," has been given many interpretations in the
past. But I believe that Socrates' interpretation of it, properly
construed, is the correct one. I also believe that Socrates and
not Plato more nearly understood what contribution philosophical reflection may make to our self-knowledge and self-
culture. That contribution is essentially the logical (or dialectical) analysis of the golden concepts, such as justice,
truth, God, through which we focus the ideals by which we
live. In a spiritual sense, we *are* our commitments. Therefore,
if these concepts provide the terms through which alone our
commitments are made manifest to ourselves and others, then
their careful study must provide a revelation of what we are,
both to ourselves and to one another. Stated in another way,
philosophical analysis is, at bottom, nothing but that device
by means of which we attempt to discover, or uncover, what
we really are. And I use the word "discover" here advisedly.
We have been made to think both by the existentialists and
by the positivists that our basic commitments and ends are
fundamentally a matter of decision or choice. Nothing could
be further from the truth. I do not choose what I mean, or
intend, by truth or by justice; nor do I decide what principles of knowledge or of justice I will live by. I *find* myself
talking and thinking in a certain way just as I find, sometimes with great difficulty, those ideals and procedures by
which I live.

If this is so, then, making due allowances for understandable shifts in perspective and for inescapable changes in
philosophical style, it no longer seems far-fetched, despite
Mr. Earle, to regard the most hard-bitten positivist as still
involved, in his own quaint way, in the ancient Socratic
quest for self-knowledge. In spite of himself he remains, in
the classical sense, a philosopher. Even the most tough-

minded exponents of "analysis" in philosophy are still not interested merely in empirical descriptions of our linguistic behavior. What concerns them, one and all, is what they variously call the "clarification," the "logically correct" or "proper" uses of expressions. And what they want to know is not what we do say, but what we ought to say or would say if we spoke well or to some purpose; or if they are interested in what we do say, then it is on the assumption that proved ways of speaking are best and that when we ignore them, as the traditional philosophers so often did, we go off the rails and so defeat our own ends. Nor are technical philosophers equally interested in all of the terms and sentences that ordinary men are prone to utter. The terms in which they are mainly interested, such as "knowledge," "truth," "validity," and "meaning," are not used in order to designate items in the world of phenomena; they are, on the contrary, normative expressions that are employed in guiding and connecting the activities, linguistic and otherwise, through which men who live in communities organize their lives. It is the procedure which concerns the philosopher, not the fact; the method, not the particular results that may be achieved through its application.

But the matter goes deeper than this. The older philosophers could regard words as mere counters precisely because they viewed both language and thought as finished photographic representations of an independent, abstract, and equally static reality. But if we take time and action seriously, then it becomes apparent that language simply does not exist save "performatively" in the living speech-acts in which men do the various specialized things we call "commending," "promising," "advising," "inferring," and "describing." In a word, language really exists only in act, so that if we would grasp the meanings of words (or ideas), we must also grasp what, in particular, men are doing with them. And conversely, when we do manage to understand what expressions mean, we must necessarily also understand to that extent what the men who use them are up to, what they are doing, intending, and aiming at. And it is partly for this reason that Wittgenstein was able to say with such profound truth that forms of words are also forms of life.

Thus, although language does not provide a mirror of the external world, as the classical philosophers supposed, it may, when properly understood, serve as a revelation of ourselves. That revelation may disappoint or even disgust us. In that case, both the forms of words and the forms of life which they reflect will appear as something to be transcended. Or it may disclose aspects of our existence which, as we thoughtfully contemplate them, are found to be immensely precious and which must be defended at all costs against those who would, witlessly, destroy them. Only from this standpoint may we begin to comprehend the underlying spiritual significance of the closet-quarrel between the ordinary-language philosophers and their opponents. On the one hand, the proponents of ideal scientific languages, the logical revisionists and reconstructionists, the rule-makers and symbol-mongers are, in effect, revolutionaries. At bottom they are dissatisfied not only with existing linguistic practices but also with the lives which are reflected in them; and they would, if they could, refashion their own lives and societies in accordance with some ideal image toward which they, perhaps hopelessly, yearn. Or, they are romantic rebels who, like Mr. Earle himself, dream of a land beyond the seas where new men may start from scratch to build the true Republic of Knowledge of which they already think they have a glimpse. On the other hand, the philosophers of ordinary language, as I envisage them, are classicists and traditionalists who, without illusions of perfection, seek to understand, and through that understanding to keep alive, the forms of language and of life which, partly by instinct and partly by conviction, determine what we are. Philosophically, the linguistic studies of these philosophers are revolutionary. Humanly and spiritually, however, their effect, if not also their intention, is to conserve practices, including linguistic usages, which may be threatened by our increasingly technological and scientific culture, but which are nonetheless essential to the survival *in any form* of spiritual concerns whose ends are not definable in purely "cognitive" terms.

The fundamental tragedy of rationalism in philosophy is that it forces its victims to misconceive their own cultural intentions. If they love art, then they must justify this love by treating the symbolic forms of art as modes of representation, in which case they cut themselves off, as Mr. Earle has done, from artistic styles which, in no obvious way at least, imitate nature. If they love the good, then they must needs justify this by representing goodness as an objective quality or relation in things, thereby risking the chance of moral cynicism when they discover, as they must, that no such quality or relation exists. If they love God, they must conceive him as a glorified "substance" or "cause," for the only form of "being" their philosophies permit them to acknowledge is the being of an object of knowledge, thus sacrificing the possibility of religious worship on a misbegotten altar of cognition. Worse than this, they are also obliged to misrepresent those who, like Augustine, Pascal, Hume, and Kierkegaard, have sporadically defended an a-gnostic and pluralistic conception of man's spiritual well-being. The latter are treated, in brief, not as a loyal opposition which merely rejects a certain philosophical conception of human culture, but as irrationalists and mystagogues who, like the Grand Inquisitor, would replace culture with an authoritarian cultus of mystery, miracle, and indoctrination. In fact, however, it is the off-beat a-gnostic rebels who have more truly understood the complex spiritual intentions of Western man and who have therefore better grasped the kinds of lucidity that are proper to each. And it is the philosophers of ordinary language who, by the slow but sure process of piecemeal logical analysis, are beginning to spell out the underlying meaning of those intentions.

I am anxious not to be misunderstood; I completely agree with Mr. Earle that the contempt of reason is a form of "blasphemy." But blasphemy has many guises, and perhaps the most insidious of all is that strange hypertrophy of reason

which, since the time of Plato, has always been the unwitting
parent of irrationalism. In our time, the same error is responsible for that romantic and ultimately barbaric mysology
which currently infects so much of our contemporary theology, criticism, and anti-analytical philosophy. Reason, it
cannot be too often said, is not a *Logos,* but an activity of
the human mind. In the course of history, it has taken many
different forms and its standards have been constantly subject to change in accordance with man's changing conception
of himself. We cannot possibly rehabilitate the gnostic cult of
reason which dominated Western philosophy until the end of
the eighteenth century. And we cannot do so because, since
Kant, the devastating criticism of that cult has undermined
the spurious mystique upon which it rests.

CONCLUSION

In conclusion, let us return to Mr. Earle's own analysis of
culture and his dreams for its new life.

In my opinion, the task of revitalizing our culture, if that is
what it needs, must be conceived in very different terms from
those which Mr. Earle employs. The metaphors of birth, life,
and death are especially misleading when applied to communal cultural activities such as art, religion, and philosophy.
For one thing, they result in stances which engender a sense
of fatality and helplessness in the presence of an irrevocable
round of vital processes which human thought and choice
are powerless to affect. Or else they encourage that revolutionary desperation which causes men to run amok, wantonly
destroying anything that reminds them of a golden youth of
culture which is beyond recall. Does Mr. Earle fully realize
how ambiguous is his own sense of direction at this fatal
crossroad between the old regime and the terror?

In one way I make no complaint. Wise men, wherever they
are, always live ambiguously in the middle way between
tradition and revolution. The part of intelligence is to conserve and reform the old patterns when we can and to
fashion new ones, gradually, as we must, creating but also

re-creating our spiritual destinies, piecemeal, as we go along. In some sense, no doubt, God, *Nous,* the work of art, and hence culture itself are "dying." It may be a fact that culture in Mr. Earle's sense is actually dead, once and for all. In that case, however, our problem is to learn to live without it. Is this prospect so bad? If we tried, we might find that we no longer really want that absolute certainty, ultimate lucidity, and communal identity to which our ancestors aspired. It has been said that our responsibilities begin in dreams. But I, for my part, am able to dream of a society (not, in Mr. Earle's sense, a community) of emancipated, civilized men who, through reticence, tact, and self-control, are able to redeem the time through consecutive acts of creation, intelligence, and love, but without insisting that each of these be viewed as part of some great communal rite. Such men, as I fancy them, would refuse to be overborne by the thought of death, either for themselves or for their civilization. On the contrary, they would find in the amenities and in the work of civilized life an honest alternative to the morbid and self-destructive preoccupation with "ultimate concern," whose objectless ends they cannot, finally, fathom. They would acknowledge the wondrous mystery of being without making a fetish of that wonder, and they would accept, without pride, the daily satisfactions that may accrue in the ordinary course from the performance of the specialized tasks which constitute their "callings." Such a dream, I realize, is very uncatholic, just as it is also very un-Hegelian and un-Marxian. So be it. If it implies, as I do not for a moment doubt, that we must in one sense live "despairingly," then we may learn to make the most of that too. Here the philosophers have much to learn from the great tragic poets who have shown us, through their art, how despair itself may be redeemed when it is finally accepted, and thus transmuted, as a condition of one's being.

I realize how much against the grain such a question may go, but it must be asked: Is not the very notion of a "whole man" itself a tragic myth, a philosophical bait unwittingly laid to make the taker mad? Organic analogies are usually acknowledged to be a mistake when applied on the social level; perhaps the mistake occurs also when such analogies are applied to the spiritual "life" of an individual person. I suggest that Mr. Earle, like all gnostics, past and present, has been victimized by the erroneous idea that the spirit or the self is an organic substance. In short, Mr. Earle's vision of culture is a bogus vision because the philosophy behind it is bad philosophy. Why should we aspire to belong to one great communal "substance" when the evidence of our senses, our hearts, and our discourse informs us that spiritual diversity is as irreducible, as ultimate, and as certain as death itself? But even if, in some sense, we all were "one," what possible spiritual comfort or nourishment could be derived from that wretched fact? What if the one were a devil, a dictator, or a rock? And if it comes to that, why, by analogy, may it not be so?

At the human level, autonomy is the prerogative of all self-respecting men. It is also the prerogative of our various concerns, each of which, so long as it does not crowd the rest, has its inviolable right to be. The spiritual life requires craft, technique, and therefore specialization. Why, then, should we deny it. A good poem is not an analysis of concepts, and talents which make for good poetry often merely come to grief when turned to the chores of philosophical midwifery. An arrangement of "meaningless" sounds in a satisfying aural pattern is not everything, but done by a master like Mozart it may serve to delight the spirit even of a Plotinus. We are not and cannot always be doing or caring about one big thing, and, thank God, we are not always doing our various little things together. Nor does doing what we do with "our whole heart" require that it should be all in all to us. Mr. Earle's "work of culture," as I call it, is not a seamless web of holy, good, and beautiful Truth, but a sentimental abstraction to which nothing in modern life corresponds. Its only conceivable analogue is a social institution, viewed in Hegel's sense as an evolving historical form of "objective spirit." But Hegel himself knew, as Earle seems to have forgotten, that art, philosophy, and religion belong to the domain of "absolute spirit" within which each individual must work out his own unique destiny according to his lights.

The fundamental difficulty with Mr. Earle's dream comes back to the matter of language. I am sure his talk of "spirit" as something which is "alive only when creating itself" and when concerned "precisely for itself, for its life," is only a manner of speaking. But it is a manner of speaking which is a philosophical booby-trap. As he himself says, at one point, "the human spirit is inevitably in individuals." Concretely this means that it has no "being" and no "substance" whatever, save in the particular activities, tasks, and aspirations which occupy individual men during their ordinary waking hours. We attain to spirituality not when we dream, but only when we try to interpret the meaning of our dreams. As Santayana put it, what we call "spirituality" is mainly a matter of wakefulness. It neither lives nor dies; it has no independent concerns, but attaches itself, willy-nilly, to any concern, ultimate or otherwise, as we become conscious of its end. It has no ideas; but any idea, when understood, becomes a spiritual thing; and it can never express itself, for it has nothing in itself to say or tell. It is neither cultured nor uncultured, civilized nor uncivilized, good or bad. Slaves and freemen, saints and sinners, nominalists and realists, gnostics and pistics, portrait painters and paper hangers may all possess it, each in his own way. That it has its troubles in the modern world I should be the last to deny. But its "death" is not due to specialization; on the contrary, specialization, like attention, is its life. Its death is due to distraction, sleepiness, boredom, and anxiety. And for these there is no single remedy.

Index